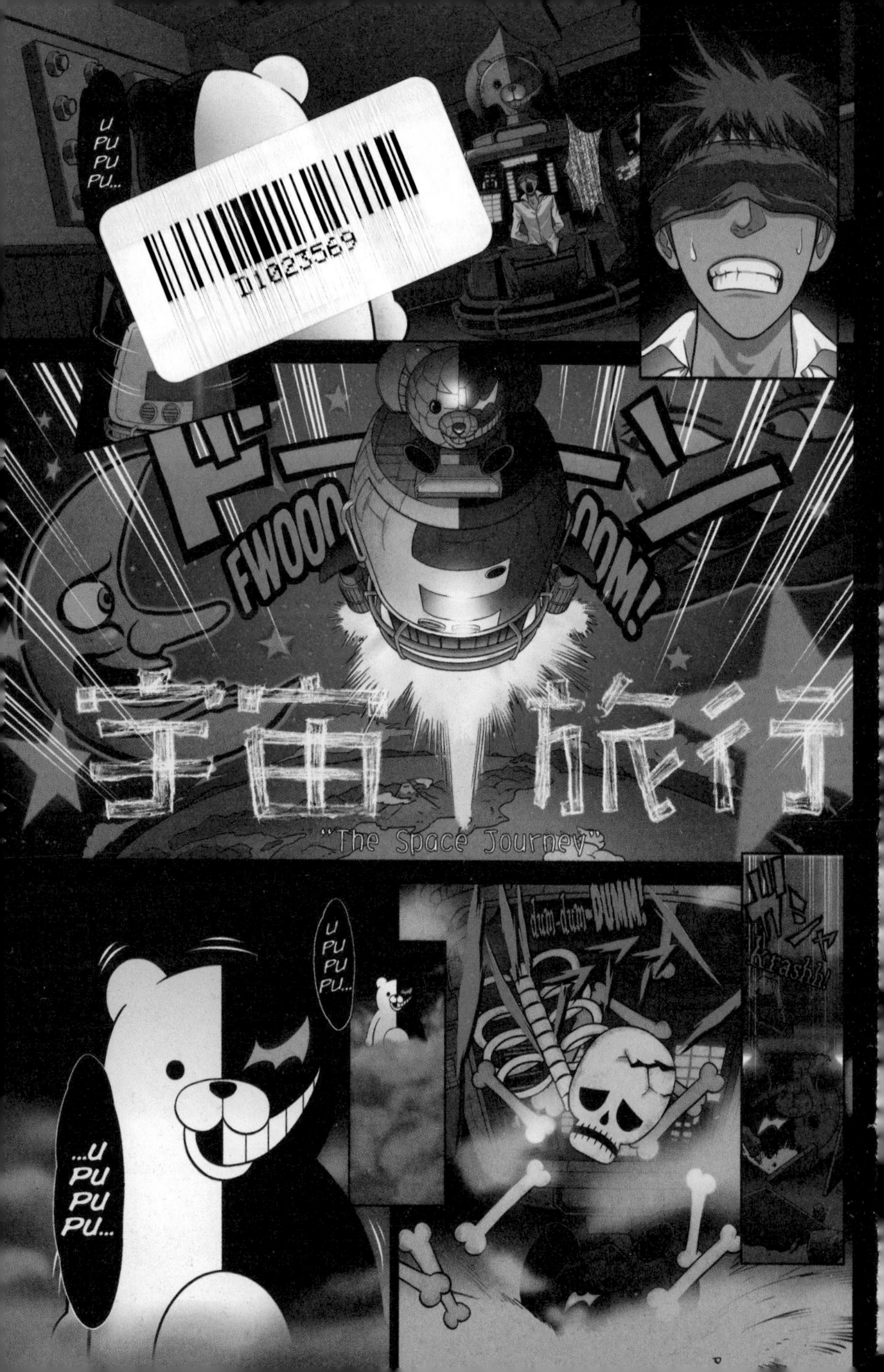
UPUPUPU...
宇宙旅行
"The Space Journey"
kerashh!
dum-dum-DUMM!
UPUPUPU...
...UPUPUPU...

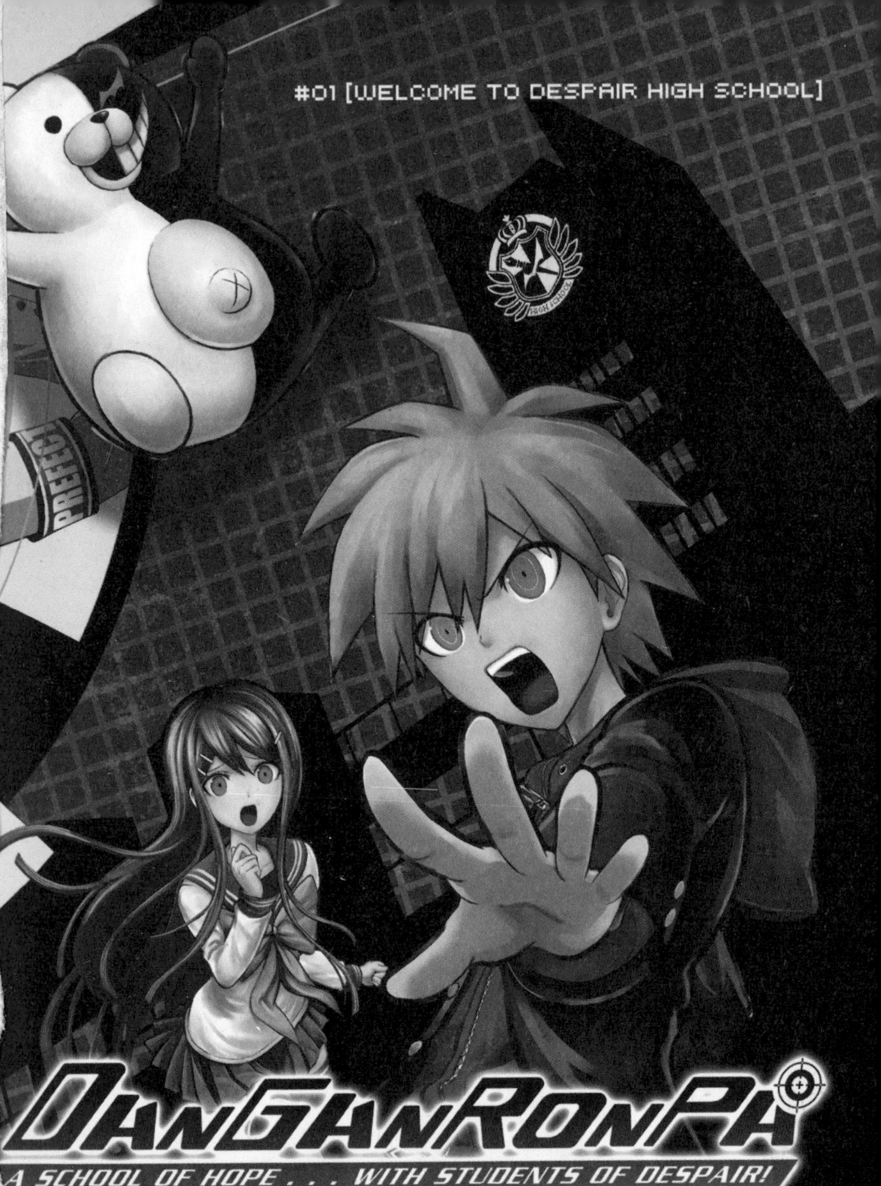
#01 [WELCOME TO DESPAIR HIGH SCHOOL]
PREFECT
DANGANRONPA
A SCHOOL OF HOPE . . . WITH STUDENTS OF DESPAIR!

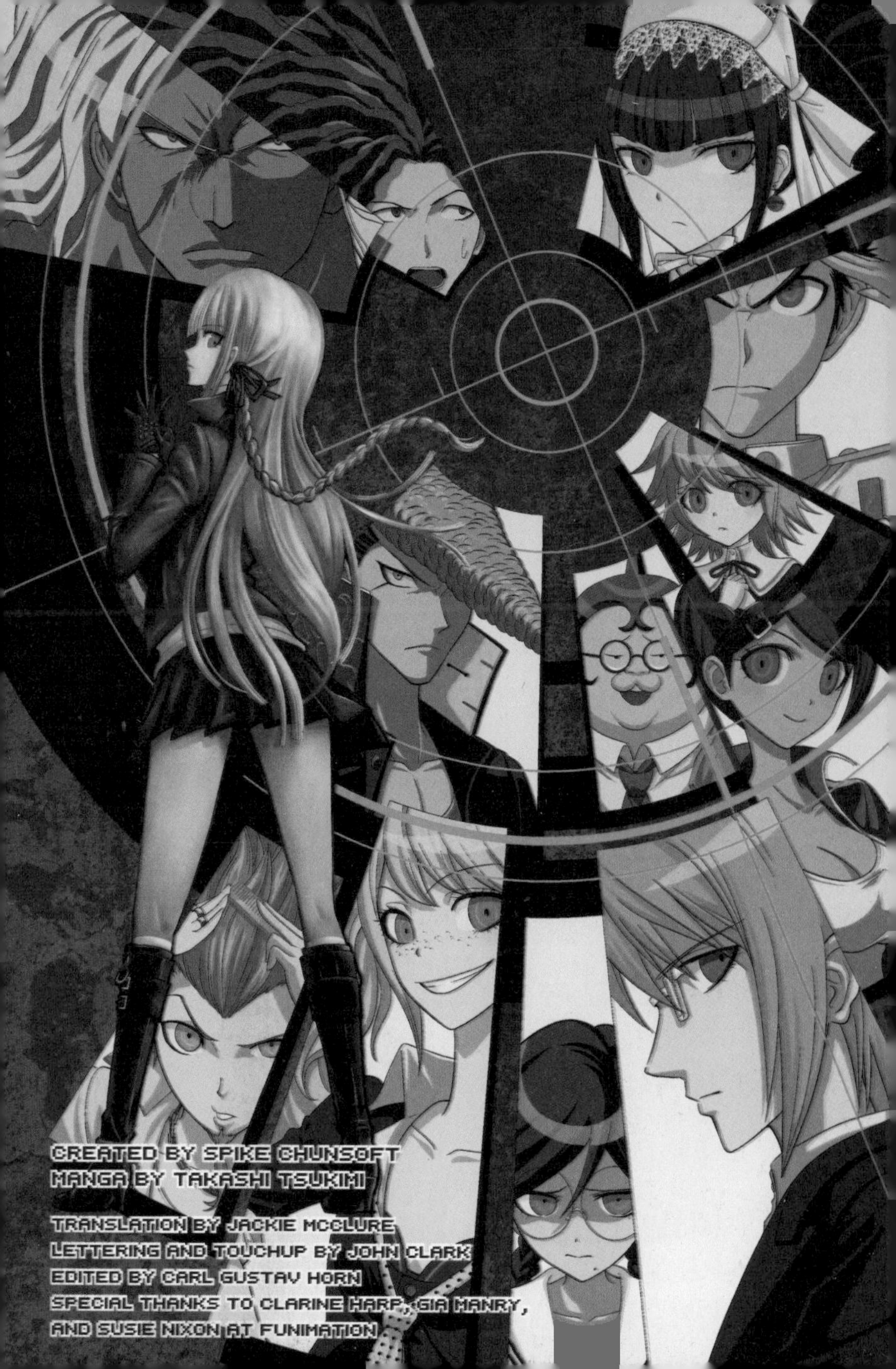

CREATED BY SPIKE CHUNSOFT
MANGA BY TAKASHI TSUKIMI

TRANSLATION BY JACKIE MCCLURE
LETTERING AND TOUCHUP BY JOHN CLARK
EDITED BY CARL GUSTAV HORN
SPECIAL THANKS TO CLARINE HARP, GIA MANRY,
AND SUSIE NIXON AT FUNIMATION

Contents

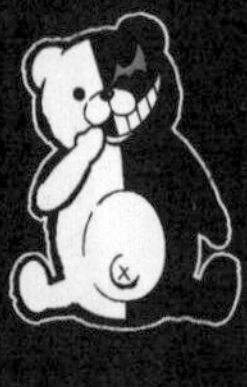

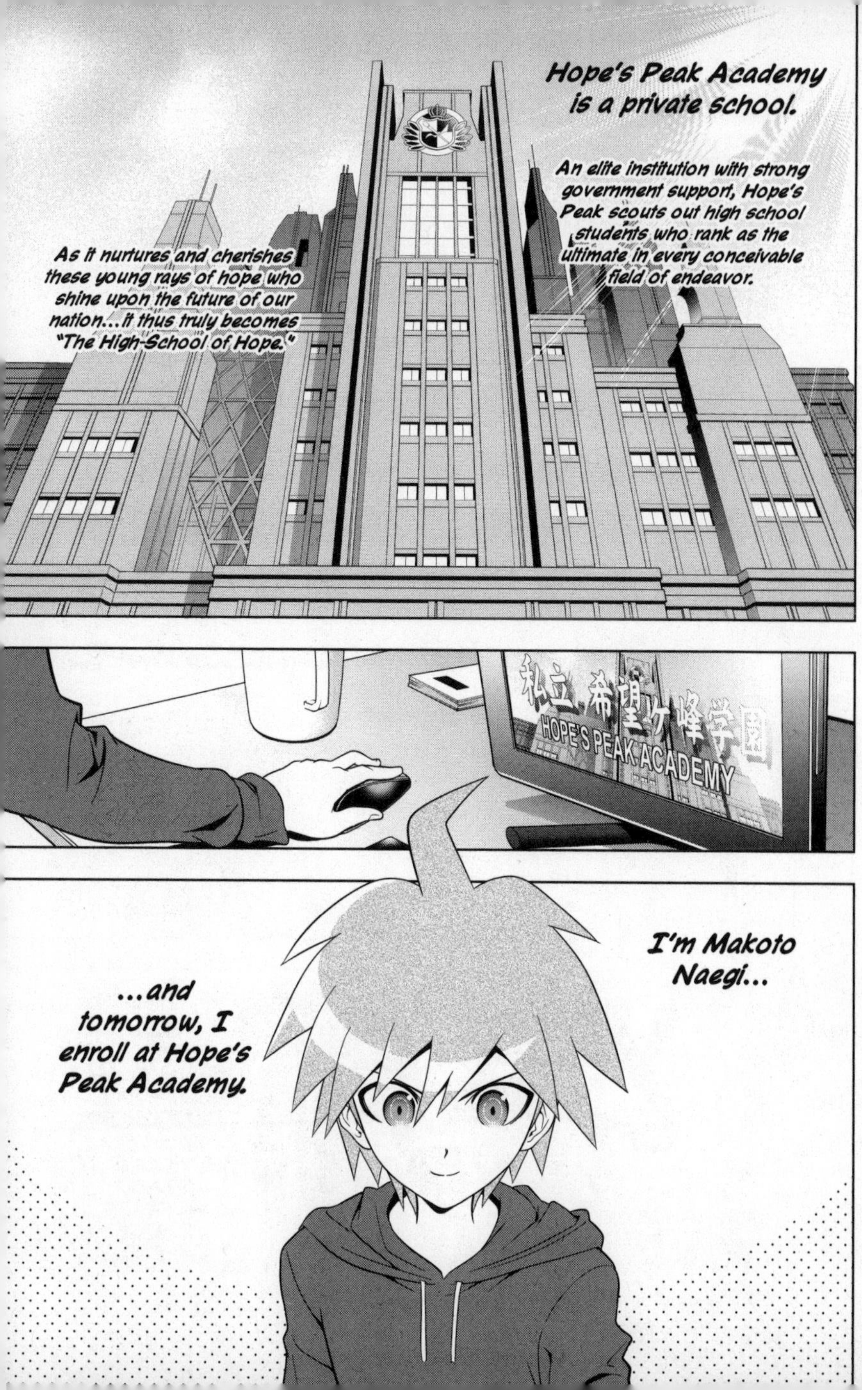
Hope's Peak Academy is a private school.
An elite institution with strong government support, Hope's Peak scouts out high school students who rank as the ultimate in every conceivable field of endeavor.
As it nurtures and cherishes these young rays of hope who shine upon the future of our nation...it thus truly becomes "The High-School of Hope."
私立 希望ヶ峰学園
HOPE'S PEAK ACADEMY
I'm Makoto Naegi...
...and tomorrow, I enroll at Hope's Peak Academy.

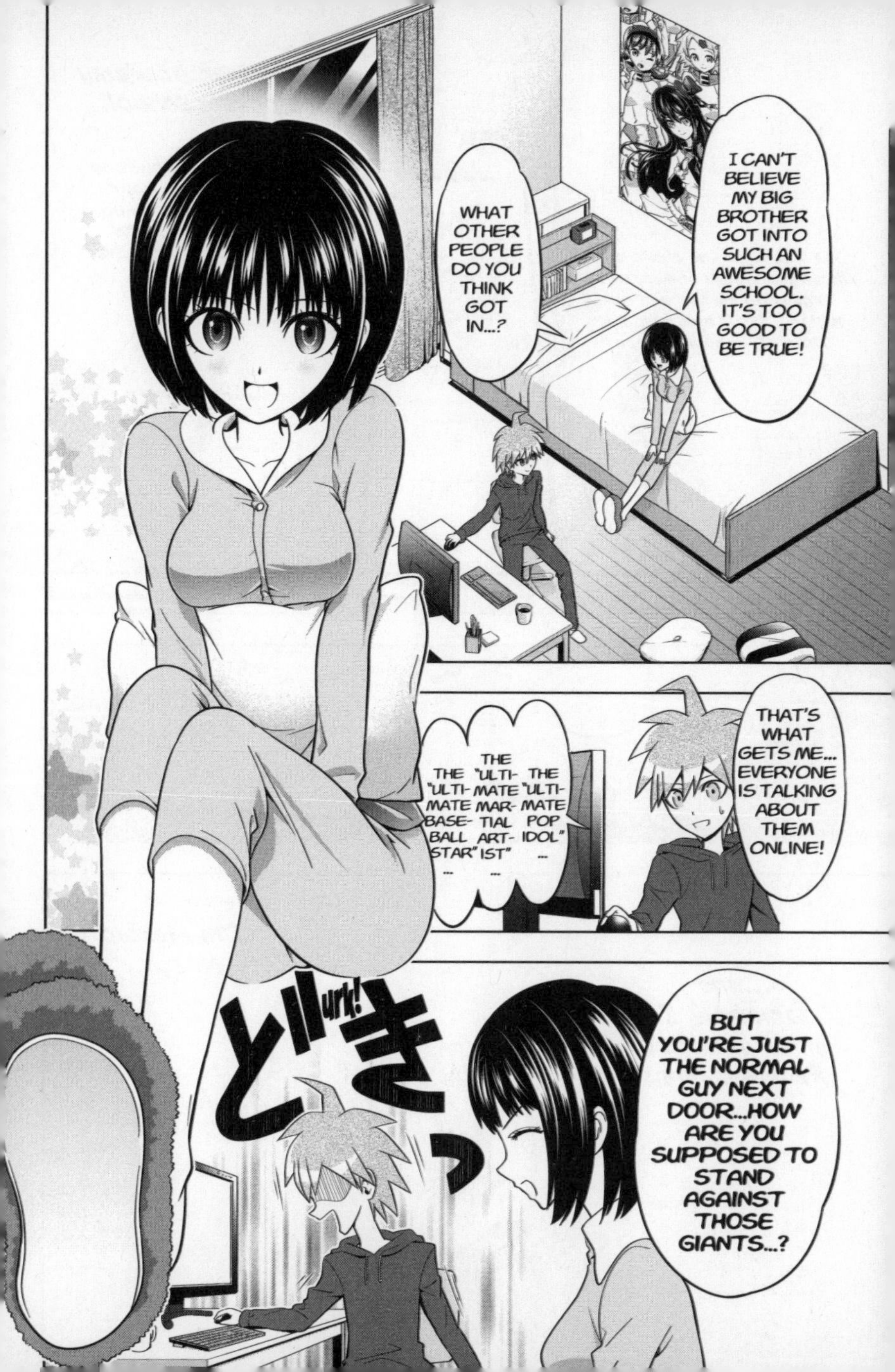

I CAN'T BELIEVE MY BIG BROTHER GOT INTO SUCH AN AWESOME SCHOOL. IT'S TOO GOOD TO BE TRUE!
WHAT OTHER PEOPLE DO YOU THINK GOT IN...?
THAT'S WHAT GETS ME... EVERYONE IS TALKING ABOUT THEM ONLINE!
THE "ULTIMATE POP IDOL"... THE "ULTIMATE MARTIAL ARTIST"... THE "ULTIMATE BASEBALL STAR"...
BUT YOU'RE JUST THE NORMAL GUY NEXT DOOR...HOW ARE YOU SUPPOSED TO STAND AGAINST THOSE GIANTS...?
どきっ
urk!

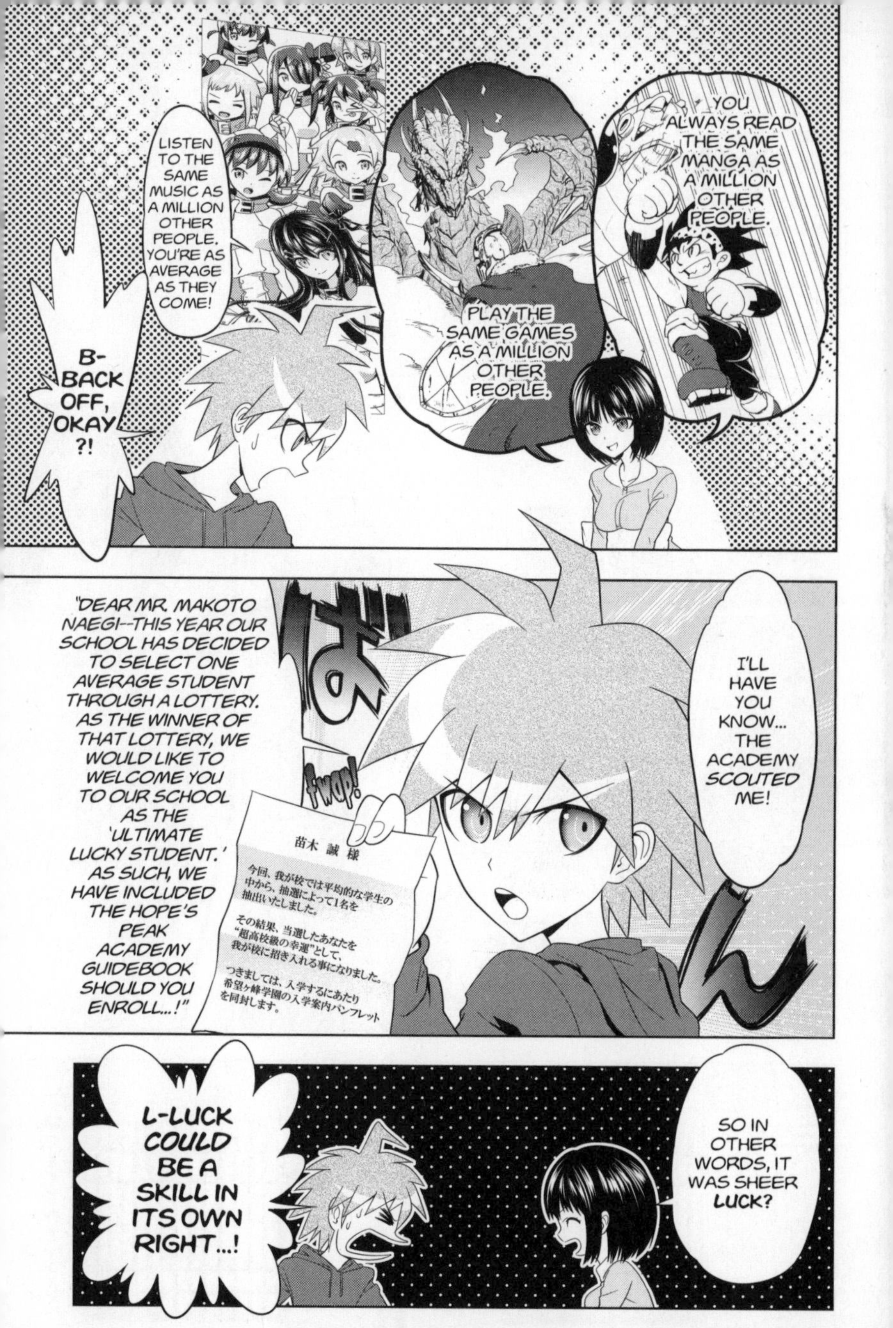
YOU ALWAYS READ THE SAME MANGA AS A MILLION OTHER PEOPLE.
PLAY THE SAME GAMES AS A MILLION OTHER PEOPLE.
LISTEN TO THE SAME MUSIC AS A MILLION OTHER PEOPLE. YOU'RE AS AVERAGE AS THEY COME!
B-BACK OFF, OKAY?!
I'LL HAVE YOU KNOW... THE ACADEMY SCOUTED ME!
ばっ
fwap!
ん
苗木 誠 様
今回、我が校では平均的な学生の中から、抽選によって1名を抽出いたしました。
その結果、当選したあなたを"超高校級の幸運"として、我が校に招き入れる事になりました。
つきましては、入学するにあたり希望ヶ峰学園の入学案内パンフレットを同封します。
"DEAR MR. MAKOTO NAEGI--THIS YEAR OUR SCHOOL HAS DECIDED TO SELECT ONE AVERAGE STUDENT THROUGH A LOTTERY. AS THE WINNER OF THAT LOTTERY, WE WOULD LIKE TO WELCOME YOU TO OUR SCHOOL AS THE 'ULTIMATE LUCKY STUDENT.' AS SUCH, WE HAVE INCLUDED THE HOPE'S PEAK ACADEMY GUIDEBOOK SHOULD YOU ENROLL...!"
SO IN OTHER WORDS, IT WAS SHEER LUCK?
L-LUCK COULD BE A SKILL IN ITS OWN RIGHT...!

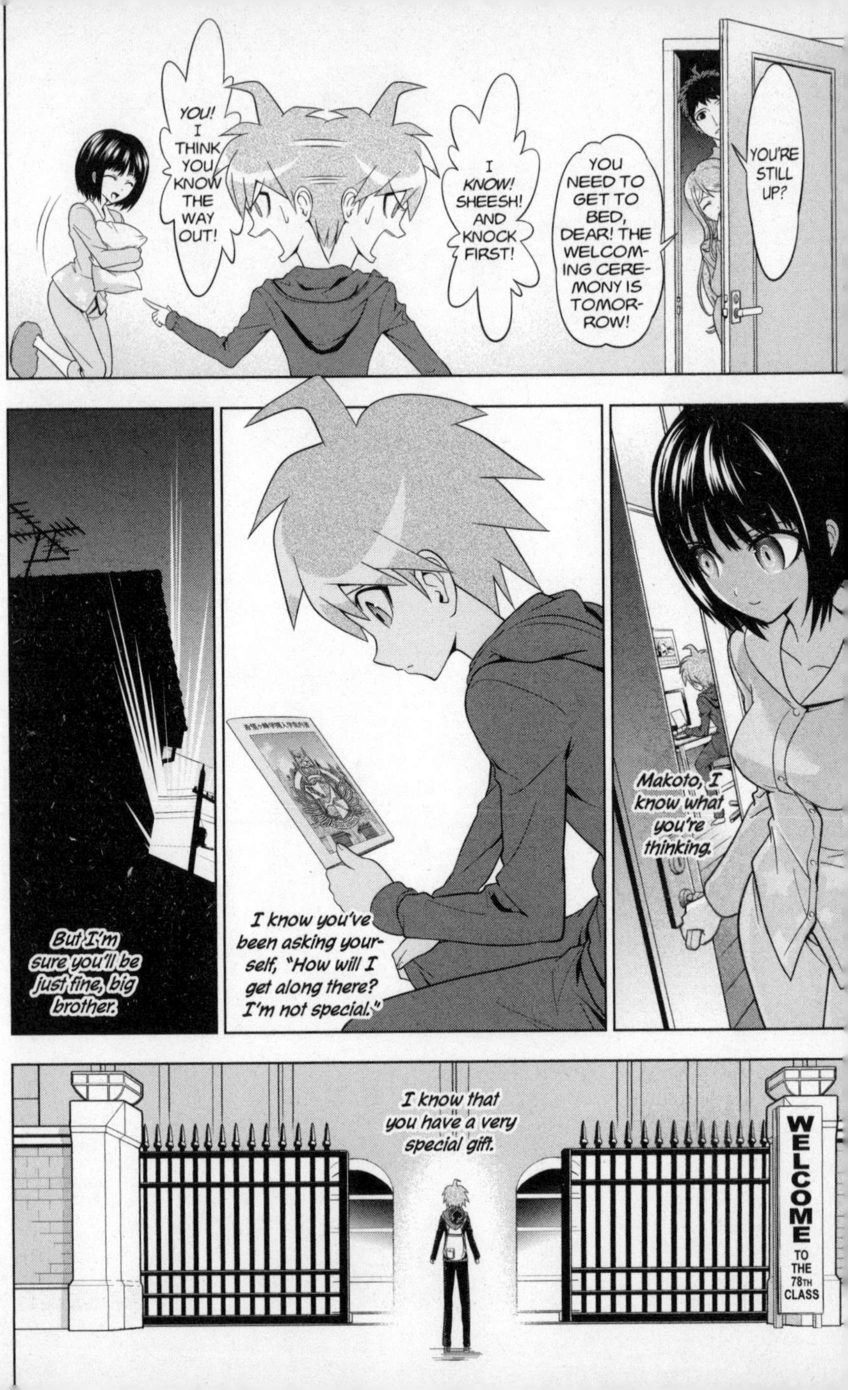
YOU'RE STILL UP?
YOU NEED TO GET TO BED, DEAR! THE WELCOMING CEREMONY IS TOMORROW!
I KNOW! SHEESH! AND KNOCK FIRST!
YOU! I THINK YOU KNOW THE WAY OUT!
Makoto, I know what you're thinking.
I know you've been asking yourself, "How will I get along there? I'm not special."
But I'm sure you'll be just fine, big brother.
I know that you have a very special gift.
WELCOME TO THE 78TH CLASS

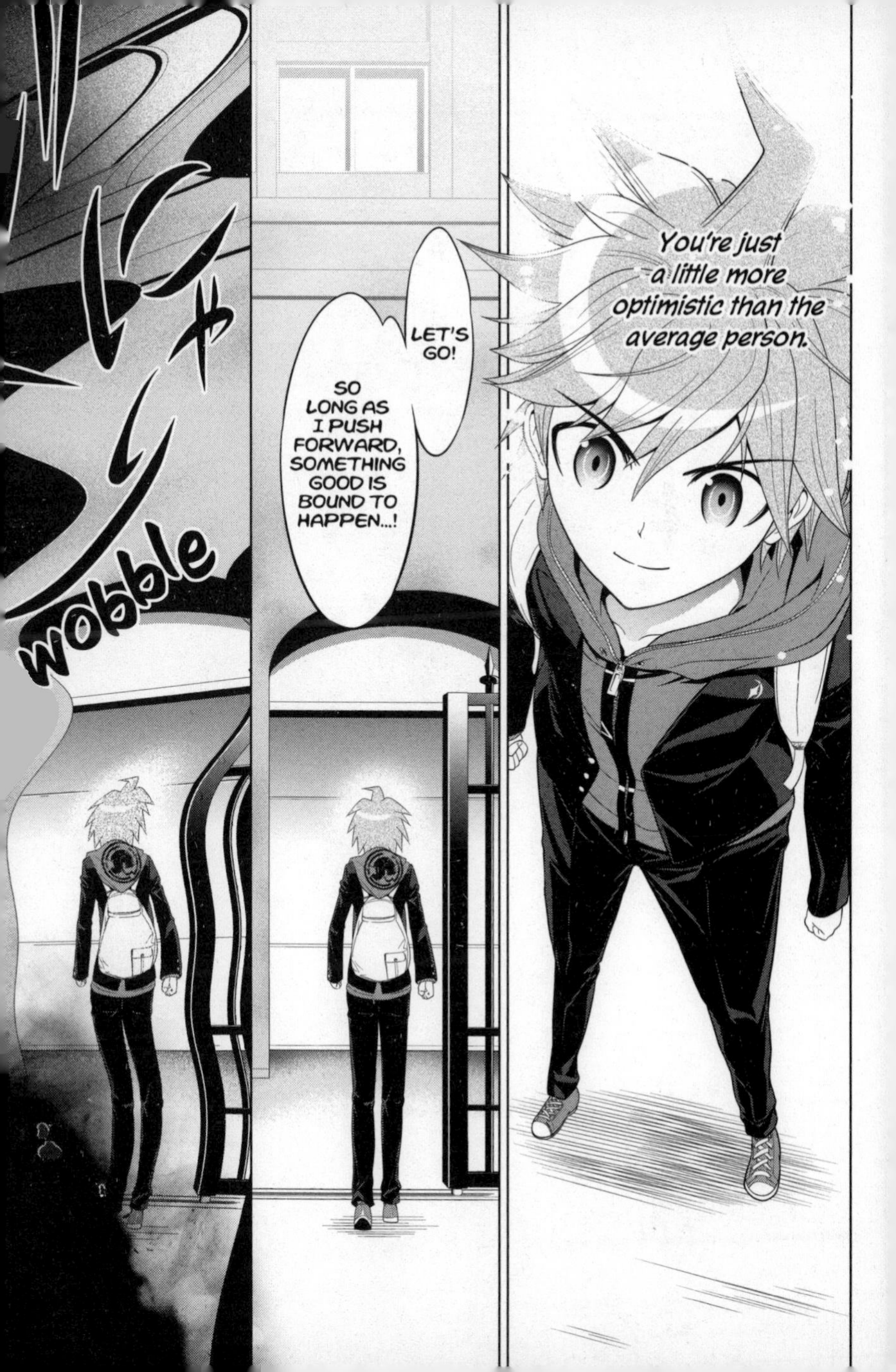
You're just a little more optimistic than the average person.
LET'S GO!
SO LONG AS I PUSH FORWARD, SOMETHING GOOD IS BOUND TO HAPPEN...!
wobble

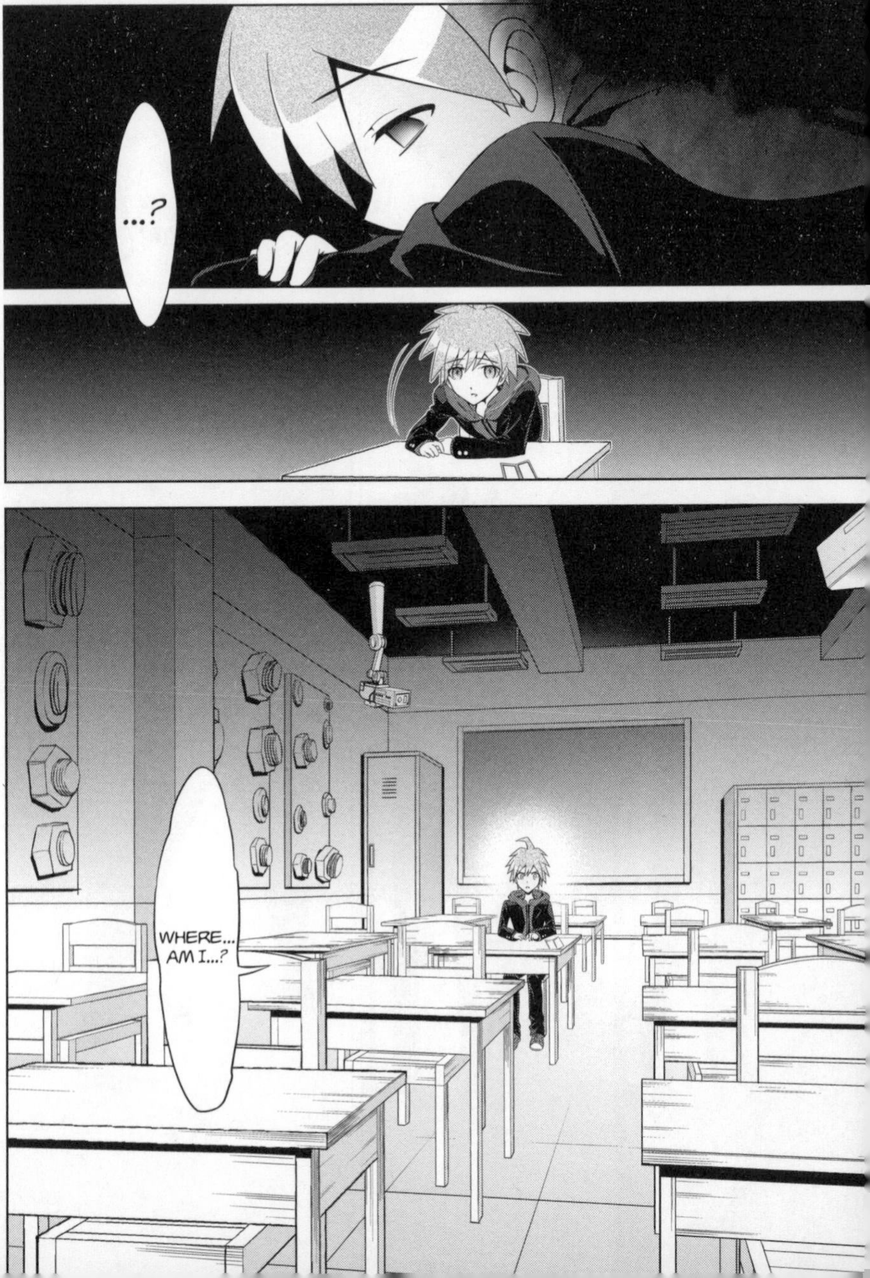
...?
WHERE... AM I...?

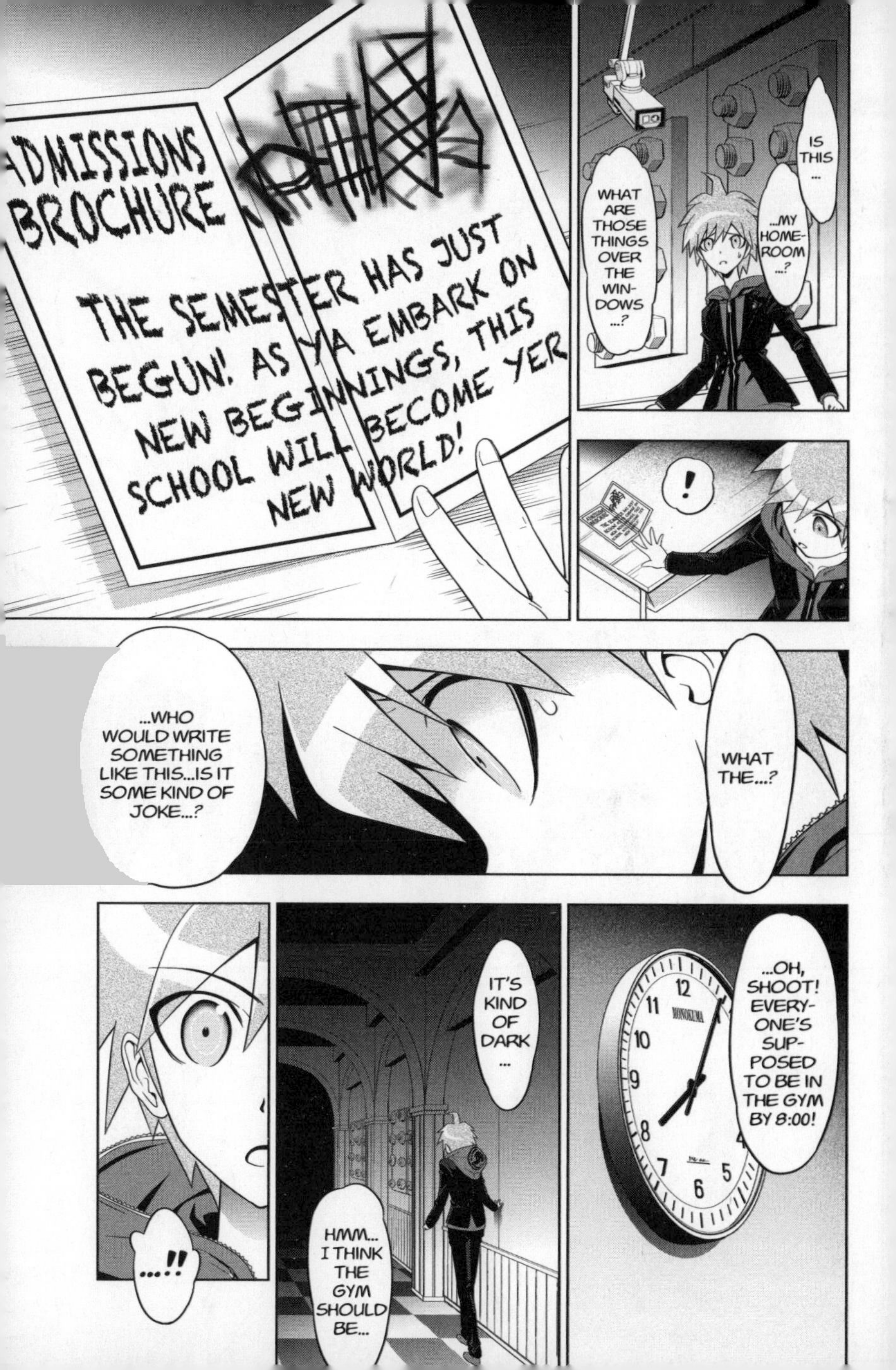
IS THIS ...
...MY HOMEROOM ...?
WHAT ARE THOSE THINGS OVER THE WINDOWS ...?
!
ADMISSIONS BROCHURE
THE SEMESTER HAS JUST BEGUN! AS YA EMBARK ON NEW BEGINNINGS, THIS SCHOOL WILL BECOME YER NEW WORLD!
WHAT THE...?
...WHO WOULD WRITE SOMETHING LIKE THIS...IS IT SOME KIND OF JOKE...?
...OH, SHOOT! EVERYONE'S SUPPOSED TO BE IN THE GYM BY 8:00!
MONOKUMA
IT'S KIND OF DARK ...
HMM... I THINK THE GYM SHOULD BE...
...!!

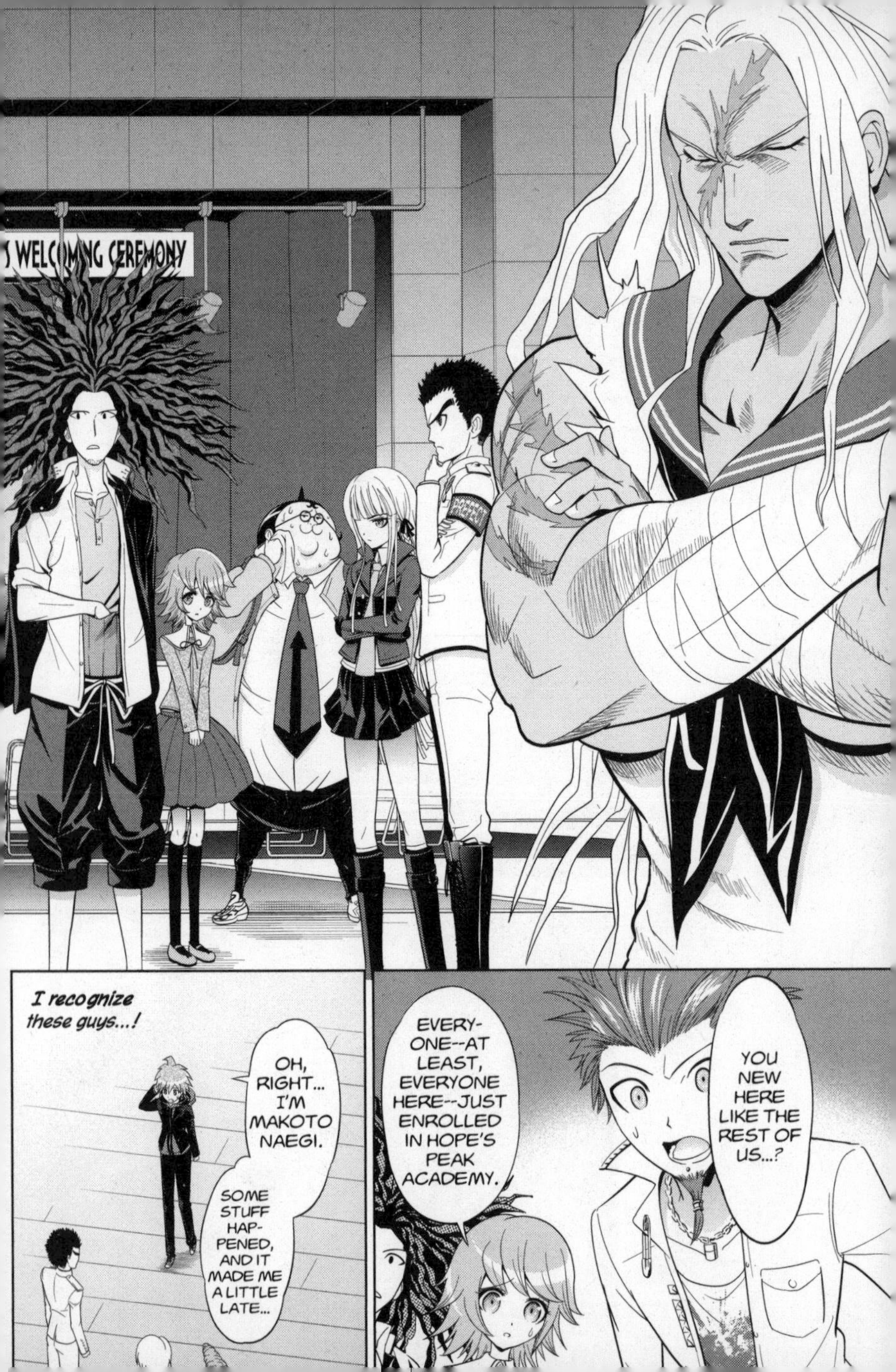

S WELCOMING CEREMONY
YOU NEW HERE LIKE THE REST OF US...?
EVERY-ONE--AT LEAST, EVERYONE HERE--JUST ENROLLED IN HOPE'S PEAK ACADEMY.
I recognize these guys...!
OH, RIGHT... I'M MAKOTO NAEGI.
SOME STUFF HAP-PENED, AND IT MADE ME A LITTLE LATE...

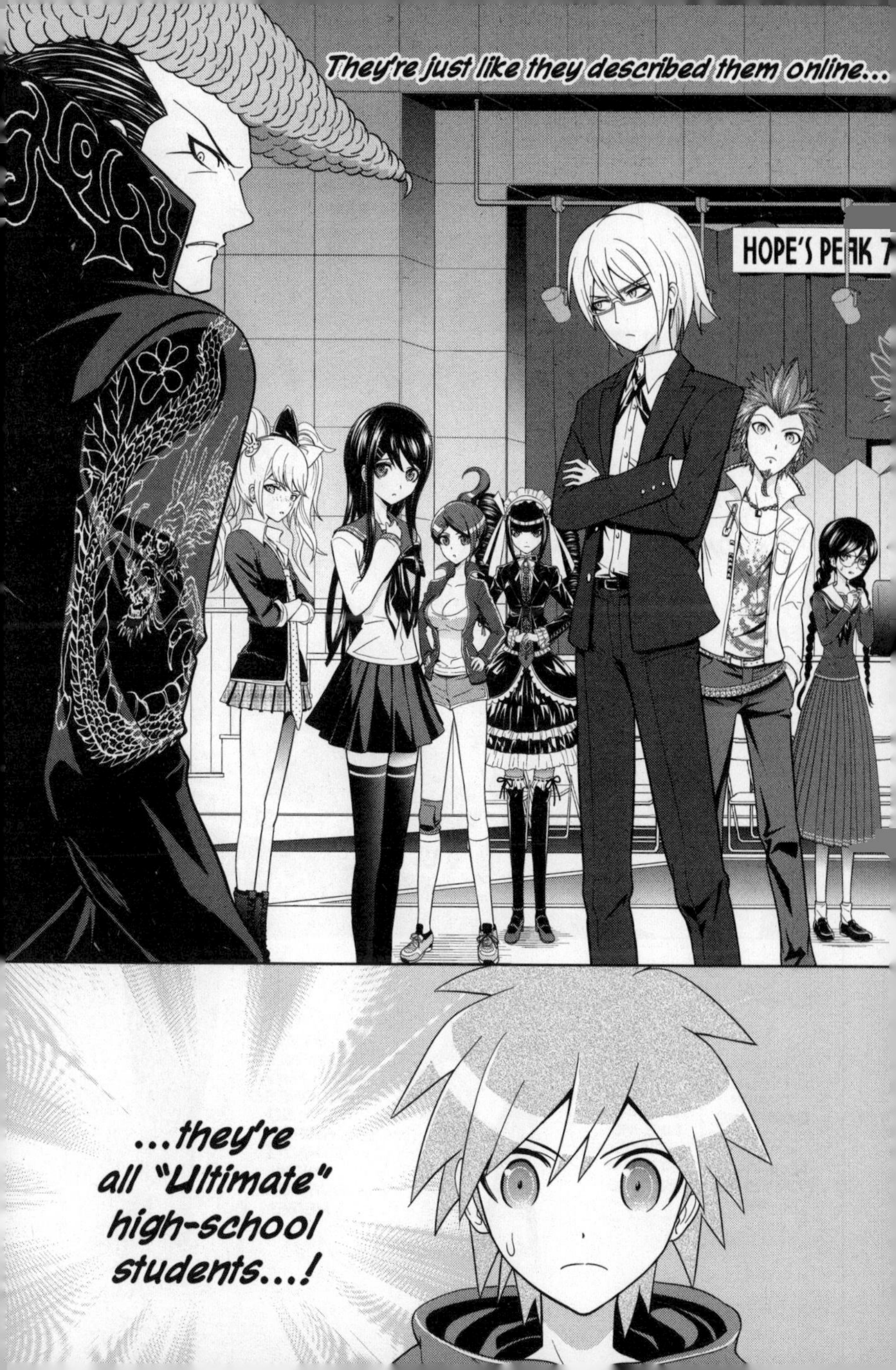
They're just like they described them online...
HOPE'S PEAK 7
...they're all "Ultimate" high-school students...!

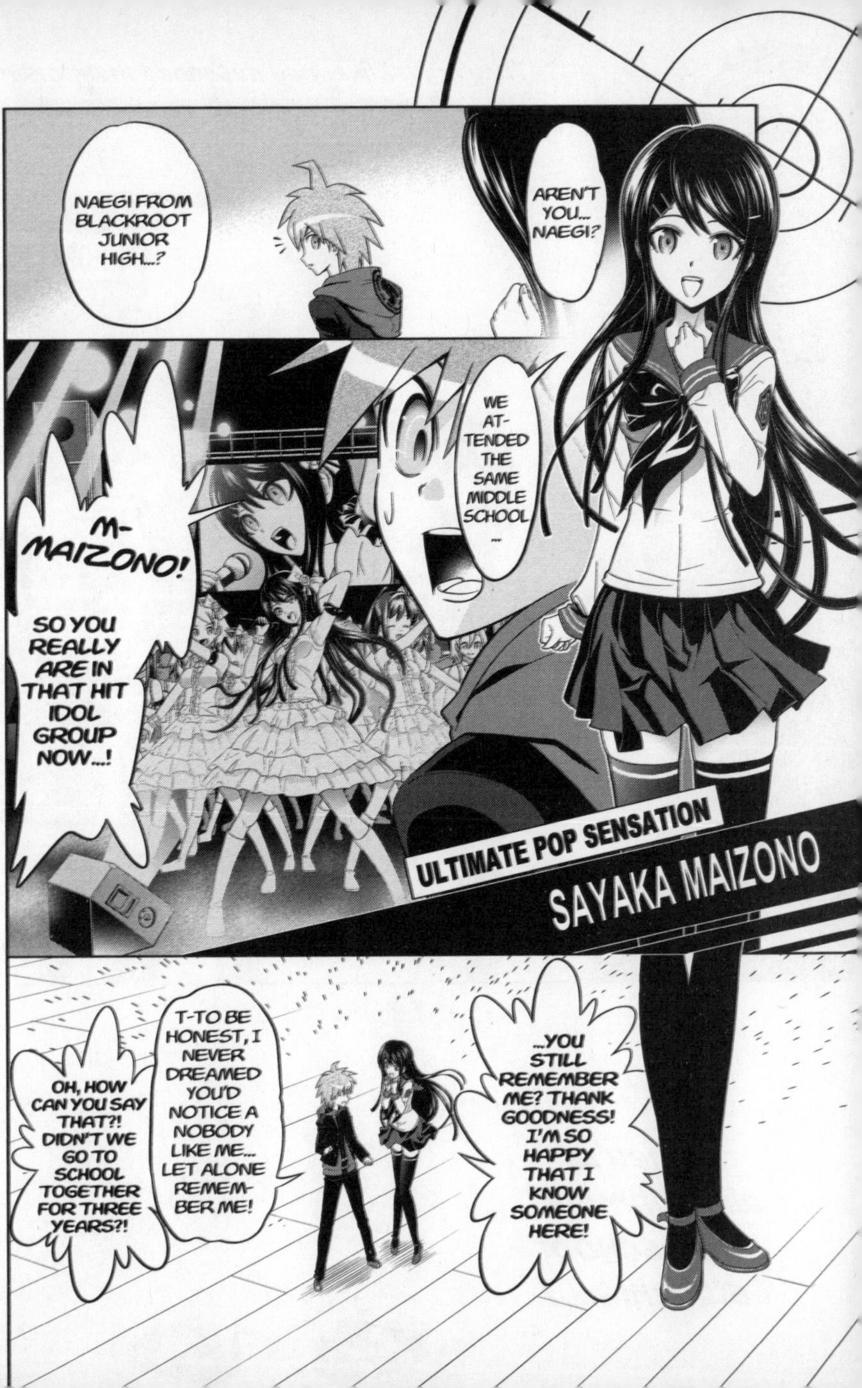
AREN'T YOU... NAEGI?
NAEGI FROM BLACKROOT JUNIOR HIGH...?
WE ATTENDED THE SAME MIDDLE SCHOOL...
M-MAIZONO!
SO YOU REALLY ARE IN THAT HIT IDOL GROUP NOW...!
ULTIMATE POP SENSATION
SAYAKA MAIZONO
...YOU STILL REMEMBER ME? THANK GOODNESS! I'M SO HAPPY THAT I KNOW SOMEONE HERE!
T-TO BE HONEST, I NEVER DREAMED YOU'D NOTICE A NOBODY LIKE ME... LET ALONE REMEMBER ME!
OH, HOW CAN YOU SAY THAT?! DIDN'T WE GO TO SCHOOL TOGETHER FOR THREE YEARS?!

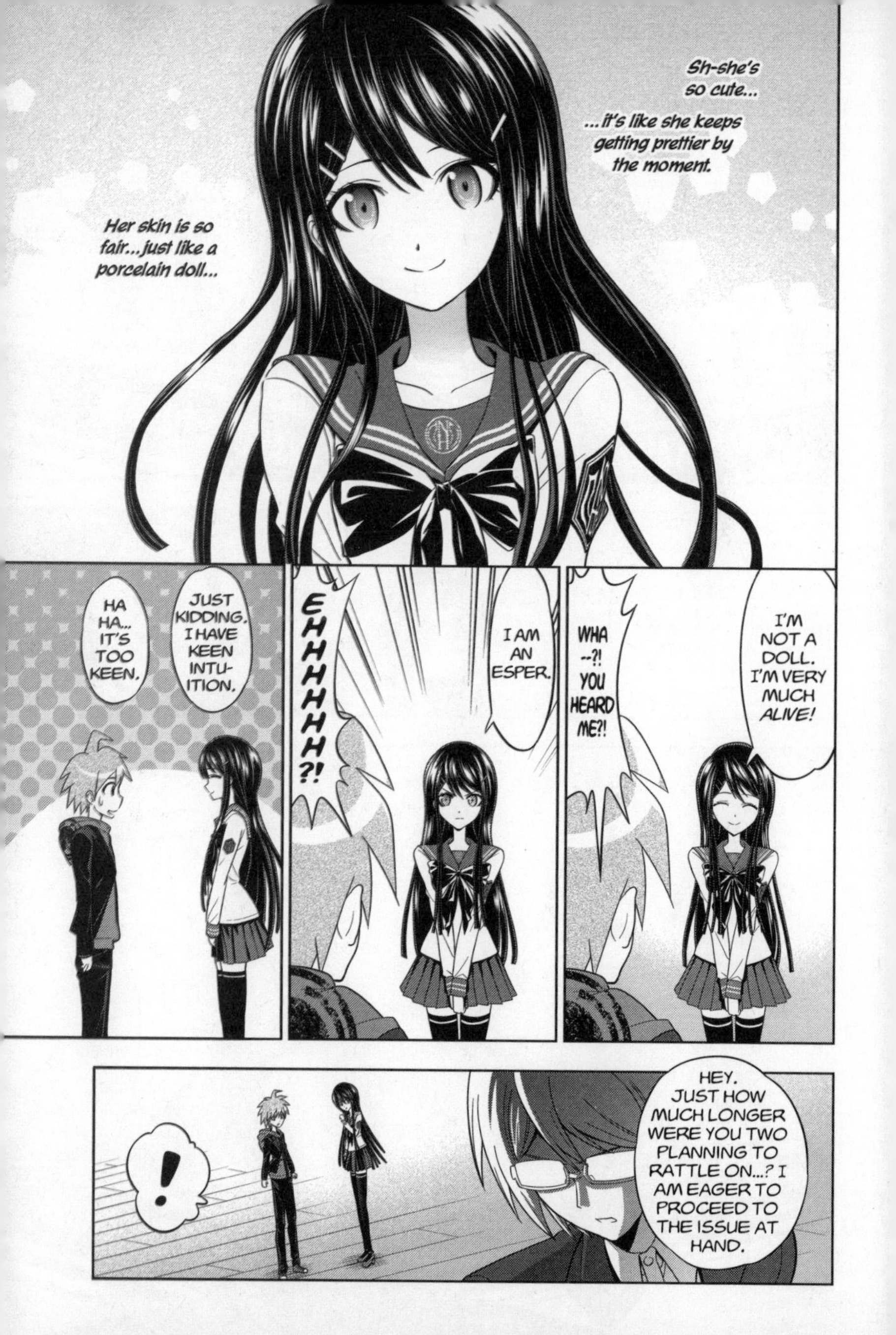
Sh-she's so cute...
...it's like she keeps getting prettier by the moment.
Her skin is so fair...just like a porcelain doll...
I'M NOT A DOLL. I'M VERY MUCH ALIVE!
WHA--?! YOU HEARD ME?!
I AM AN ESPER.
EHHHHHHHH?!
JUST KIDDING. I HAVE KEEN INTUITION.
HA HA... IT'S TOO KEEN.
HEY. JUST HOW MUCH LONGER WERE YOU TWO PLANNING TO RATTLE ON...? I AM EAGER TO PROCEED TO THE ISSUE AT HAND.
!

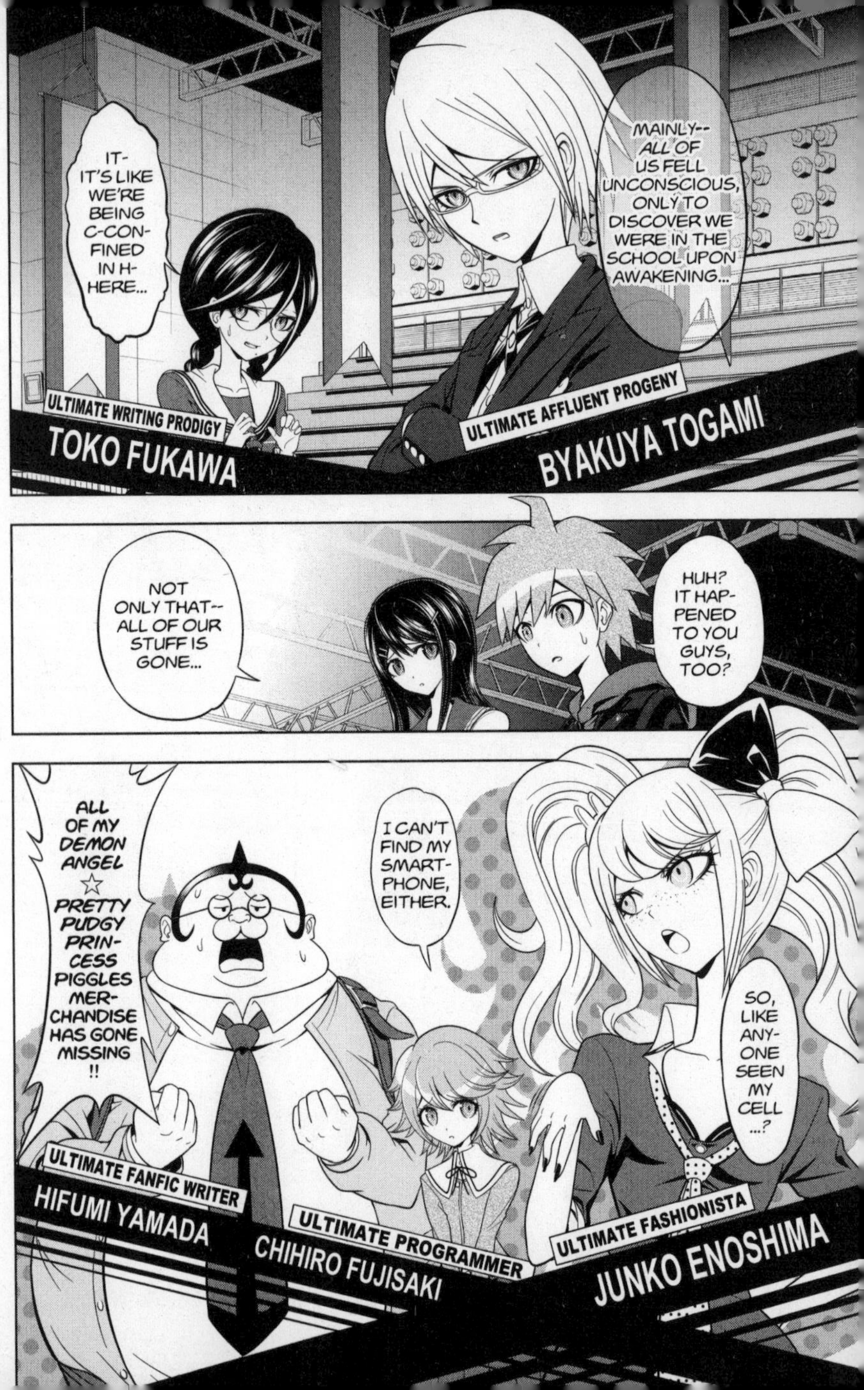
MAINLY-- ALL OF US FELL UNCONSCIOUS, ONLY TO DISCOVER WE WERE IN THE SCHOOL UPON AWAKENING...
IT- IT'S LIKE WE'RE BEING C-CON-FINED IN H-HERE...
ULTIMATE AFFLUENT PROGENY
BYAKUYA TOGAMI
ULTIMATE WRITING PRODIGY
TOKO FUKAWA
HUH? IT HAP-PENED TO YOU GUYS, TOO?
NOT ONLY THAT-- ALL OF OUR STUFF IS GONE...
SO, LIKE ANY-ONE SEEN MY CELL ...?
I CAN'T FIND MY SMART-PHONE, EITHER.
ALL OF MY DEMON ANGEL ☆ PRETTY PUDGY PRIN-CESS PIGGLES MER-CHANDISE HAS GONE MISSING !!
ULTIMATE FASHIONISTA
JUNKO ENOSHIMA
ULTIMATE PROGRAMMER
CHIHIRO FUJISAKI
ULTIMATE FANFIC WRITER
HIFUMI YAMADA

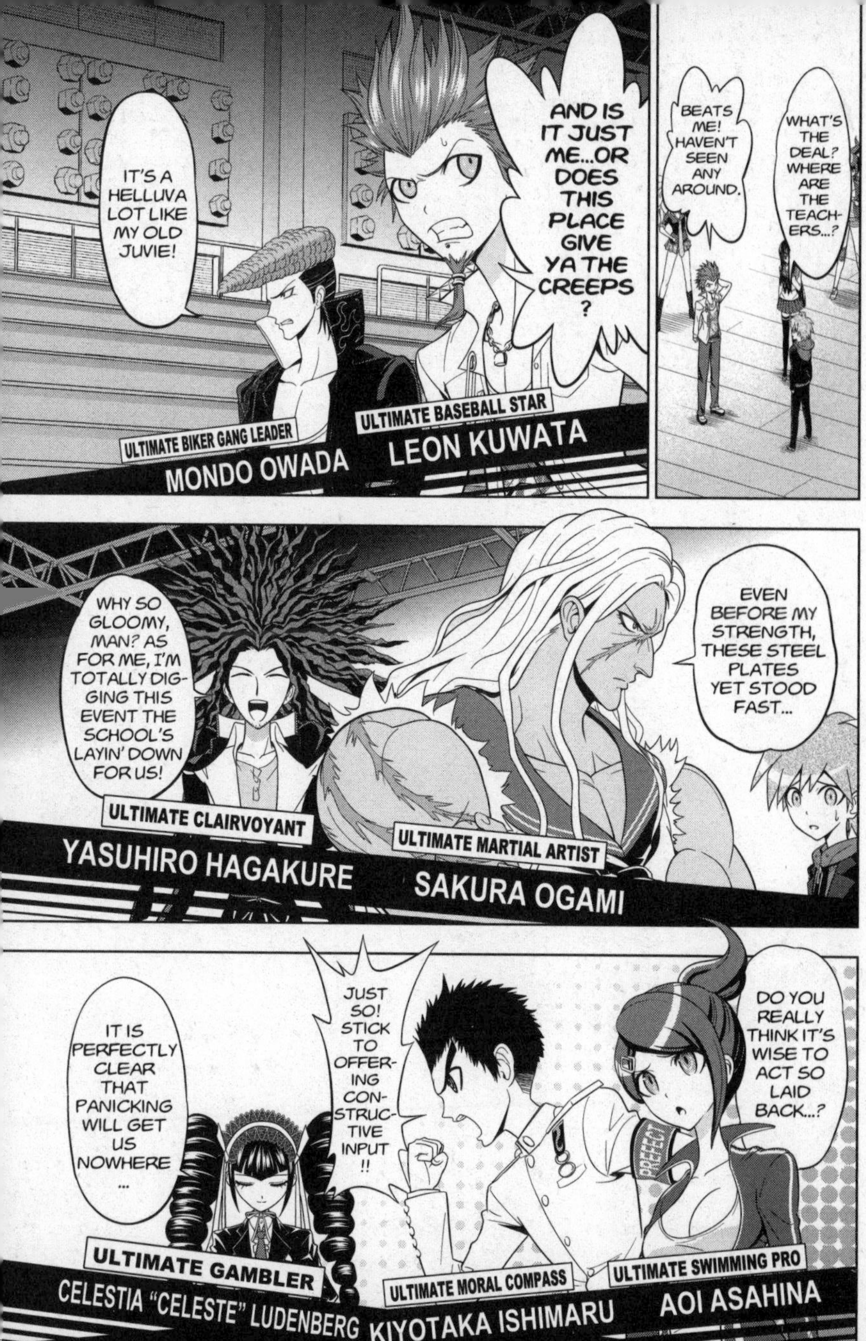
WHAT'S THE DEAL? WHERE ARE THE TEACHERS...?
BEATS ME! HAVEN'T SEEN ANY AROUND.
AND IS IT JUST ME...OR DOES THIS PLACE GIVE YA THE CREEPS?
ULTIMATE BASEBALL STAR
LEON KUWATA
IT'S A HELLUVA LOT LIKE MY OLD JUVIE!
ULTIMATE BIKER GANG LEADER
MONDO OWADA
EVEN BEFORE MY STRENGTH, THESE STEEL PLATES YET STOOD FAST...
ULTIMATE MARTIAL ARTIST
SAKURA OGAMI
WHY SO GLOOMY, MAN? AS FOR ME, I'M TOTALLY DIGGING THIS EVENT THE SCHOOL'S LAYIN' DOWN FOR US!
ULTIMATE CLAIRVOYANT
YASUHIRO HAGAKURE
DO YOU REALLY THINK IT'S WISE TO ACT SO LAID BACK...?
ULTIMATE SWIMMING PRO
AOI ASAHINA
JUST SO! STICK TO OFFERING CONSTRUCTIVE INPUT!!
ULTIMATE MORAL COMPASS
KIYOTAKA ISHIMARU
IT IS PERFECTLY CLEAR THAT PANICKING WILL GET US NOWHERE...
ULTIMATE GAMBLER
CELESTIA "CELESTE" LUDENBERG

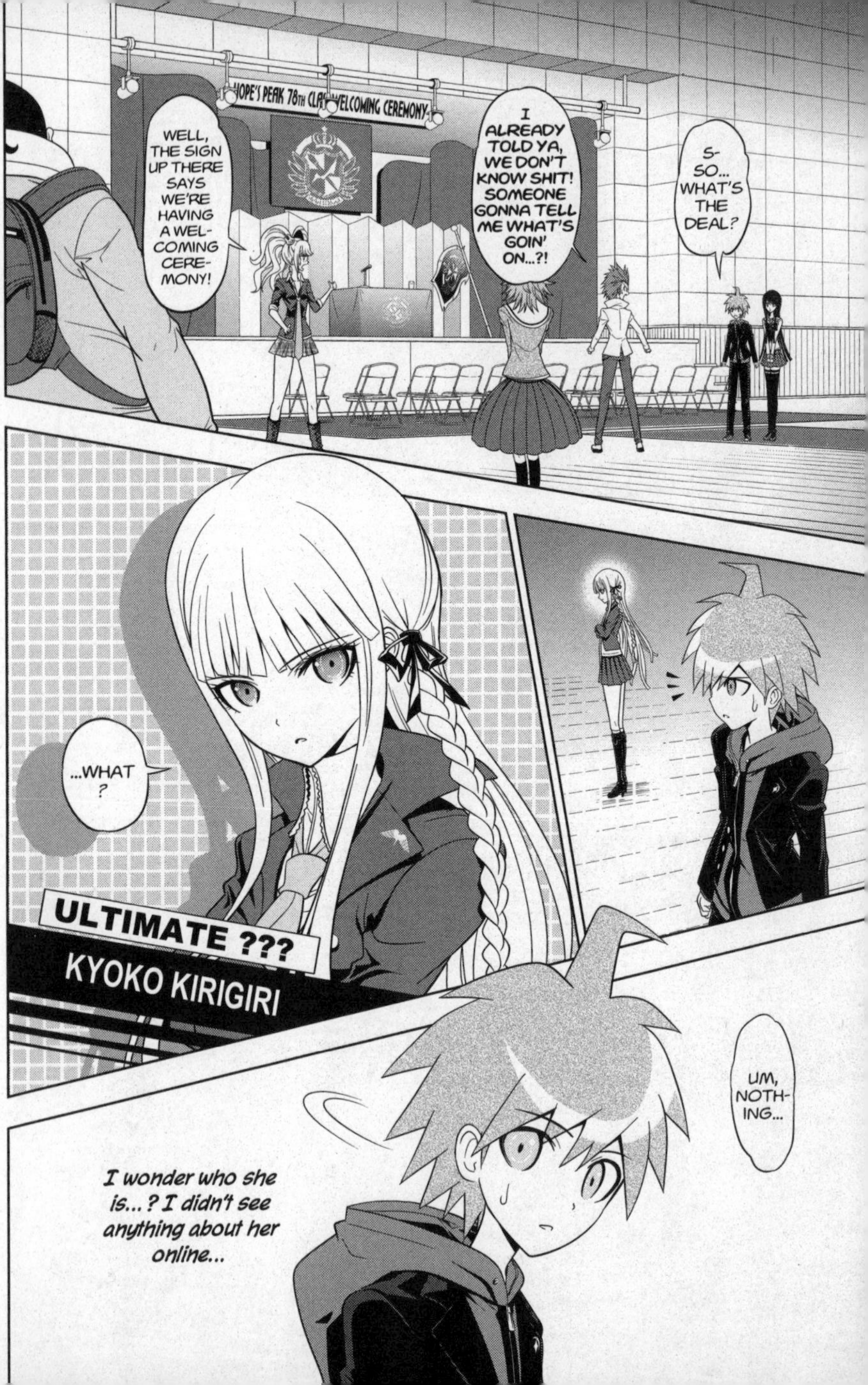
HOPE'S PEAK 78TH CLA WELCOMING CEREMONY
S-SO... WHAT'S THE DEAL?
I ALREADY TOLD YA, WE DON'T KNOW SHIT! SOMEONE GONNA TELL ME WHAT'S GOIN' ON...?!
WELL, THE SIGN UP THERE SAYS WE'RE HAVING A WEL-COMING CERE-MONY!
...WHAT?
ULTIMATE ???
KYOKO KIRIGIRI
UM, NOTH-ING...
I wonder who she is...? I didn't see anything about her online...

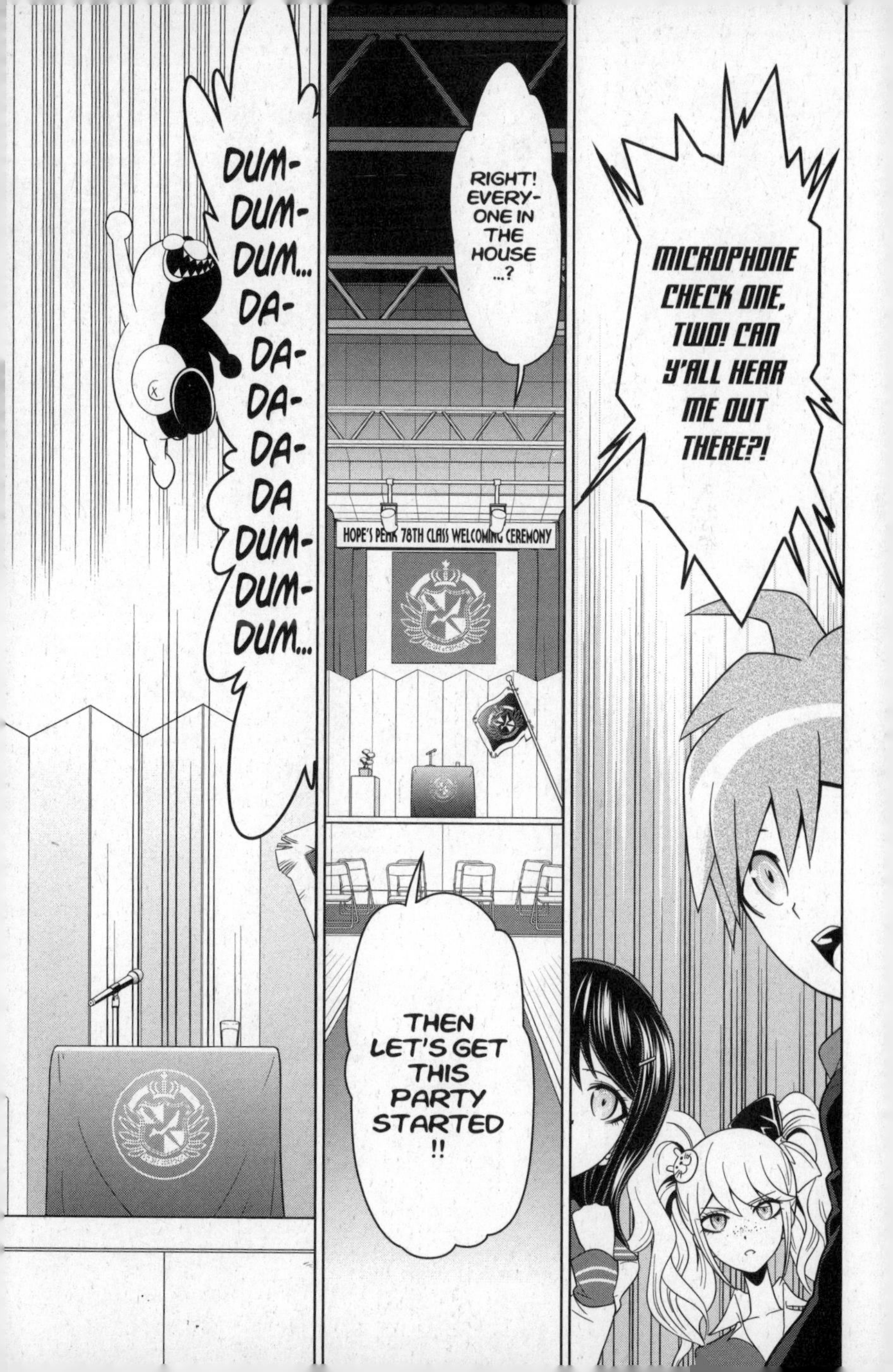
MICROPHONE CHECK ONE, TWO! CAN Y'ALL HEAR ME OUT THERE?!
RIGHT! EVERYONE IN THE HOUSE ...?
HOPE'S PEAK 78TH CLASS WELCOMING CEREMONY
THEN LET'S GET THIS PARTY STARTED!!
DUM-DUM-DUM... DA-DA-DA-DA-DA DUM-DUM-DUM...

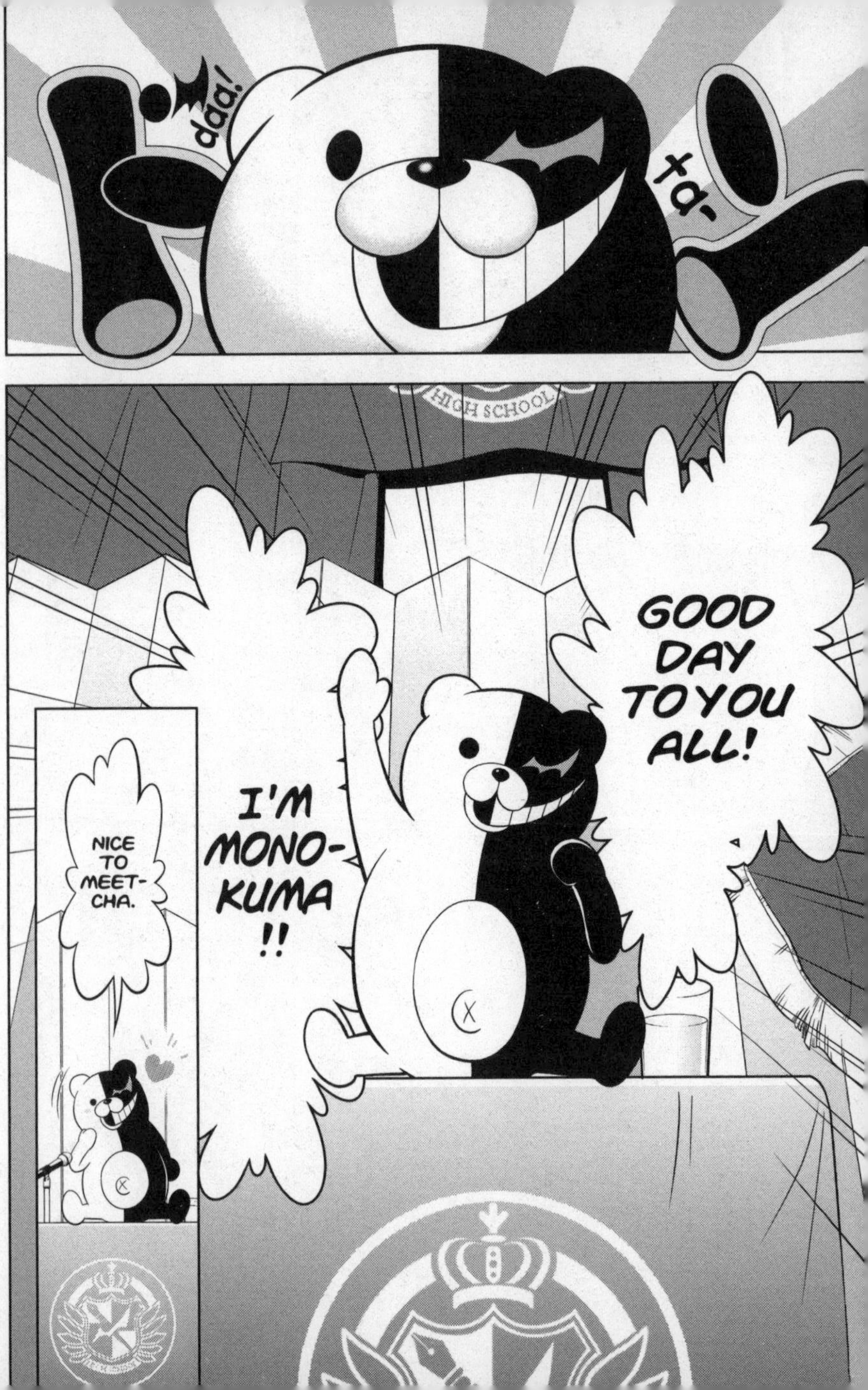
ta-
daa!
HIGH SCHOOL
GOOD DAY TO YOU ALL!
I'M MONO-KUMA!!
NICE TO MEET-CHA.

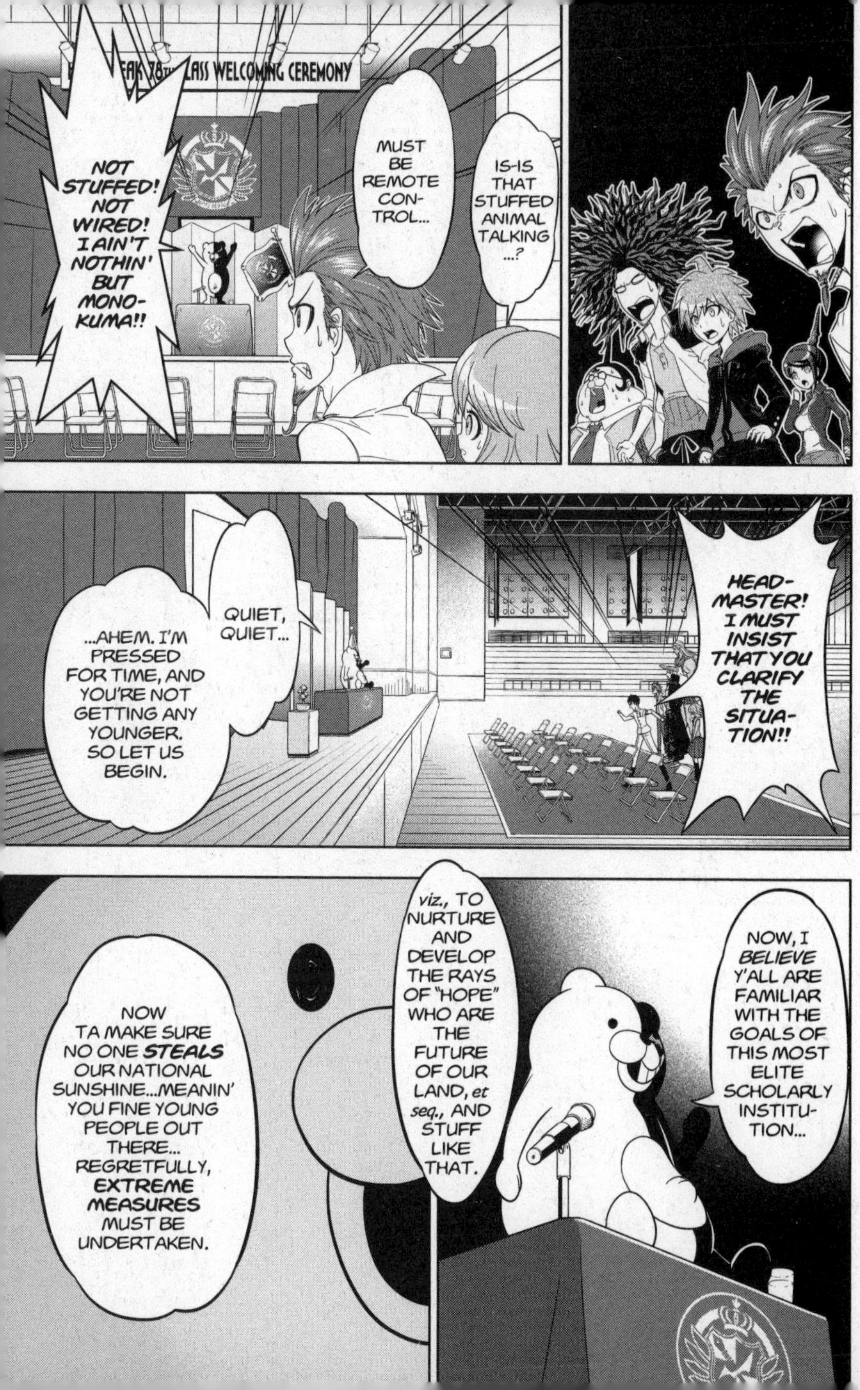
WELCOMING CEREMONY
IS-IS THAT STUFFED ANIMAL TALKING...?
MUST BE REMOTE CONTROL...
NOT STUFFED! NOT WIRED! I AIN'T NOTHIN' BUT MONOKUMA!!
HEADMASTER! I MUST INSIST THAT YOU CLARIFY THE SITUATION!!
QUIET, QUIET...
...AHEM. I'M PRESSED FOR TIME, AND YOU'RE NOT GETTING ANY YOUNGER. SO LET US BEGIN.
NOW, I *BELIEVE* Y'ALL ARE FAMILIAR WITH THE GOALS OF THIS MOST ELITE SCHOLARLY INSTITUTION...
viz., TO NURTURE AND DEVELOP THE RAYS OF "HOPE" WHO ARE THE FUTURE OF OUR LAND, *et seq.*, AND STUFF LIKE THAT.
NOW TA MAKE SURE NO ONE **STEALS** OUR NATIONAL SUNSHINE...MEANIN' YOU FINE YOUNG PEOPLE OUT THERE... REGRETFULLY, **EXTREME MEASURES** MUST BE UNDERTAKEN.

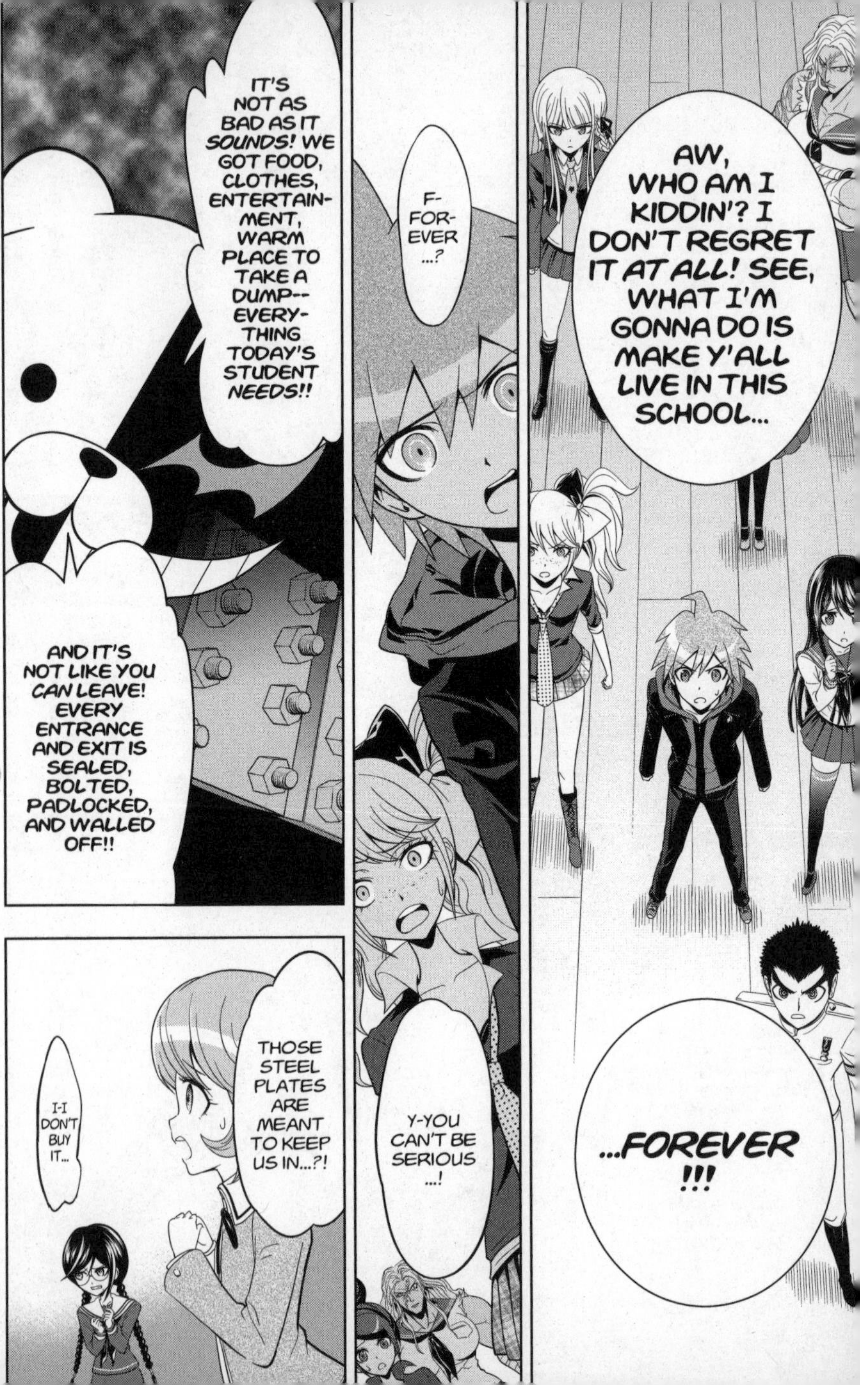
AW, WHO AM I KIDDIN'? I DON'T REGRET IT AT ALL! SEE, WHAT I'M GONNA DO IS MAKE Y'ALL LIVE IN THIS SCHOOL...
...FOREVER!!!
F-FOR-EVER...?
Y-YOU CAN'T BE SERIOUS...!
IT'S NOT AS BAD AS IT SOUNDS! WE GOT FOOD, CLOTHES, ENTERTAIN-MENT, WARM PLACE TO TAKE A DUMP-- EVERY-THING TODAY'S STUDENT NEEDS!!
AND IT'S NOT LIKE YOU CAN LEAVE! EVERY ENTRANCE AND EXIT IS SEALED, BOLTED, PADLOCKED, AND WALLED OFF!!
THOSE STEEL PLATES ARE MEANT TO KEEP US IN...?!
I-I DON'T BUY IT...

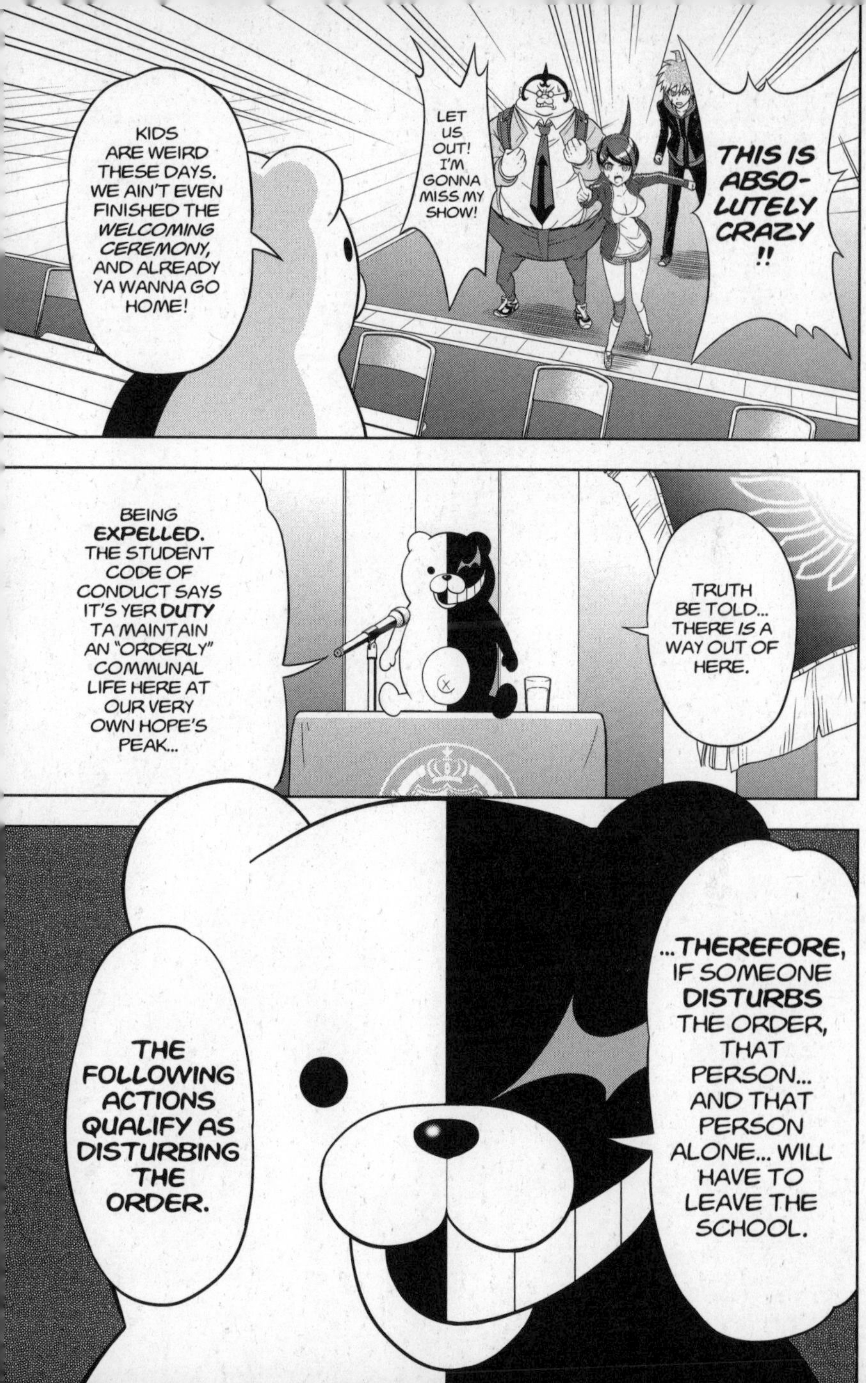
THIS IS ABSOLUTELY CRAZY!!
LET US OUT! I'M GONNA MISS MY SHOW!
KIDS ARE WEIRD THESE DAYS. WE AIN'T EVEN FINISHED THE *WELCOMING CEREMONY*, AND ALREADY YA WANNA GO HOME!
TRUTH BE TOLD... THERE *IS* A WAY OUT OF HERE.
BEING **EXPELLED**. THE STUDENT CODE OF CONDUCT SAYS IT'S YER **DUTY** TA MAINTAIN AN "ORDERLY" COMMUNAL LIFE HERE AT OUR VERY OWN HOPE'S PEAK...
...THEREFORE, IF SOMEONE **DISTURBS** THE ORDER, THAT PERSON... AND THAT PERSON ALONE... WILL HAVE TO LEAVE THE SCHOOL.
THE FOLLOWING ACTIONS QUALIFY AS DISTURBING THE ORDER.

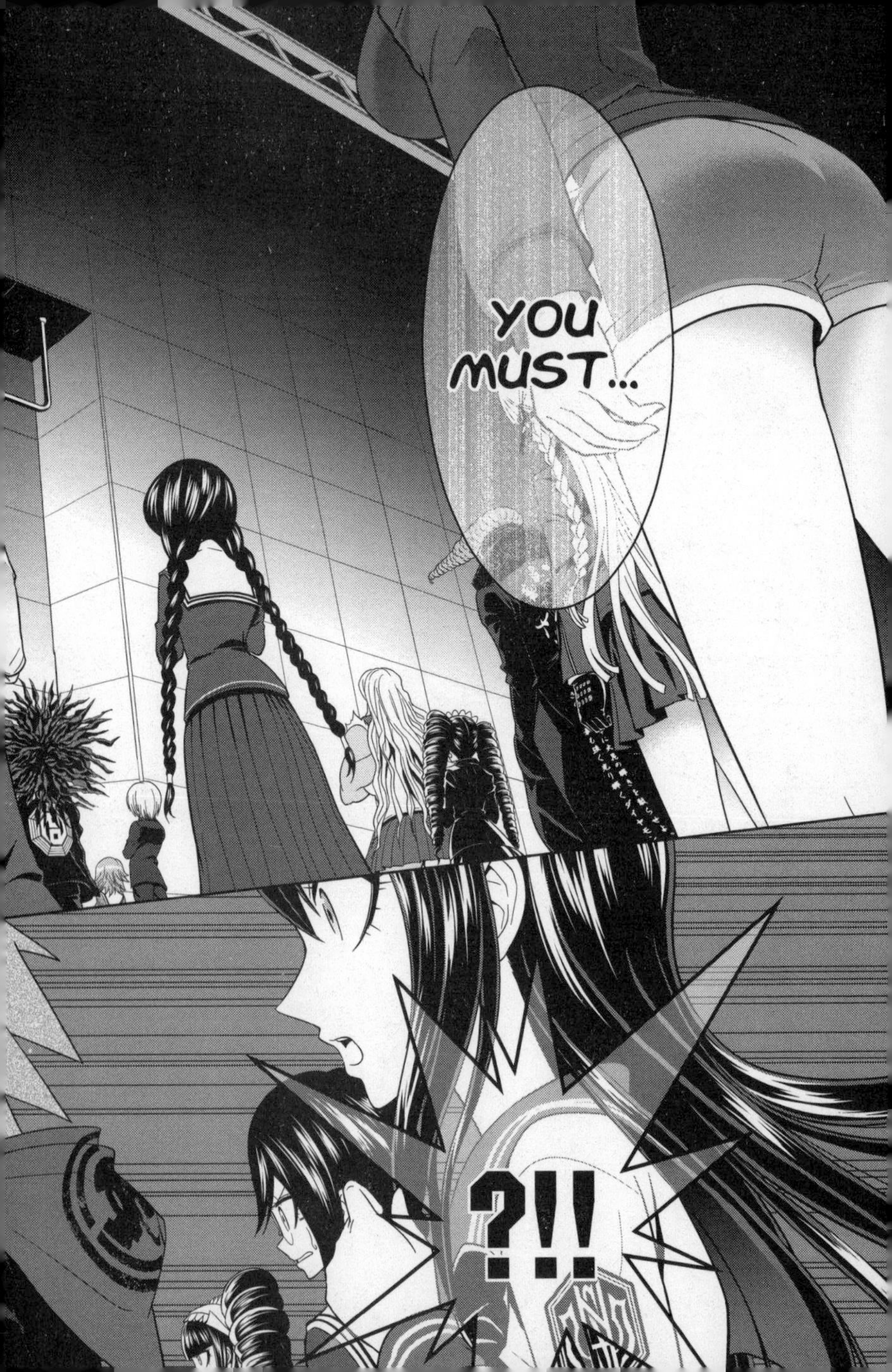
YOU MUST...
?!!

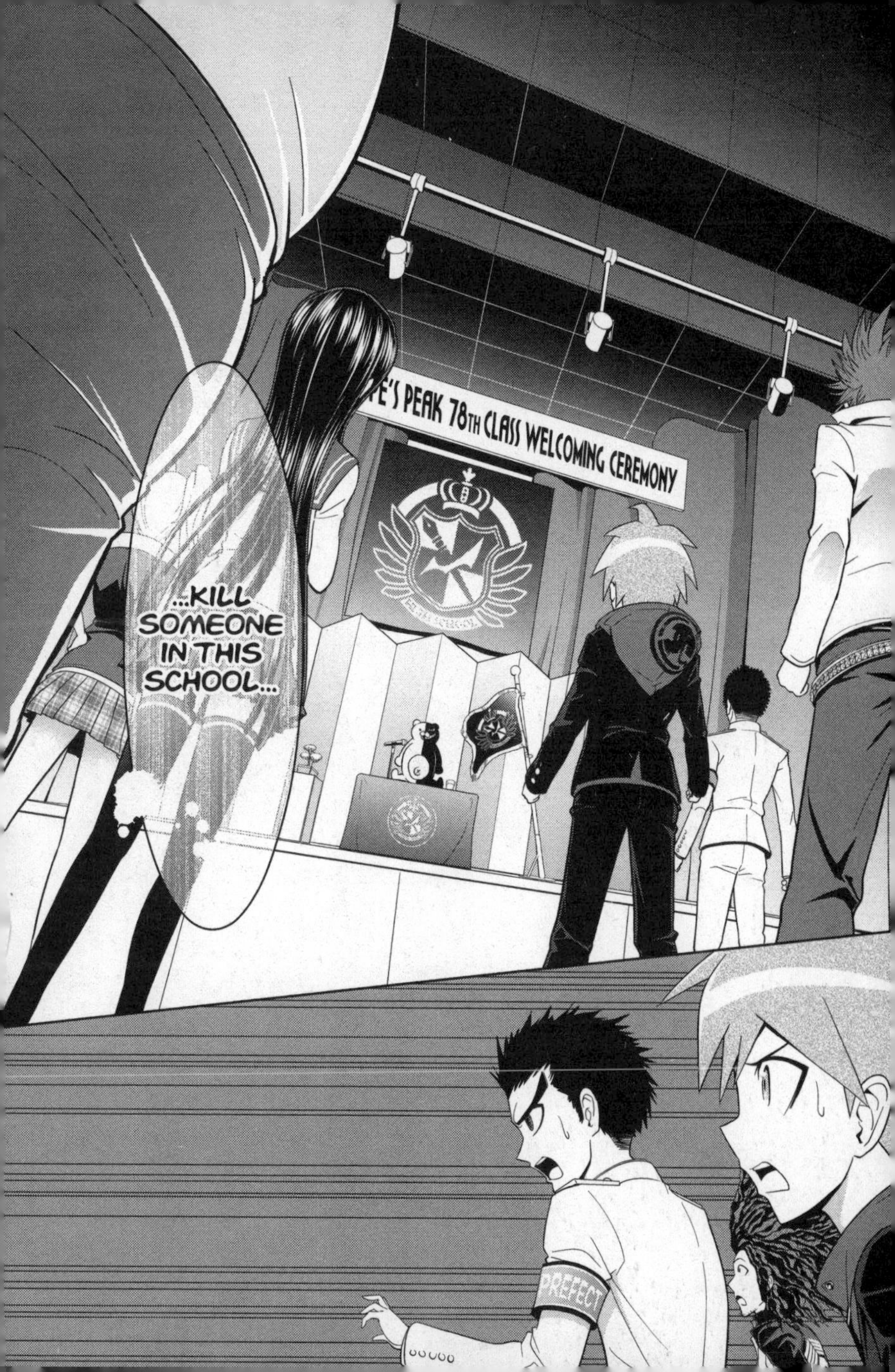
PE'S PEAK 78TH CLASS WELCOMING CEREMONY
...KILL SOMEONE IN THIS SCHOOL...
PREFECT

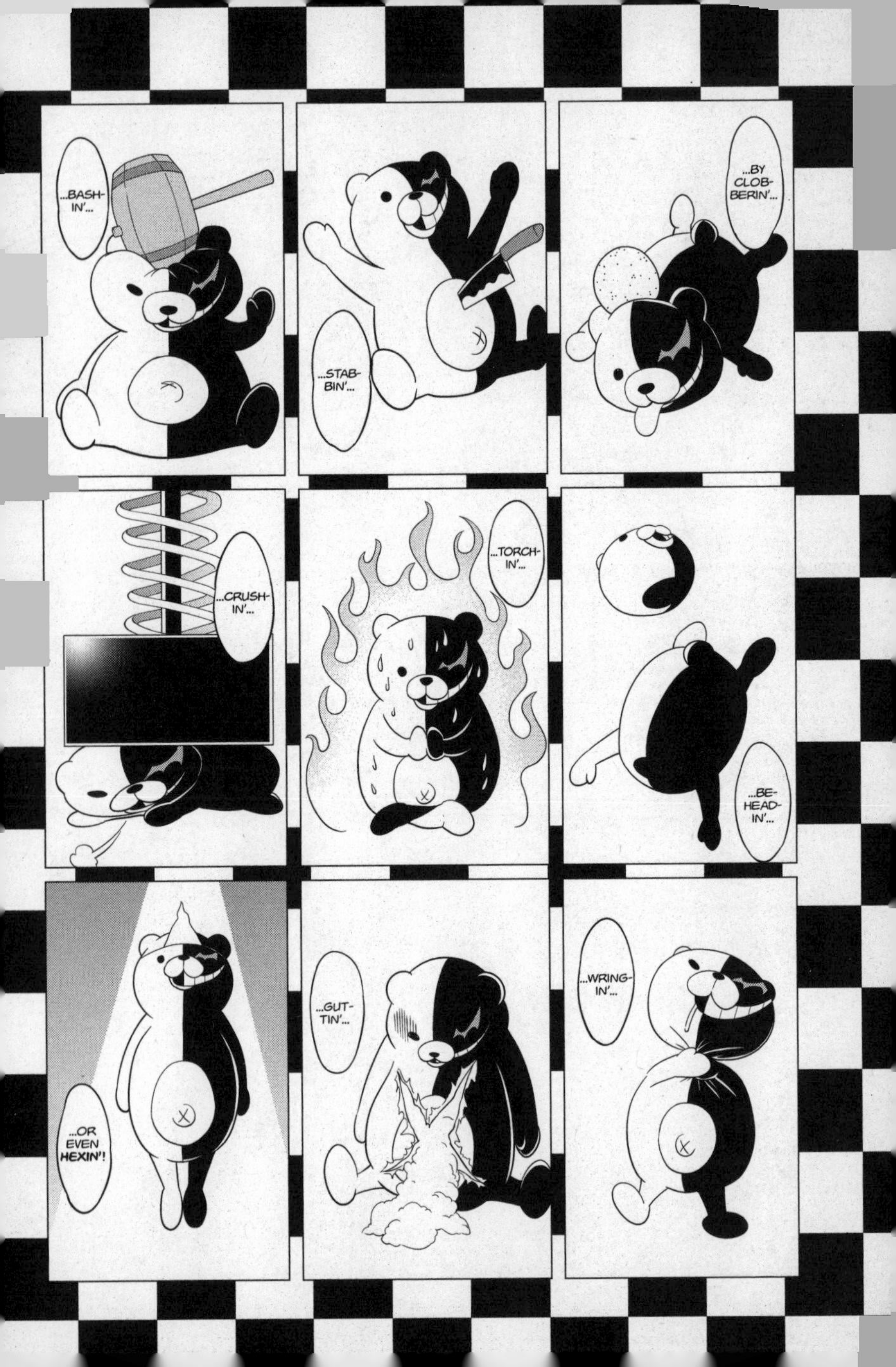
...BY CLOBBERIN'...
...STABBIN'...
...BASHIN'...
...BEHEADIN'...
...TORCHIN'...
...CRUSHIN'...
...WRINGIN'...
...GUTTIN'...
...OR EVEN HEXIN'!

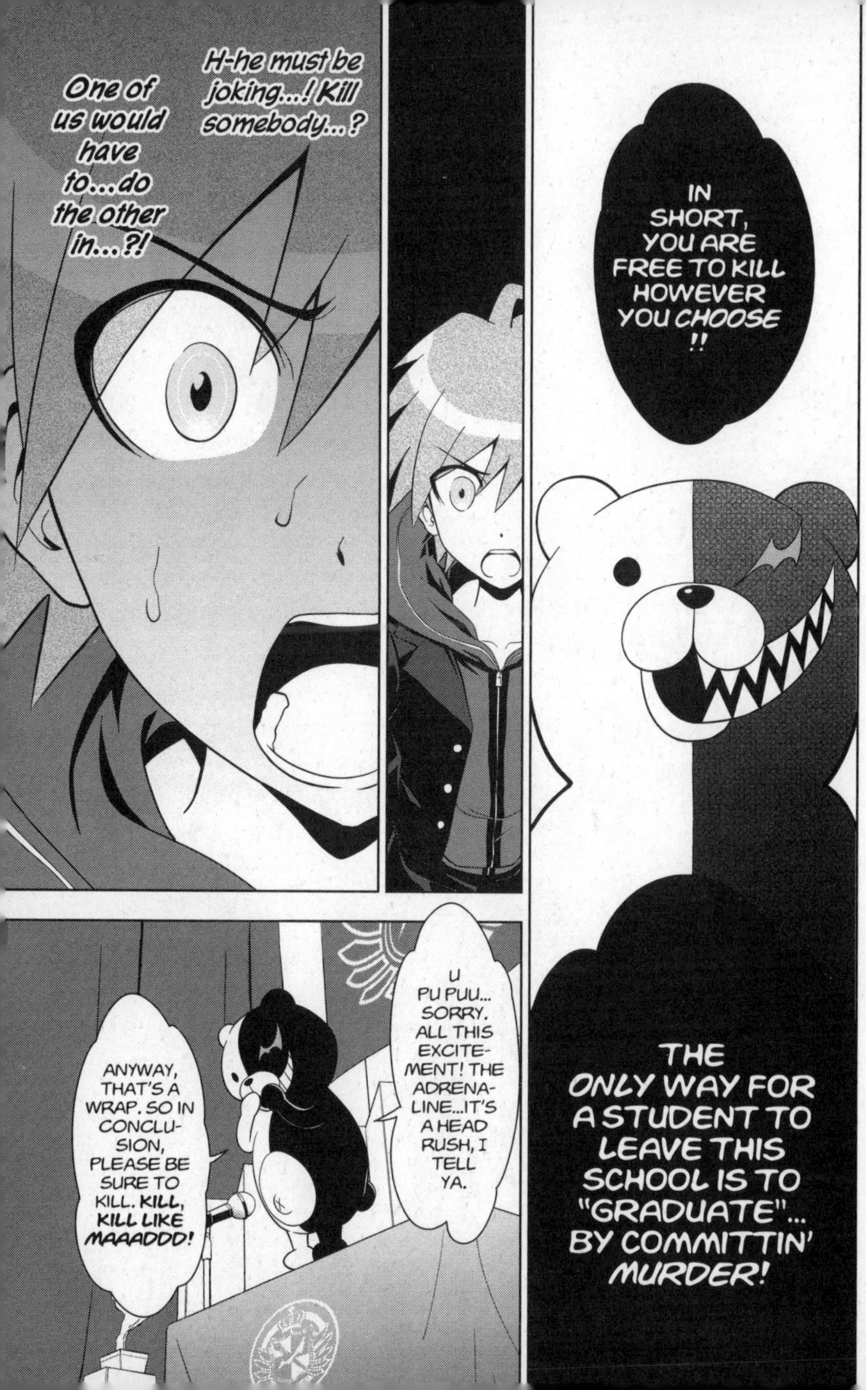
IN SHORT, YOU ARE FREE TO KILL HOWEVER YOU CHOOSE !!
THE ONLY WAY FOR A STUDENT TO LEAVE THIS SCHOOL IS TO "GRADUATE"... BY COMMITTIN' MURDER!
H-he must be joking...! Kill somebody...?
One of us would have to...do the other in...?!
U PU PUU... SORRY. ALL THIS EXCITE-MENT! THE ADRENA-LINE...IT'S A HEAD RUSH, I TELL YA.
ANYWAY, THAT'S A WRAP. SO IN CONCLU-SION, PLEASE BE SURE TO KILL. KILL, KILL LIKE MAAADDD!

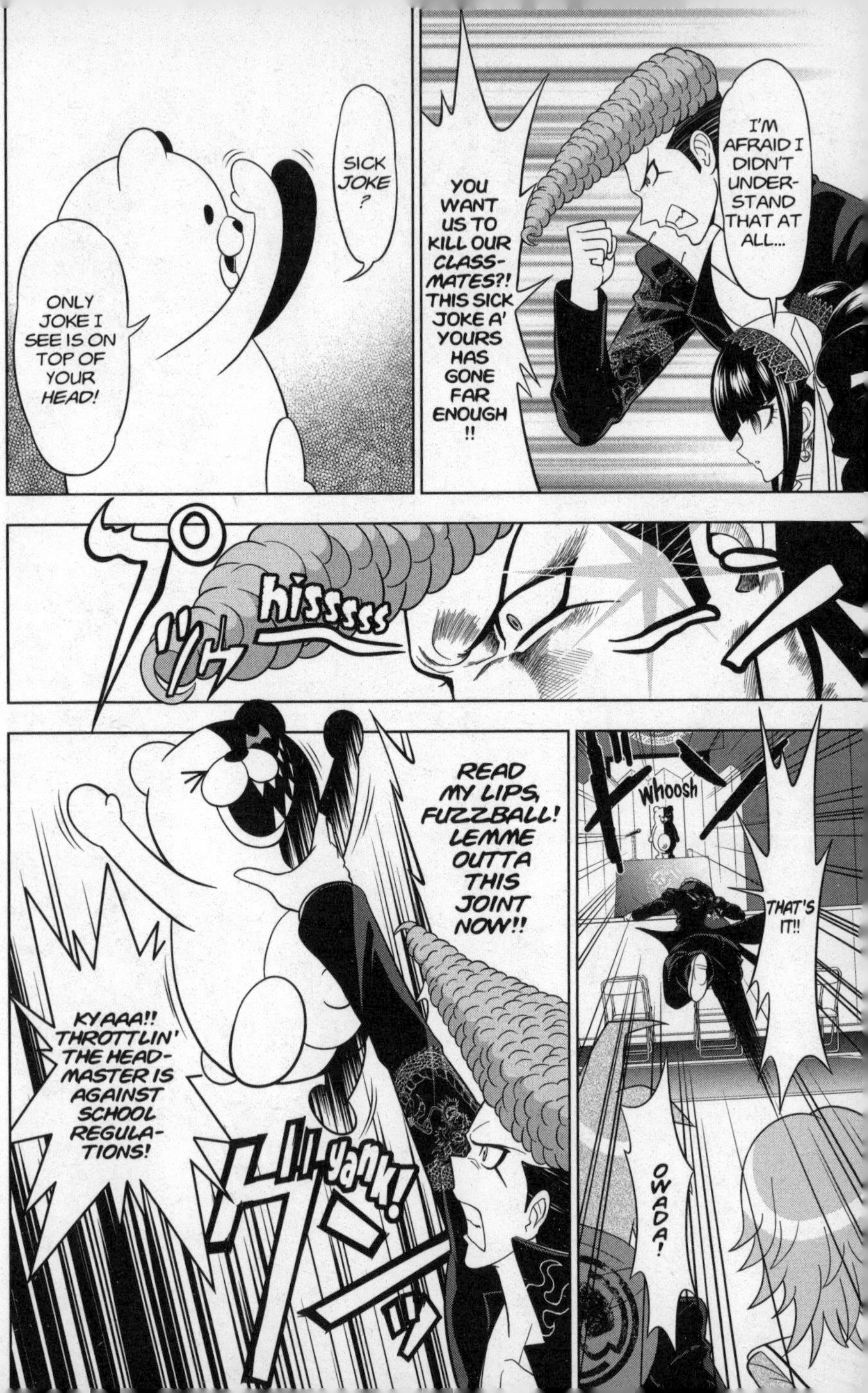
I'M AFRAID I DIDN'T UNDER-STAND THAT AT ALL...
YOU WANT US TO KILL OUR CLASS-MATES?! THIS SICK JOKE A' YOURS HAS GONE FAR ENOUGH!!
SICK JOKE?
ONLY JOKE I SEE IS ON TOP OF YOUR HEAD!
hissssss
whoosh
THAT'S IT!!
OWADA!
READ MY LIPS, FUZZBALL! LEMME OUTTA THIS JOINT NOW!!
KYAAA!! THROTTLIN' THE HEAD-MASTER IS AGAINST SCHOOL REGULA-TIONS!
yank!

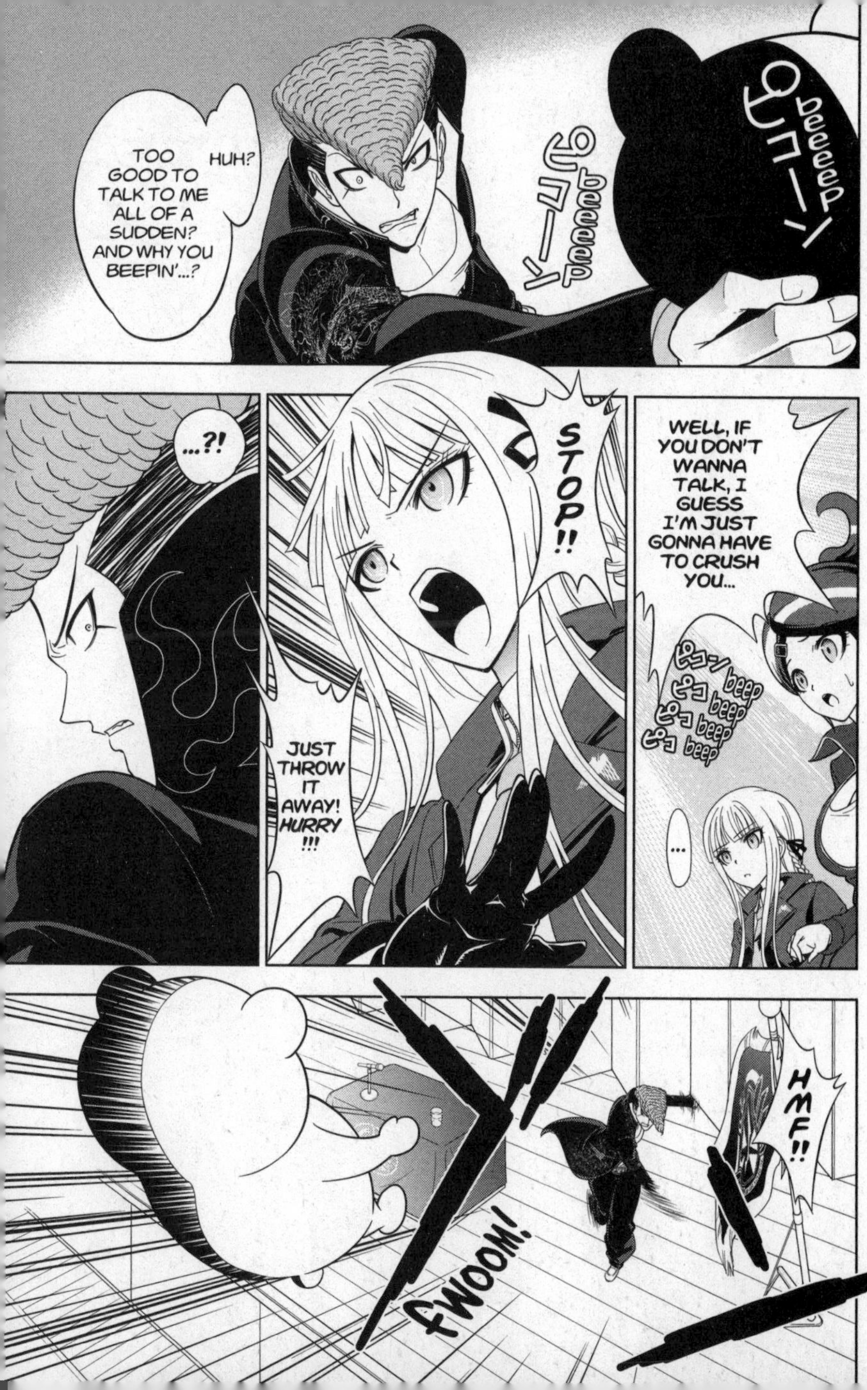
beeeep ピコーン
beeeeep ピコーン
HUH?
TOO GOOD TO TALK TO ME ALL OF A SUDDEN? AND WHY YOU BEEPIN'...?
WELL, IF YOU DON'T WANNA TALK, I GUESS I'M JUST GONNA HAVE TO CRUSH YOU...
ピコーン beep
ピコ beep
ピコ beep
ピコ beep
...
STOP!!
JUST THROW IT AWAY! HURRY!!!
...?!
HMF!!
FWOOM!

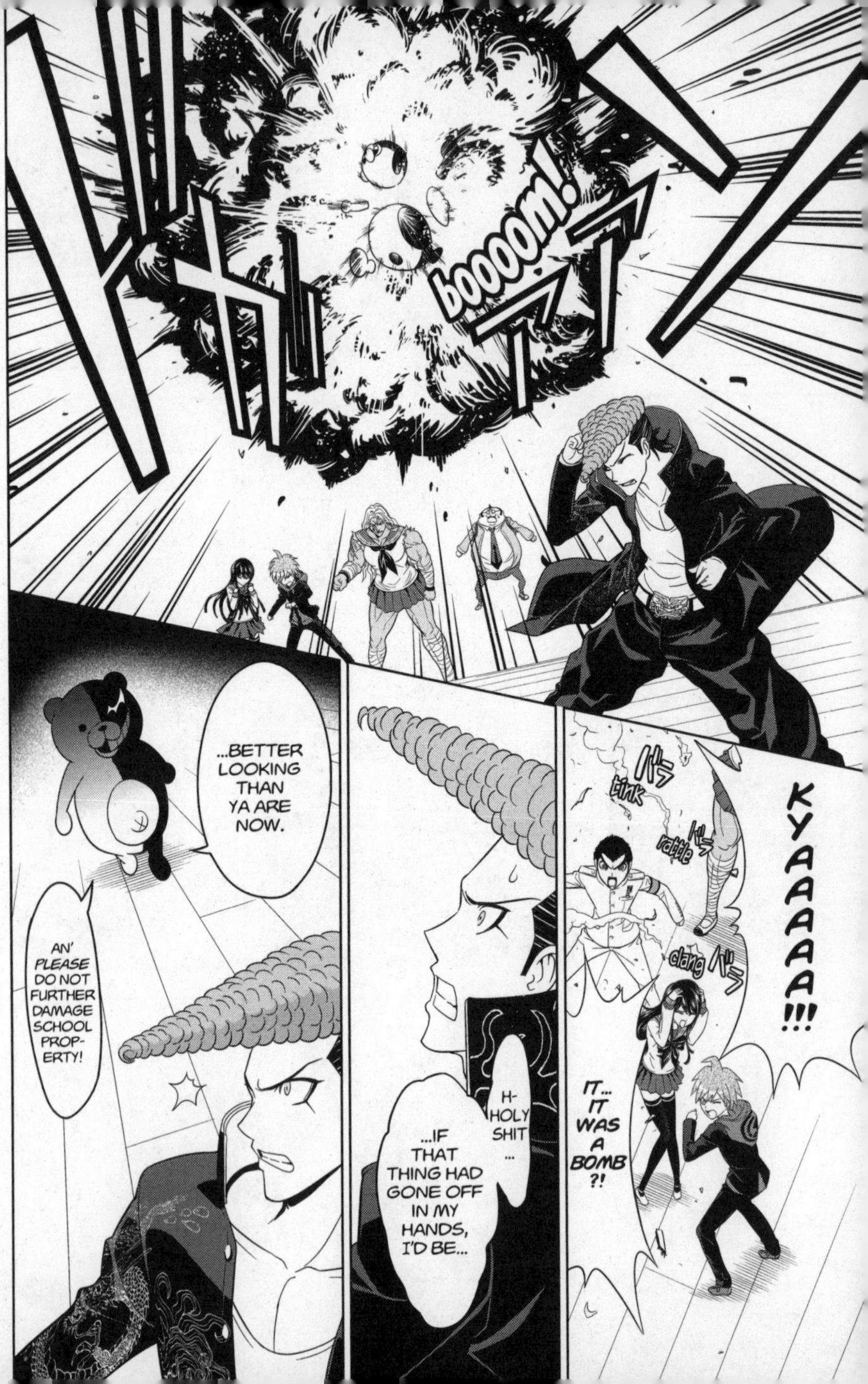
booom!
tink
rattle
clang
KYAAAAAA!!!
IT... IT WAS A BOMB?!
H-HOLY SHIT...
...IF THAT THING HAD GONE OFF IN MY HANDS, I'D BE...
...BETTER LOOKING THAN YA ARE NOW.
AN' PLEASE DO NOT FURTHER DAMAGE SCHOOL PROP-ERTY!

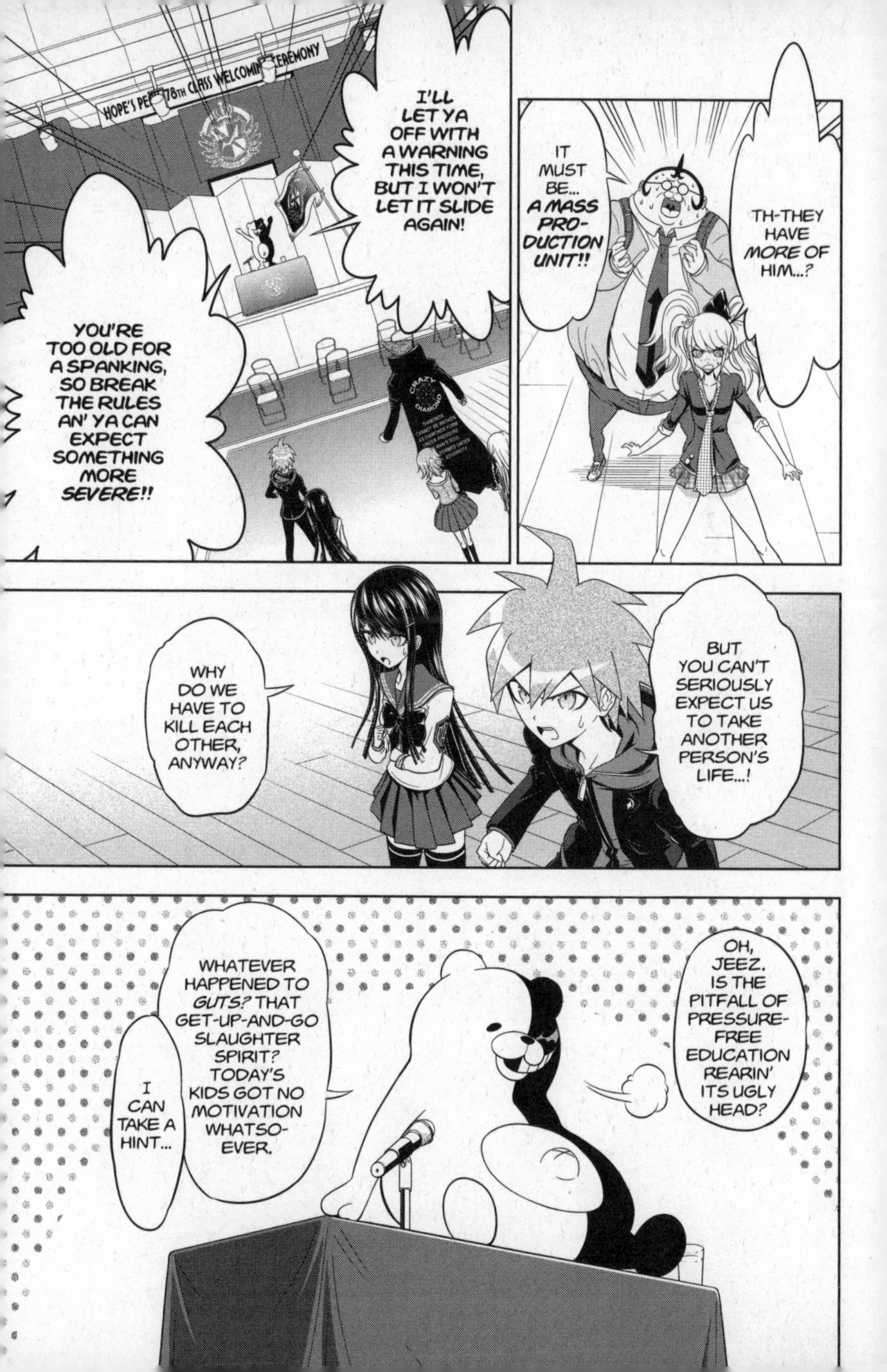
TH-THEY HAVE MORE OF HIM...?
IT MUST BE... A MASS PRODUCTION UNIT!!
I'LL LET YA OFF WITH A WARNING THIS TIME, BUT I WON'T LET IT SLIDE AGAIN!
CRAZY DIAMOND
YOU'RE TOO OLD FOR A SPANKING, SO BREAK THE RULES AN' YA CAN EXPECT SOMETHING MORE SEVERE!!
BUT YOU CAN'T SERIOUSLY EXPECT US TO TAKE ANOTHER PERSON'S LIFE...!
WHY DO WE HAVE TO KILL EACH OTHER, ANYWAY?
OH, JEEZ. IS THE PITFALL OF PRESSURE-FREE EDUCATION REARIN' ITS UGLY HEAD?
WHATEVER HAPPENED TO GUTS? THAT GET-UP-AND-GO SLAUGHTER SPIRIT? TODAY'S KIDS GOT NO MOTIVATION WHATSO-EVER.
I CAN TAKE A HINT...

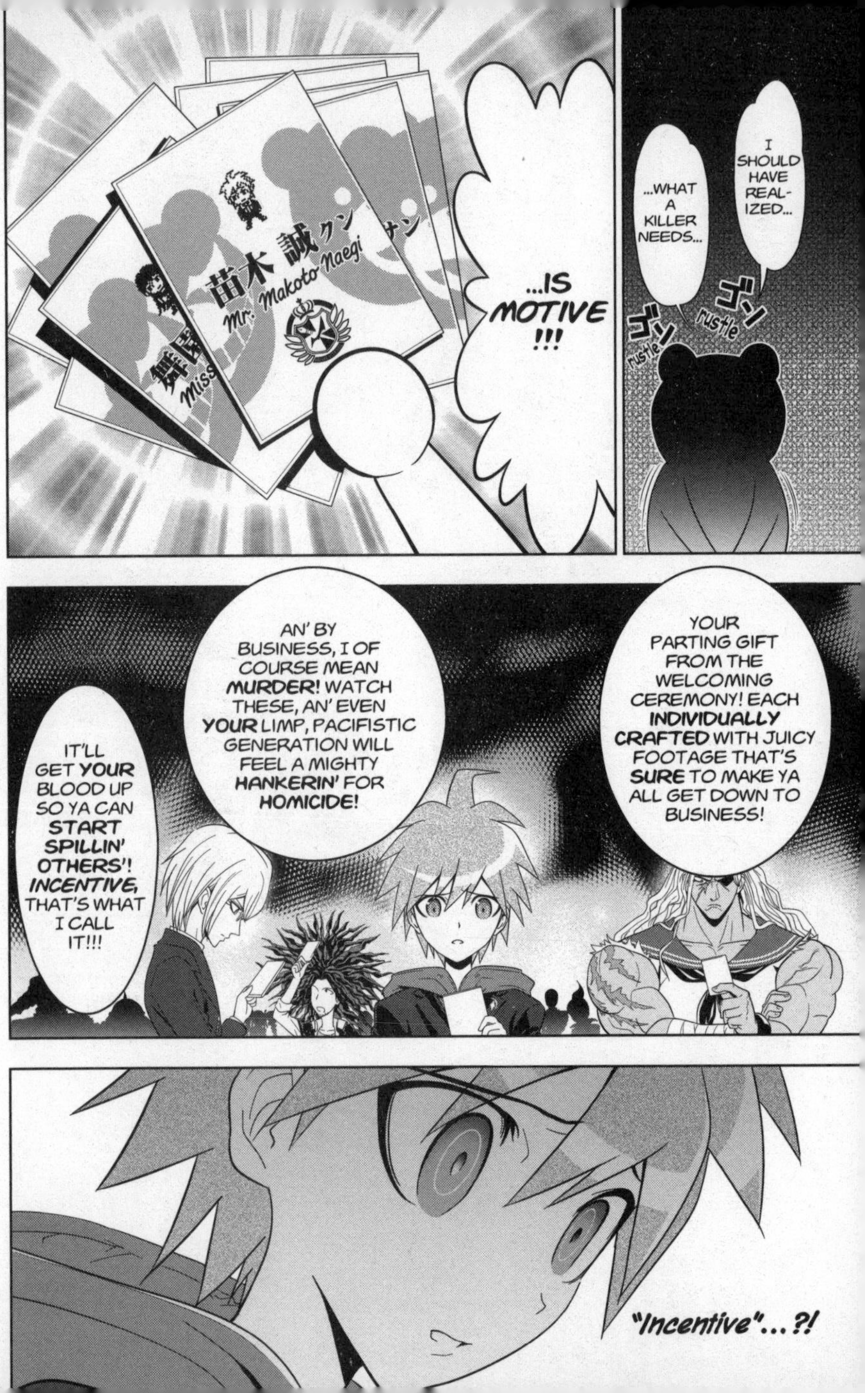
I SHOULD HAVE REALIZED...
...WHAT A KILLER NEEDS...
rustle
rustle
...IS MOTIVE!!!
苗木 誠クン
Mr. Makoto Naegi
Miss
YOUR PARTING GIFT FROM THE WELCOMING CEREMONY! EACH INDIVIDUALLY CRAFTED WITH JUICY FOOTAGE THAT'S SURE TO MAKE YA ALL GET DOWN TO BUSINESS!
AN' BY BUSINESS, I OF COURSE MEAN MURDER! WATCH THESE, AN' EVEN YOUR LIMP, PACIFISTIC GENERATION WILL FEEL A MIGHTY HANKERIN' FOR HOMICIDE!
IT'LL GET YOUR BLOOD UP SO YA CAN START SPILLIN' OTHERS'! INCENTIVE, THAT'S WHAT I CALL IT!!!
"Incentive"...?!

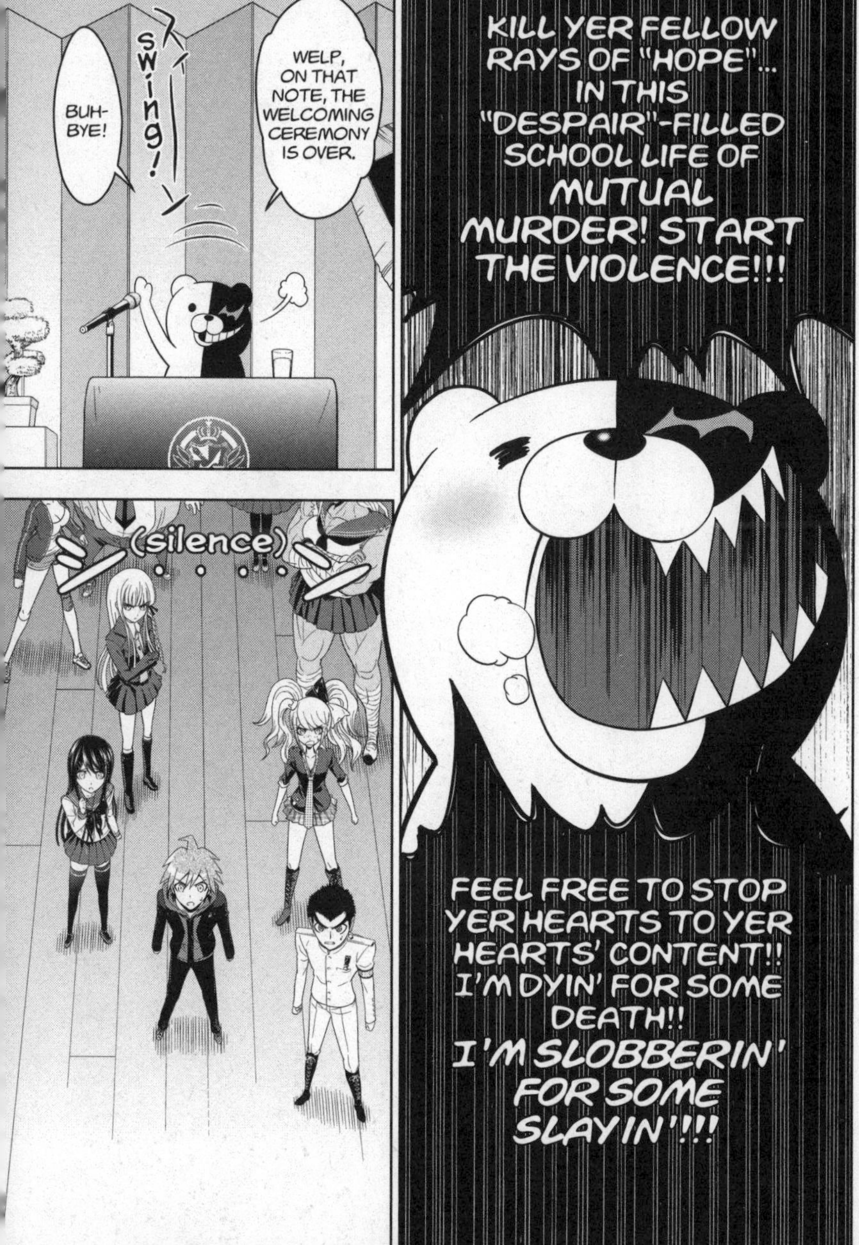
KILL YER FELLOW RAYS OF "HOPE"... IN THIS "DESPAIR"-FILLED SCHOOL LIFE OF MUTUAL MURDER! START THE VIOLENCE!!!
FEEL FREE TO STOP YER HEARTS TO YER HEARTS' CONTENT!! I'M DYIN' FOR SOME DEATH!!
I'M SLOBBERIN' FOR SOME SLAYIN'!!!
WELP, ON THAT NOTE, THE WELCOMING CEREMONY IS OVER.
SWING!
BUH-BYE!
(silence)
....

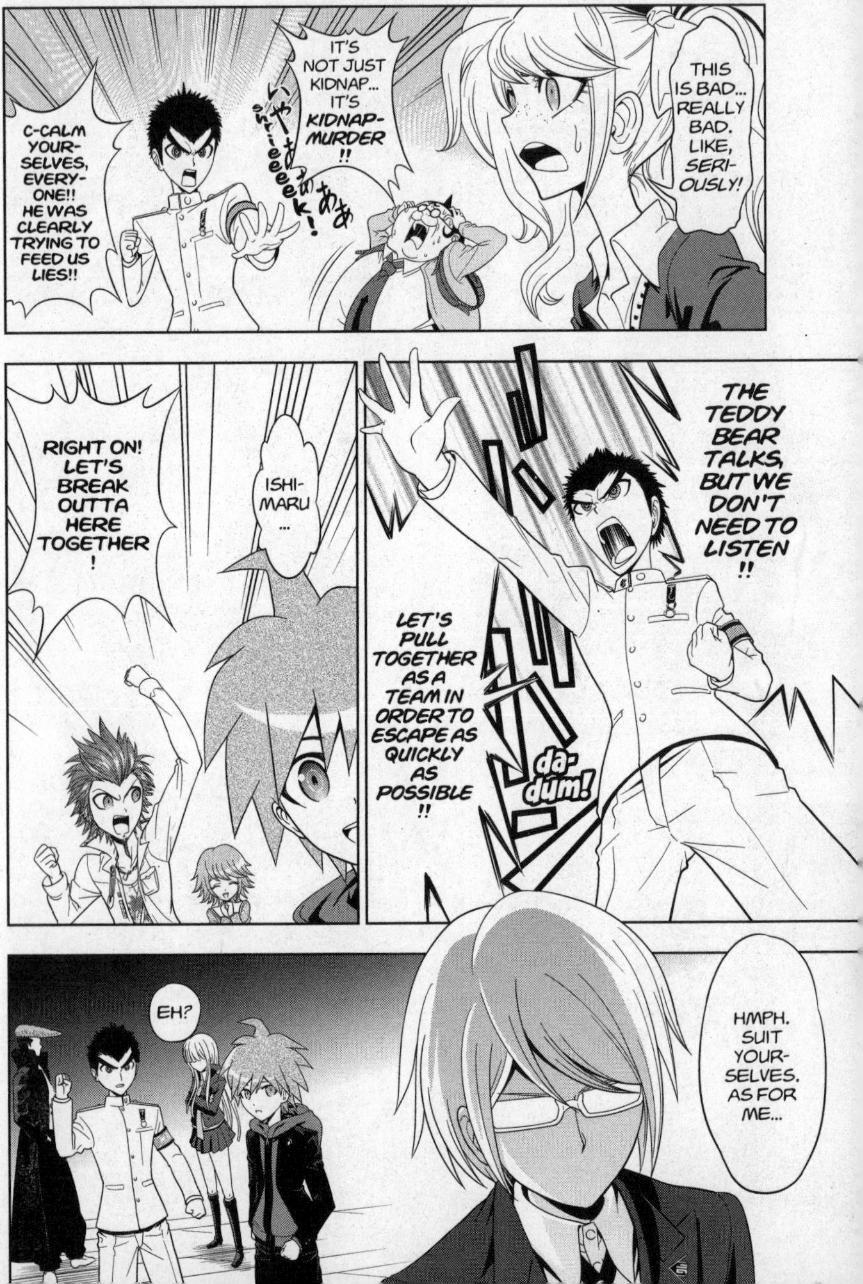
THIS IS BAD... REALLY BAD. LIKE, SERIOUSLY!
IT'S NOT JUST KIDNAP... IT'S KIDNAP-MURDER!!
いやあああ
shrieeeeek!
C-CALM YOURSELVES, EVERYONE!! HE WAS CLEARLY TRYING TO FEED US LIES!!
THE TEDDY BEAR TALKS, BUT WE DON'T NEED TO LISTEN!!
LET'S PULL TOGETHER AS A TEAM IN ORDER TO ESCAPE AS QUICKLY AS POSSIBLE!!
da-dum!
ISHIMARU...
RIGHT ON! LET'S BREAK OUTTA HERE TOGETHER!
HMPH. SUIT YOURSELVES. AS FOR ME...
EH?

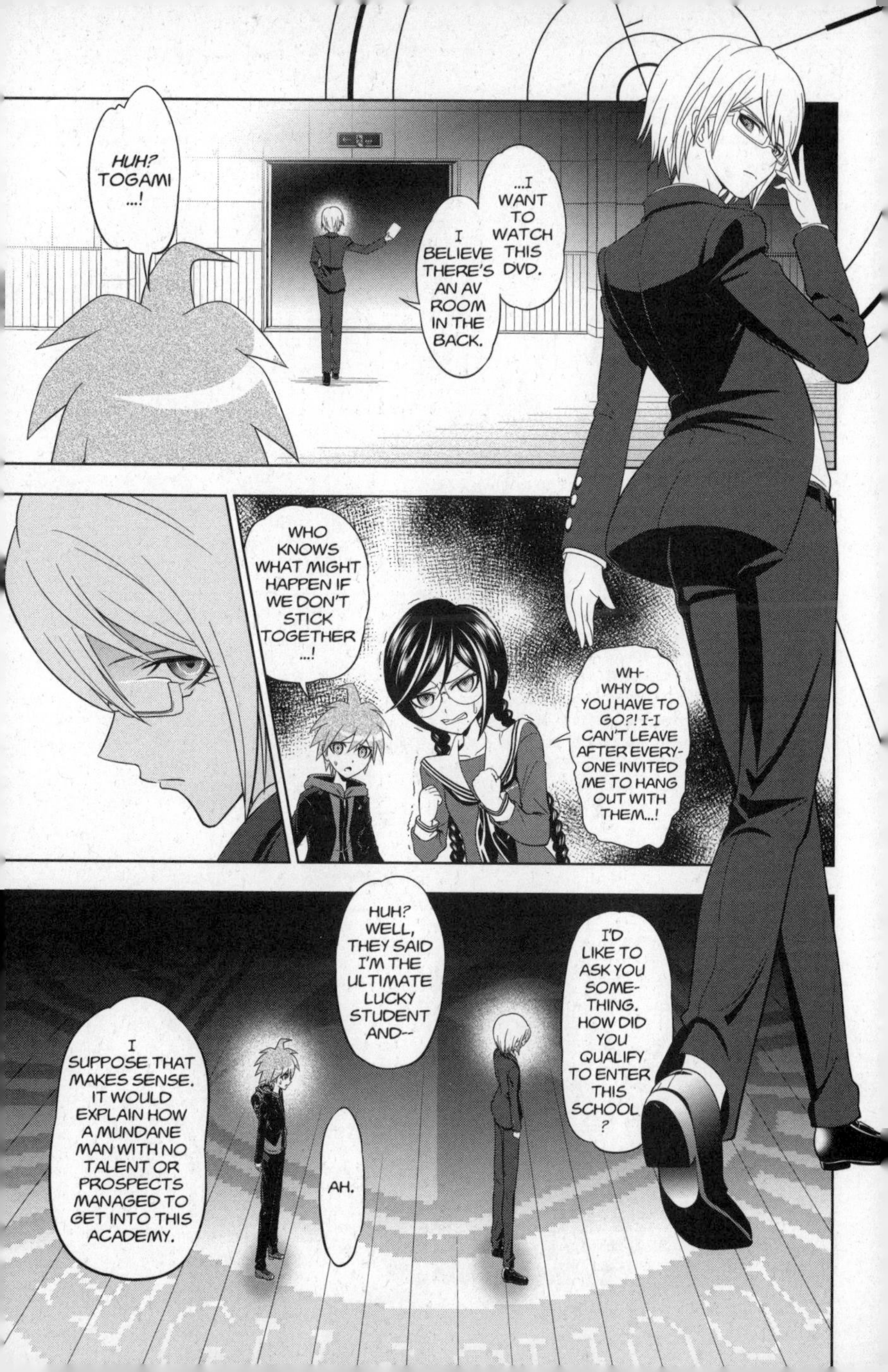
...I WANT TO WATCH THIS DVD.
I BELIEVE THERE'S AN AV ROOM IN THE BACK.
HUH? TOGAMI ...!
WH- WHY DO YOU HAVE TO GO?! I-I CAN'T LEAVE AFTER EVERY-ONE INVITED ME TO HANG OUT WITH THEM...!
WHO KNOWS WHAT MIGHT HAPPEN IF WE DON'T STICK TOGETHER ...!
I'D LIKE TO ASK YOU SOME-THING. HOW DID YOU QUALIFY TO ENTER THIS SCHOOL ?
HUH? WELL, THEY SAID I'M THE ULTIMATE LUCKY STUDENT AND--
AH.
I SUPPOSE THAT MAKES SENSE. IT WOULD EXPLAIN HOW A MUNDANE MAN WITH NO TALENT OR PROSPECTS MANAGED TO GET INTO THIS ACADEMY.

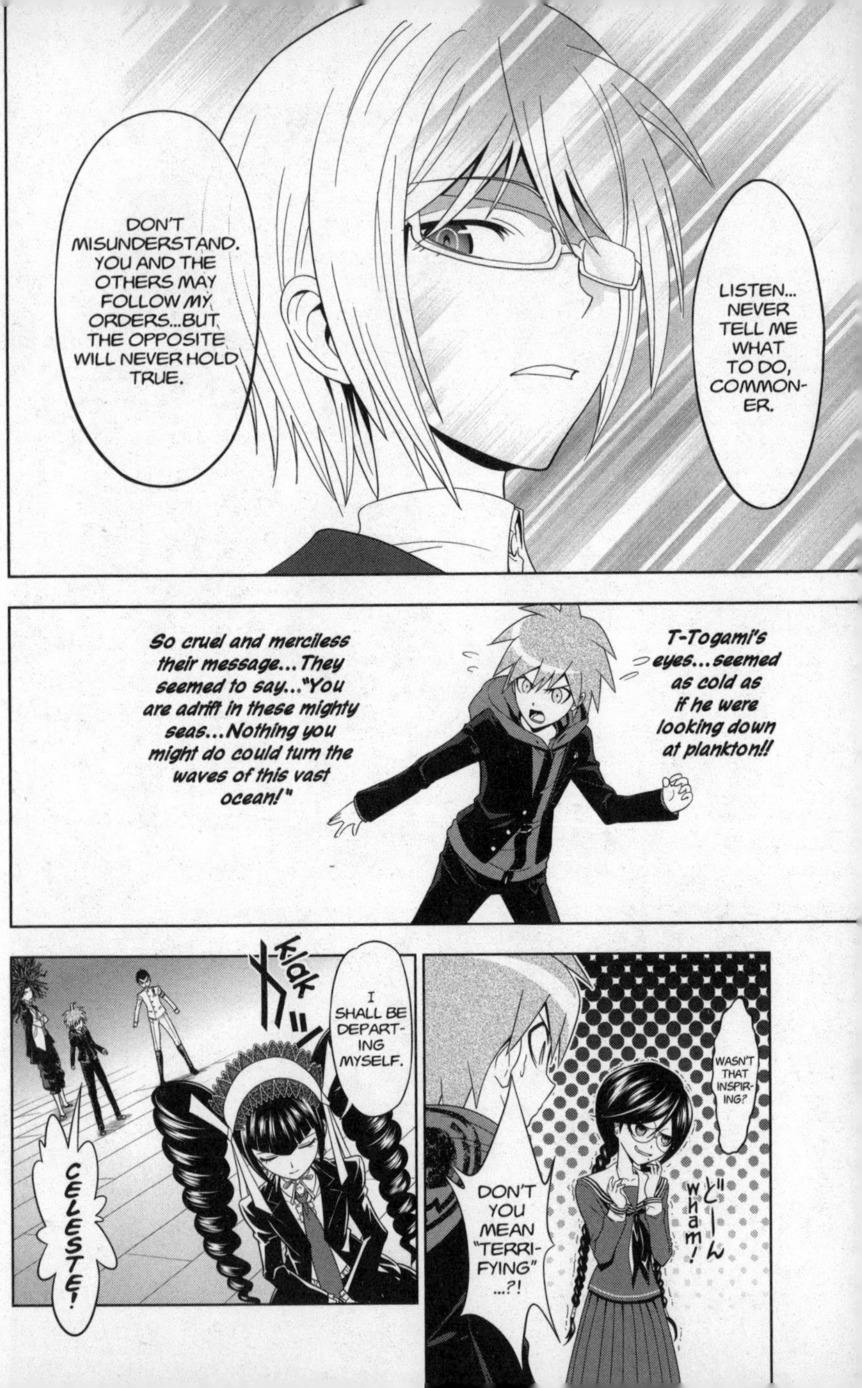
LISTEN... NEVER TELL ME WHAT TO DO, COMMONER.
DON'T MISUNDERSTAND. YOU AND THE OTHERS MAY FOLLOW MY ORDERS...BUT THE OPPOSITE WILL NEVER HOLD TRUE.
T-Togami's eyes...seemed as cold as if he were looking down at plankton!!
So cruel and merciless their message...They seemed to say..."You are adrift in these mighty seas...Nothing you might do could turn the waves of this vast ocean!"
WASN'T THAT INSPIRING?
wham!
DON'T YOU MEAN "TERRIFYING" ...?!
klak
I SHALL BE DEPARTING MYSELF.
CELESTE!

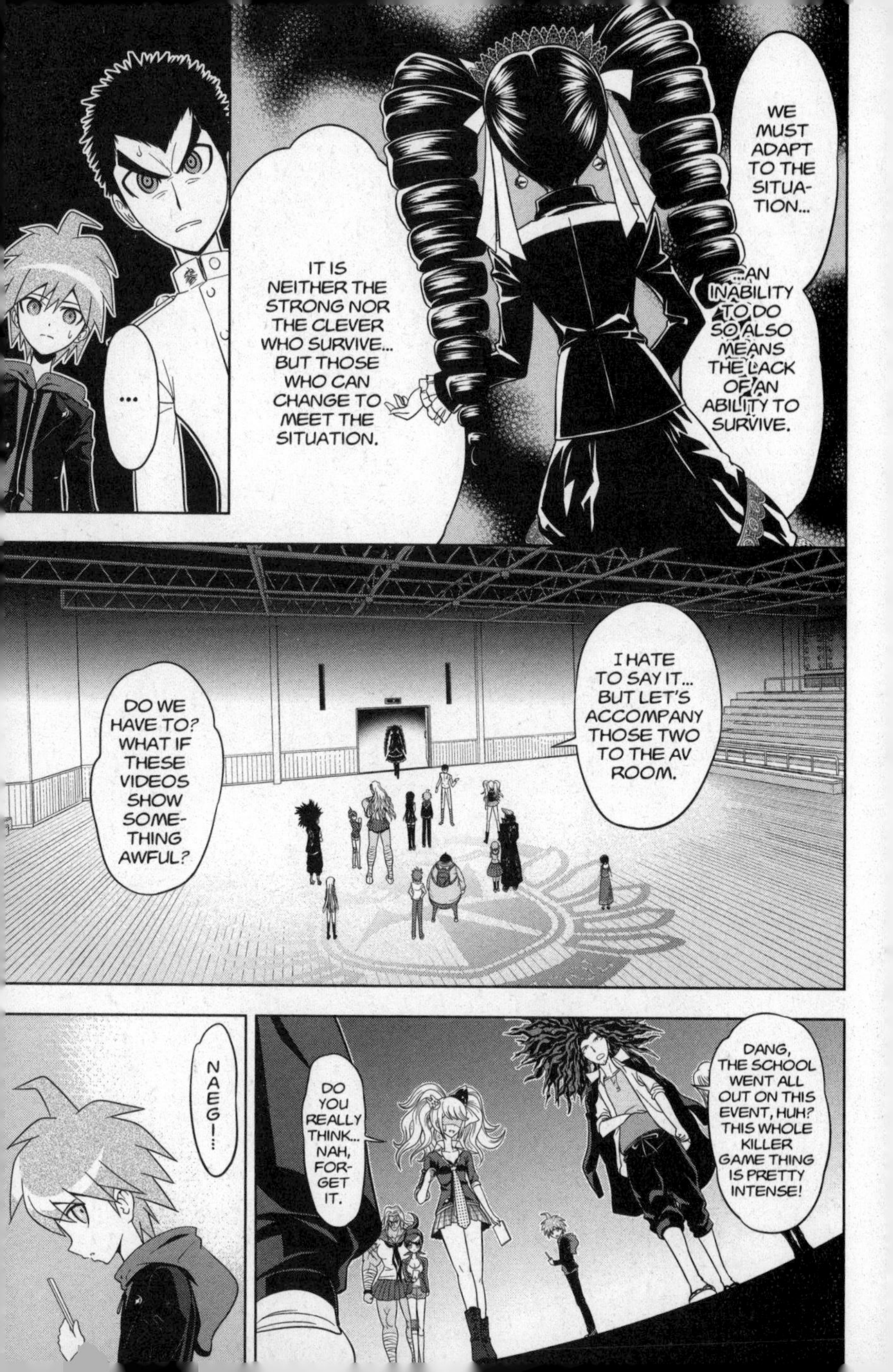
WE MUST ADAPT TO THE SITUATION...
...AN INABILITY TO DO SO ALSO MEANS THE LACK OF AN ABILITY TO SURVIVE.
IT IS NEITHER THE STRONG NOR THE CLEVER WHO SURVIVE... BUT THOSE WHO CAN CHANGE TO MEET THE SITUATION.
...
I HATE TO SAY IT... BUT LET'S ACCOMPANY THOSE TWO TO THE AV ROOM.
DO WE HAVE TO? WHAT IF THESE VIDEOS SHOW SOME-THING AWFUL?
DANG, THE SCHOOL WENT ALL OUT ON THIS EVENT, HUH? THIS WHOLE KILLER GAME THING IS PRETTY INTENSE!
DO YOU REALLY THINK... NAH, FOR-GET IT.
NAEGI!

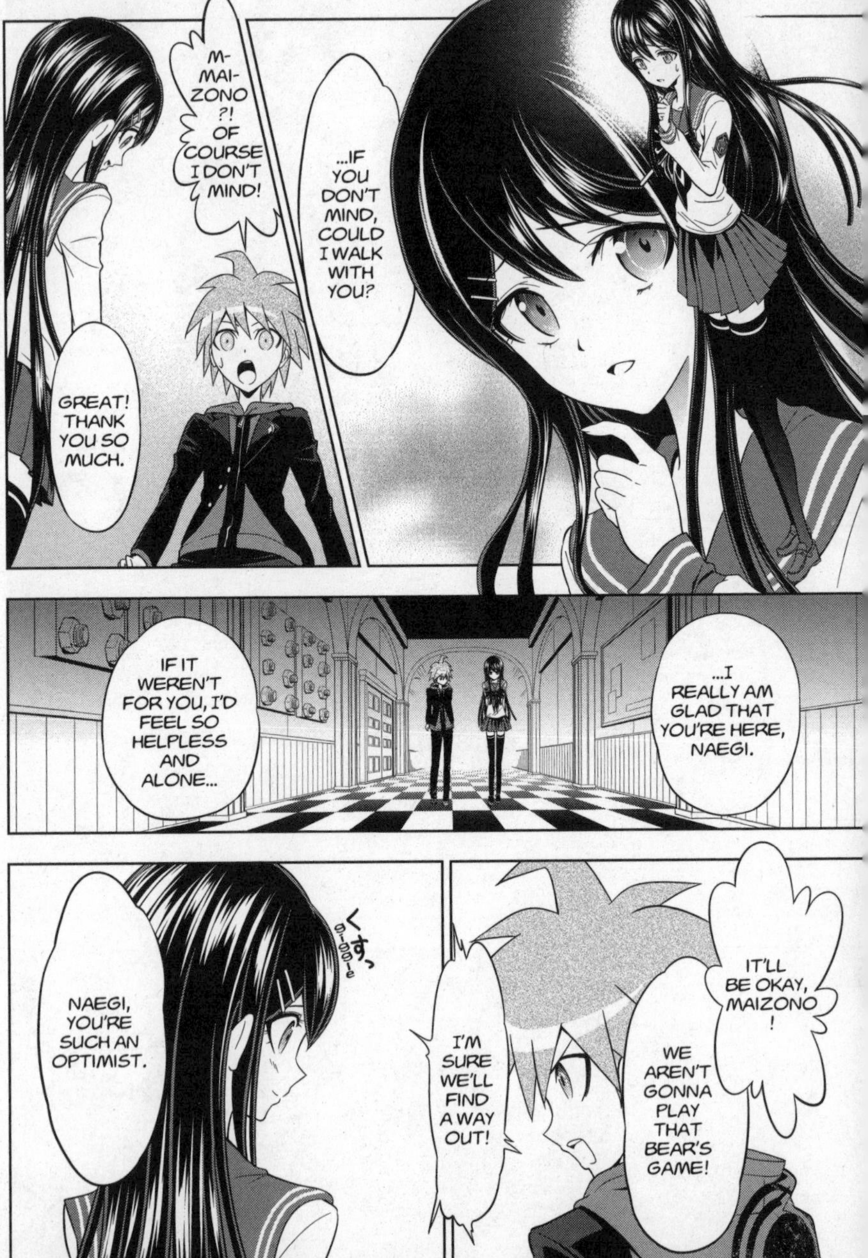
...IF YOU DON'T MIND, COULD I WALK WITH YOU?
M-MAI-ZONO?! OF COURSE I DON'T MIND!
GREAT! THANK YOU SO MUCH.
...I REALLY AM GLAD THAT YOU'RE HERE, NAEGI.
IF IT WEREN'T FOR YOU, I'D FEEL SO HELPLESS AND ALONE...
IT'LL BE OKAY, MAIZONO!
WE AREN'T GONNA PLAY THAT BEAR'S GAME!
I'M SURE WE'LL FIND A WAY OUT!
くすっ giggle
NAEGI, YOU'RE SUCH AN OPTIMIST.

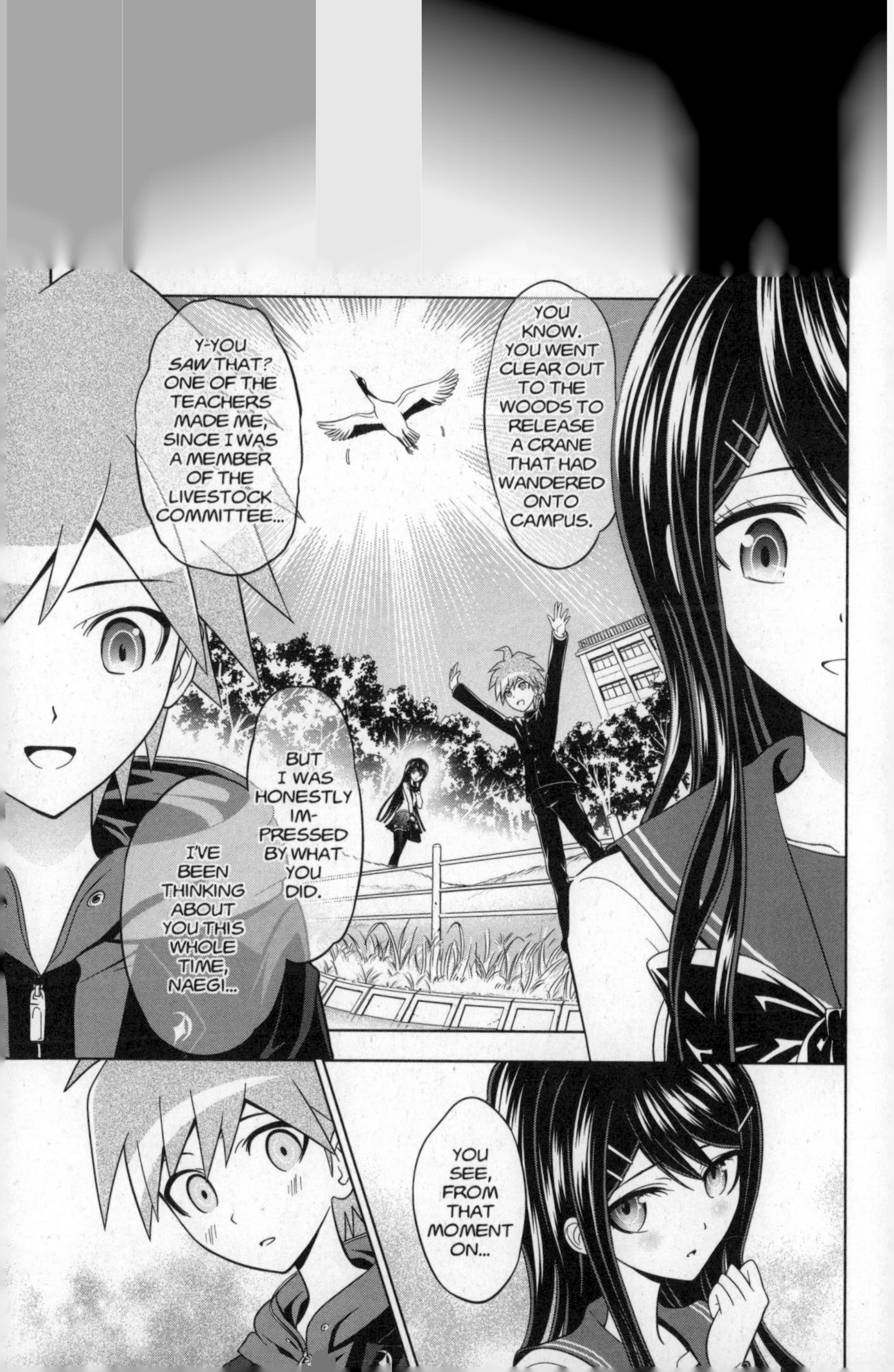
YOU KNOW. YOU WENT CLEAR OUT TO THE WOODS TO RELEASE A CRANE THAT HAD WANDERED ONTO CAMPUS.
Y-YOU *SAW* THAT? ONE OF THE TEACHERS MADE ME, SINCE I WAS A MEMBER OF THE LIVESTOCK COMMITTEE...
BUT I WAS HONESTLY IM-PRESSED BY WHAT YOU DID.
I'VE BEEN THINKING ABOUT YOU THIS WHOLE TIME, NAEGI...
YOU SEE, FROM THAT MOMENT ON...

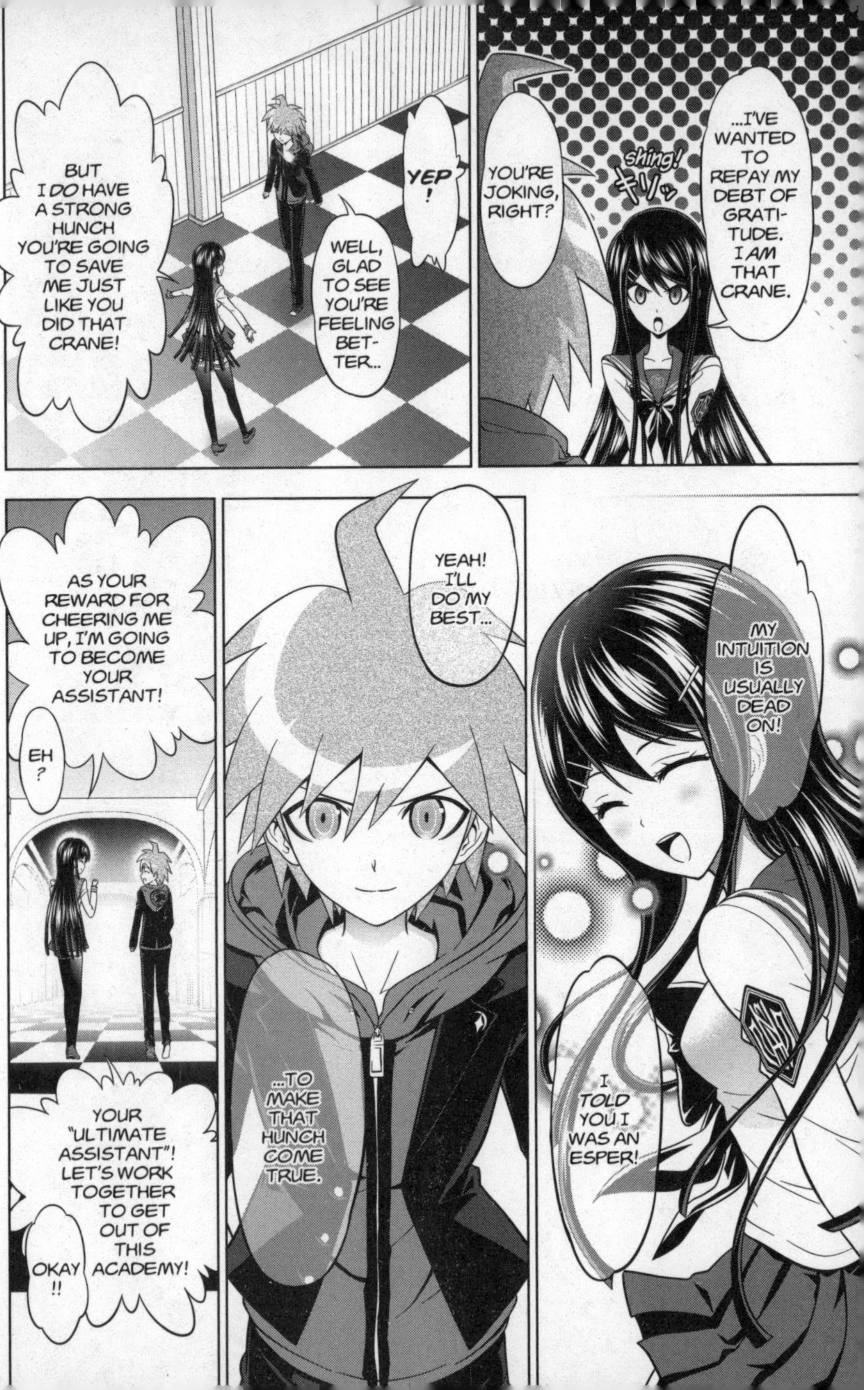
...I'VE WANTED TO REPAY MY DEBT OF GRATITUDE. I AM THAT CRANE.
shing!
キリッ
YOU'RE JOKING, RIGHT?
YEP!
WELL, GLAD TO SEE YOU'RE FEELING BETTER...
BUT I DO HAVE A STRONG HUNCH YOU'RE GOING TO SAVE ME JUST LIKE YOU DID THAT CRANE!
MY INTUITION IS USUALLY DEAD ON!
I TOLD YOU I WAS AN ESPER!
YEAH! I'LL DO MY BEST...
...TO MAKE THAT HUNCH COME TRUE.
AS YOUR REWARD FOR CHEERING ME UP, I'M GOING TO BECOME YOUR ASSISTANT!
EH?
YOUR "ULTIMATE ASSISTANT"! LET'S WORK TOGETHER TO GET OUT OF THIS ACADEMY!
OKAY!!

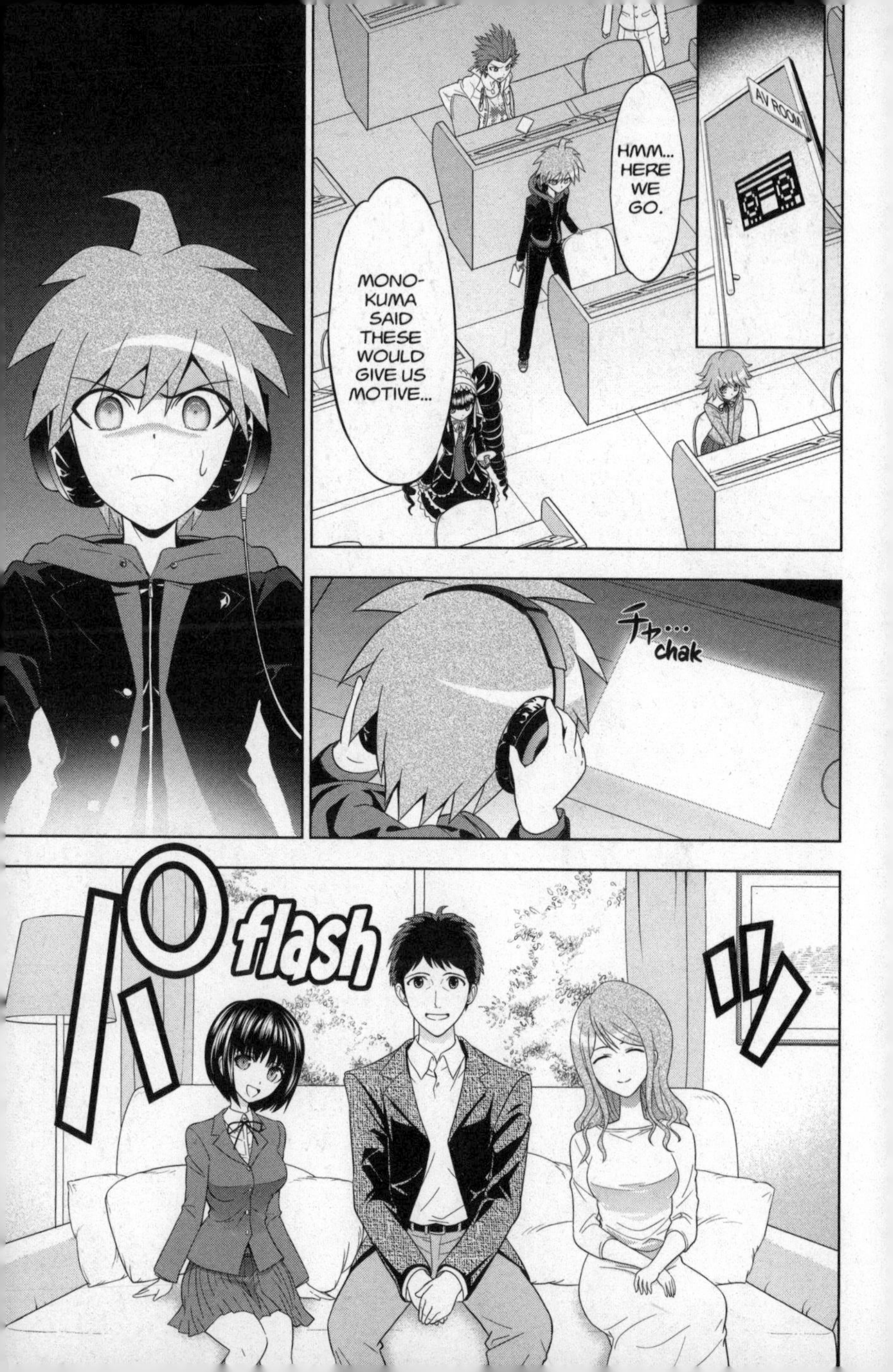
AV ROOM
HMM... HERE WE GO.
MONO-KUMA SAID THESE WOULD GIVE US MOTIVE...
チャ...
chak
パッ
flash

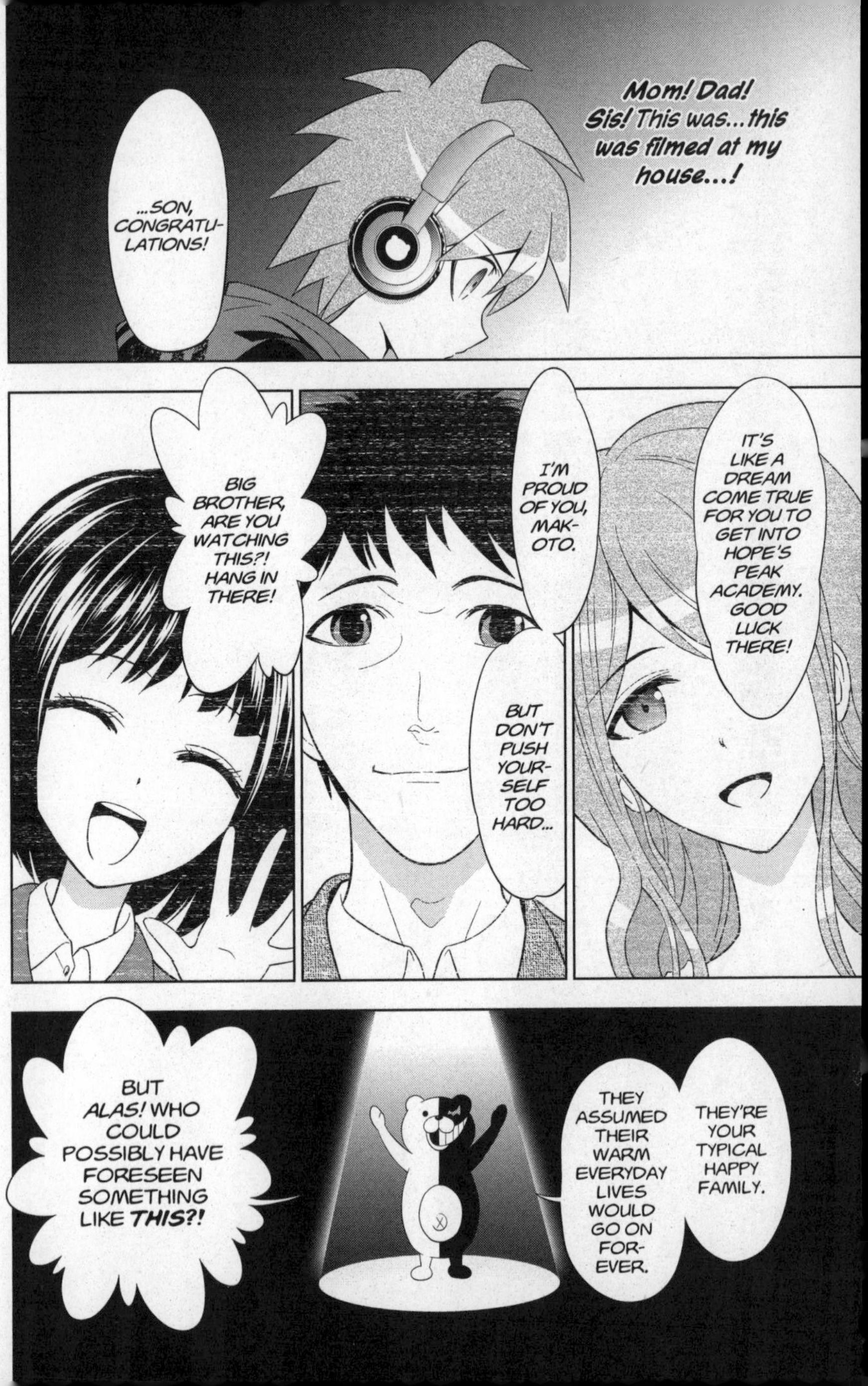
Mom! Dad! Sis! This was...this was filmed at my house...!
...SON, CONGRATULATIONS!
IT'S LIKE A DREAM COME TRUE FOR YOU TO GET INTO HOPE'S PEAK ACADEMY. GOOD LUCK THERE!
I'M PROUD OF YOU, MAKOTO.
BUT DON'T PUSH YOURSELF TOO HARD...
BIG BROTHER, ARE YOU WATCHING THIS?! HANG IN THERE!
THEY'RE YOUR TYPICAL HAPPY FAMILY.
THEY ASSUMED THEIR WARM EVERYDAY LIVES WOULD GO ON FOREVER.
BUT ALAS! WHO COULD POSSIBLY HAVE FORESEEN SOMETHING LIKE THIS?!

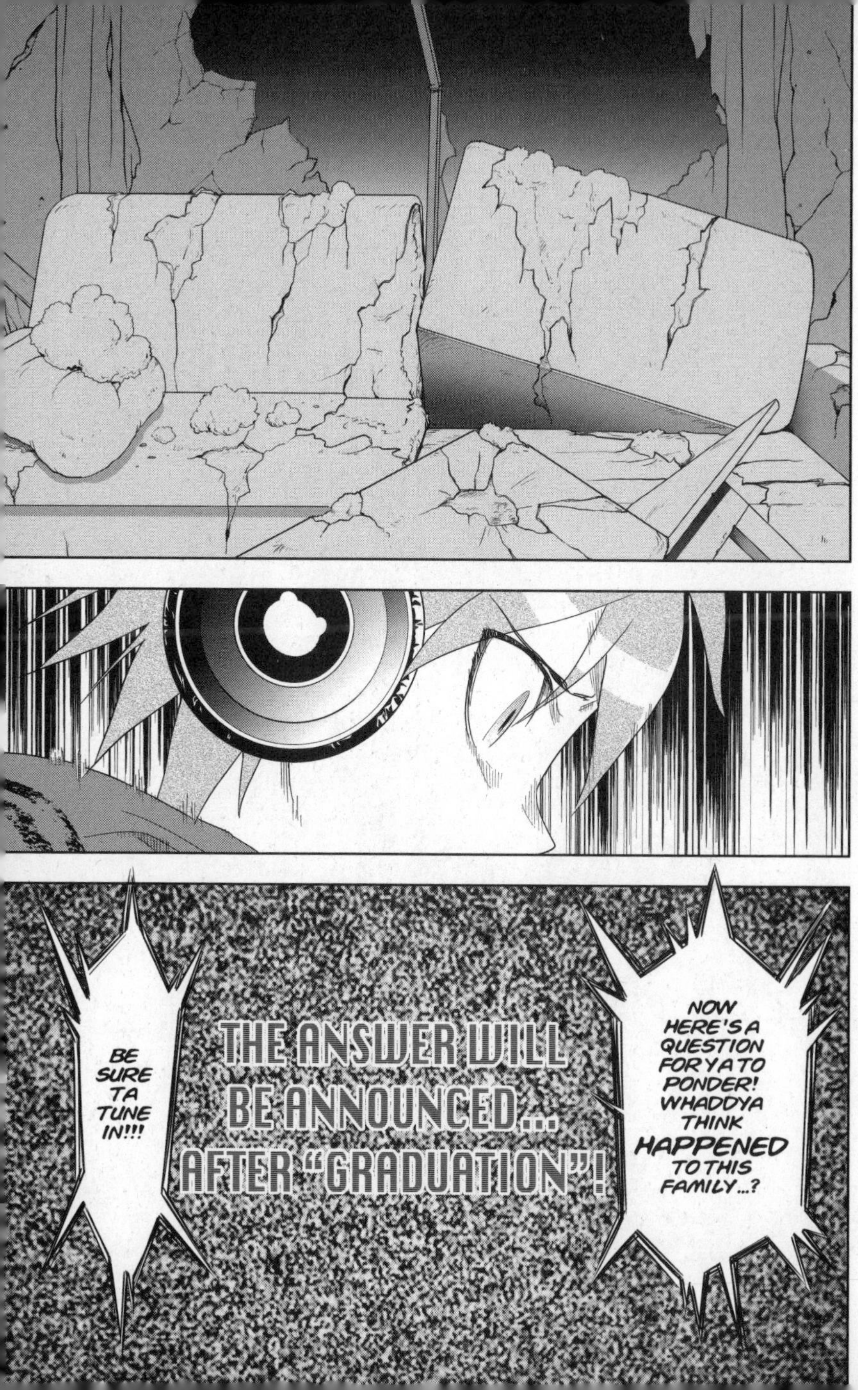
NOW HERE'S A QUESTION FOR YA TO PONDER! WHADDYA THINK HAPPENED TO THIS FAMILY...?
THE ANSWER WILL BE ANNOUNCED... AFTER "GRADUATION"!
BE SURE TA TUNE IN!!!

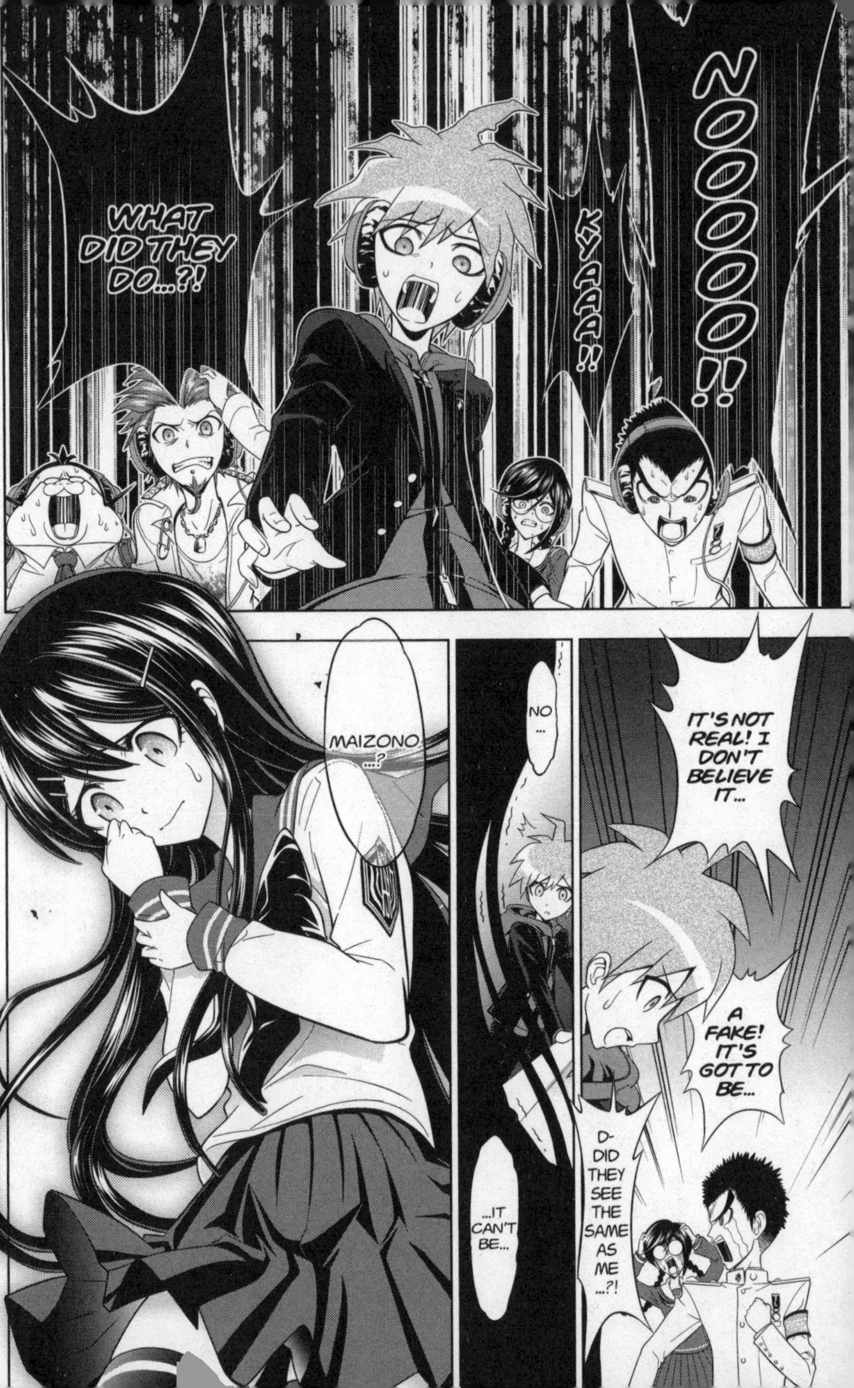
NOOOOOOO!!
KYAAAA!!
WHAT DID THEY DO...?!
IT'S NOT REAL! I DON'T BELIEVE IT...
A FAKE! IT'S GOT TO BE...
D-DID THEY SEE THE SAME AS ME...?!
NO...
...IT CAN'T BE...
MAIZONO...?

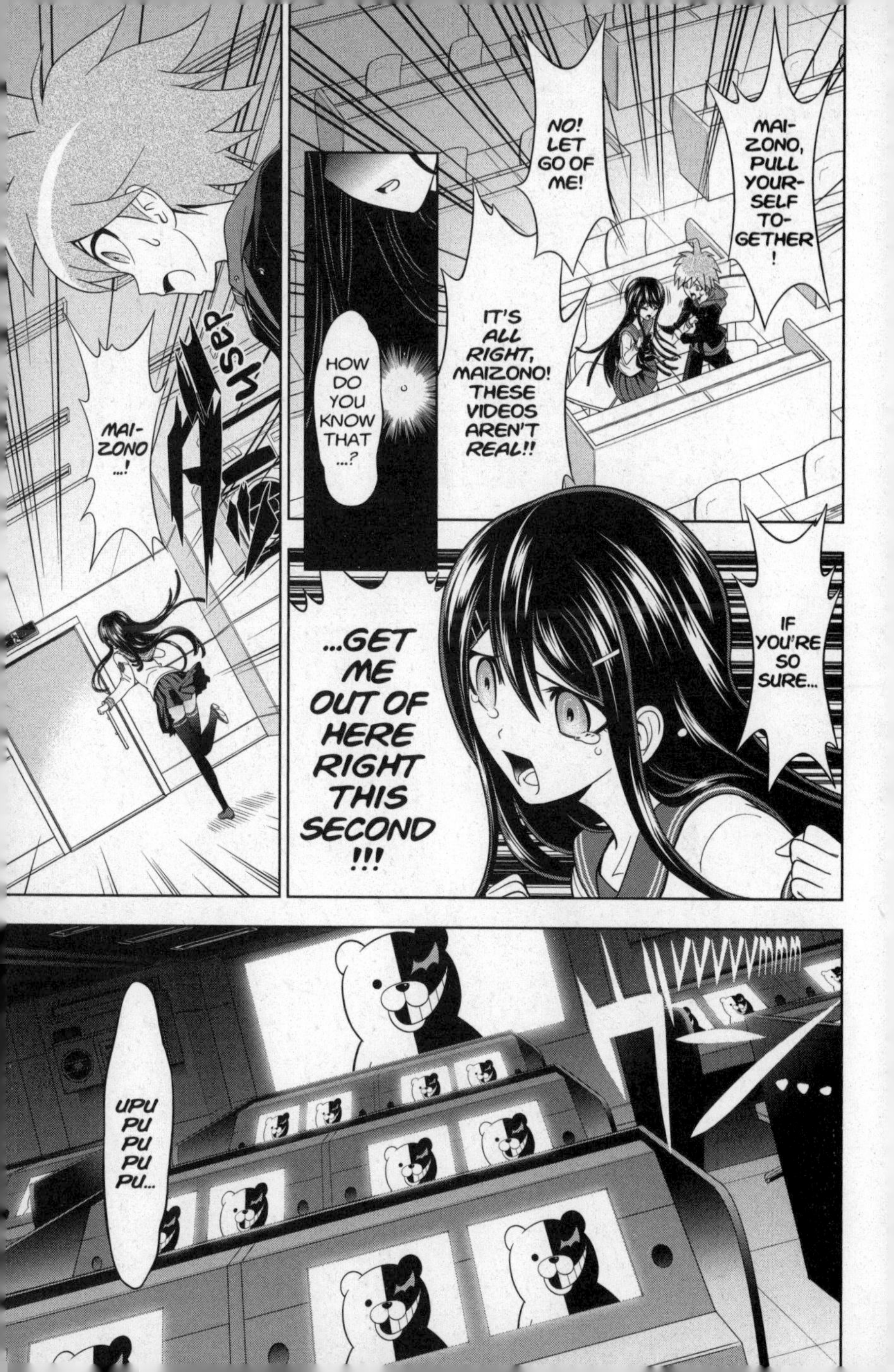
MAI-ZONO, PULL YOUR-SELF TO-GETHER!
NO! LET GO OF ME!
IT'S ALL RIGHT, MAIZONO! THESE VIDEOS AREN'T REAL!!
HOW DO YOU KNOW THAT ...?
IF YOU'RE SO SURE...
...GET ME OUT OF HERE RIGHT THIS SECOND!!!
dash
MAI-ZONO ...!
VVVVVMMM
UPU PU PU PU PU...

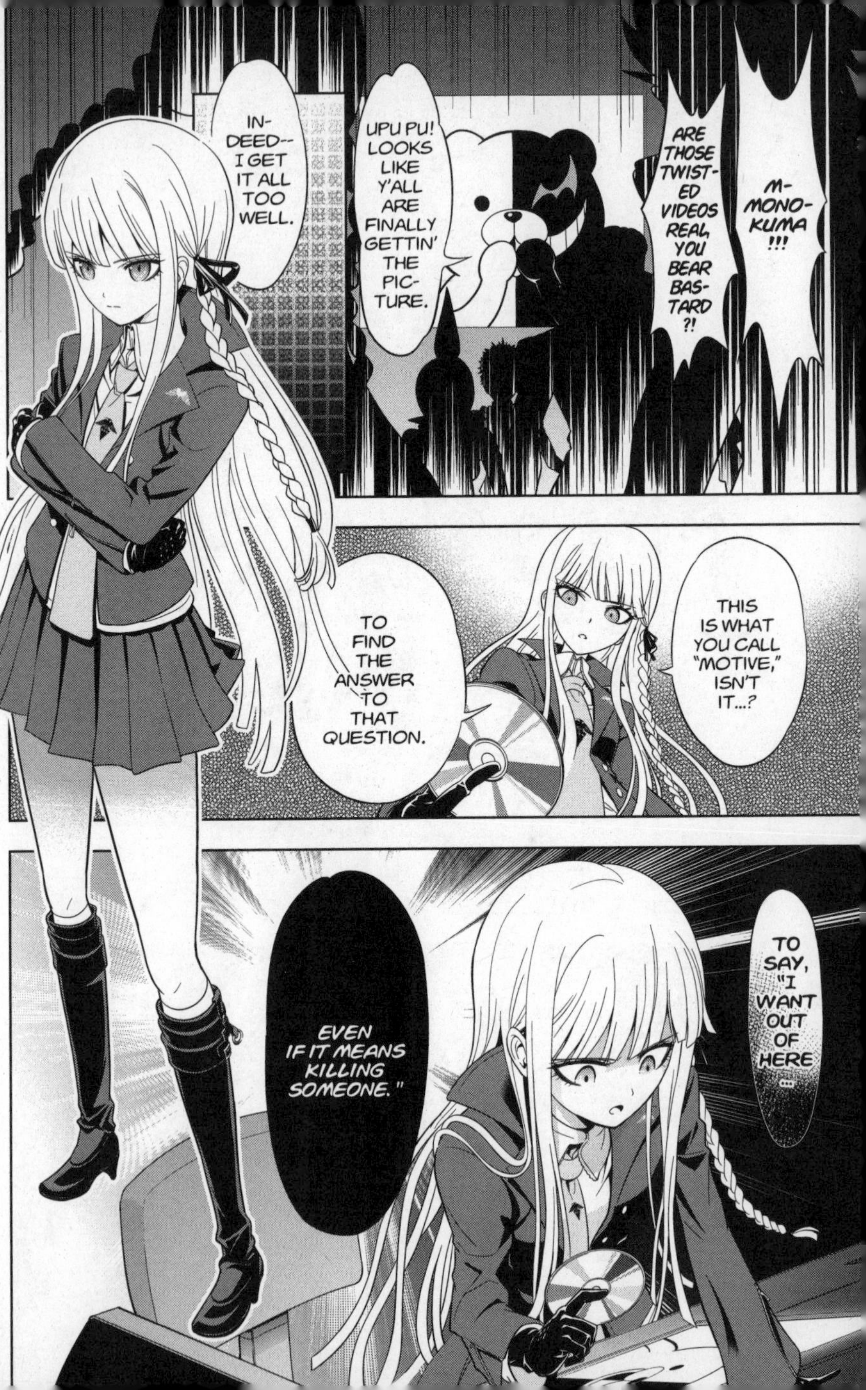
M-MONOKUMA!!!
ARE THOSE TWISTED VIDEOS REAL, YOU BEAR BASTARD?!
UPU PU! LOOKS LIKE Y'ALL ARE FINALLY GETTIN' THE PICTURE.
INDEED-- I GET IT ALL TOO WELL.
THIS IS WHAT YOU CALL "MOTIVE," ISN'T IT...?
TO FIND THE ANSWER TO THAT QUESTION.
TO SAY, "I WANT OUT OF HERE...
EVEN IF IT MEANS KILLING SOMEONE."

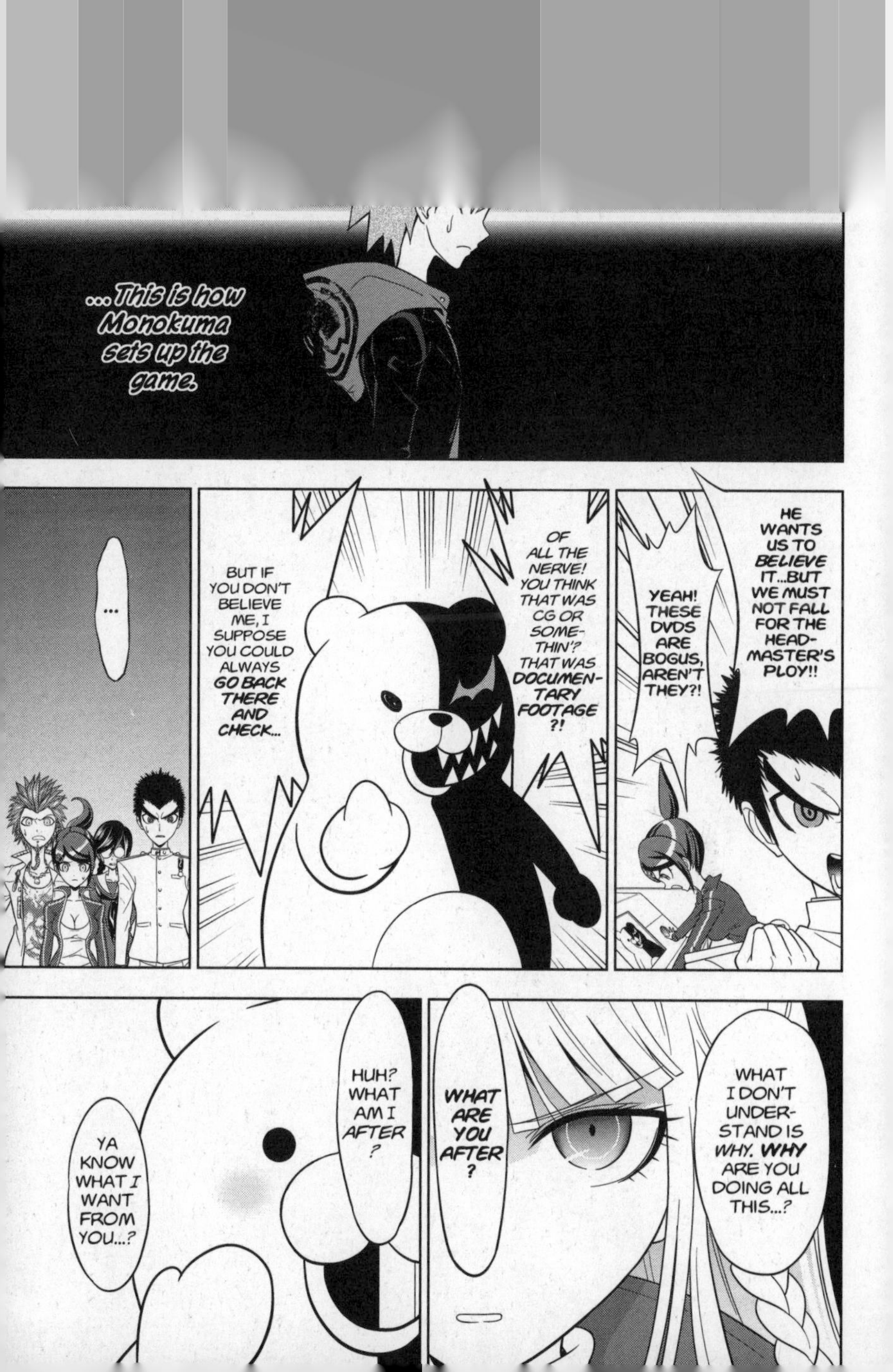
...This is how Monokuma sets up the game.
HE WANTS US TO *BELIEVE* IT...BUT WE MUST NOT FALL FOR THE HEADMASTER'S PLOY!!
YEAH! THESE DVDS ARE BOGUS, AREN'T THEY?!
OF ALL THE NERVE! YOU THINK THAT WAS CG OR SOMETHIN'? THAT WAS **DOCUMENTARY FOOTAGE**?!
BUT IF YOU DON'T BELIEVE ME, I SUPPOSE YOU COULD ALWAYS **GO BACK THERE AND CHECK...**
...
WHAT I DON'T UNDERSTAND IS WHY. ***WHY*** ARE YOU DOING ALL THIS...?
WHAT ARE YOU AFTER?
HUH? WHAT AM I *AFTER*?
YA KNOW WHAT *I* WANT FROM YOU...?

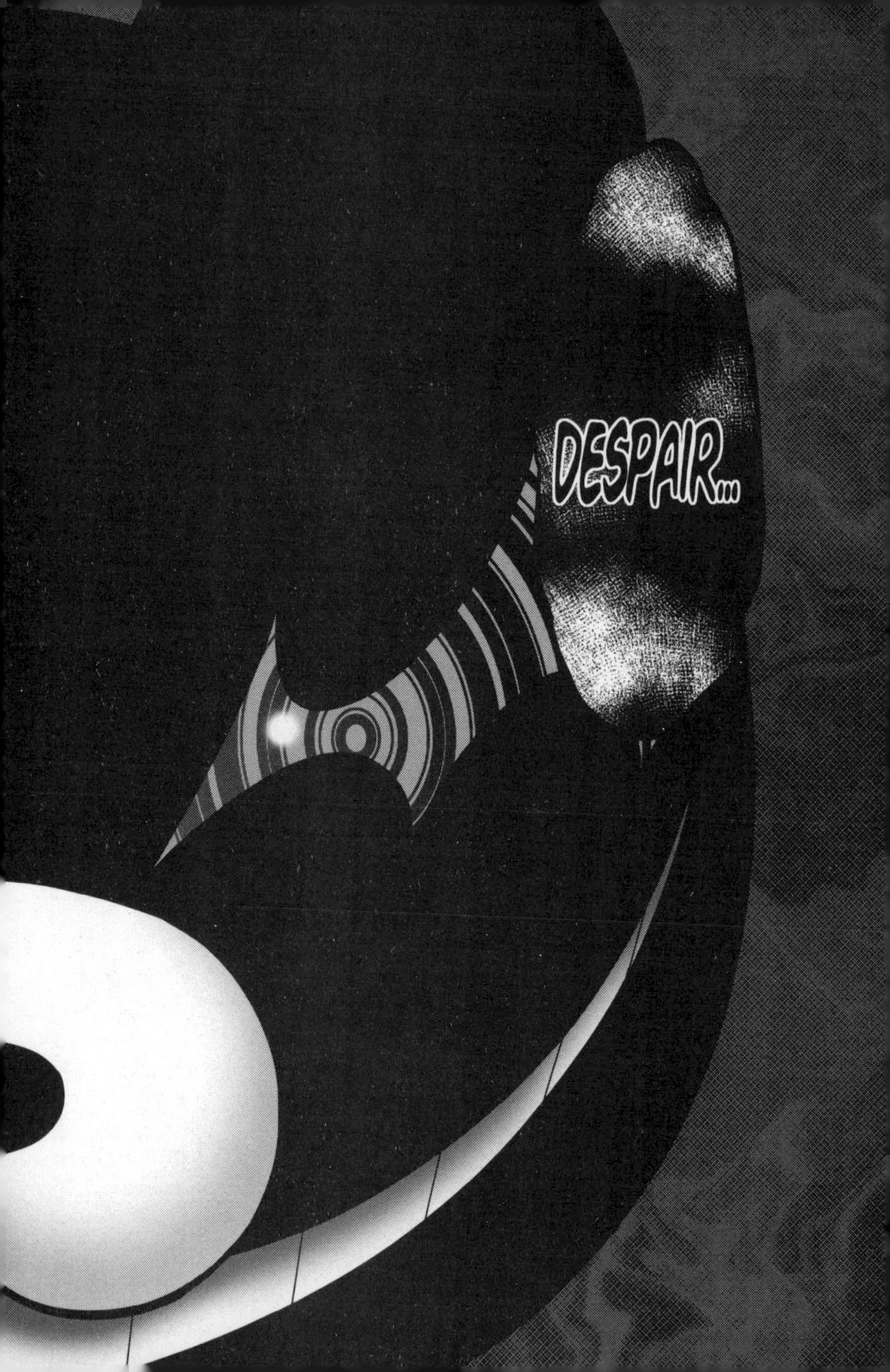
DESPAIR...

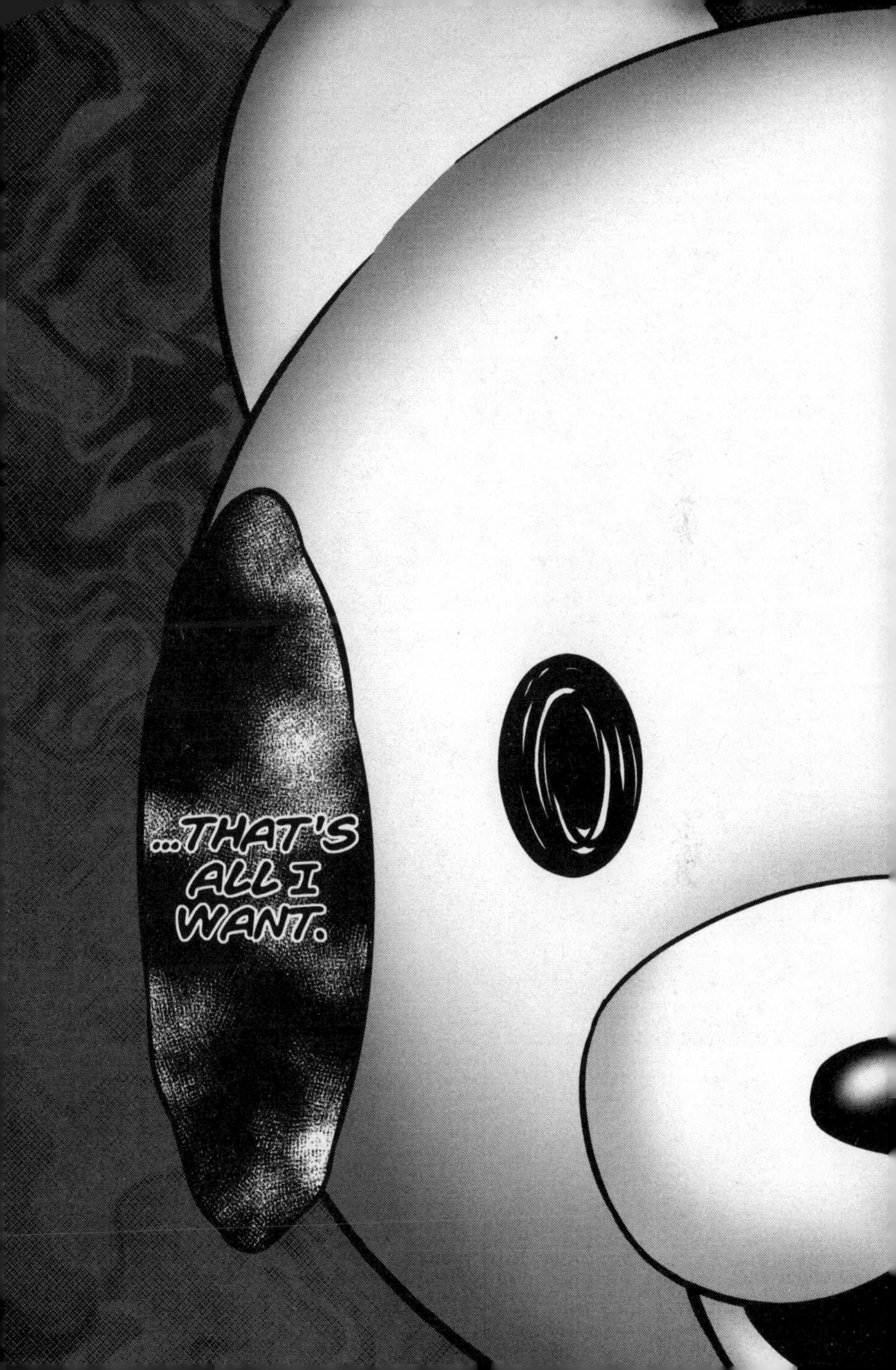
...THAT'S ALL I WANT.

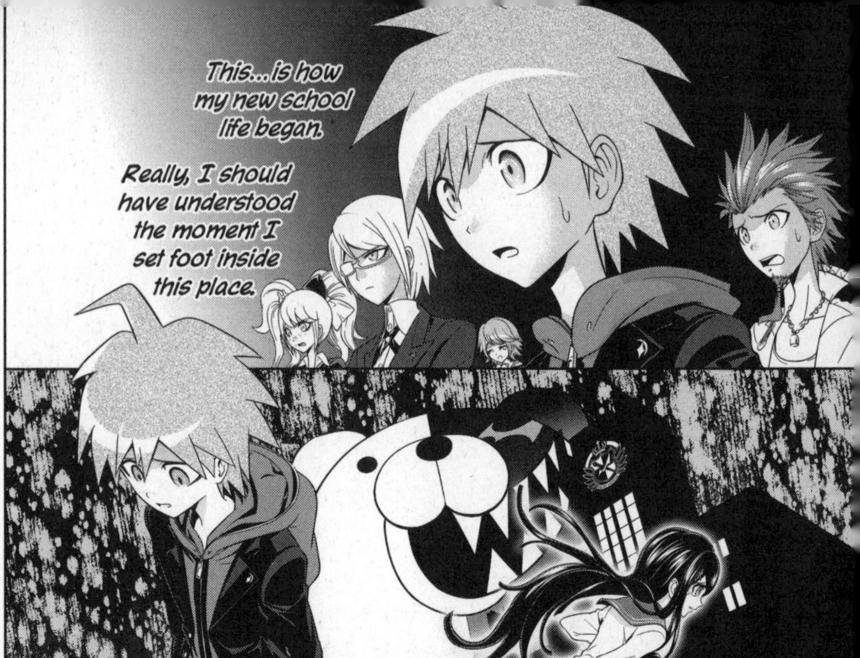
This...is how my new school life began.
Really, I should have understood the moment I set foot inside this place.
I didn't come to Hope's Peak Academy because I was the "Ultimate Lucky Student"...
...but because I was the ultimate unlucky one.

SURVIVING STUDENTS: 15

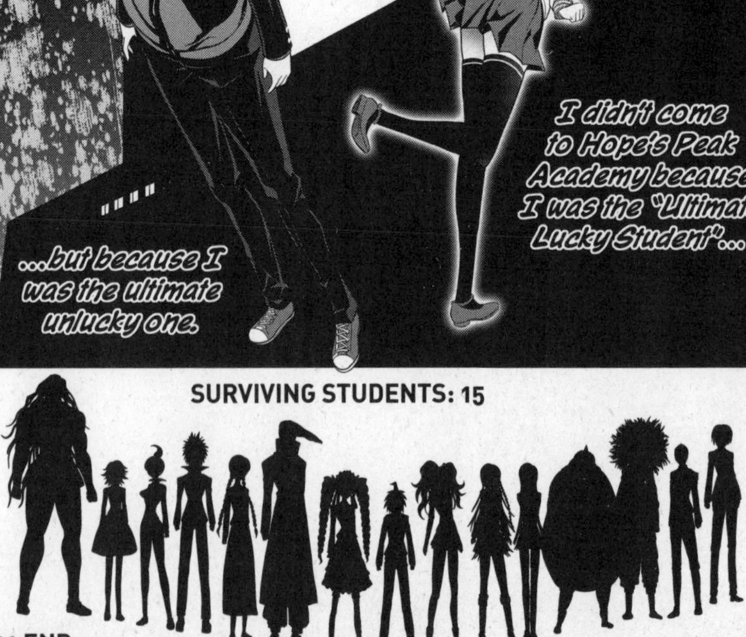

#01 END

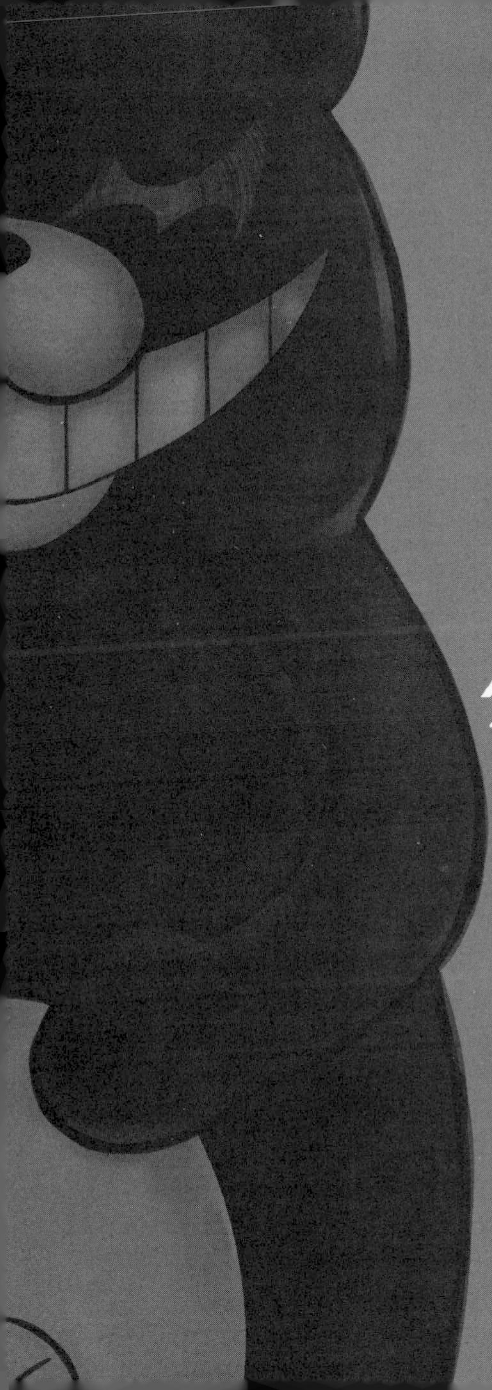

ダンガンロンパ
DANGANRONPA 希望の学園と絶望の高校生
THE ANIMATION

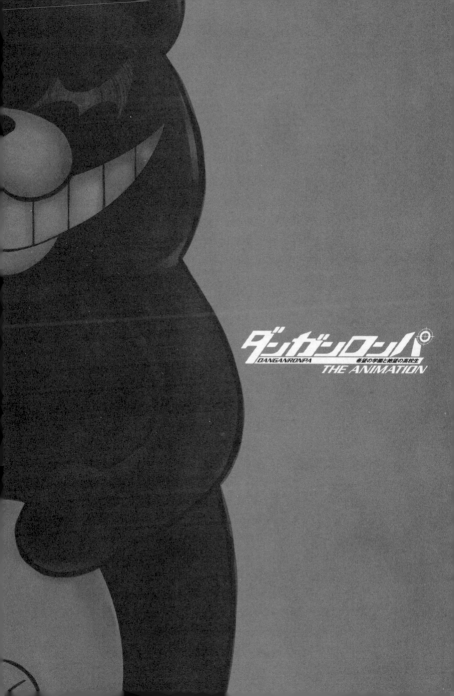

DANGANRONPA
A SCHOOL OF HOPE . . . WITH STUDENTS OF DESPAIR!
THE ANIMATION

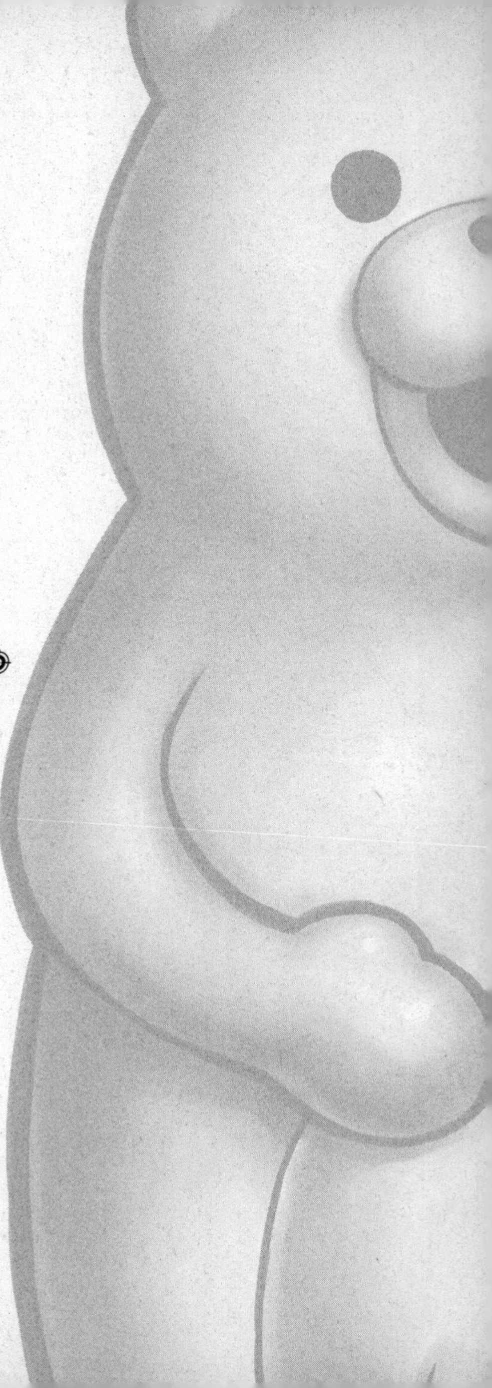

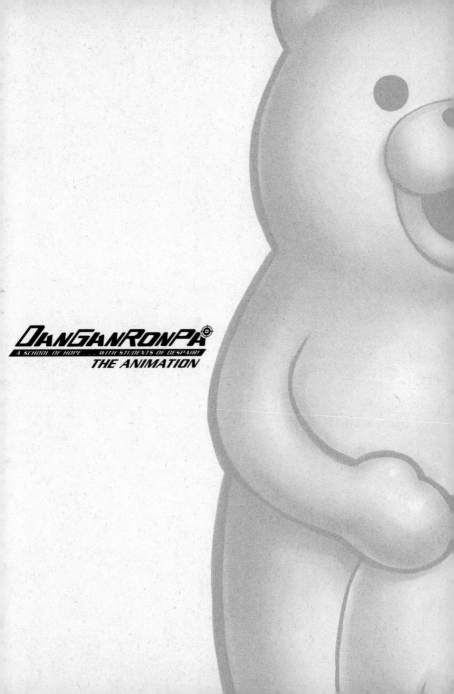

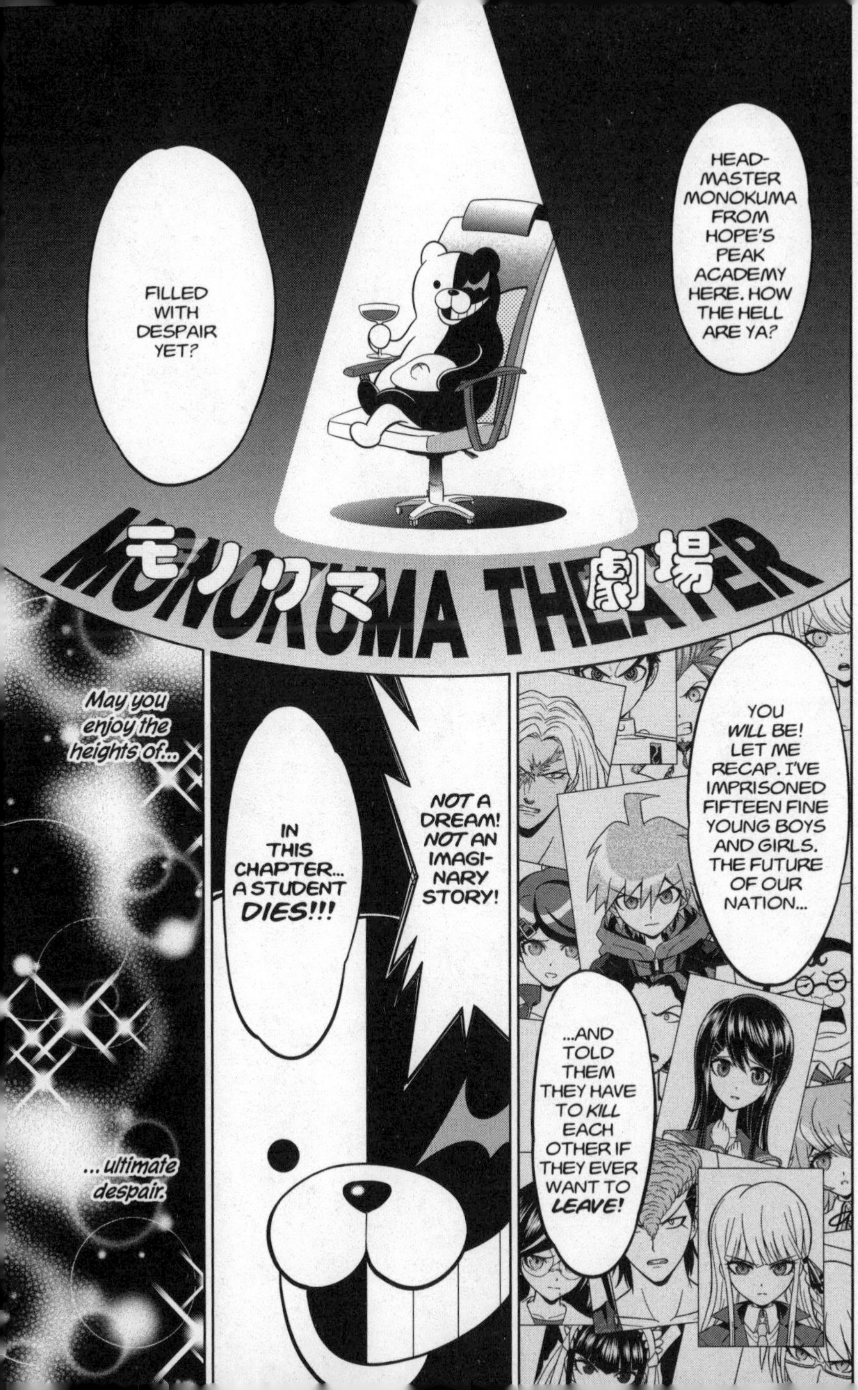
HEAD-MASTER MONOKUMA FROM HOPE'S PEAK ACADEMY HERE. HOW THE HELL ARE YA?
FILLED WITH DESPAIR YET?
モノクマ劇場
MONOKUMA THEATER
YOU WILL BE! LET ME RECAP. I'VE IMPRISONED FIFTEEN FINE YOUNG BOYS AND GIRLS. THE FUTURE OF OUR NATION...
...AND TOLD THEM THEY HAVE TO *KILL* EACH OTHER IF THEY EVER WANT TO *LEAVE!*
NOT A DREAM! *NOT* AN IMAGINARY STORY!
IN THIS CHAPTER... A STUDENT *DIES!!!*
May you enjoy the heights of...
... ultimate despair.

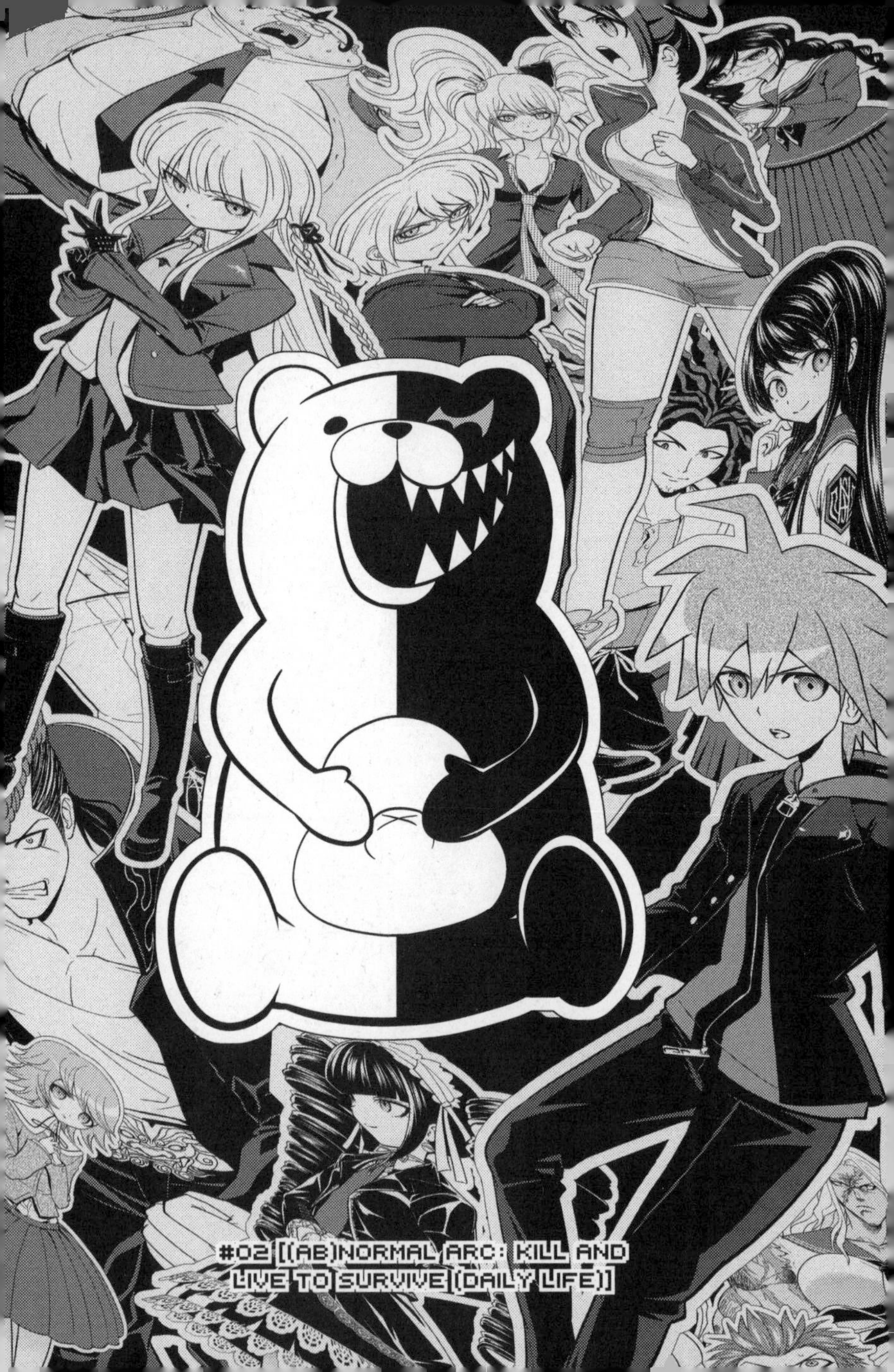
#02 [(AB)NORMAL ARC: KILL AND
LIVE TO SURVIVE (DAILY LIFE)]

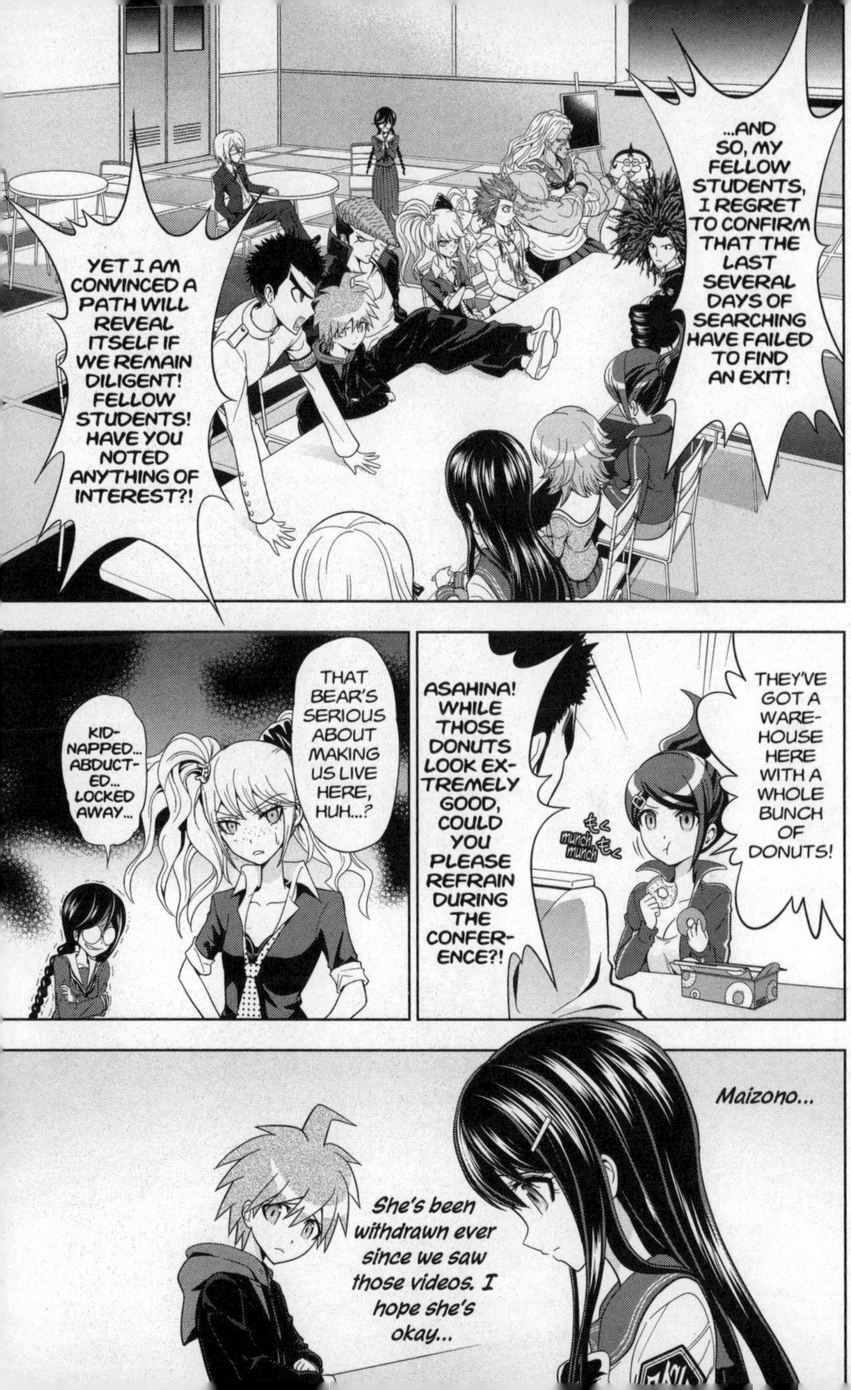
...AND SO, MY FELLOW STUDENTS, I REGRET TO CONFIRM THAT THE LAST SEVERAL DAYS OF SEARCHING HAVE FAILED TO FIND AN EXIT!
YET I AM CONVINCED A PATH WILL REVEAL ITSELF IF WE REMAIN DILIGENT! FELLOW STUDENTS! HAVE YOU NOTED ANYTHING OF INTEREST?!
THEY'VE GOT A WARE-HOUSE HERE WITH A WHOLE BUNCH OF DONUTS!
もく munch もく munch
ASAHINA! WHILE THOSE DONUTS LOOK EX-TREMELY GOOD, COULD YOU PLEASE REFRAIN DURING THE CONFER-ENCE?!
THAT BEAR'S SERIOUS ABOUT MAKING US LIVE HERE, HUH...?
KID-NAPPED... ABDUCT-ED... LOCKED AWAY...
Maizono...
She's been withdrawn ever since we saw those videos. I hope she's okay...

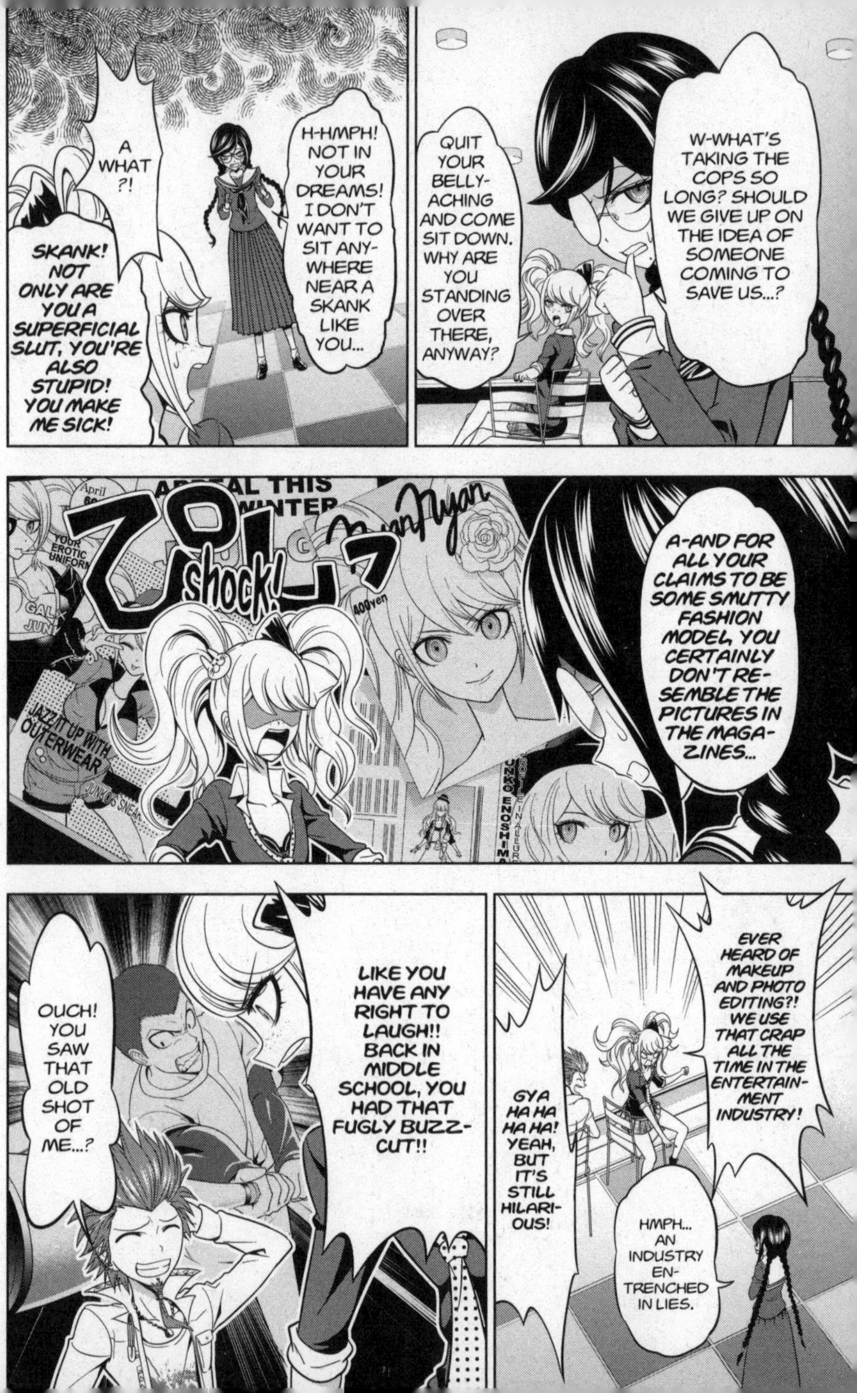
W-WHAT'S TAKING THE COPS SO LONG? SHOULD WE GIVE UP ON THE IDEA OF SOMEONE COMING TO SAVE US...?
QUIT YOUR BELLY-ACHING AND COME SIT DOWN. WHY ARE YOU STANDING OVER THERE, ANYWAY?
H-HMPH! NOT IN YOUR DREAMS! I DON'T WANT TO SIT ANY-WHERE NEAR A SKANK LIKE YOU...
A WHAT?!
SKANK! NOT ONLY ARE YOU A SUPERFICIAL SLUT, YOU'RE ALSO STUPID! YOU MAKE ME SICK!
A-AND FOR ALL YOUR CLAIMS TO BE SOME SMUTTY FASHION MODEL, YOU CERTAINLY DON'T RE-SEMBLE THE PICTURES IN THE MAGA-ZINES...
shock!
400yen
YOUR EROTIC UNIFORM
JAZZ IT UP WITH OUTERWEAR
JUNKO ENOSHIMA
EVER HEARD OF MAKEUP AND PHOTO EDITING?! WE USE THAT CRAP ALL THE TIME IN THE ENTERTAIN-MENT INDUSTRY!
GYA HA HA HA! YEAH, BUT IT'S STILL HILARI-OUS!
HMPH... AN INDUSTRY EN-TRENCHED IN LIES.
LIKE YOU HAVE ANY RIGHT TO LAUGH!! BACK IN MIDDLE SCHOOL, YOU HAD THAT FUGLY BUZZ-CUT!!
OUCH! YOU SAW THAT OLD SHOT OF ME...?

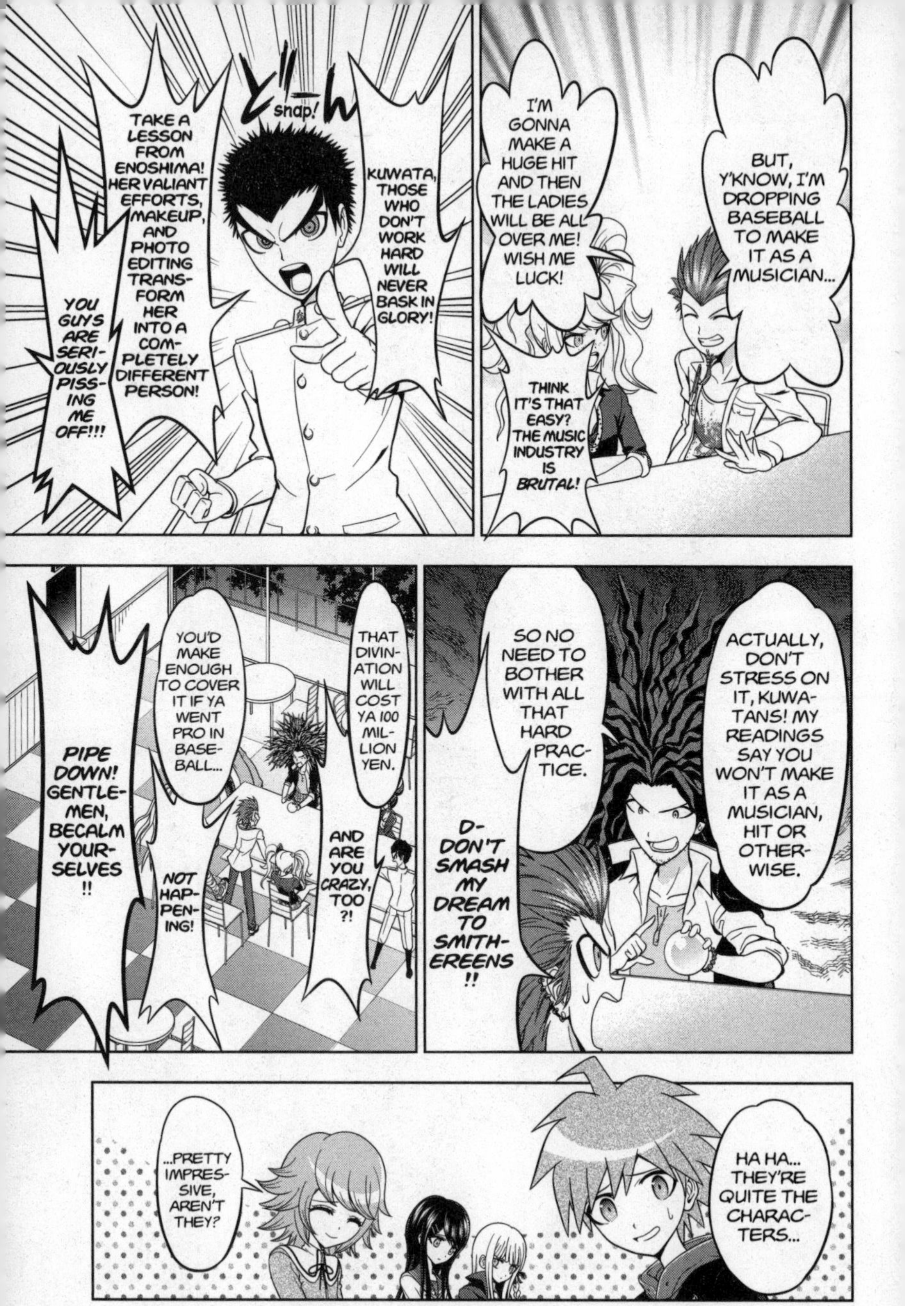
BUT, Y'KNOW, I'M DROPPING BASEBALL TO MAKE IT AS A MUSICIAN...
I'M GONNA MAKE A HUGE HIT AND THEN THE LADIES WILL BE ALL OVER ME! WISH ME LUCK!
THINK IT'S THAT EASY? THE MUSIC INDUSTRY IS *BRUTAL!*
snap!
KUWATA, THOSE WHO DON'T WORK HARD WILL NEVER BASK IN GLORY!
TAKE A LESSON FROM ENOSHIMA! HER VALIANT EFFORTS, MAKEUP, AND PHOTO EDITING TRANSFORM HER INTO A COMPLETELY DIFFERENT PERSON!
YOU GUYS ARE SERIOUSLY PISSING ME OFF!!!
ACTUALLY, DON'T STRESS ON IT, KUWATANS! MY READINGS SAY YOU WON'T MAKE IT AS A MUSICIAN, HIT OR OTHERWISE.
SO NO NEED TO BOTHER WITH ALL THAT HARD PRACTICE.
D-DON'T SMASH MY DREAM TO SMITHEREENS!!
THAT DIVINATION WILL COST YA 100 MILLION YEN.
YOU'D MAKE ENOUGH TO COVER IT IF YA WENT PRO IN BASEBALL...
AND ARE YOU CRAZY, TOO?!
NOT HAPPENING!
PIPE DOWN! GENTLEMEN, BECALM YOURSELVES!!
HA HA... THEY'RE QUITE THE CHARACTERS...
...PRETTY IMPRESSIVE, AREN'T THEY?

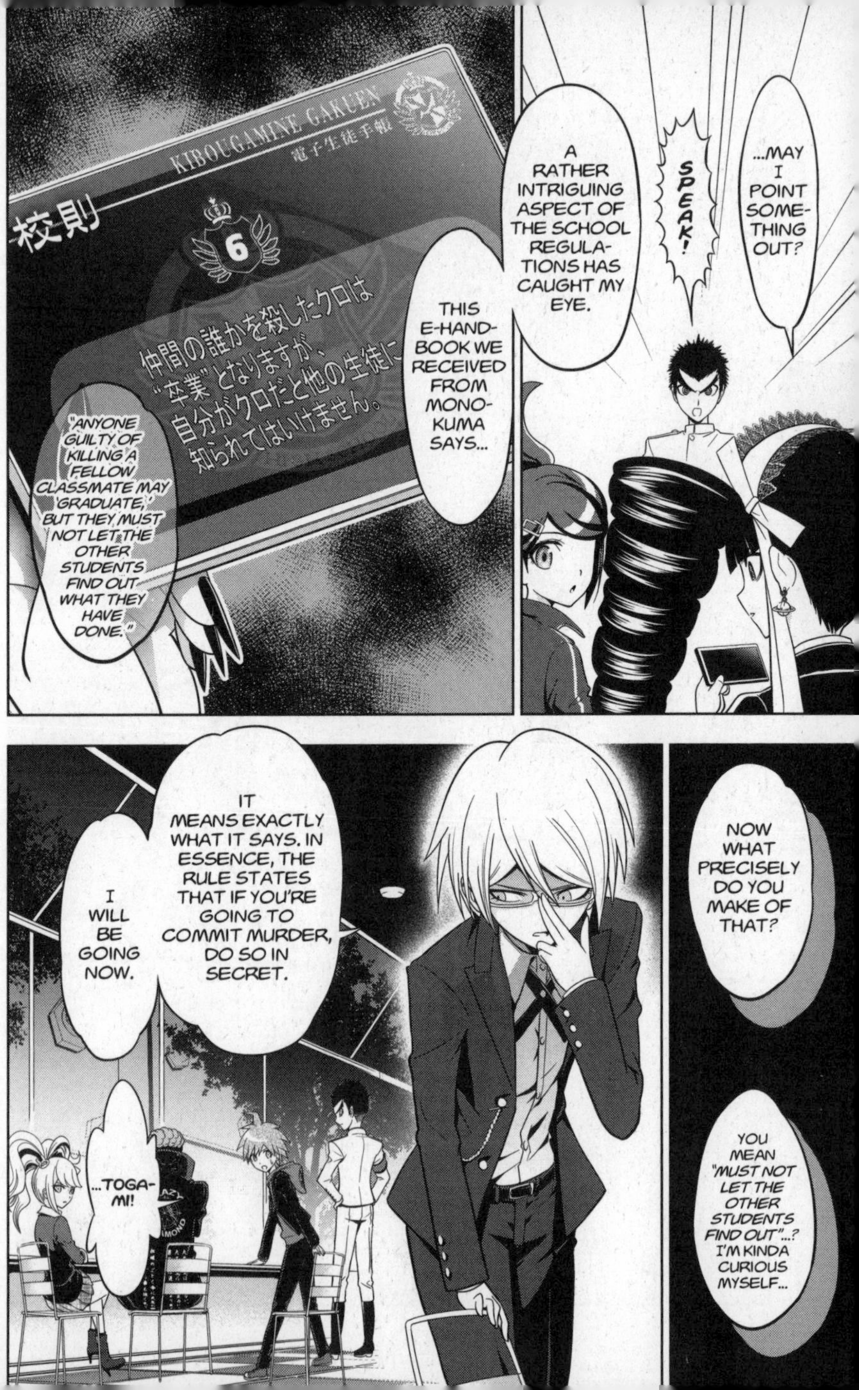

...MAY I POINT SOMETHING OUT?
SPEAK!
A RATHER INTRIGUING ASPECT OF THE SCHOOL REGULATIONS HAS CAUGHT MY EYE.
THIS E-HANDBOOK WE RECEIVED FROM MONOKUMA SAYS...
KIBOUGAMINE GAKUEN
電子生徒手帳
校則
6
仲間の誰かを殺したクロは
"卒業"となりますが、
自分がクロだと他の生徒に
知られてはいけません。
"ANYONE GUILTY OF KILLING A FELLOW CLASSMATE MAY 'GRADUATE,' BUT THEY MUST NOT LET THE OTHER STUDENTS FIND OUT WHAT THEY HAVE DONE."
NOW WHAT PRECISELY DO YOU MAKE OF THAT?
YOU MEAN "MUST NOT LET THE OTHER STUDENTS FIND OUT"...? I'M KINDA CURIOUS MYSELF...
IT MEANS EXACTLY WHAT IT SAYS. IN ESSENCE, THE RULE STATES THAT IF YOU'RE GOING TO COMMIT MURDER, DO SO IN SECRET.
I WILL BE GOING NOW.
...TOGAMI!

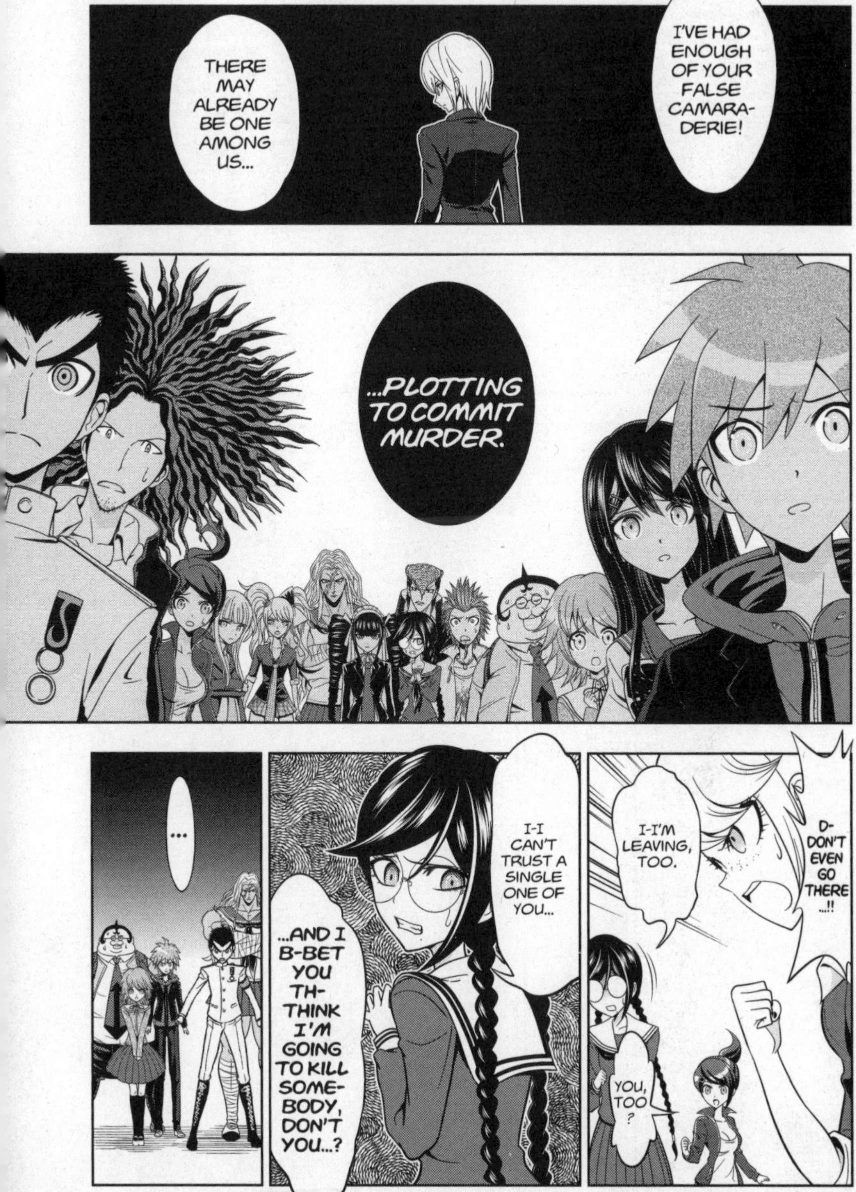
I'VE HAD ENOUGH OF YOUR FALSE CAMARA-DERIE!
THERE MAY ALREADY BE ONE AMONG US...
...PLOTTING TO COMMIT MURDER.
D-DON'T EVEN GO THERE...!!
I-I'M LEAVING, TOO.
YOU, TOO?
I-I CAN'T TRUST A SINGLE ONE OF YOU...
...AND I B-BET YOU TH-THINK I'M GOING TO KILL SOME-BODY, DON'T YOU...?
...

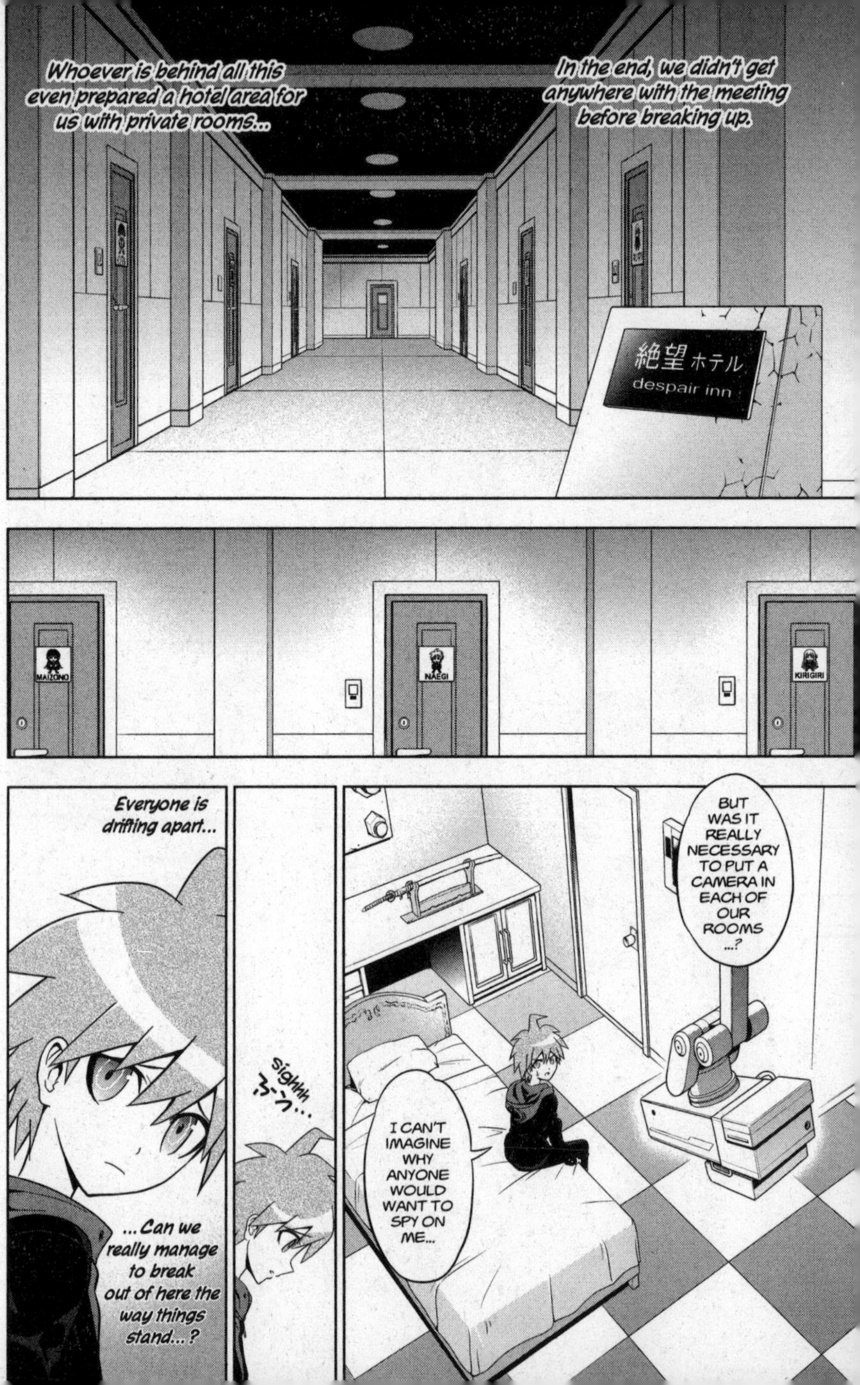
In the end, we didn't get anywhere with the meeting before breaking up.
Whoever is behind all this even prepared a hotel area for us with private rooms...
絶望ホテル
despair inn
KIRIGIRI
NAEGI
MAIZONO
BUT WAS IT REALLY NECESSARY TO PUT A CAMERA IN EACH OF OUR ROOMS ...?
I CAN'T IMAGINE WHY ANYONE WOULD WANT TO SPY ON ME...
sighhh
ふーっ…
Everyone is drifting apart...
...Can we really manage to break out of here the way things stand...?

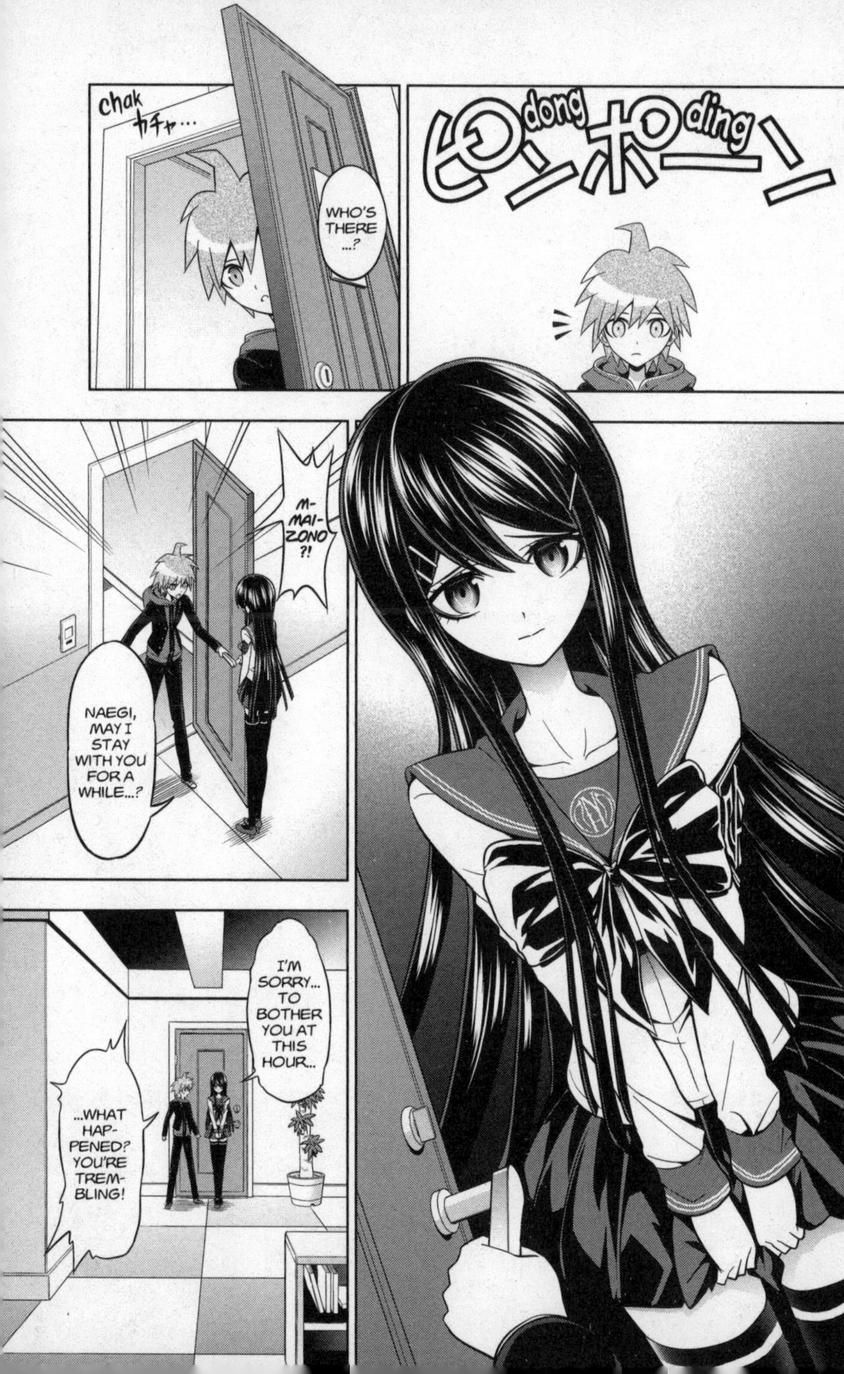
ピンポーン
dong
ding
chak
カチャ…
WHO'S THERE ...?
M-MAIZONO?!
NAEGI, MAY I STAY WITH YOU FOR A WHILE...?
I'M SORRY... TO BOTHER YOU AT THIS HOUR...
...WHAT HAPPENED? YOU'RE TREMBLING!

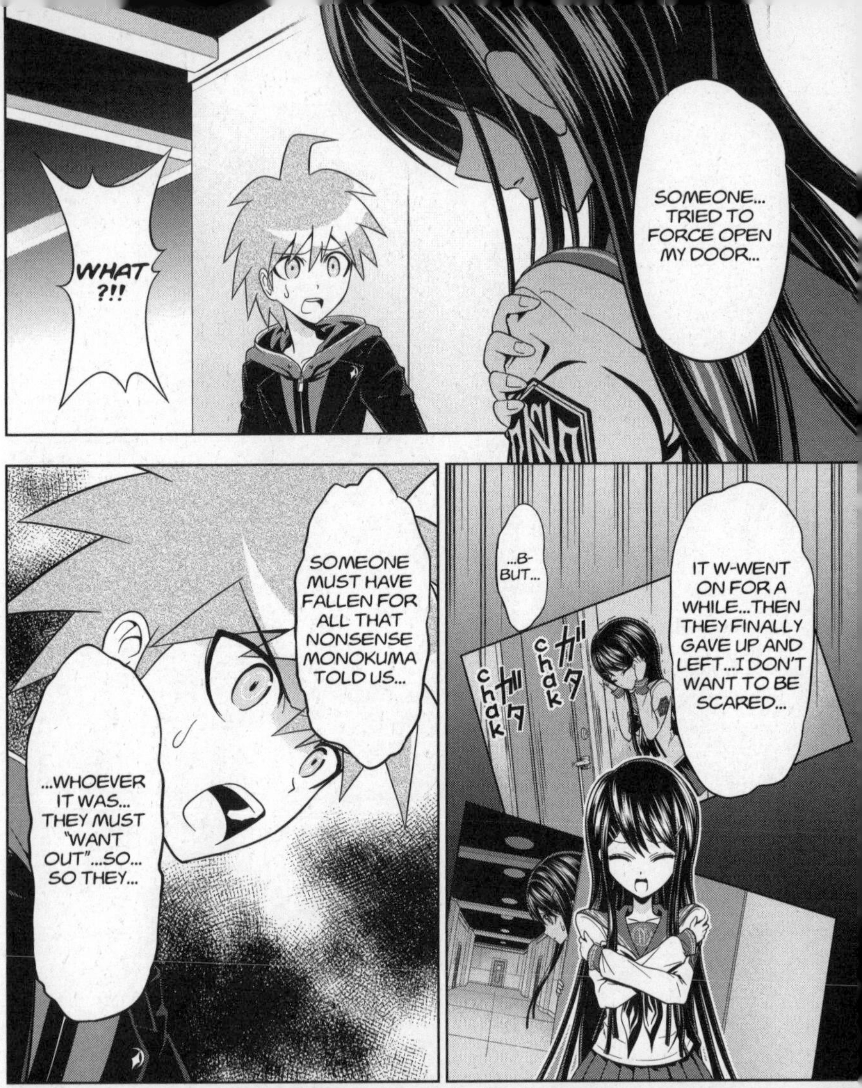
SOMEONE... TRIED TO FORCE OPEN MY DOOR...
WHAT?!!
IT W-WENT ON FOR A WHILE...THEN THEY FINALLY GAVE UP AND LEFT...I DON'T WANT TO BE SCARED...
...B-BUT...
ガタ chak
ガタ chak
SOMEONE MUST HAVE FALLEN FOR ALL THAT NONSENSE MONOKUMA TOLD US...
...WHOEVER IT WAS... THEY MUST "WANT OUT"...SO... SO THEY...

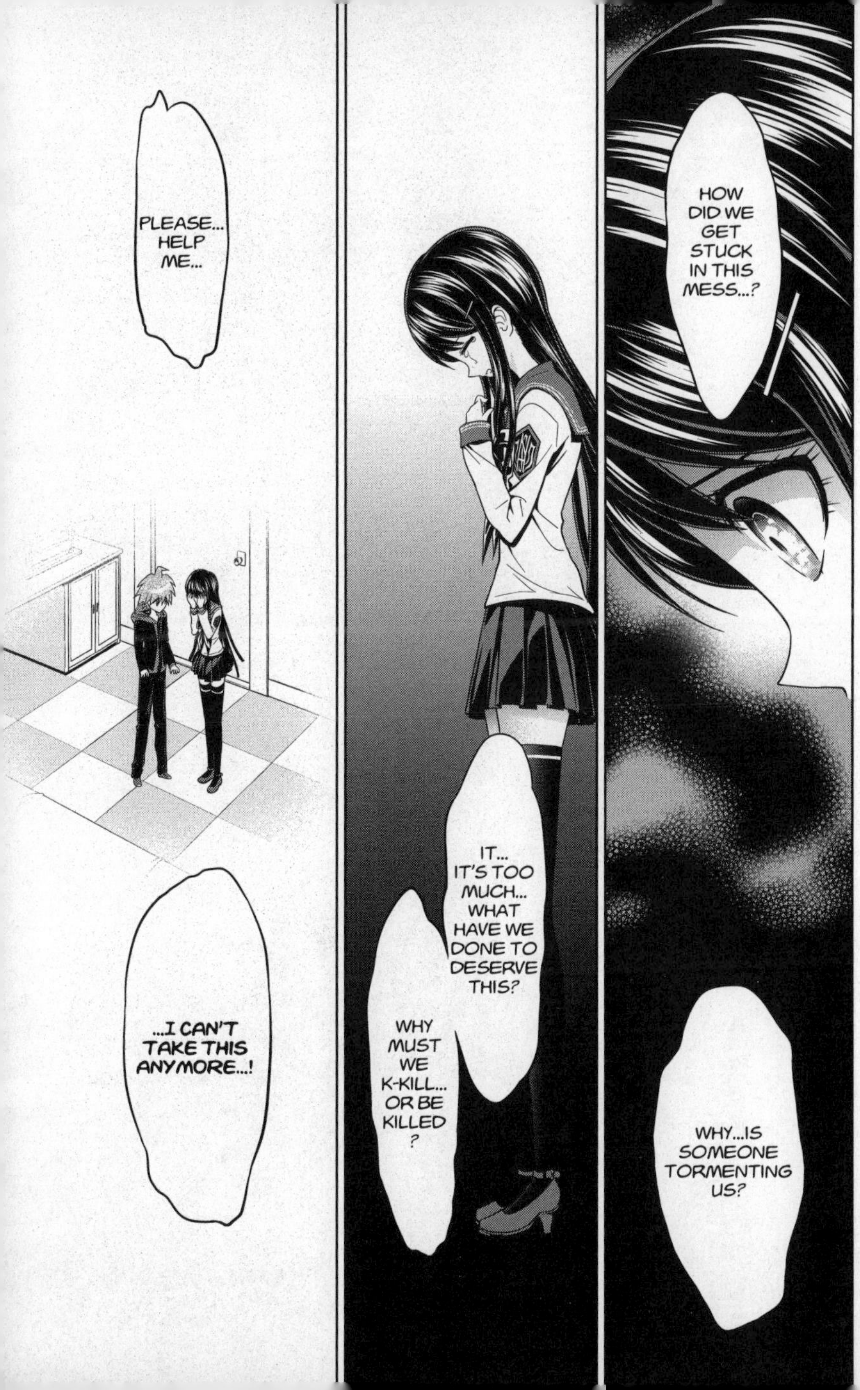

HOW DID WE GET STUCK IN THIS MESS...?
WHY...IS SOMEONE TORMENTING US?
IT... IT'S TOO MUCH... WHAT HAVE WE DONE TO DESERVE THIS?
WHY MUST WE K-KILL... OR BE KILLED?
PLEASE... HELP ME...
...I CAN'T TAKE THIS ANYMORE...!

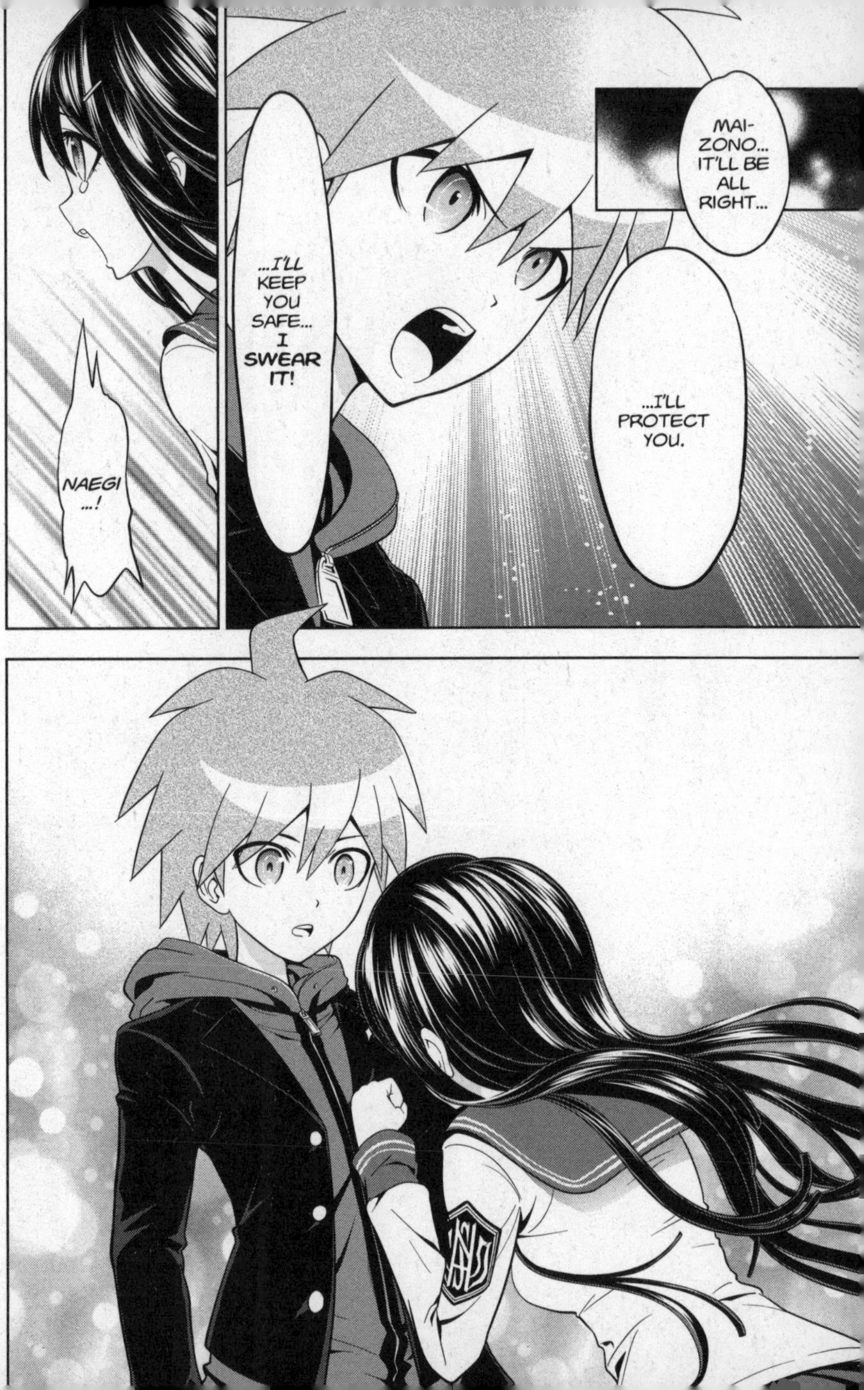
MAI-ZONO... IT'LL BE ALL RIGHT...
...I'LL PROTECT YOU.
...I'LL KEEP YOU SAFE... I SWEAR IT!
NAEGI ...!

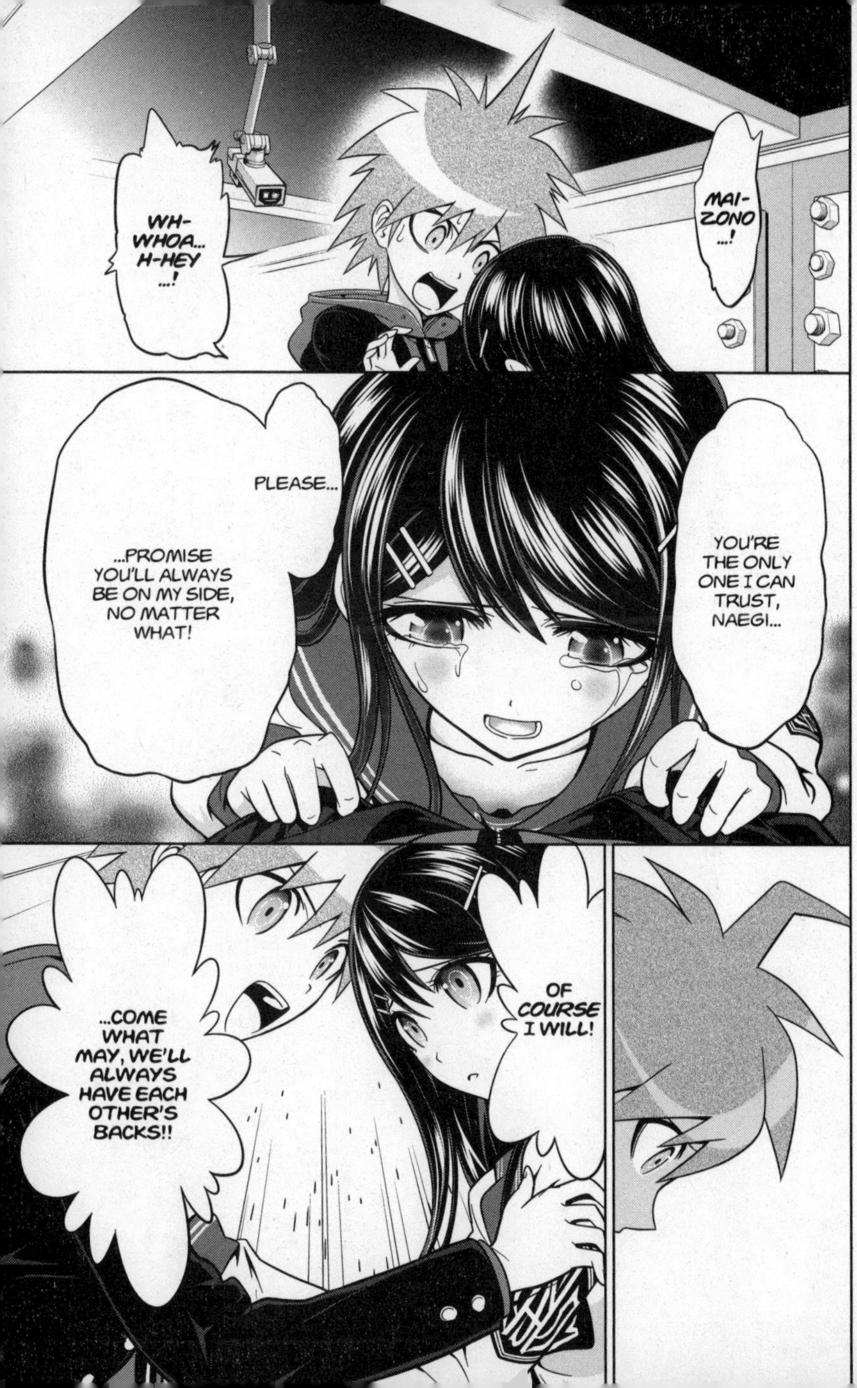
MAI-ZONO ...!
WH-WHOA... H-HEY ...!
YOU'RE THE ONLY ONE I CAN TRUST, NAEGI...
PLEASE... ...PROMISE YOU'LL ALWAYS BE ON MY SIDE, NO MATTER WHAT!
OF COURSE I WILL!
...COME WHAT MAY, WE'LL ALWAYS HAVE EACH OTHER'S BACKS!!

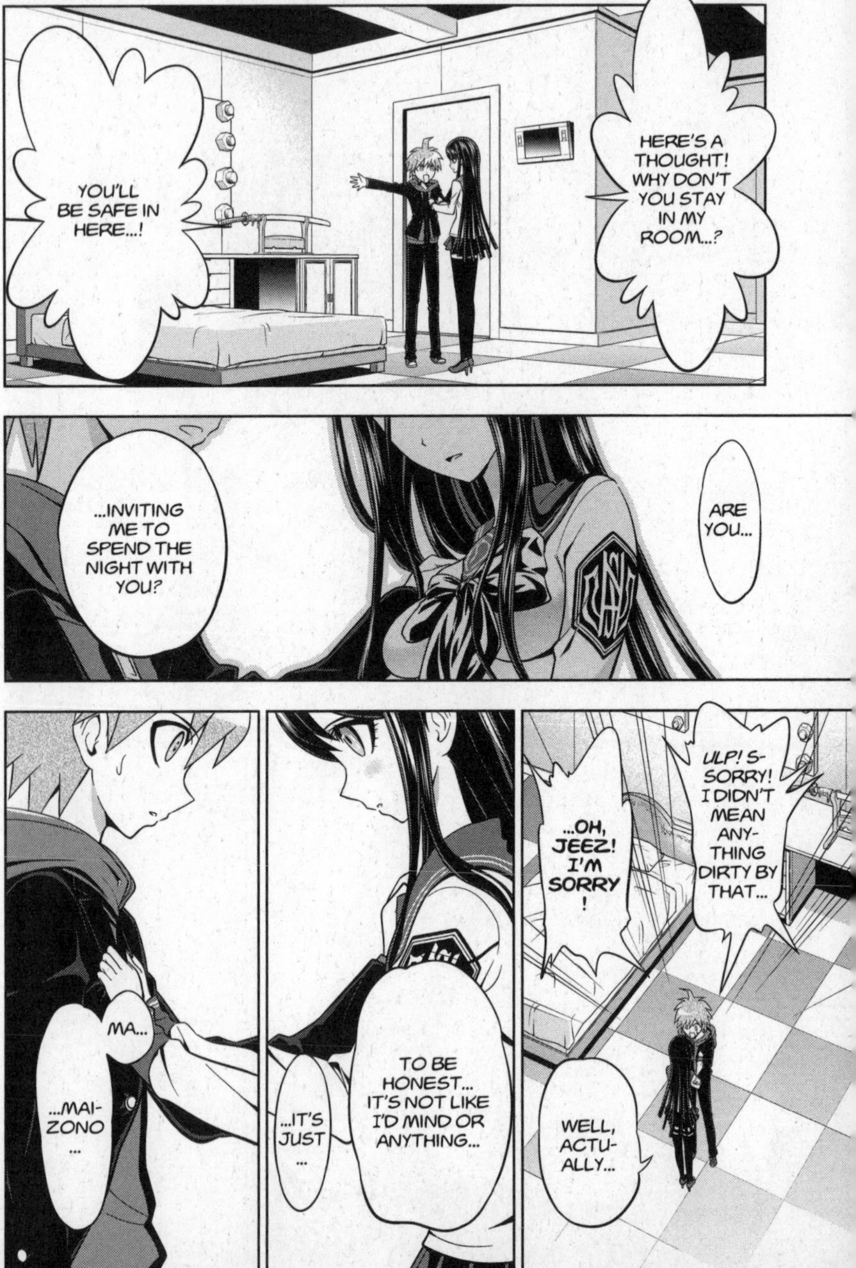
HERE'S A THOUGHT! WHY DON'T YOU STAY IN MY ROOM...?
YOU'LL BE SAFE IN HERE...!
ARE YOU...
...INVITING ME TO SPEND THE NIGHT WITH YOU?
ULP! S-SORRY! I DIDN'T MEAN ANY-THING DIRTY BY THAT...
...OH, JEEZ! I'M SORRY!
WELL, ACTU-ALLY...
TO BE HONEST... IT'S NOT LIKE I'D MIND OR ANYTHING...
...IT'S JUST ...
MA...
...MAI-ZONO ...

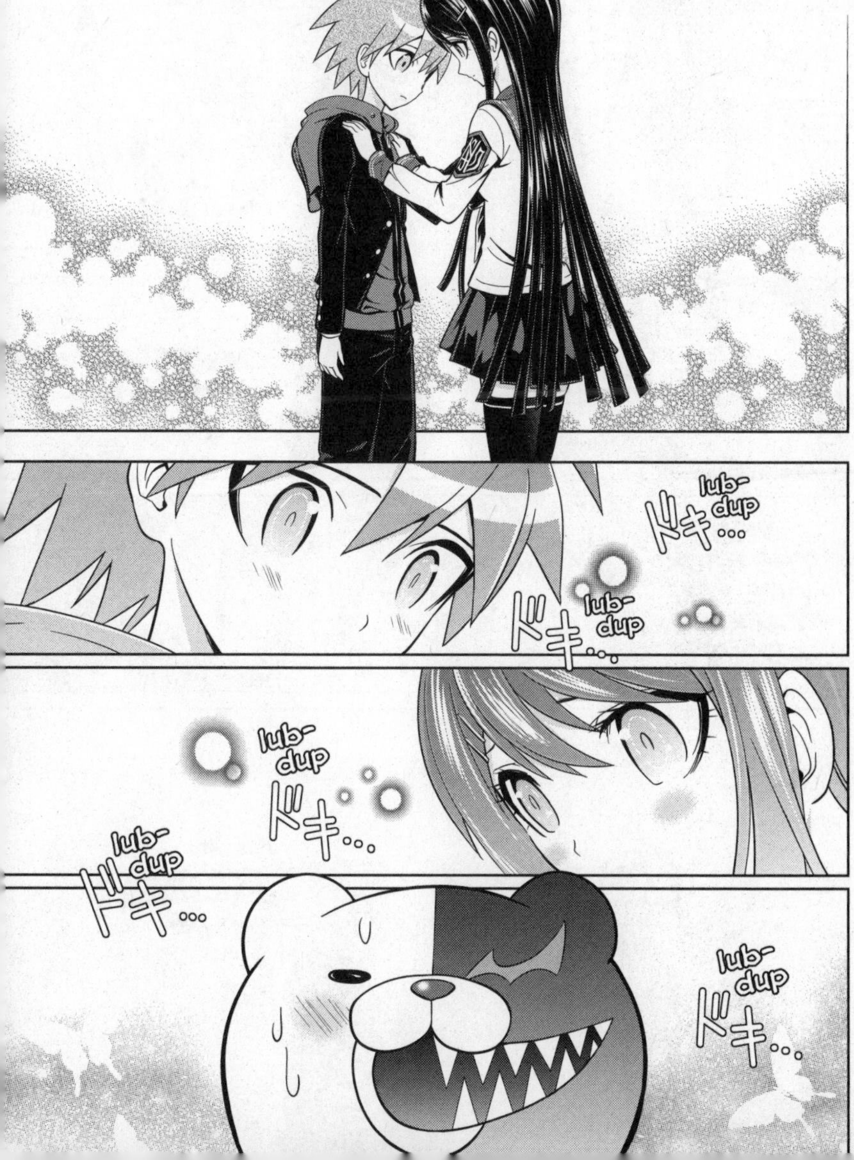
ドキ…
lub-dup
ドキ…
lub-dup
ドキ…
lub-dup
ドキ…
lub-dup
ドキ…
lub-dup

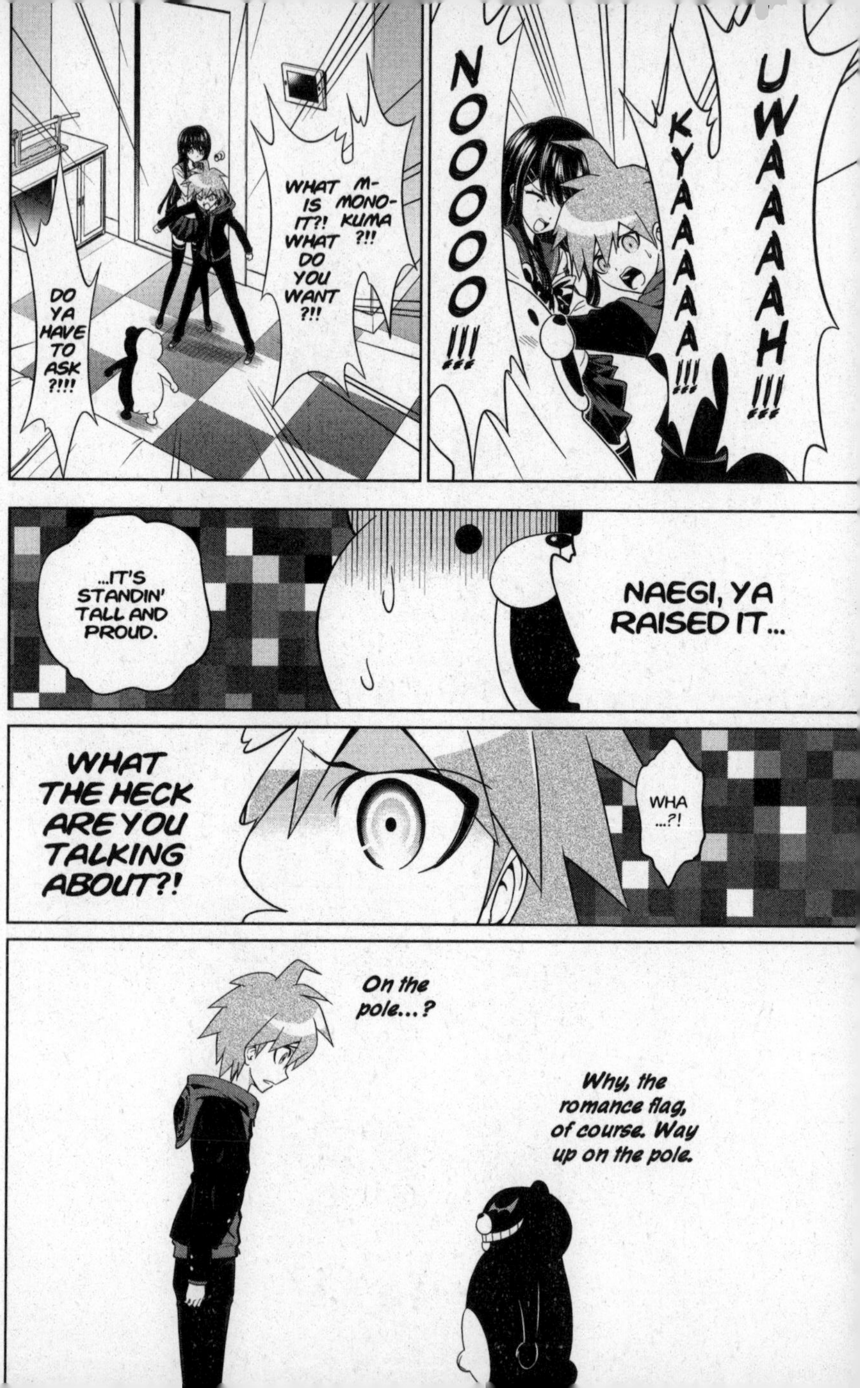
UWAAAAAH!!!
KYAAAAAA!!!
NOOOOO!!!
M-MONOKUMA?!!
WHAT IS IT?! WHAT DO YOU WANT?!!
DO YA HAVE TO ASK?!!!
NAEGI, YA RAISED IT...
...IT'S STANDIN' TALL AND PROUD.
WHA...?!
WHAT THE HECK ARE YOU TALKING ABOUT?!
On the pole...?
Why, the romance flag, of course. Way up on the pole.

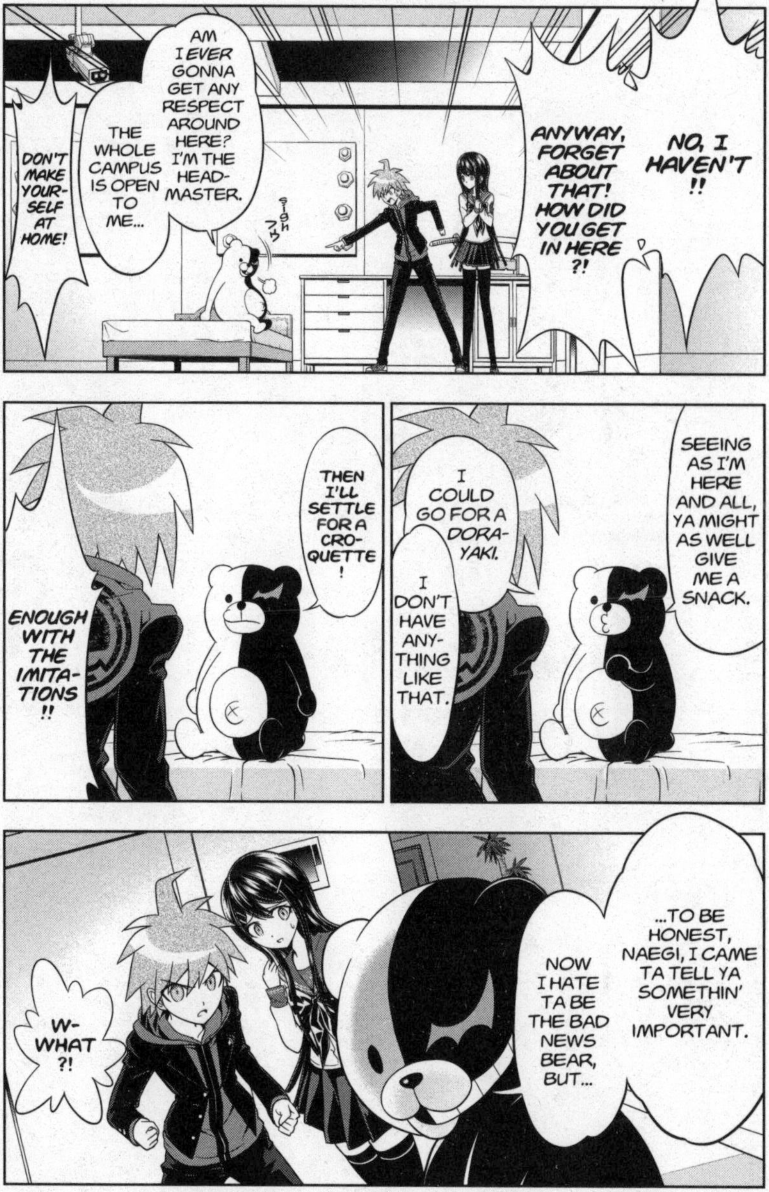
NO, I HAVEN'T!!
ANYWAY, FORGET ABOUT THAT! HOW DID YOU GET IN HERE?!
AM I EVER GONNA GET ANY RESPECT AROUND HERE? I'M THE HEADMASTER.
THE WHOLE CAMPUS IS OPEN TO ME...
sigh
DON'T MAKE YOURSELF AT HOME!
SEEING AS I'M HERE AND ALL, YA MIGHT AS WELL GIVE ME A SNACK.
I COULD GO FOR A DORAYAKI.
I DON'T HAVE ANYTHING LIKE THAT.
THEN I'LL SETTLE FOR A CROQUETTE!
ENOUGH WITH THE IMITATIONS!!
...TO BE HONEST, NAEGI, I CAME TA TELL YA SOMETHIN' VERY IMPORTANT.
NOW I HATE TA BE THE BAD NEWS BEAR, BUT...
W-WHAT?!

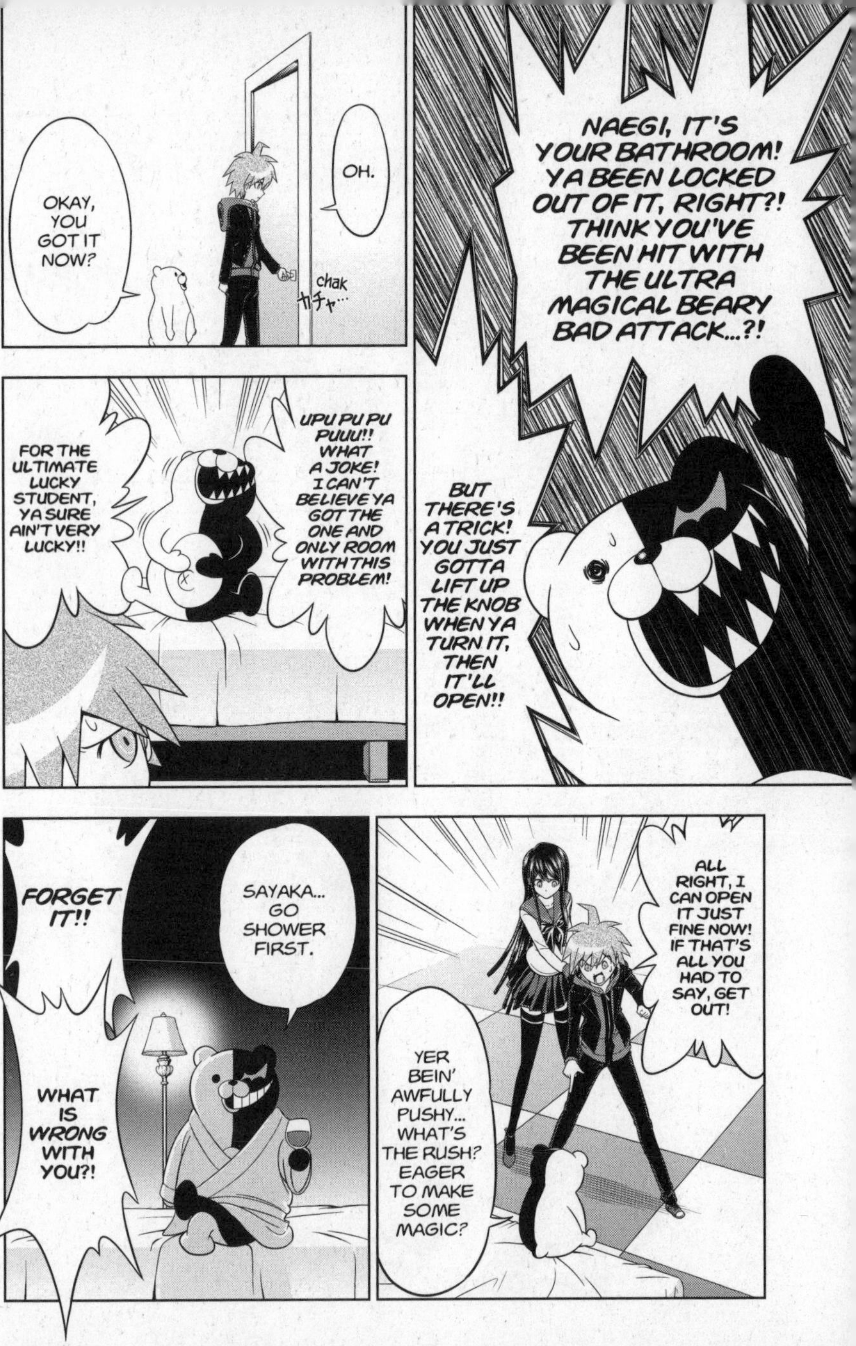
NAEGI, IT'S YOUR BATHROOM! YA BEEN LOCKED OUT OF IT, RIGHT?! THINK YOU'VE BEEN HIT WITH THE ULTRA MAGICAL BEARY BAD ATTACK...?!
BUT THERE'S A TRICK! YOU JUST GOTTA LIFT UP THE KNOB WHEN YA TURN IT, THEN IT'LL OPEN!!
OH.
OKAY, YOU GOT IT NOW?
chak カチャ…
UPU PU PU PUUU!! WHAT A JOKE! I CAN'T BELIEVE YA GOT THE ONE AND ONLY ROOM WITH THIS PROBLEM!
FOR THE ULTIMATE LUCKY STUDENT, YA SURE AIN'T VERY LUCKY!!
ALL RIGHT, I CAN OPEN IT JUST FINE NOW! IF THAT'S ALL YOU HAD TO SAY, GET OUT!
YER BEIN' AWFULLY PUSHY... WHAT'S THE RUSH? EAGER TO MAKE SOME MAGIC?
SAYAKA... GO SHOWER FIRST.
FORGET IT!!
WHAT IS WRONG WITH YOU?!

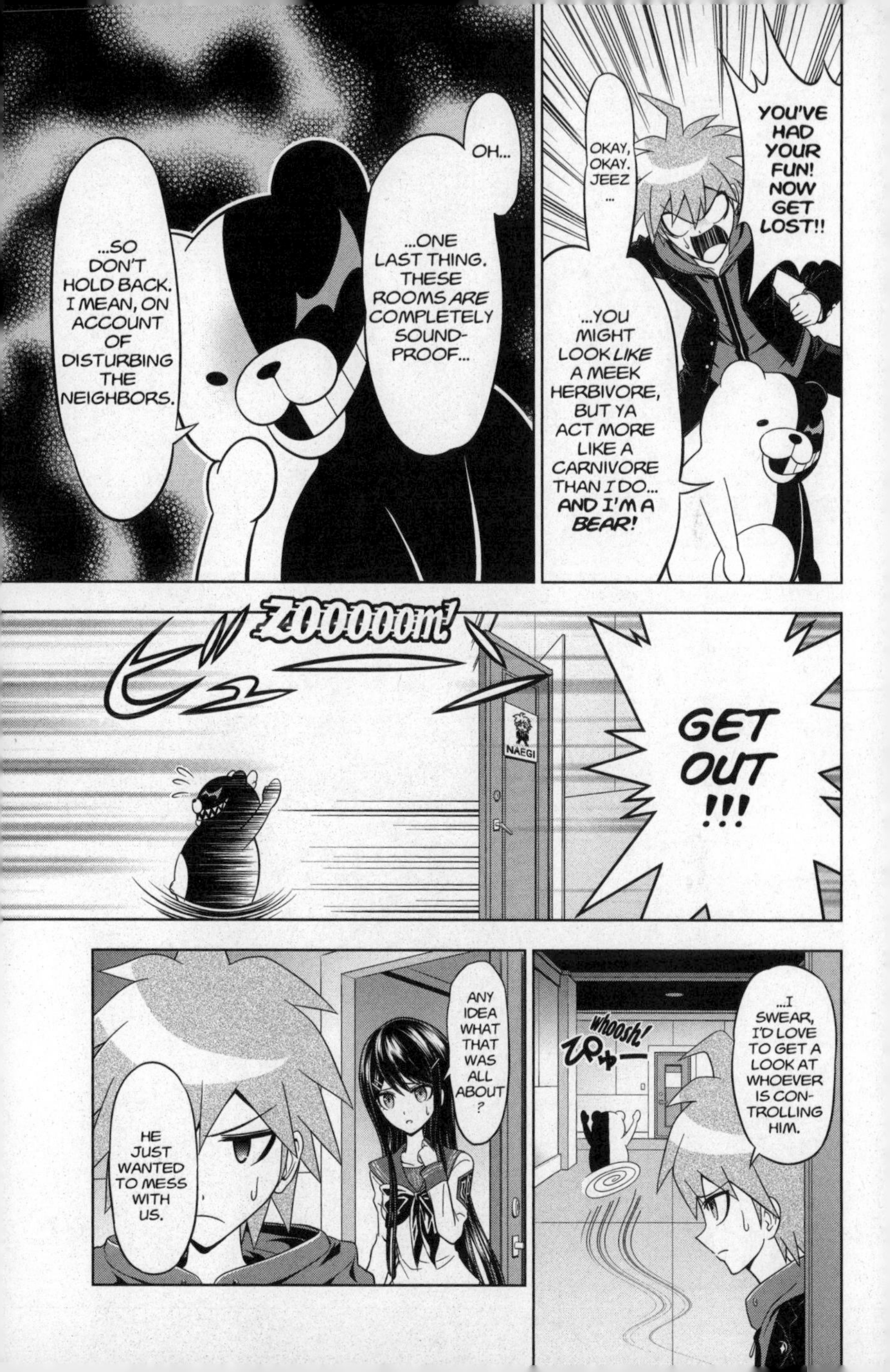
YOU'VE HAD YOUR FUN! NOW GET LOST!!
OKAY, OKAY. JEEZ ...
...YOU MIGHT LOOK LIKE A MEEK HERBIVORE, BUT YA ACT MORE LIKE A CARNIVORE THAN I DO... AND I'M A BEAR!
OH...
...ONE LAST THING. THESE ROOMS ARE COMPLETELY SOUND-PROOF...
...SO DON'T HOLD BACK. I MEAN, ON ACCOUNT OF DISTURBING THE NEIGHBORS.
GET OUT !!!
NAEGI
ZOOOOOOM!
...I SWEAR, I'D LOVE TO GET A LOOK AT WHOEVER IS CON-TROLLING HIM.
whoosh!
ANY IDEA WHAT THAT WAS ALL ABOUT ?
HE JUST WANTED TO MESS WITH US.

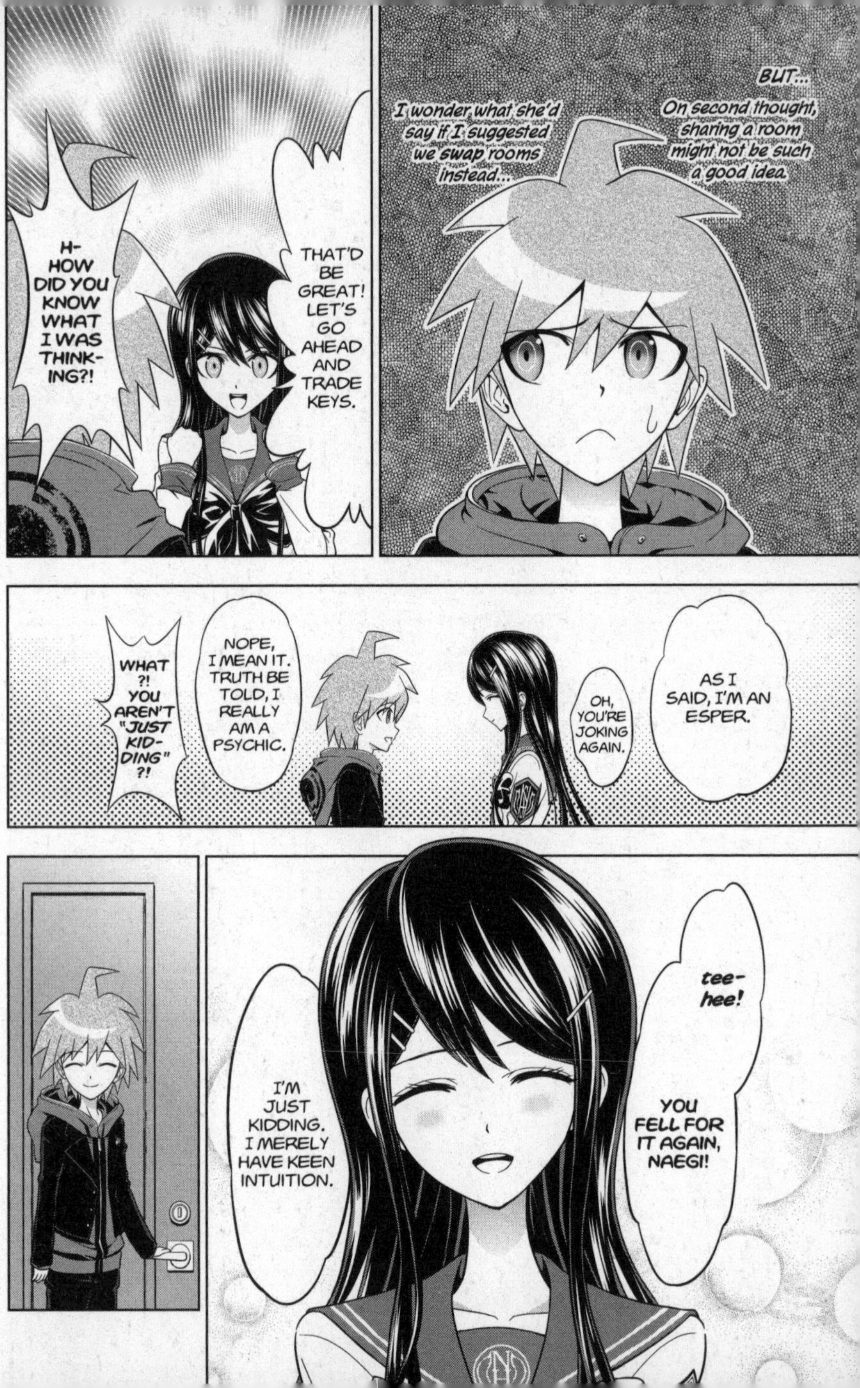
BUT...
On second thought, sharing a room might not be such a good idea.
I wonder what she'd say if I suggested we swap rooms instead...
THAT'D BE GREAT! LET'S GO AHEAD AND TRADE KEYS.
H-HOW DID YOU KNOW WHAT I WAS THINKING?!
AS I SAID, I'M AN ESPER.
OH, YOU'RE JOKING AGAIN.
NOPE, I MEAN IT. TRUTH BE TOLD, I REALLY AM A PSYCHIC.
WHAT?! YOU AREN'T "JUST KIDDING"?!
tee-hee!
YOU FELL FOR IT AGAIN, NAEGI!
I'M JUST KIDDING. I MERELY HAVE KEEN INTUITION.

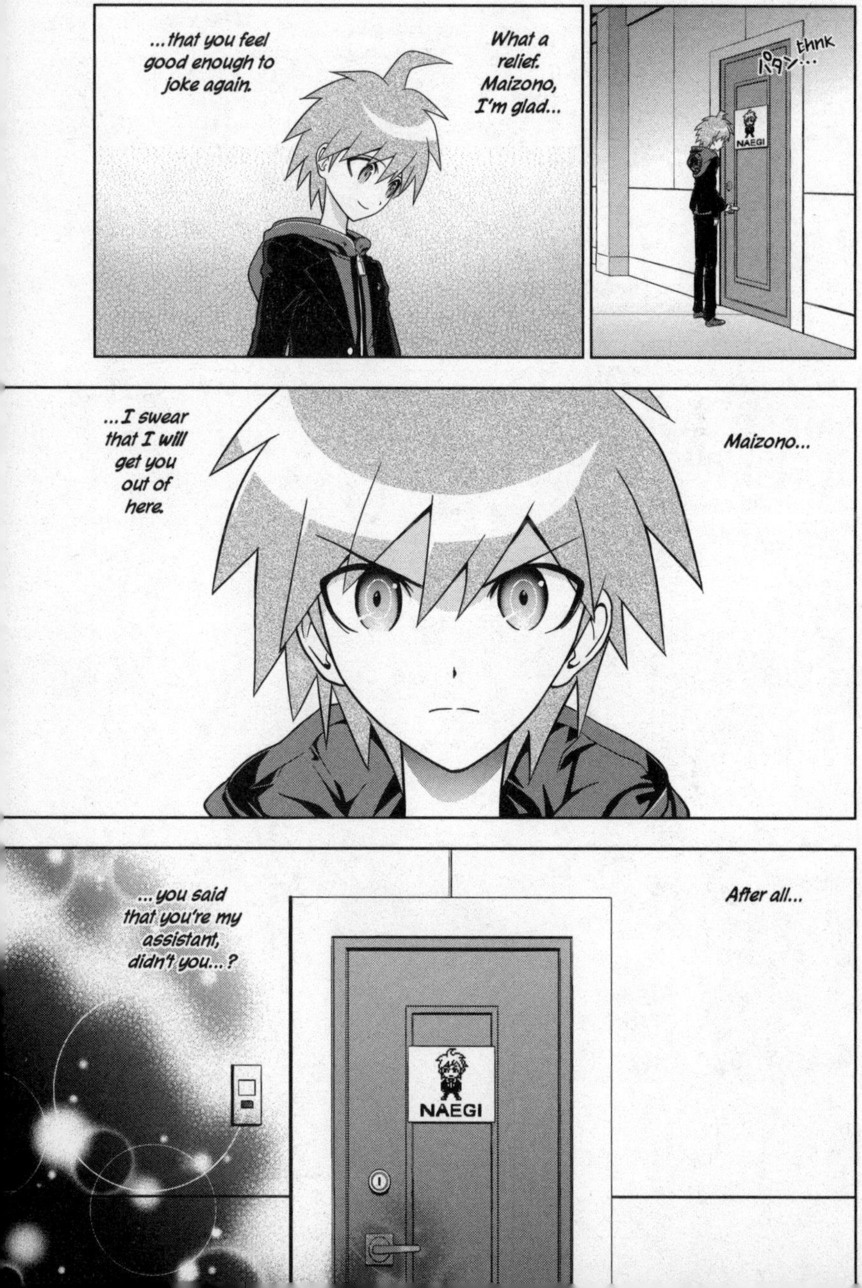
thnk
パタン…
NAEGI
What a relief. Maizono, I'm glad...
...that you feel good enough to joke again.
Maizono...
...I swear that I will get you out of here.
After all...
...you said that you're my assistant, didn't you...?
NAEGI

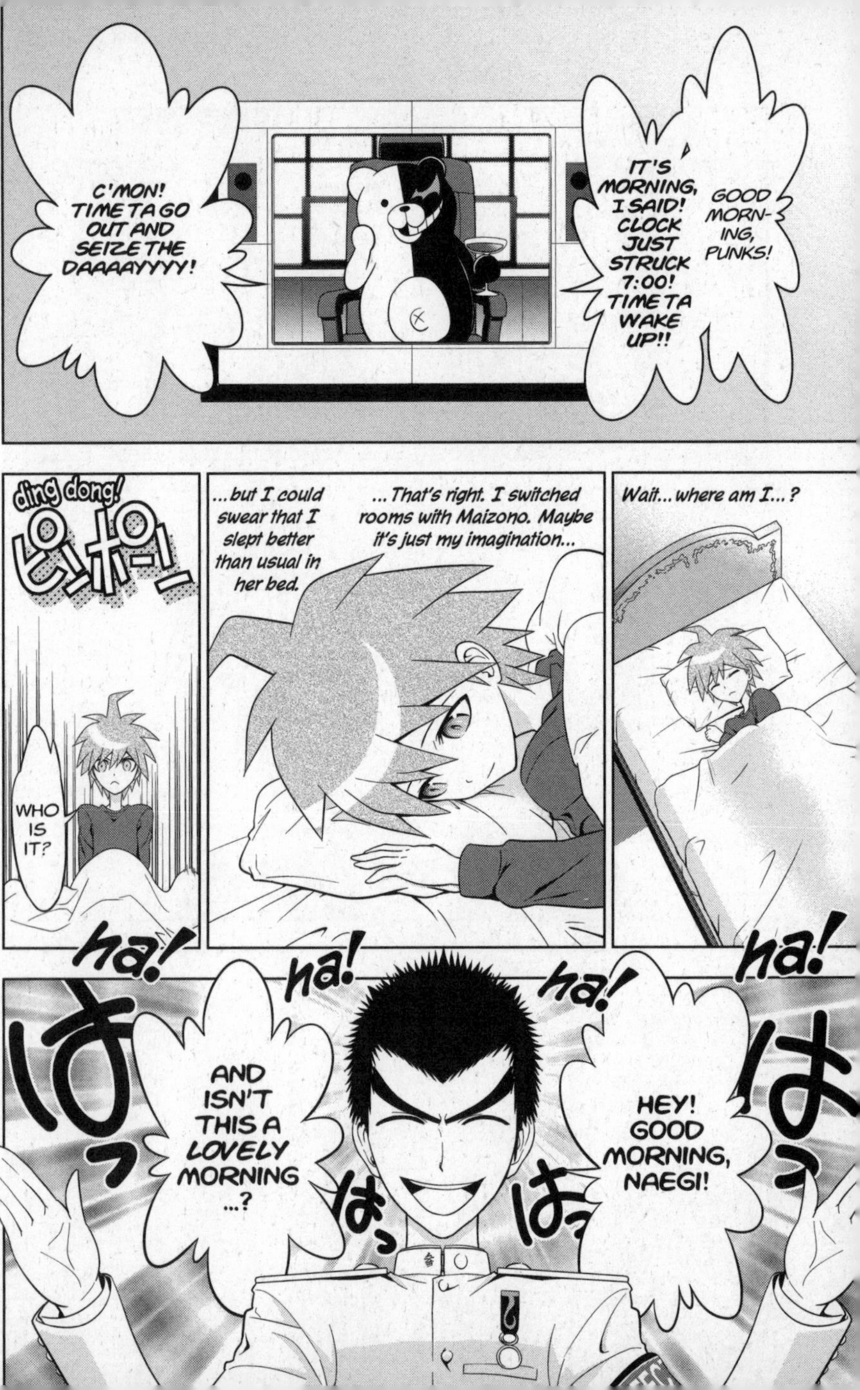
GOOD MORNING, PUNKS!
IT'S MORNING, I SAID! CLOCK JUST STRUCK 7:00! TIME TA WAKE UP!!
C'MON! TIME TA GO OUT AND SEIZE THE DAAAAYYYY!
Wait...where am I...?
...That's right. I switched rooms with Maizono. Maybe it's just my imagination...
...but I could swear that I slept better than usual in her bed.
ding dong!
ピンポーン
WHO IS IT?
ha! ha! ha! ha!
はっ はっ はっ はっ
HEY! GOOD MORNING, NAEGI!
AND ISN'T THIS A LOVELY MORNING...?

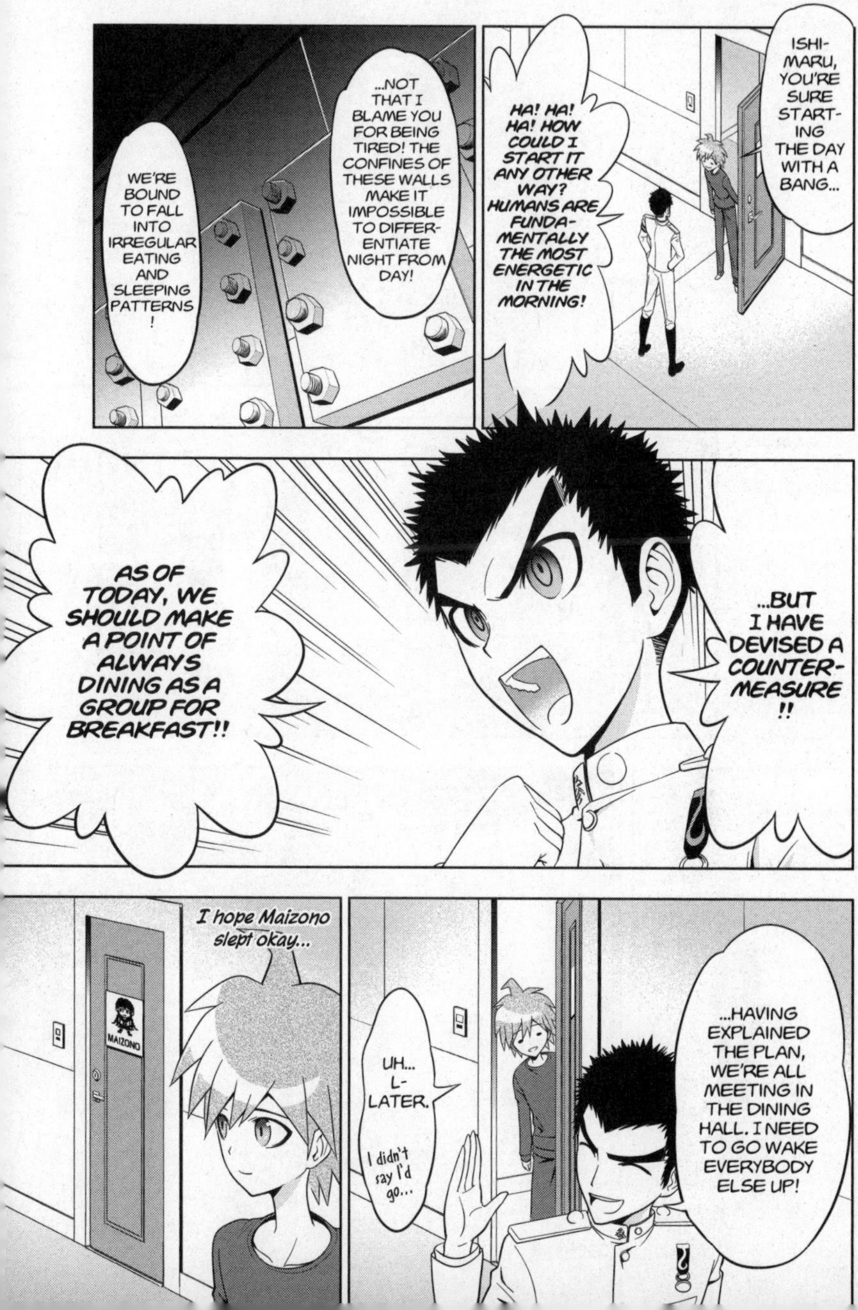
ISHIMARU, YOU'RE SURE STARTING THE DAY WITH A BANG...
HA! HA! HA! HOW COULD I START IT ANY OTHER WAY? HUMANS ARE FUNDAMENTALLY THE MOST ENERGETIC IN THE MORNING!
...NOT THAT I BLAME YOU FOR BEING TIRED! THE CONFINES OF THESE WALLS MAKE IT IMPOSSIBLE TO DIFFERENTIATE NIGHT FROM DAY!
WE'RE BOUND TO FALL INTO IRREGULAR EATING AND SLEEPING PATTERNS!
...BUT I HAVE DEVISED A COUNTER-MEASURE!!
AS OF TODAY, WE SHOULD MAKE A POINT OF ALWAYS DINING AS A GROUP FOR BREAKFAST!!
...HAVING EXPLAINED THE PLAN, WE'RE ALL MEETING IN THE DINING HALL. I NEED TO GO WAKE EVERYBODY ELSE UP!
UH... L-LATER.
I didn't say I'd go...
I hope Maizono slept okay...
MAIZONO

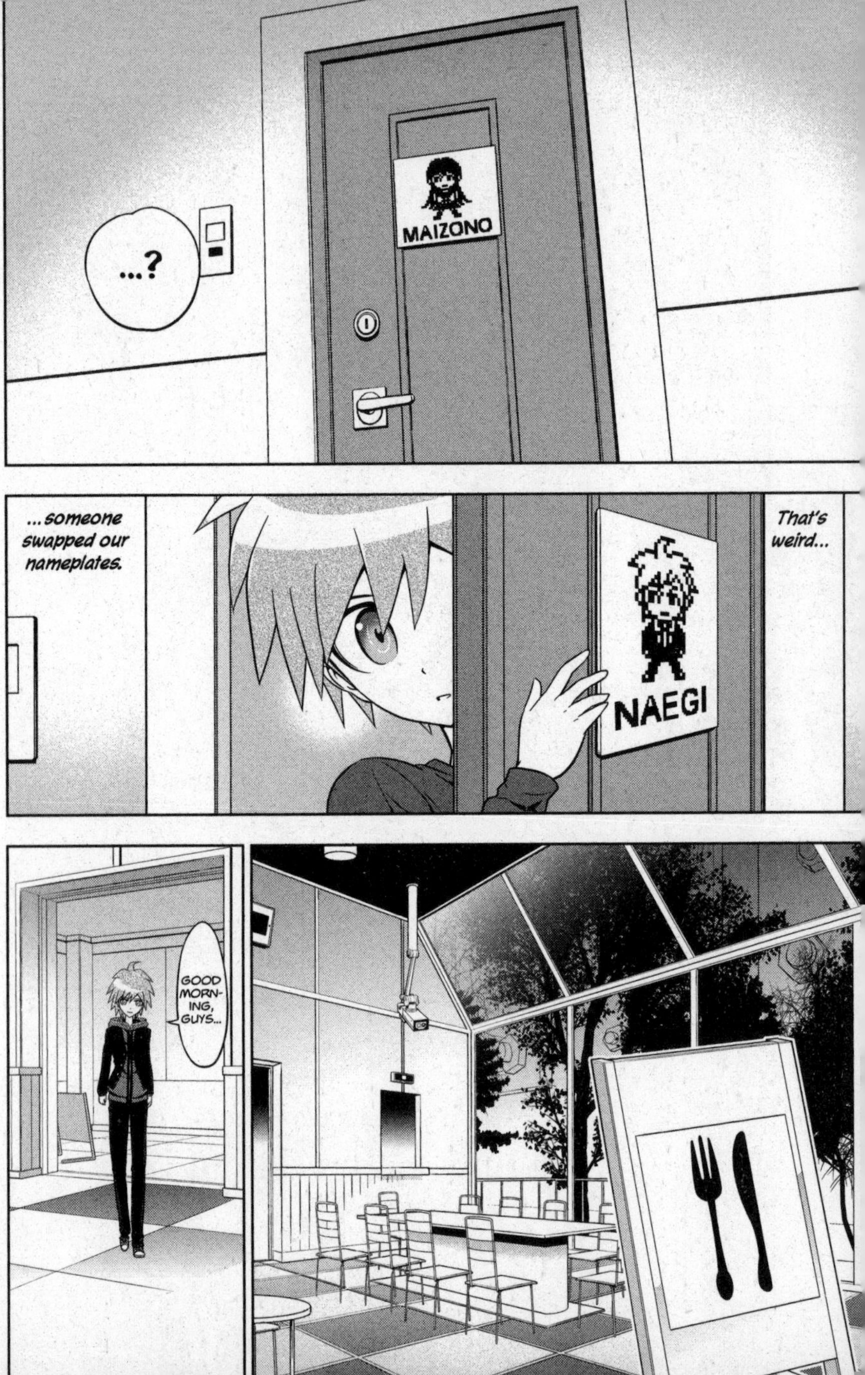
...?
MAIZONO
That's weird...
...someone swapped our nameplates.
NAEGI
GOOD MORN-ING, GUYS...

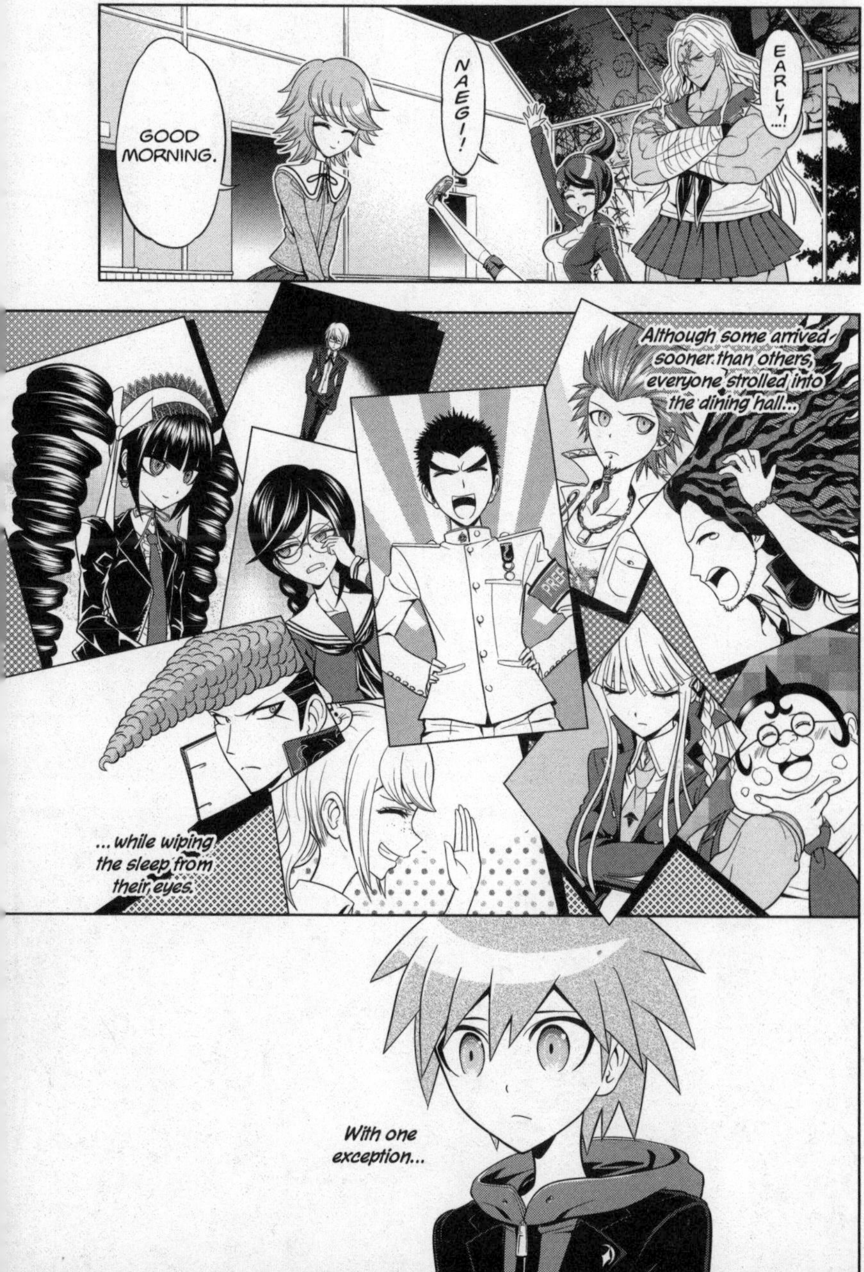
EARLY...!
NAEGI!
GOOD MORNING.
Although some arrived sooner than others, everyone strolled into the dining hall...
...while wiping the sleep from their eyes.
With one exception...

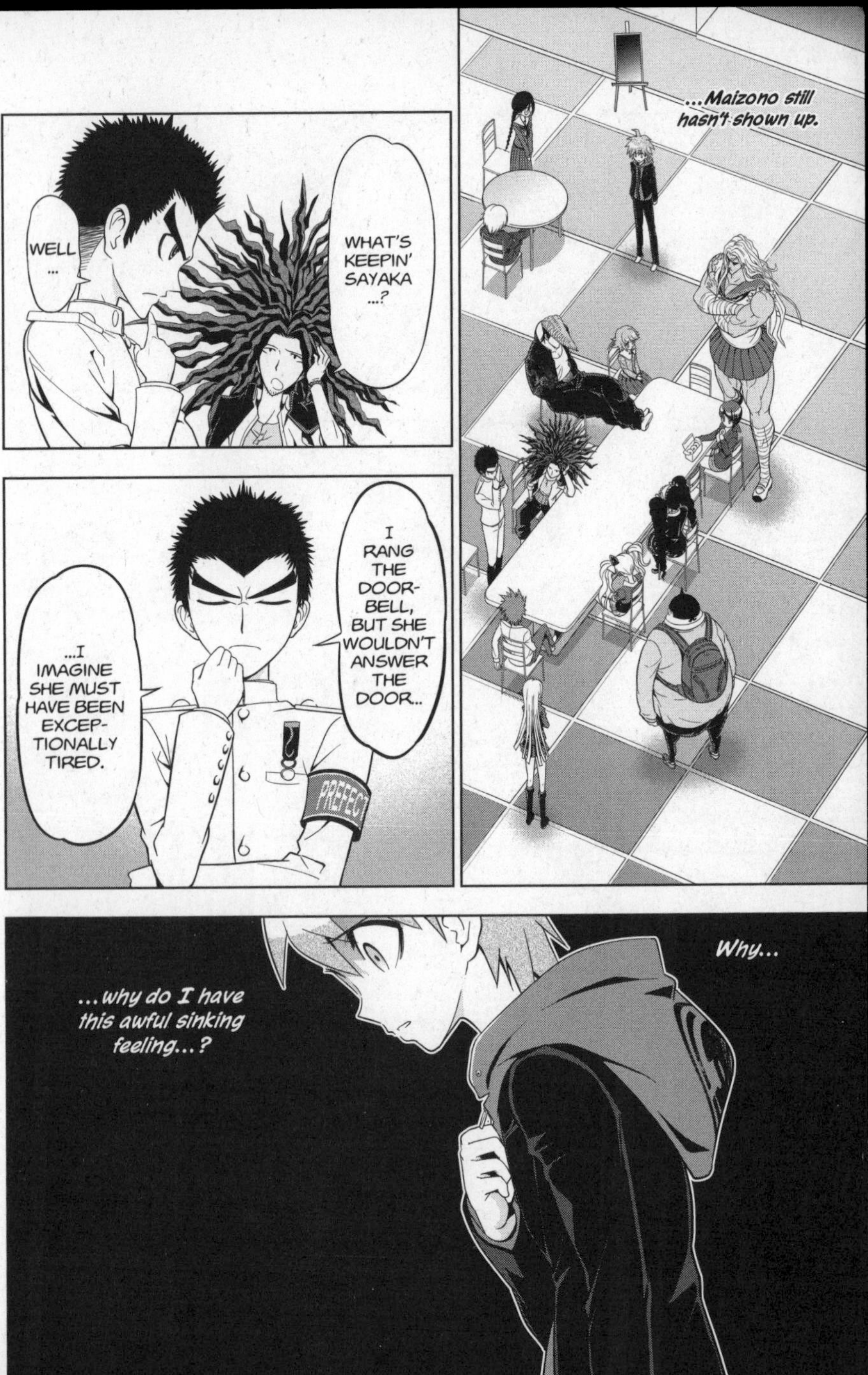
...Maizono still hasn't shown up.
WHAT'S KEEPIN' SAYAKA ...?
WELL ...
I RANG THE DOOR-BELL, BUT SHE WOULDN'T ANSWER THE DOOR..
...I IMAGINE SHE MUST HAVE BEEN EXCEP-TIONALLY TIRED.
PREFECT
Why...
...why do I have this awful sinking feeling...?

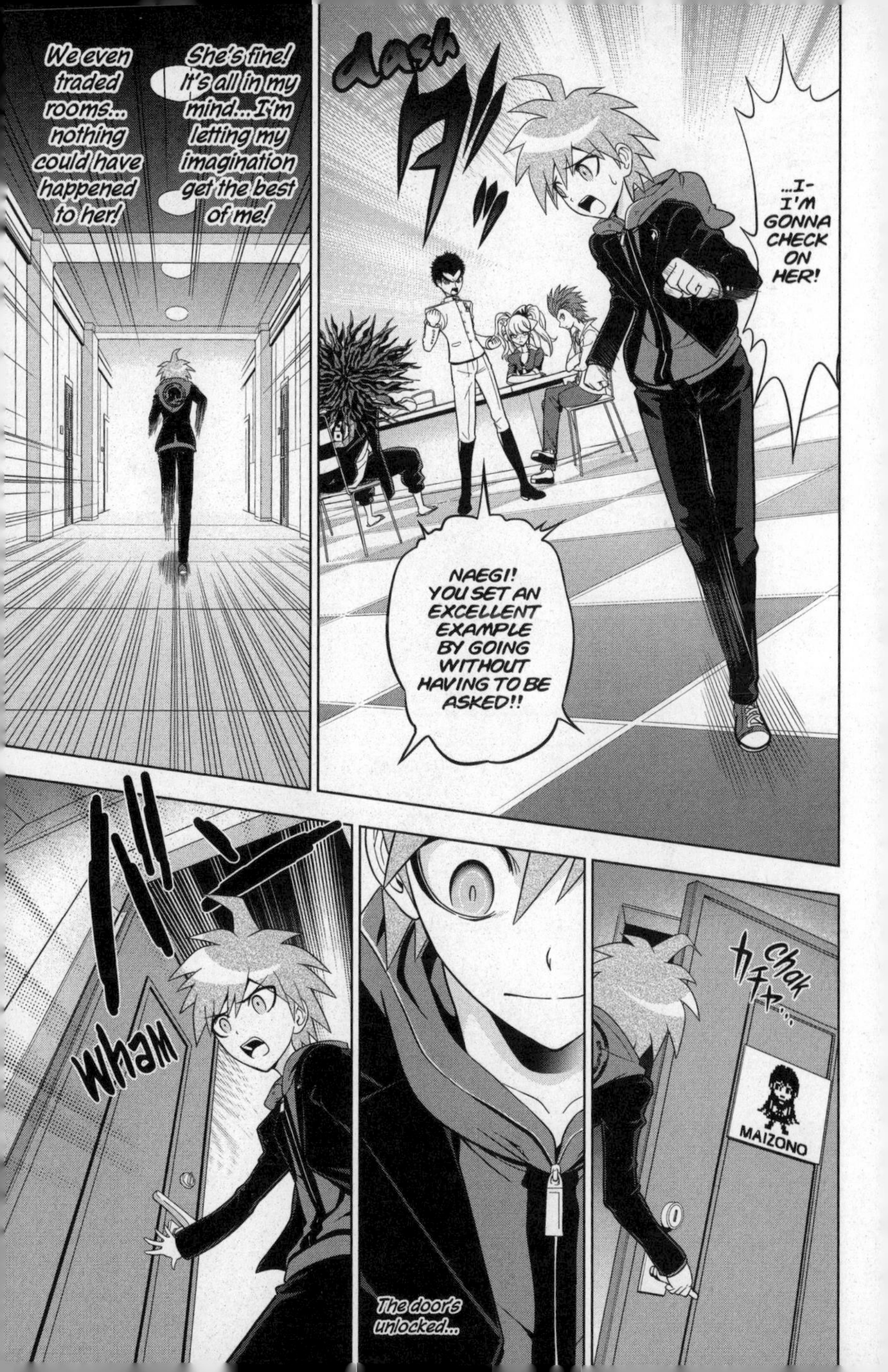
dash
...I- I'M GONNA CHECK ON HER!
NAEGI! YOU SET AN EXCELLENT EXAMPLE BY GOING WITHOUT HAVING TO BE ASKED!!
She's fine! It's all in my mind...I'm letting my imagination get the best of me!
We even traded rooms... nothing could have happened to her!
Chak
MAIZONO
The door's unlocked...
Wham

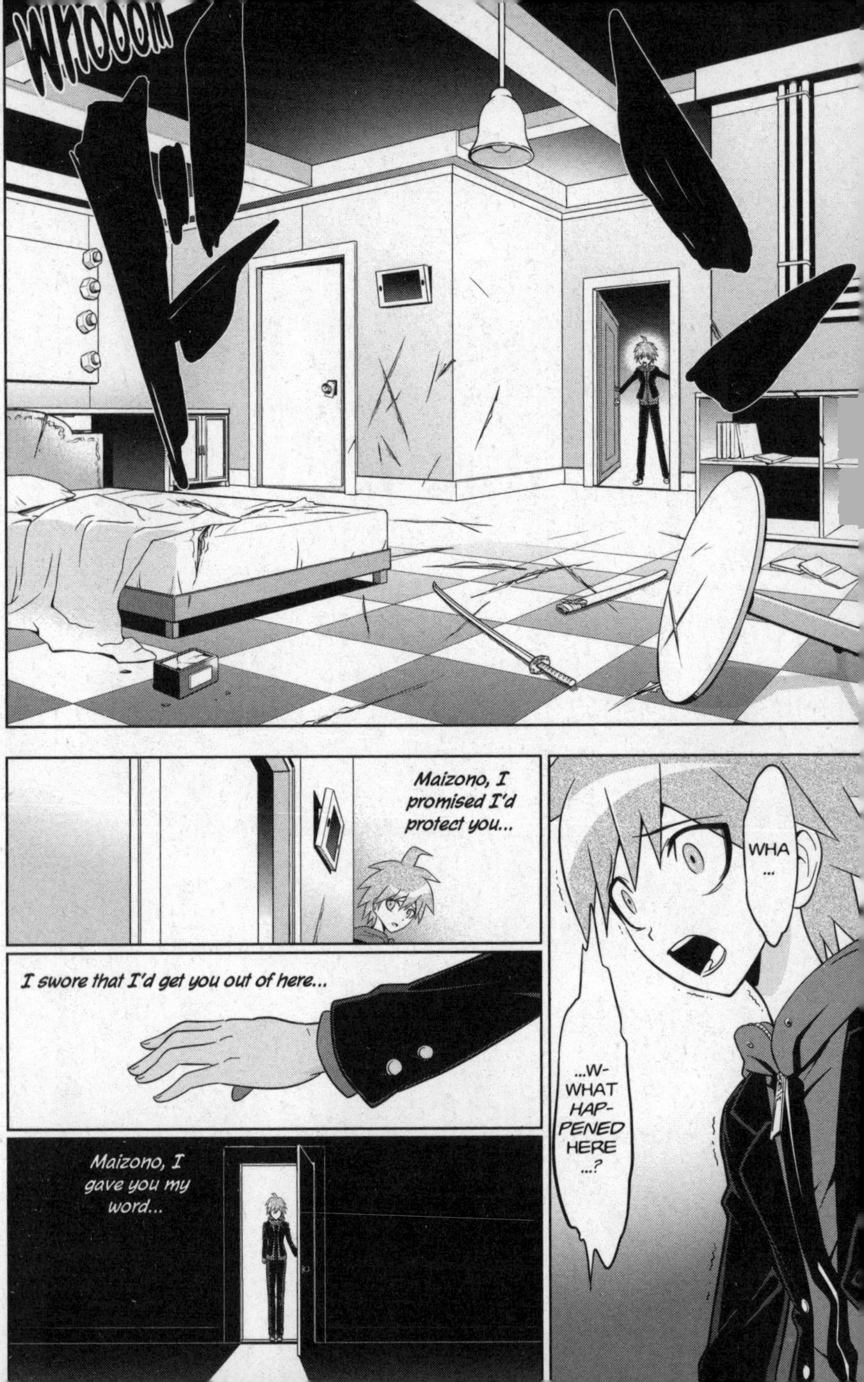
WHOOOM
WHA ...
...W-WHAT HAPPENED HERE ...?
Maizono, I promised I'd protect you...
I swore that I'd get you out of here...
Maizono, I gave you my word...

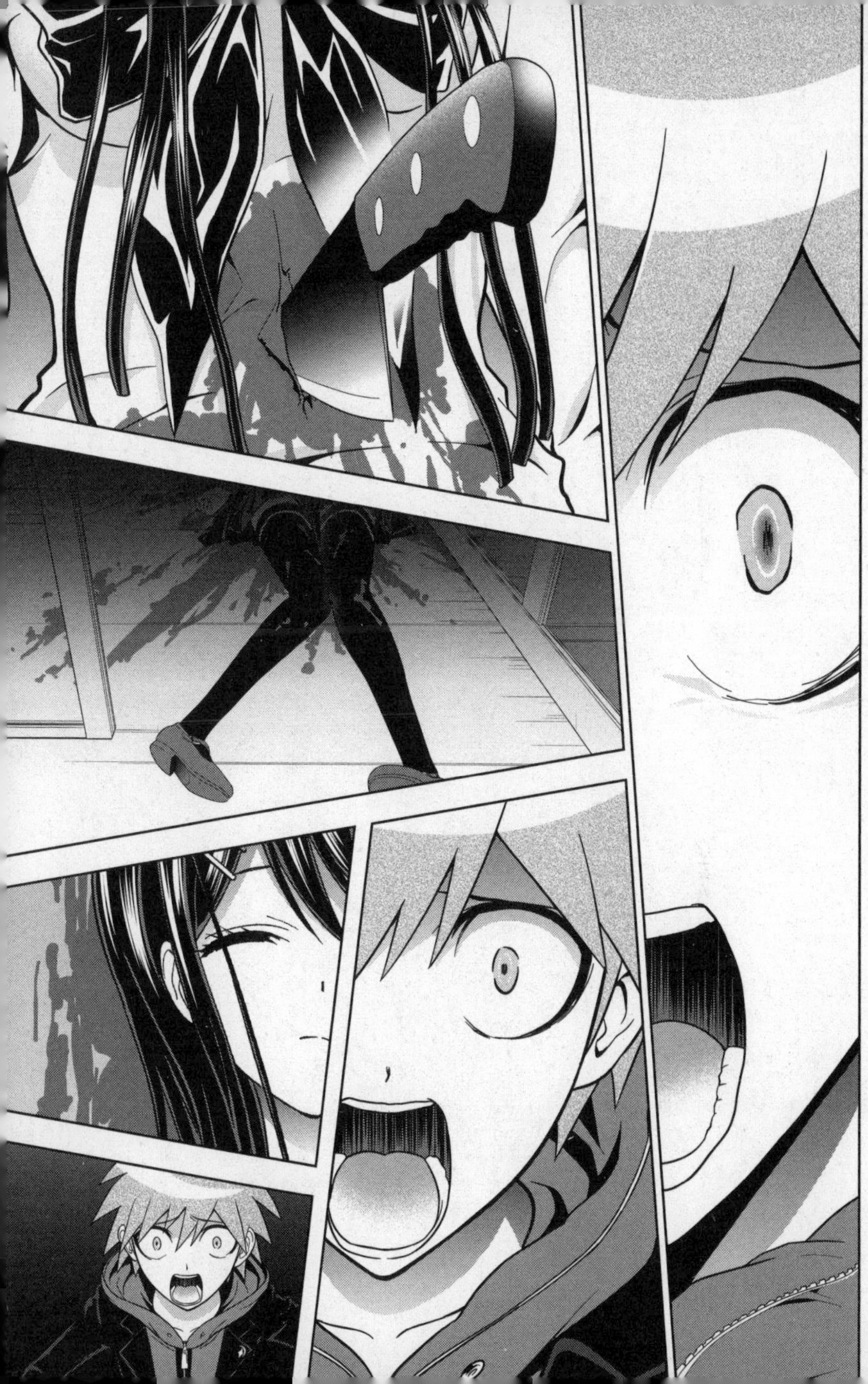

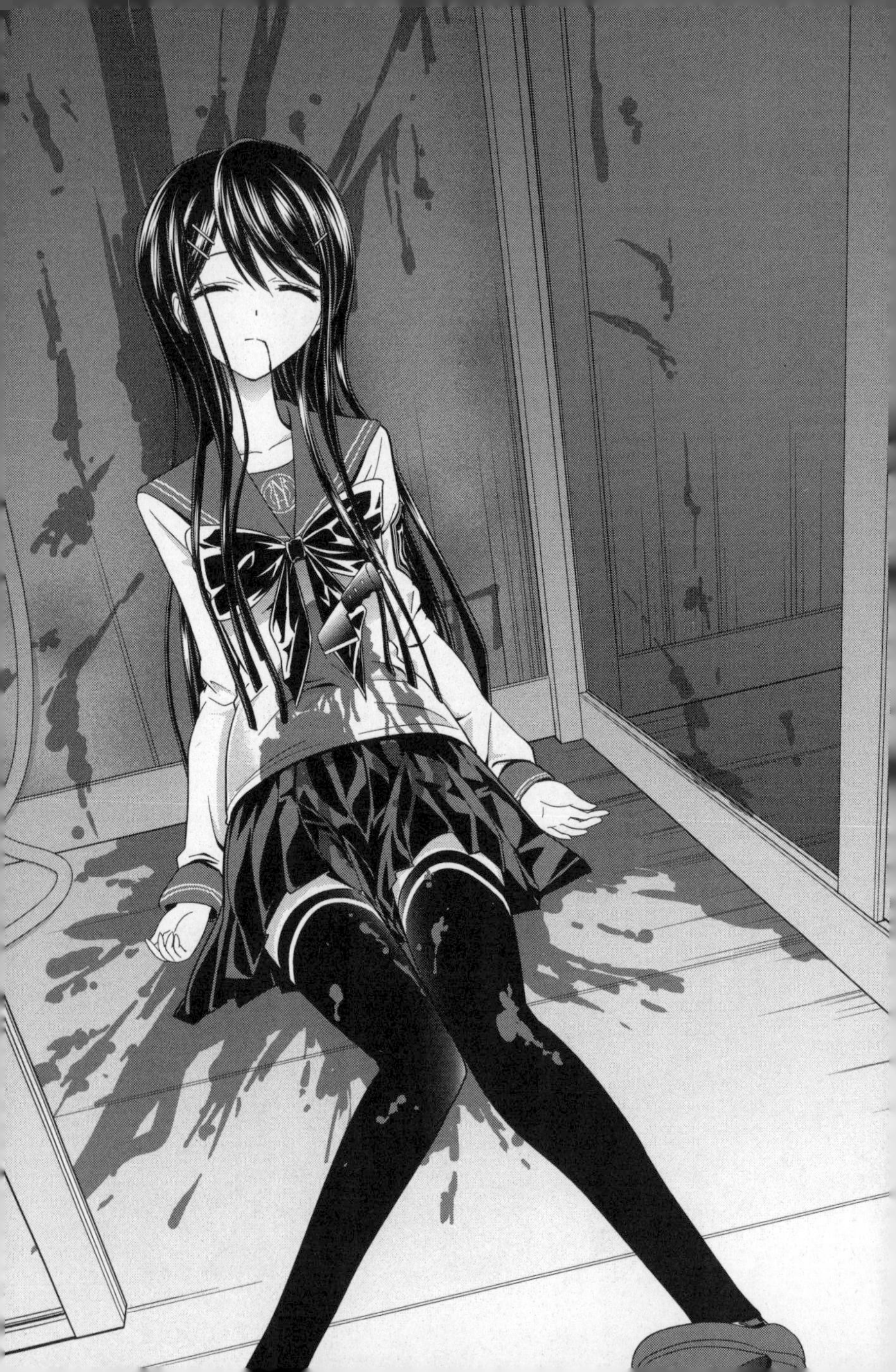

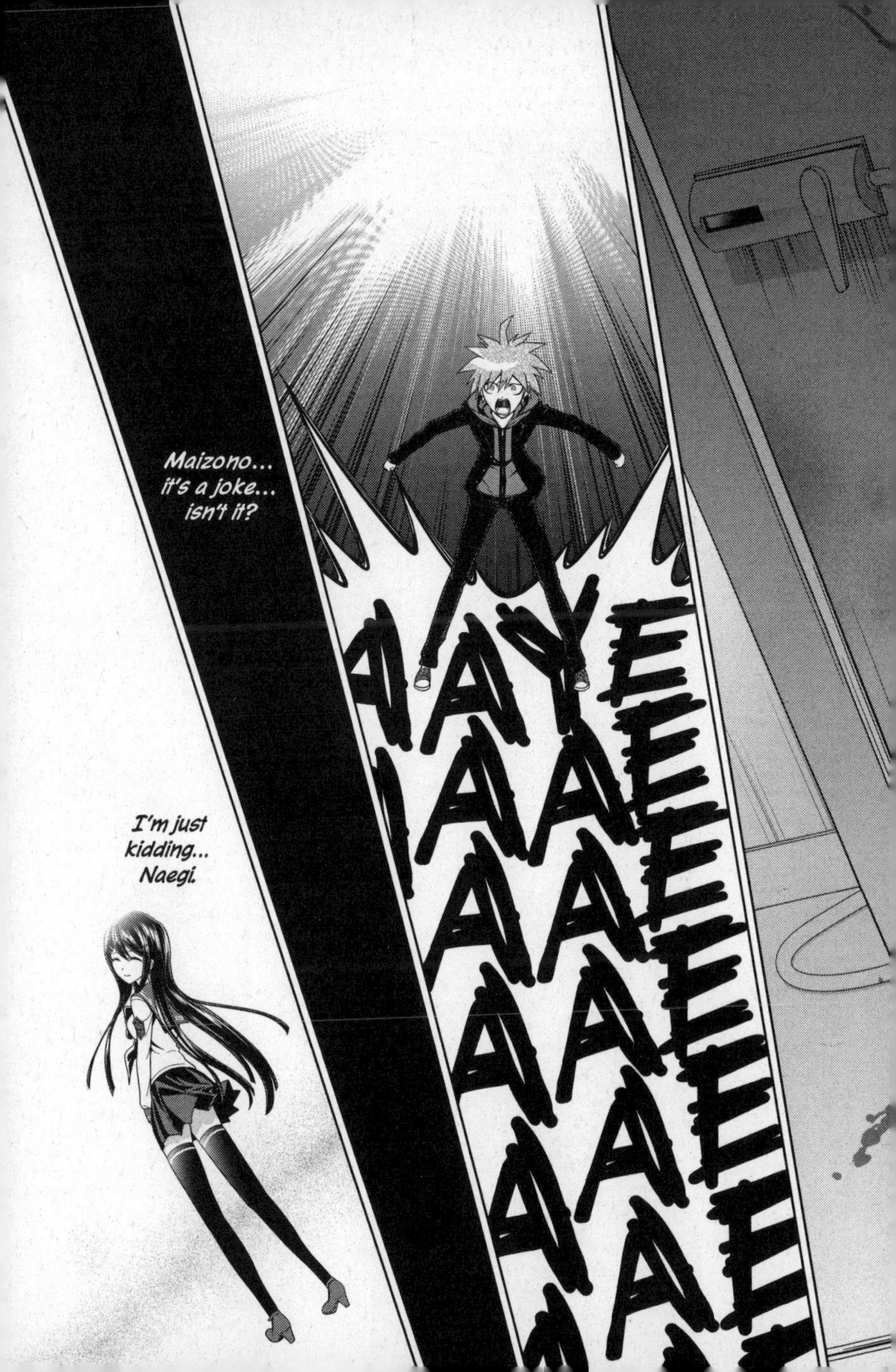
Maizono... it's a joke... isn't it?
I'm just kidding... Naegi.

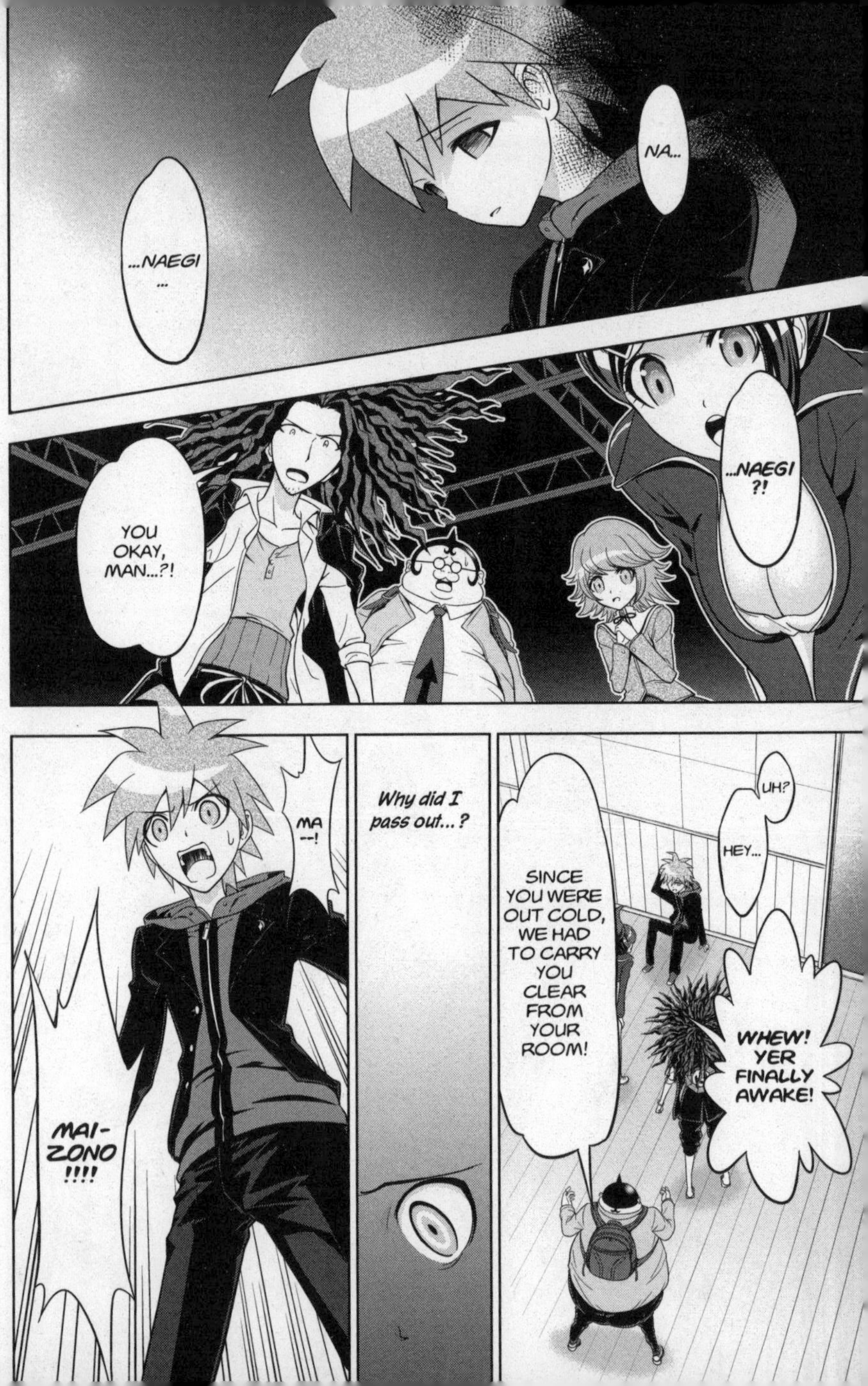
NA...
...NAEGI ...
...NAEGI ?!
YOU OKAY, MAN...?!
UH?
HEY...
WHEW! YER FINALLY AWAKE!
SINCE YOU WERE OUT COLD, WE HAD TO CARRY YOU CLEAR FROM YOUR ROOM!
Why did I pass out...?
MA--!
MAI-ZONO!!!!

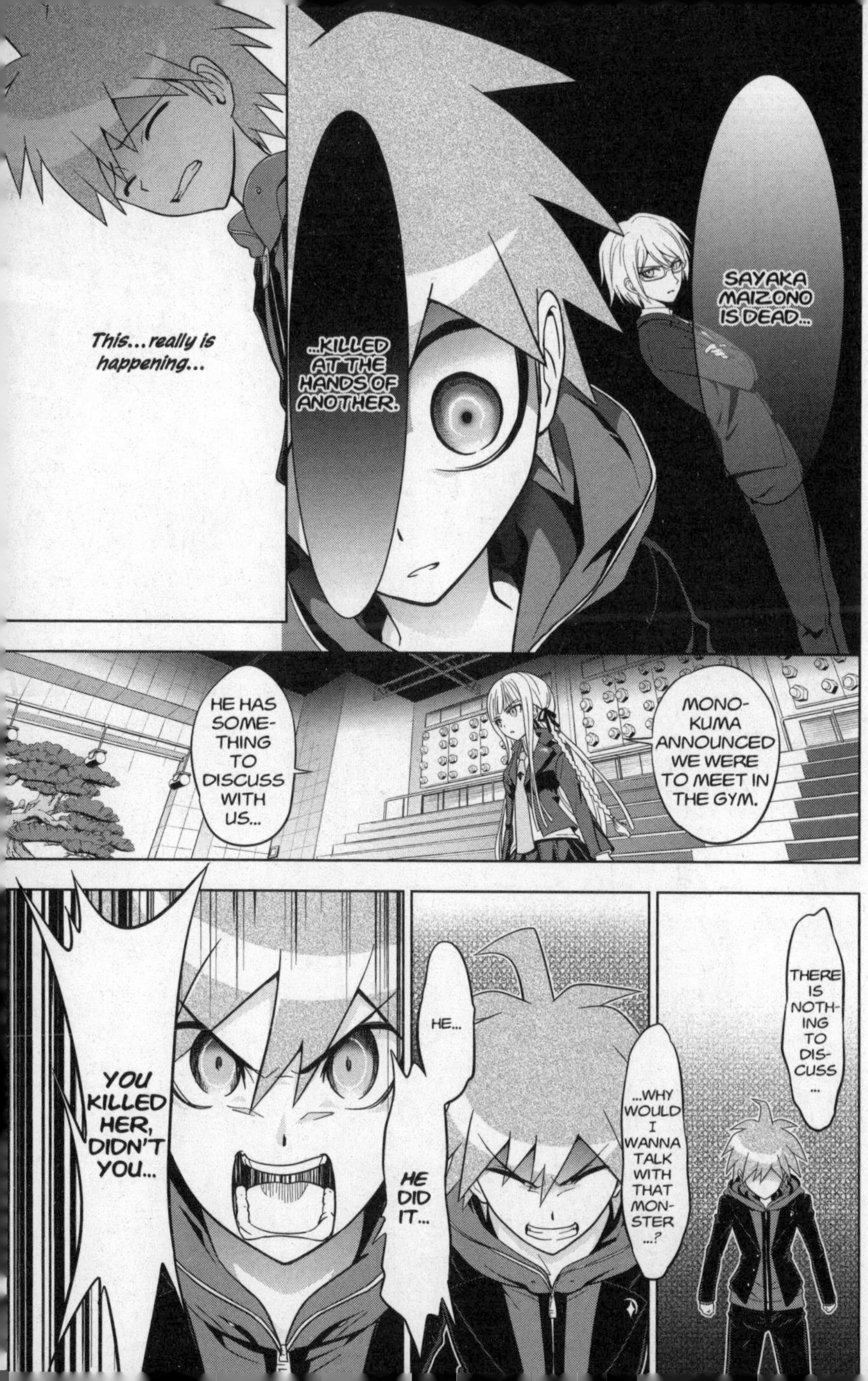
SAYAKA MAIZONO IS DEAD...
...KILLED AT THE HANDS OF ANOTHER.
This...really is happening...
MONOKUMA ANNOUNCED WE WERE TO MEET IN THE GYM.
HE HAS SOMETHING TO DISCUSS WITH US...
THERE IS NOTHING TO DISCUSS...
...WHY WOULD I WANNA TALK WITH THAT MONSTER...?
HE...
HE DID IT...
YOU KILLED HER, DIDN'T YOU...

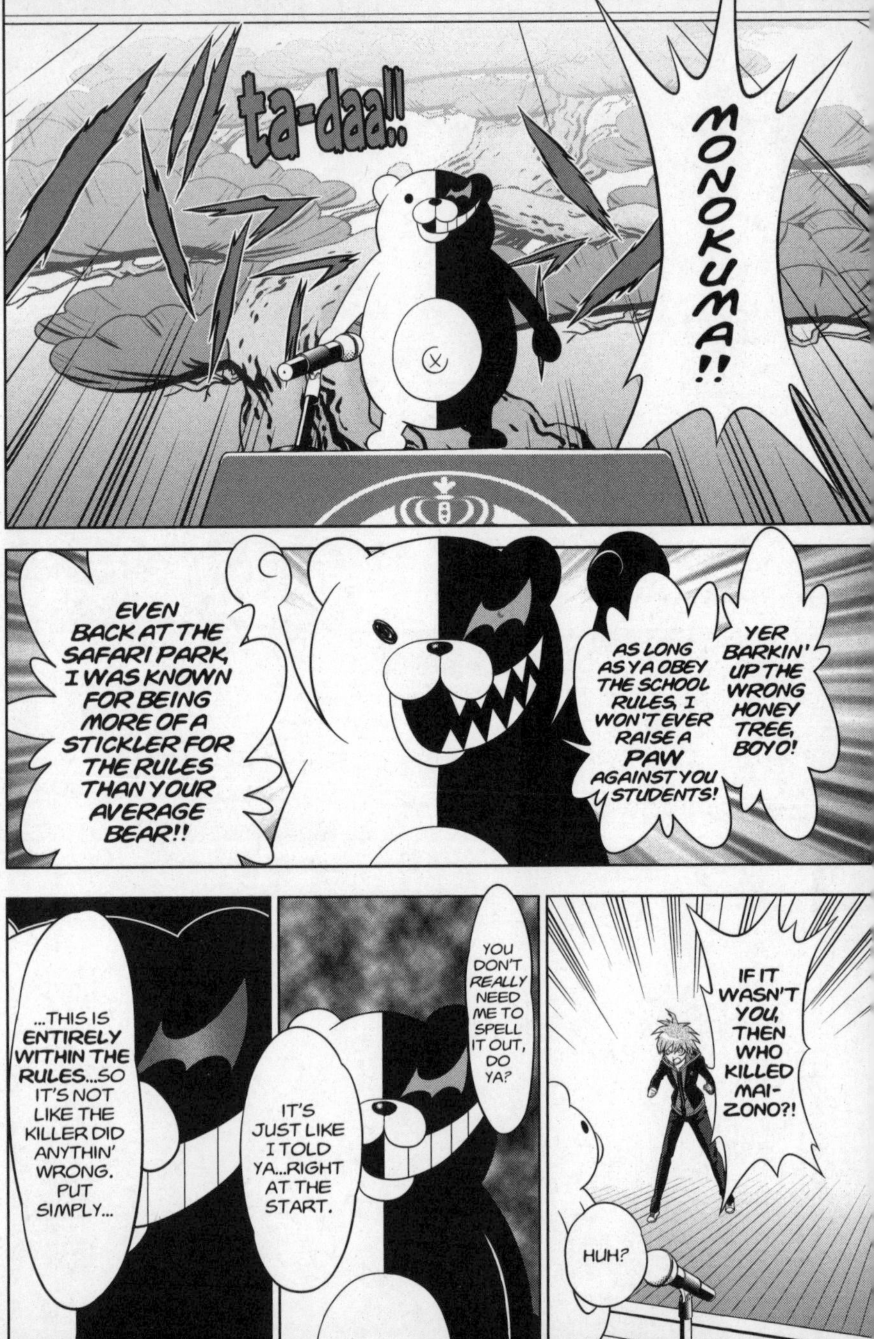
MONOKUMA!!
ta-daa!!
YER BARKIN' UP THE WRONG HONEY TREE, BOYO!
AS LONG AS YA OBEY THE SCHOOL RULES, I WON'T EVER RAISE A PAW AGAINST YOU STUDENTS!
EVEN BACK AT THE SAFARI PARK, I WAS KNOWN FOR BEING MORE OF A STICKLER FOR THE RULES THAN YOUR AVERAGE BEAR!!
IF IT WASN'T YOU, THEN WHO KILLED MAI-ZONO?!
HUH?
YOU DON'T REALLY NEED ME TO SPELL IT OUT, DO YA?
IT'S JUST LIKE I TOLD YA...RIGHT AT THE START.
...THIS IS ENTIRELY WITHIN THE RULES...SO IT'S NOT LIKE THE KILLER DID ANYTHIN' WRONG. PUT SIMPLY...

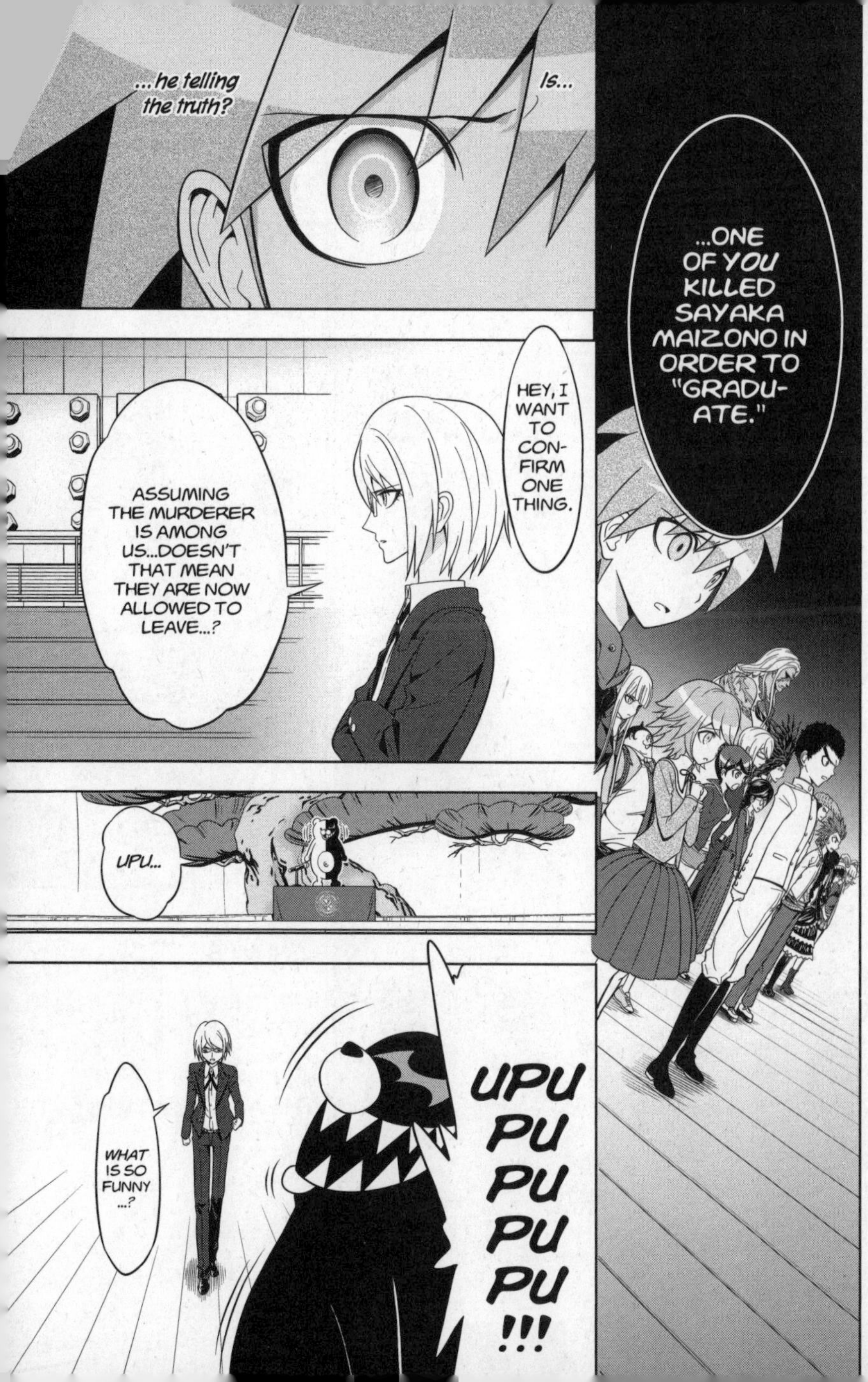
...ONE OF YOU KILLED SAYAKA MAIZONO IN ORDER TO "GRADUATE."
Is...
...he telling the truth?
HEY, I WANT TO CONFIRM ONE THING.
ASSUMING THE MURDERER IS AMONG US...DOESN'T THAT MEAN THEY ARE NOW ALLOWED TO LEAVE...?
UPU...
UPUPUPUPUPUPU!!!
WHAT IS SO FUNNY...?

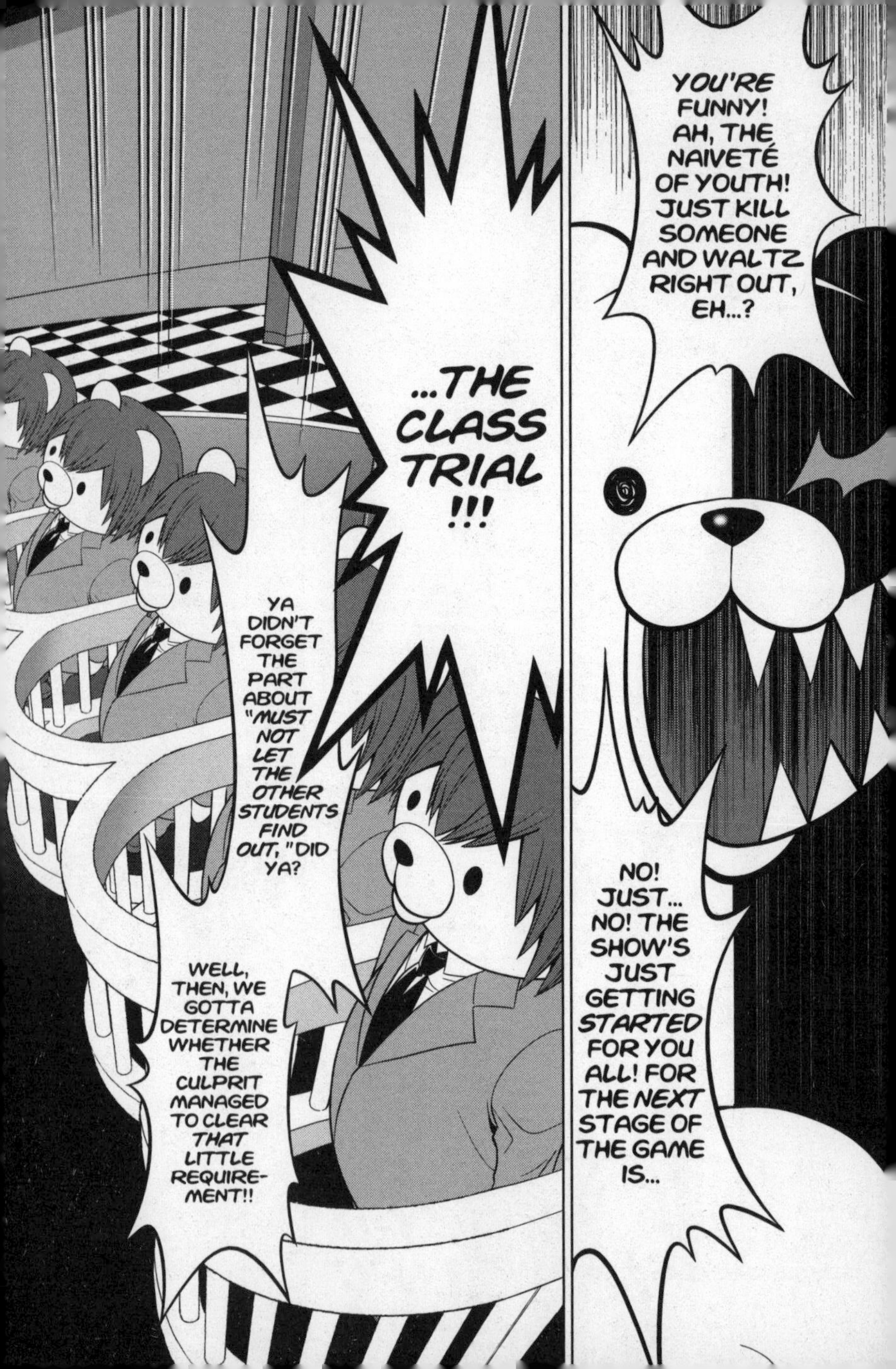
YOU'RE FUNNY! AH, THE NAIVETÉ OF YOUTH! JUST KILL SOMEONE AND WALTZ RIGHT OUT, EH...?
NO! JUST... NO! THE SHOW'S JUST GETTING *STARTED* FOR YOU ALL! FOR THE *NEXT* STAGE OF THE GAME IS...
...THE CLASS TRIAL!!!
YA DIDN'T FORGET THE PART ABOUT "*MUST NOT LET THE OTHER STUDENTS FIND OUT*," DID YA?
WELL, THEN, WE GOTTA DETERMINE WHETHER THE CULPRIT MANAGED TO CLEAR *THAT* LITTLE REQUIRE-MENT!!

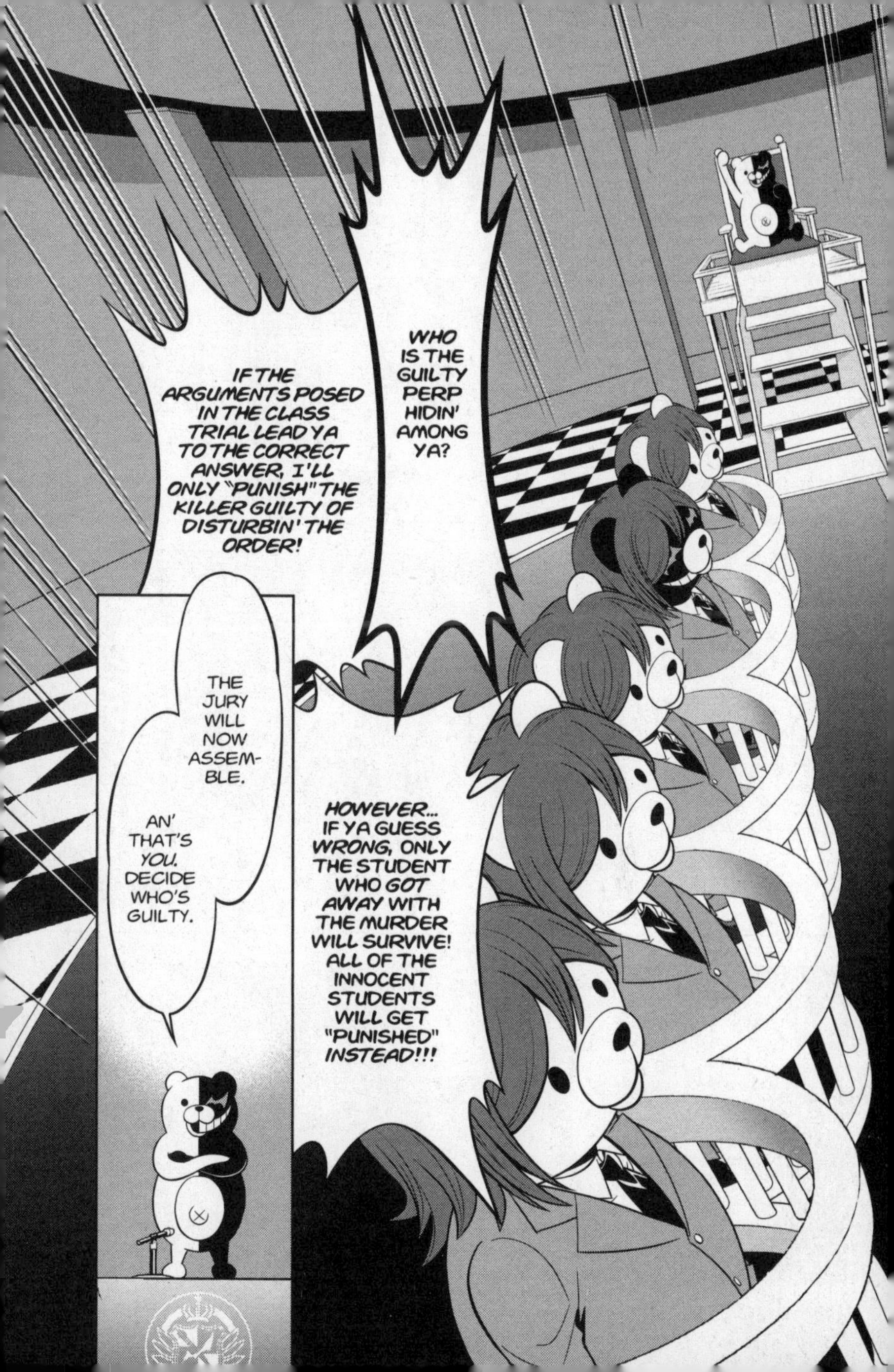
WHO IS THE GUILTY PERP HIDIN' AMONG YA?
IF THE ARGUMENTS POSED IN THE CLASS TRIAL LEAD YA TO THE CORRECT ANSWER, I'LL ONLY "PUNISH" THE KILLER GUILTY OF DISTURBIN' THE ORDER!
HOWEVER... IF YA GUESS WRONG, ONLY THE STUDENT WHO GOT AWAY WITH THE MURDER WILL SURVIVE! ALL OF THE INNOCENT STUDENTS WILL GET "PUNISHED" INSTEAD!!!
THE JURY WILL NOW ASSEM-BLE.
AN' THAT'S YOU. DECIDE WHO'S GUILTY.

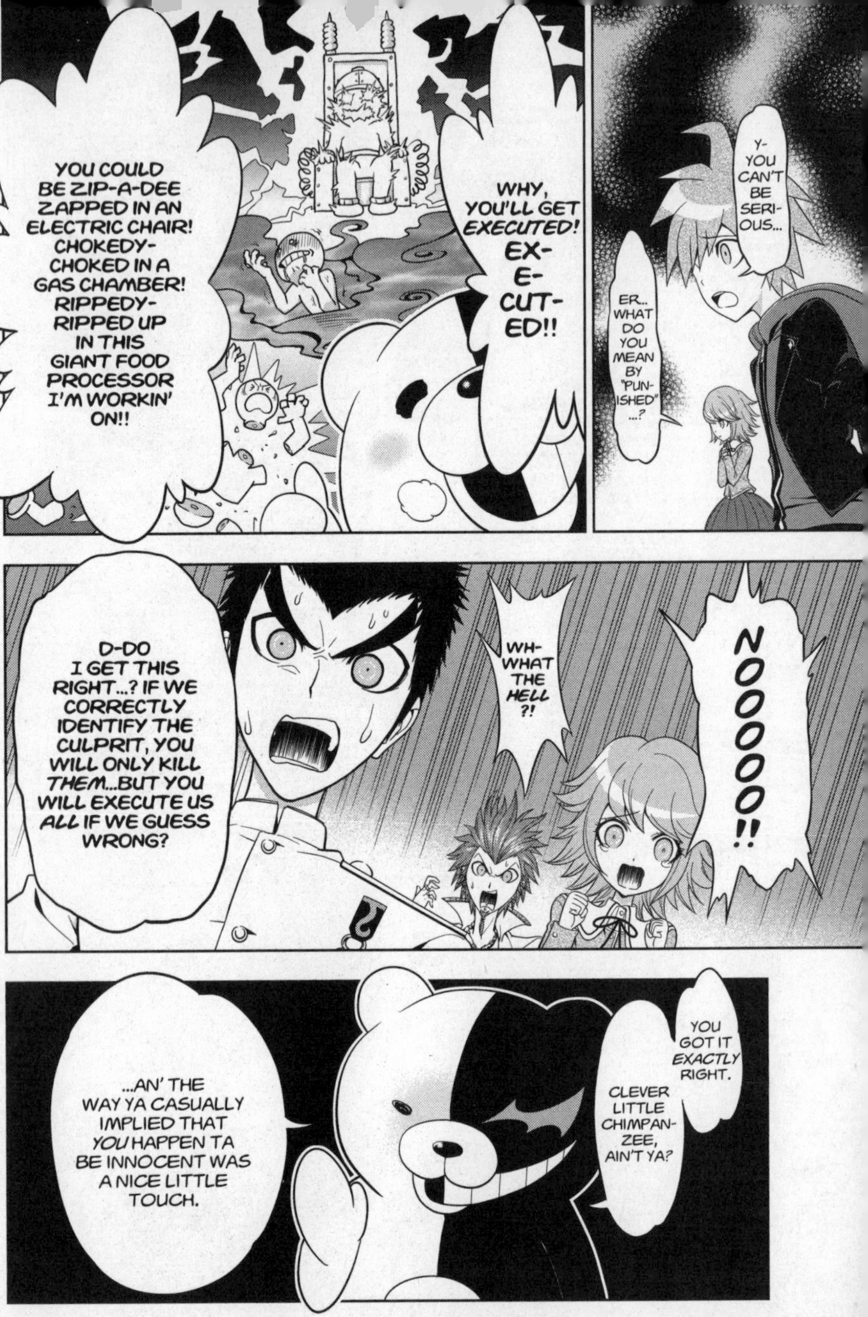
Y-YOU CAN'T BE SERIOUS...
ER... WHAT DO YOU MEAN BY "PUNISHED"...?
WHY, YOU'LL GET *EXECUTED!* EX-E-CUT-ED!!
YOU COULD BE ZIP-A-DEE ZAPPED IN AN ELECTRIC CHAIR! CHOKEDY-CHOKED IN A GAS CHAMBER! RIPPEDY-RIPPED UP IN THIS GIANT FOOD PROCESSOR I'M WORKIN' ON!!
NOOOOOO!!
WH-WHAT THE *HELL* ?!
D-DO I GET THIS RIGHT...? IF WE CORRECTLY IDENTIFY THE CULPRIT, YOU WILL ONLY KILL *THEM*...BUT YOU WILL EXECUTE US *ALL* IF WE GUESS WRONG?
YOU GOT IT *EXACTLY* RIGHT.
CLEVER LITTLE CHIMPANZEE, AIN'T YA?
...AN' THE WAY YA CASUALLY IMPLIED THAT *YOU* HAPPEN TA BE INNOCENT WAS A NICE LITTLE TOUCH.

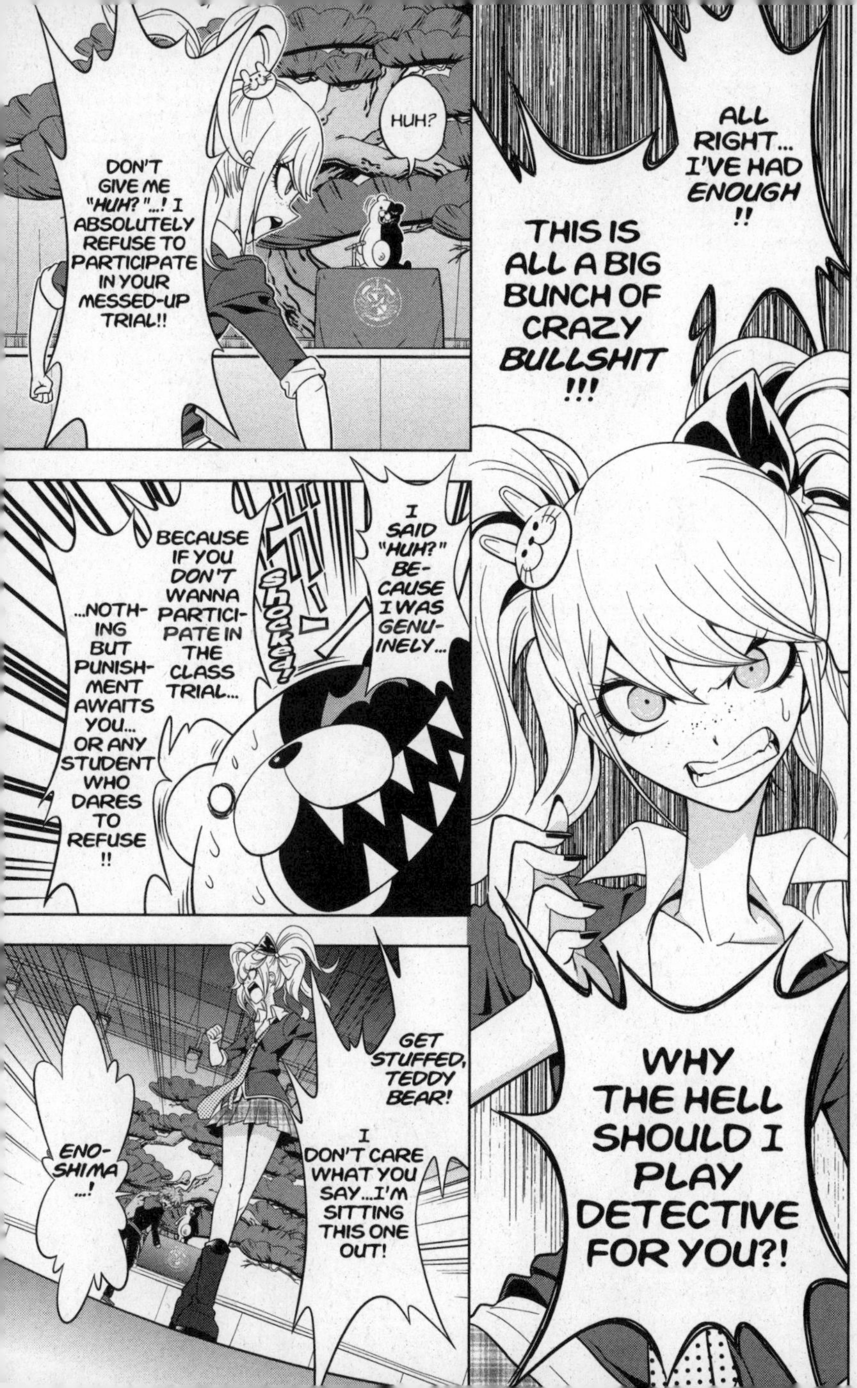
ALL RIGHT... I'VE HAD *ENOUGH* !!
THIS IS ALL A BIG BUNCH OF CRAZY *BULLSHIT* !!!
WHY THE HELL SHOULD I PLAY DETECTIVE FOR YOU?!
HUH?
DON'T GIVE ME "*HUH?*"...! I ABSOLUTELY REFUSE TO PARTICIPATE IN YOUR MESSED-UP TRIAL!!
I SAID "*HUH?*" BE-CAUSE I WAS GENU-INELY...
Shocked!
BECAUSE IF YOU DON'T WANNA PARTICI-PATE IN THE CLASS TRIAL...
...NOTH-ING BUT PUNISH-MENT AWAITS YOU... OR ANY STUDENT WHO DARES TO REFUSE !!
GET STUFFED, TEDDY BEAR!
I DON'T CARE WHAT YOU SAY...I'M SITTING THIS ONE OUT!
ENO-SHIMA ...!

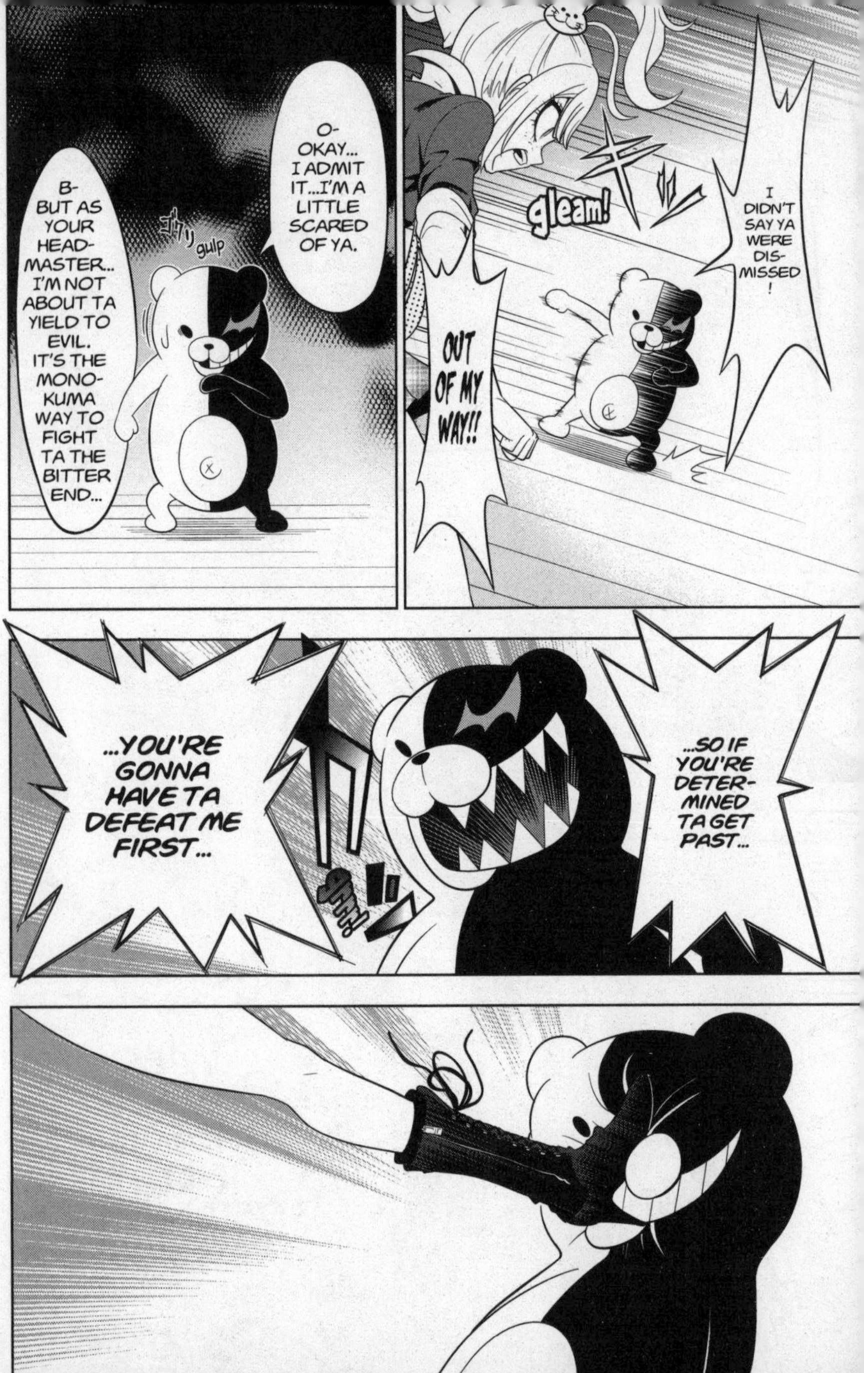
I DIDN'T SAY YA WERE DIS-MISSED!
gleam!
OUT OF MY WAY!!
O-OKAY... I ADMIT IT...I'M A LITTLE SCARED OF YA.
gulp
B-BUT AS YOUR HEAD-MASTER... I'M NOT ABOUT TA YIELD TO EVIL. IT'S THE MONO-KUMA WAY TO FIGHT TA THE BITTER END...
...SO IF YOU'RE DETER-MINED TA GET PAST...
...YOU'RE GONNA HAVE TA DEFEAT ME FIRST...

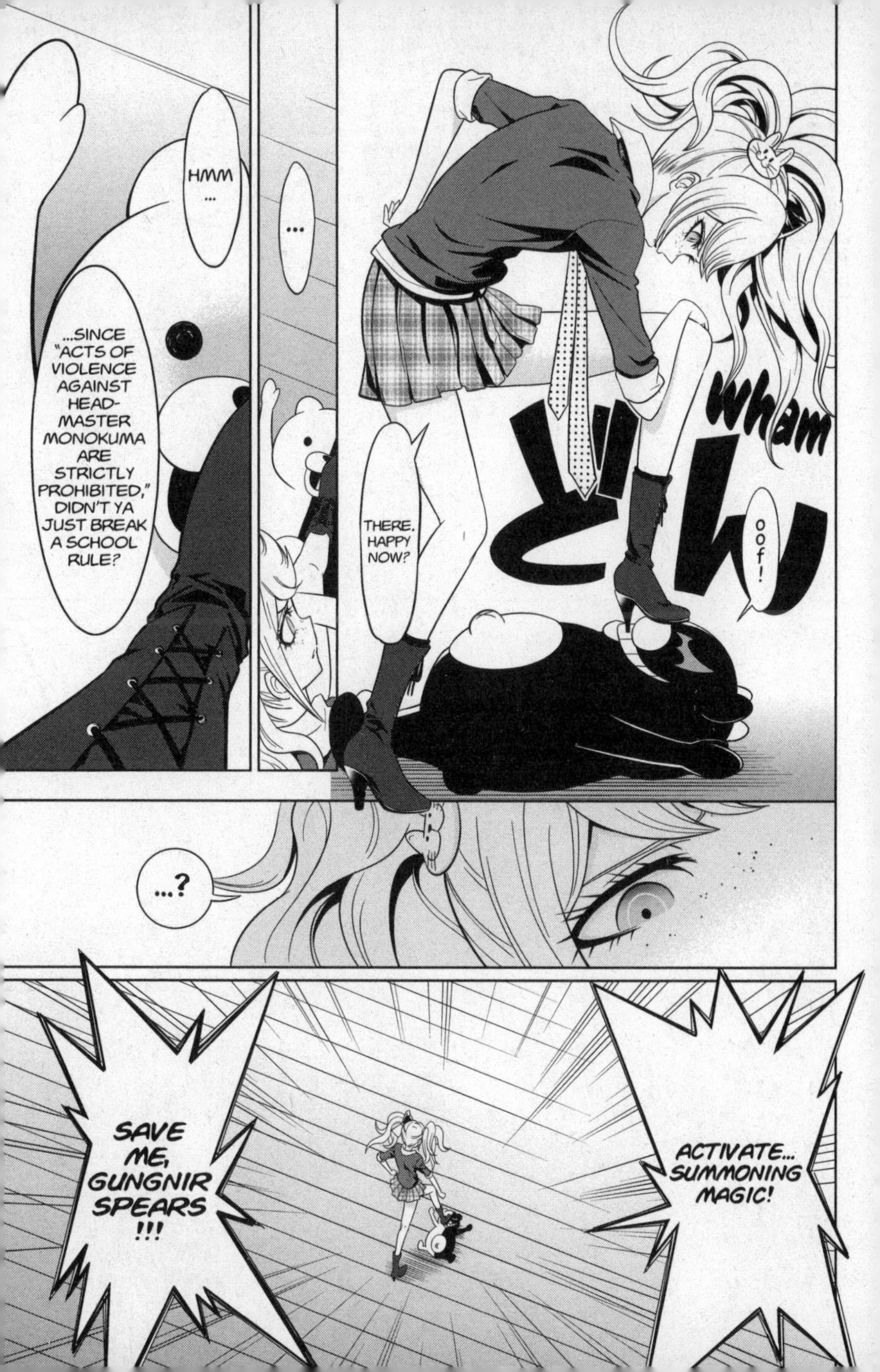
wham
どん
oof!
THERE. HAPPY NOW?
...
HMM ...
...SINCE "ACTS OF VIOLENCE AGAINST HEAD-MASTER MONOKUMA ARE STRICTLY PROHIBITED," DIDN'T YA JUST BREAK A SCHOOL RULE?
...?
ACTIVATE... SUMMONING MAGIC!
SAVE ME, GUNGNIR SPEARS !!!

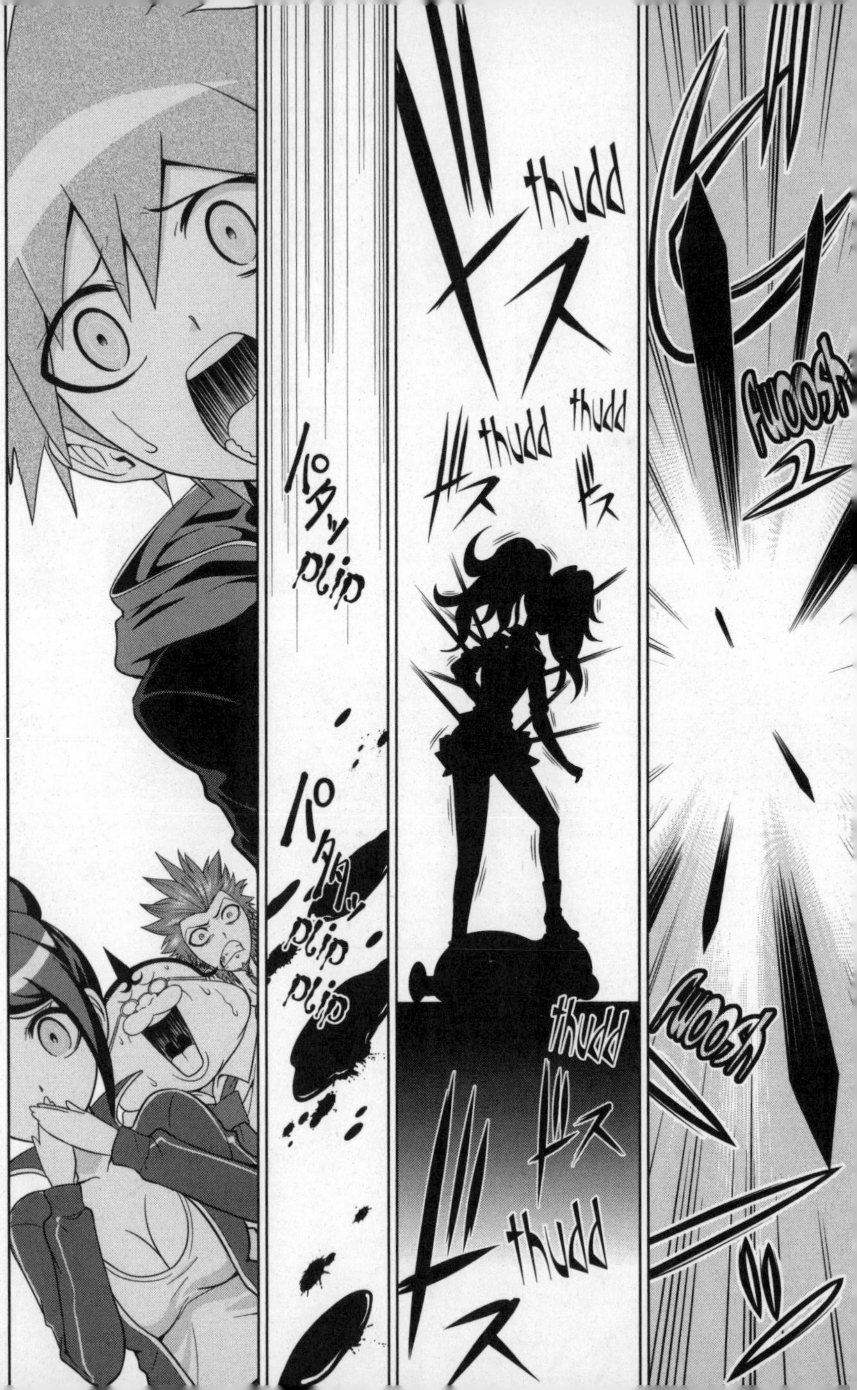
fwoosh
fwoosh
ドス
thudd
thudd
thudd
thudd
thudd
パタッ
plip
パタタッ
plip plip

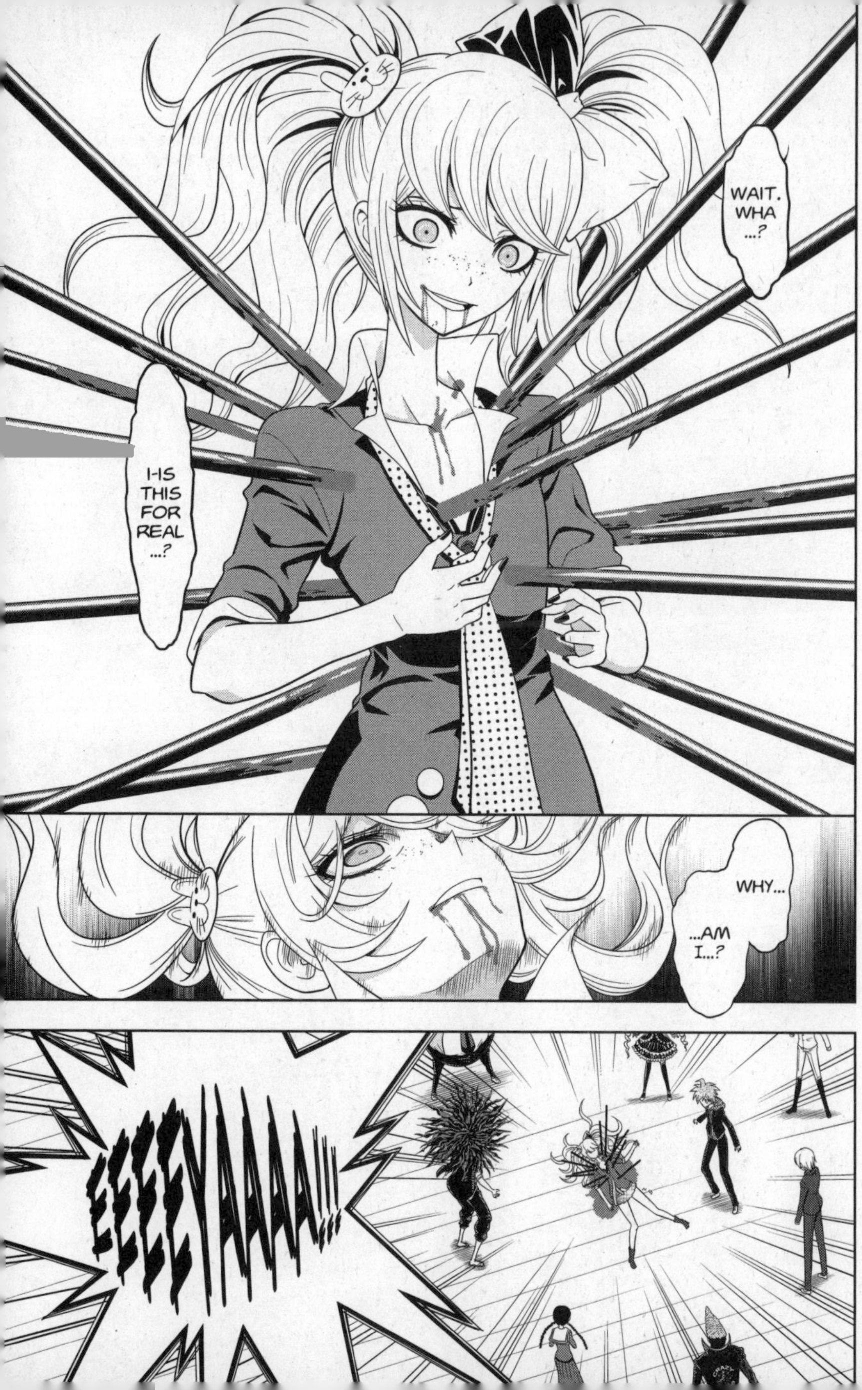
WAIT. WHA ...?
I-IS THIS FOR REAL ...?
WHY...
...AM I...?
EEEEYAAAA!!!

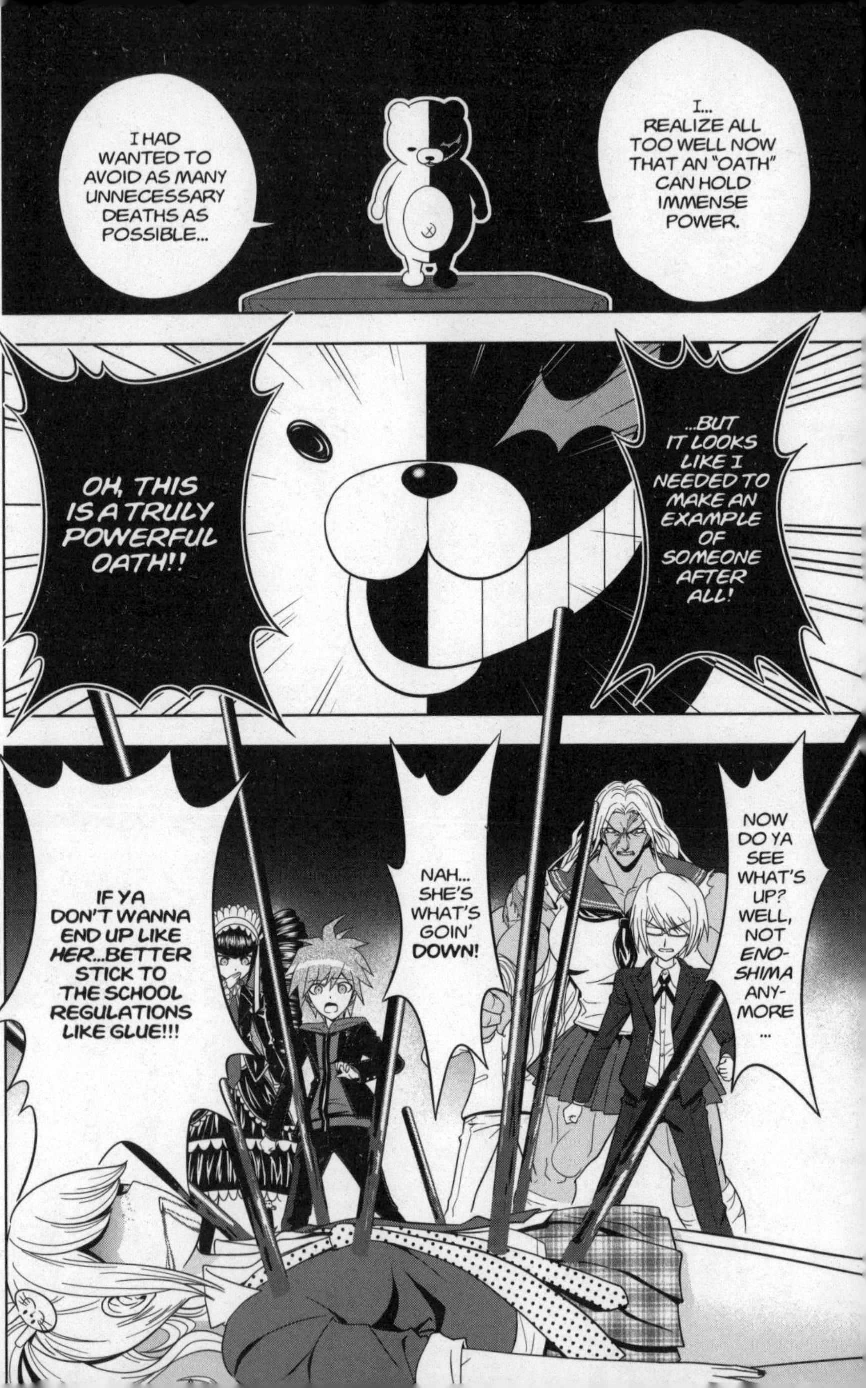
I... REALIZE ALL TOO WELL NOW THAT AN "OATH" CAN HOLD IMMENSE POWER.
I HAD WANTED TO AVOID AS MANY UNNECESSARY DEATHS AS POSSIBLE...
...BUT IT LOOKS LIKE I NEEDED TO MAKE AN EXAMPLE OF SOMEONE AFTER ALL!
OH, THIS IS A TRULY POWERFUL OATH!!
NOW DO YA SEE WHAT'S UP? WELL, NOT ENO-SHIMA ANY-MORE...
NAH... SHE'S WHAT'S GOIN' DOWN!
IF YA DON'T WANNA END UP LIKE HER...BETTER STICK TO THE SCHOOL REGULATIONS LIKE GLUE!!!

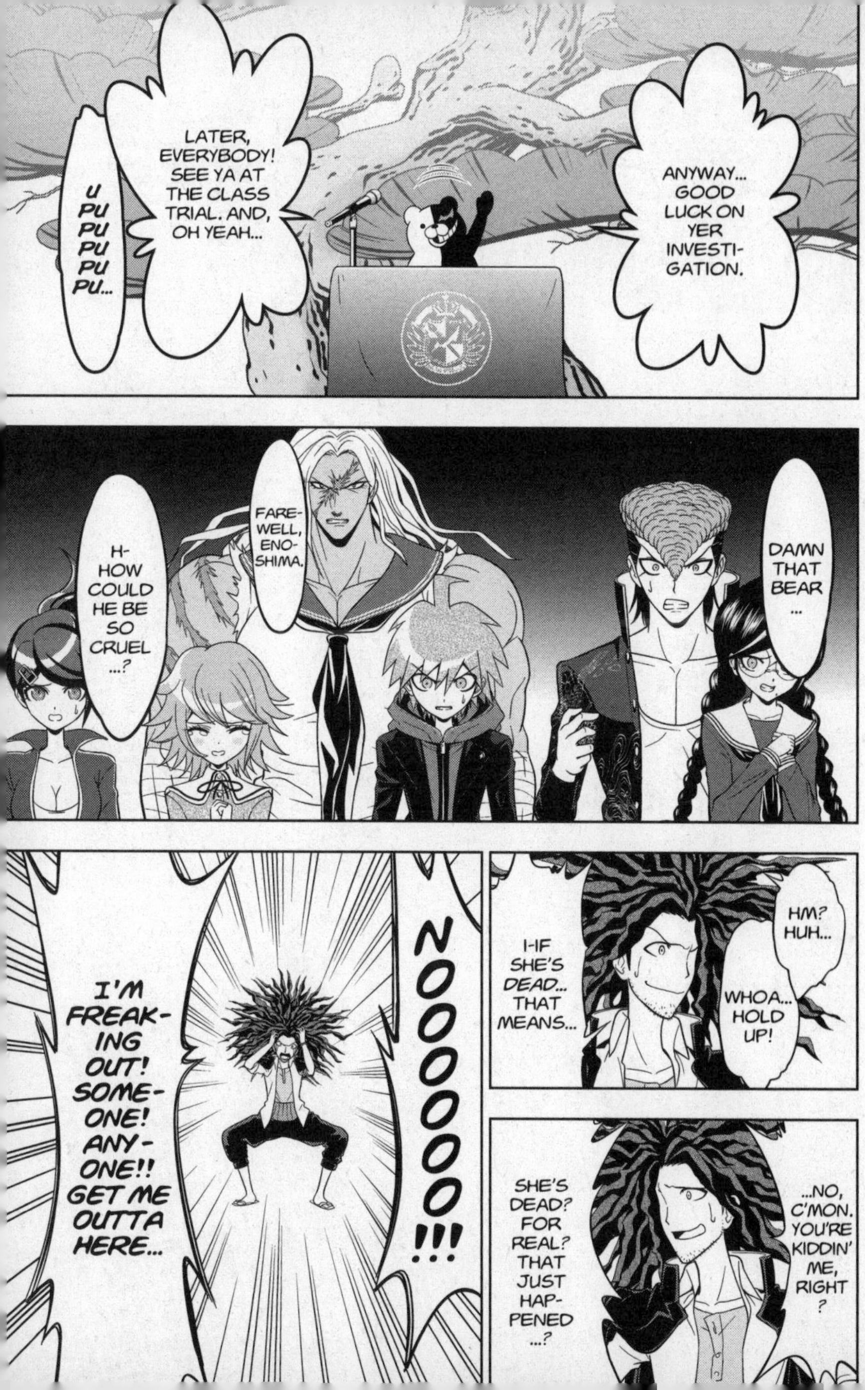

ANYWAY... GOOD LUCK ON YER INVESTIGATION.
LATER, EVERYBODY! SEE YA AT THE CLASS TRIAL. AND, OH YEAH...
UPUPUPUPUPU...
DAMN THAT BEAR...
FAREWELL, ENOSHIMA.
H-HOW COULD HE BE SO CRUEL...?
HM? HUH...
WHOA... HOLD UP!
I-IF SHE'S DEAD... THAT MEANS...
...NO, C'MON. YOU'RE KIDDIN' ME, RIGHT?
SHE'S DEAD? FOR REAL? THAT JUST HAPPENED...?
NOOOOOOO!!!
I'M FREAKING OUT! SOMEONE! ANYONE!! GET ME OUTTA HERE...

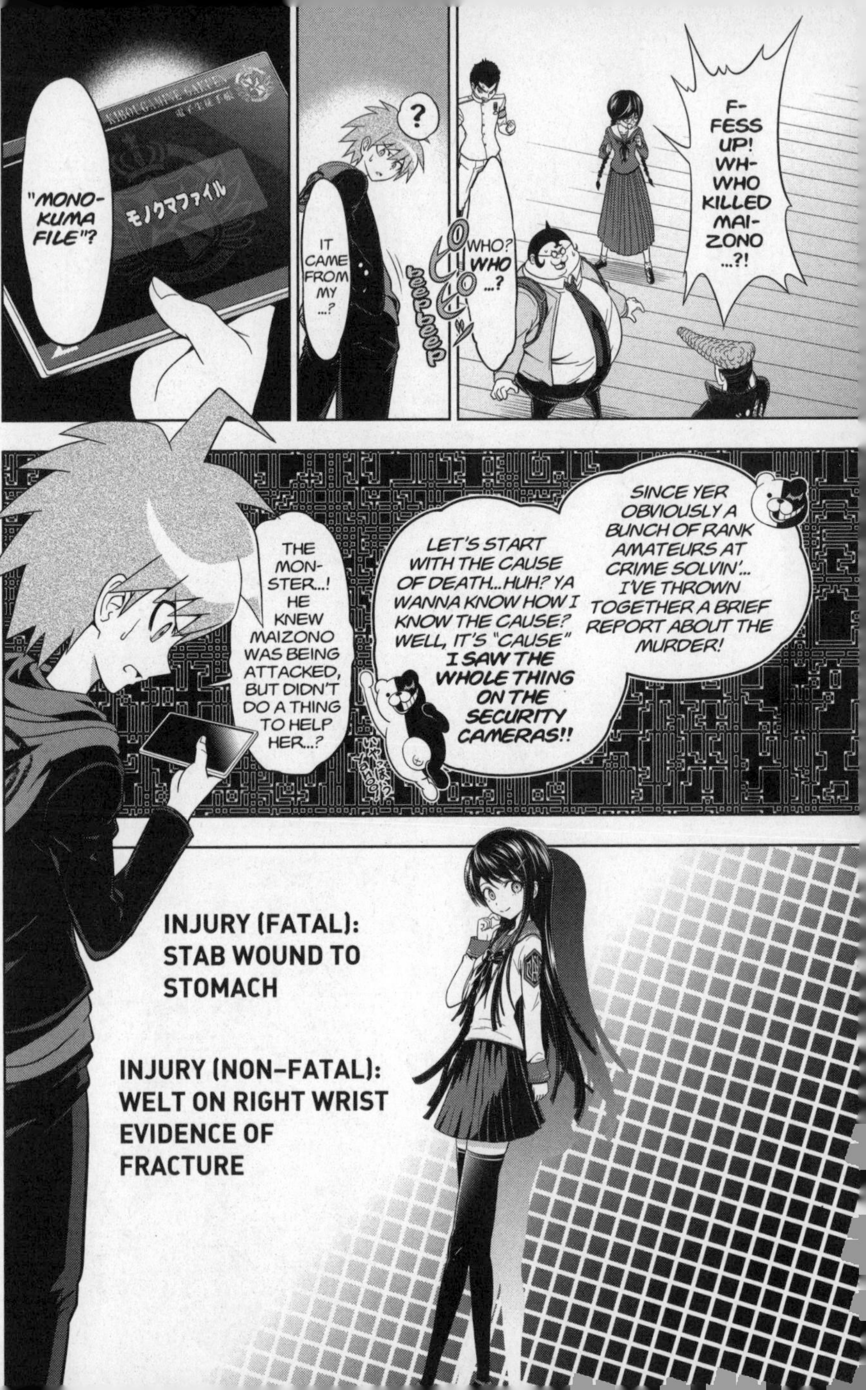
F-FESS UP! WH-WHO KILLED MAI-ZONO ...?!
WHO? WHO ...?
BEEP BEEP
?
IT CAME FROM MY ...?
"MONO-KUMA FILE"?
モノクマファイル
SINCE YER OBVIOUSLY A BUNCH OF RANK AMATEURS AT CRIME SOLVIN'... I'VE THROWN TOGETHER A BRIEF REPORT ABOUT THE MURDER!
LET'S START WITH THE CAUSE OF DEATH...HUH? YA WANNA KNOW HOW I KNOW THE CAUSE? WELL, IT'S "CAUSE" I SAW THE WHOLE THING ON THE SECURITY CAMERAS!!
THE MON-STER...! HE KNEW MAIZONO WAS BEING ATTACKED, BUT DIDN'T DO A THING TO HELP HER...?
INJURY (FATAL): STAB WOUND TO STOMACH
INJURY (NON-FATAL): WELT ON RIGHT WRIST EVIDENCE OF FRACTURE

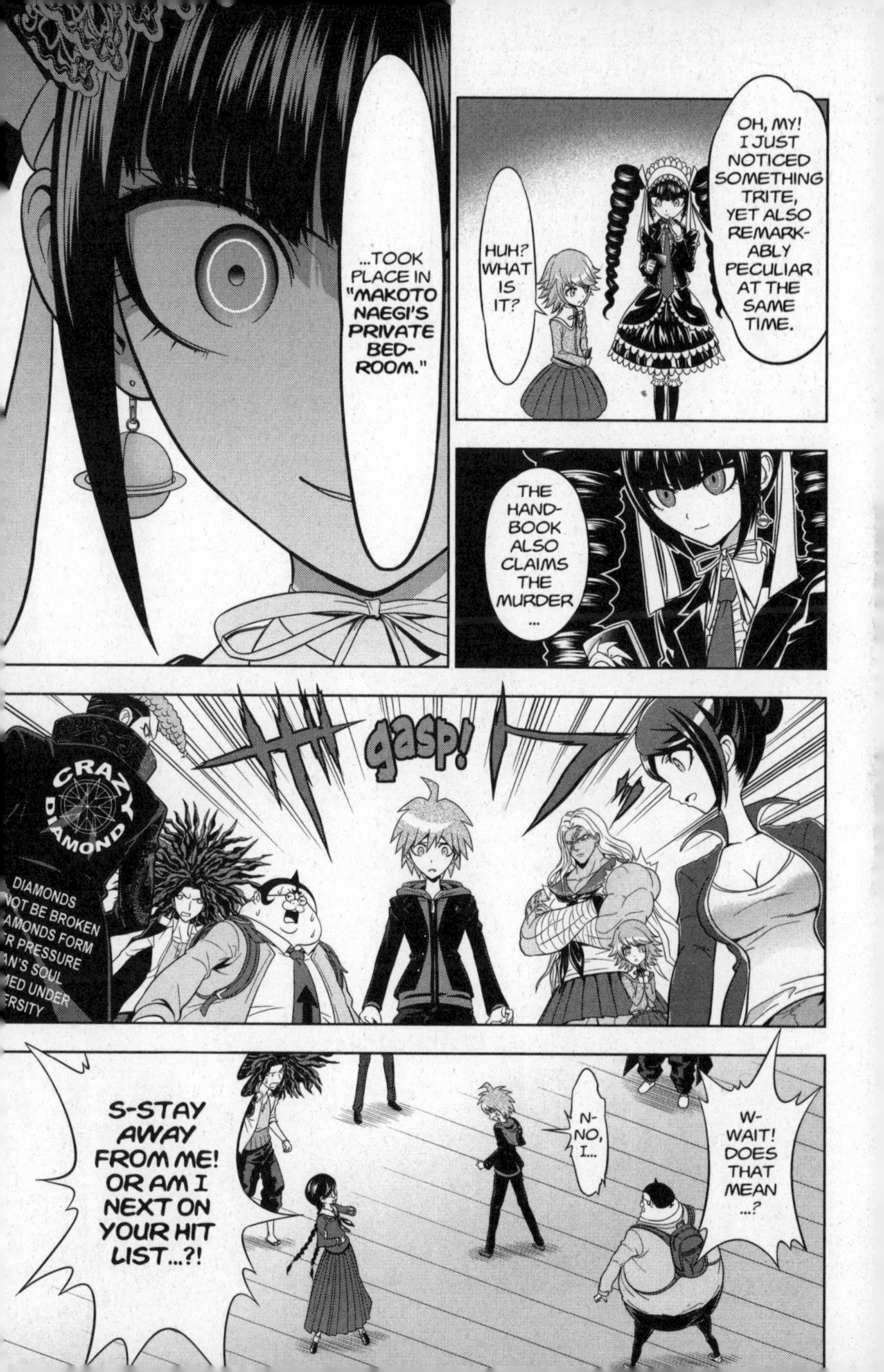
OH, MY! I JUST NOTICED SOMETHING TRITE, YET ALSO REMARKABLY PECULIAR AT THE SAME TIME.
HUH? WHAT IS IT?
THE HANDBOOK ALSO CLAIMS THE MURDER...
...TOOK PLACE IN "MAKOTO NAEGI'S PRIVATE BEDROOM."
gasp!
CRAZY DIAMOND
DIAMONDS
W-WAIT! DOES THAT MEAN...?
N-NO, I...
S-STAY AWAY FROM ME! OR AM I NEXT ON YOUR HIT LIST...?!

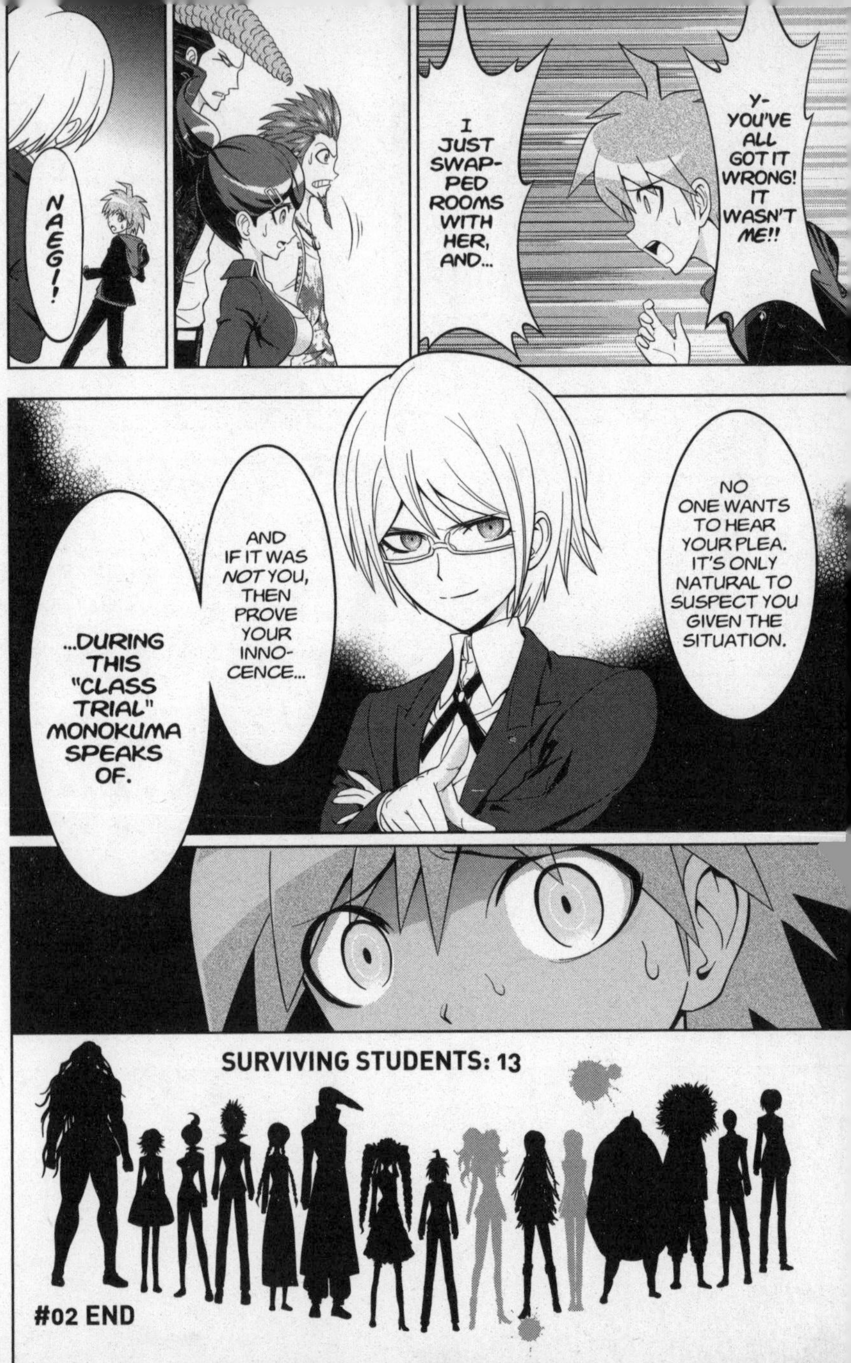

Y-YOU'VE ALL GOT IT WRONG! IT WASN'T ME!!
I JUST SWAP-PED ROOMS WITH HER, AND...
NAEGI!
NO ONE WANTS TO HEAR YOUR PLEA. IT'S ONLY NATURAL TO SUSPECT YOU GIVEN THE SITUATION.
AND IF IT WAS NOT YOU, THEN PROVE YOUR INNO-CENCE...
...DURING THIS "CLASS TRIAL" MONOKUMA SPEAKS OF.
SURVIVING STUDENTS: 13
#02 END

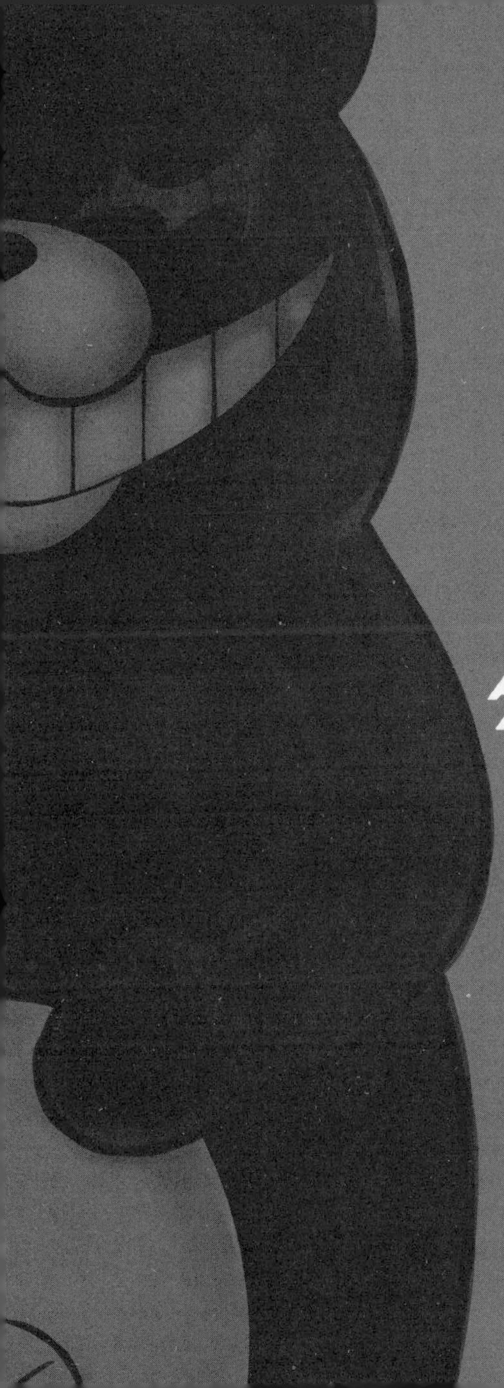

ダンガンロンパ
DANGANRONPA 希望の学園と絶望の高校生
THE ANIMATION

DANGANRONPA

A SCHOOL OF HOPE . . . WITH STUDENTS OF DESPAIR!

THE ANIMATION

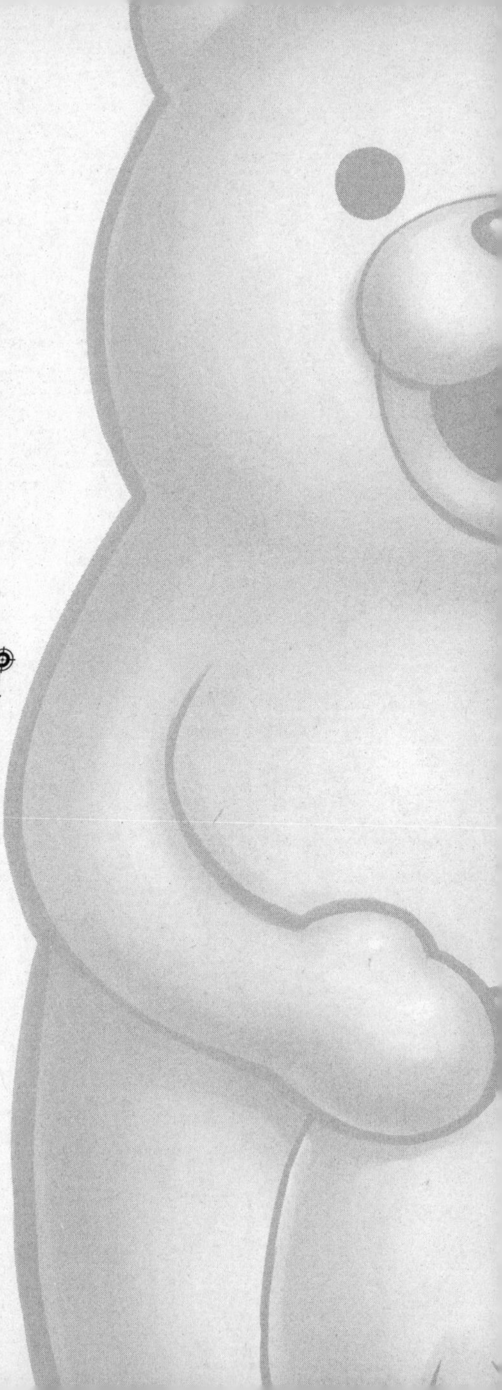

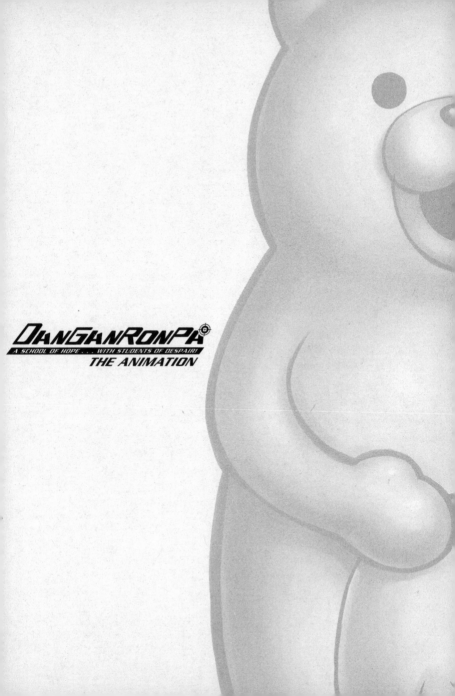

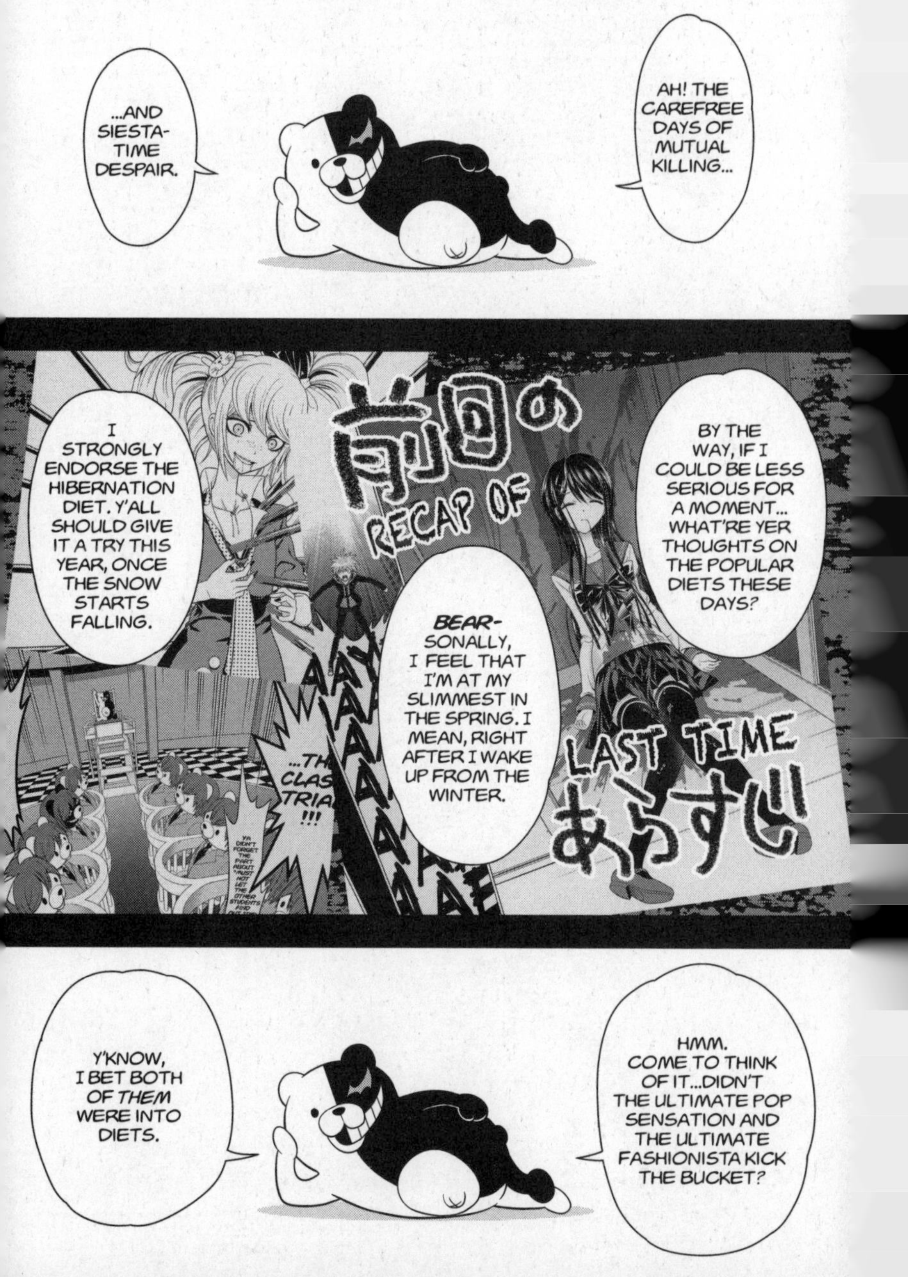
AH! THE CAREFREE DAYS OF MUTUAL KILLING...
...AND SIESTA-TIME DESPAIR.
前回のあらすじ
RECAP OF LAST TIME
BY THE WAY, IF I COULD BE LESS SERIOUS FOR A MOMENT... WHAT'RE YER THOUGHTS ON THE POPULAR DIETS THESE DAYS?
BEAR-SONALLY, I FEEL THAT I'M AT MY SLIMMEST IN THE SPRING. I MEAN, RIGHT AFTER I WAKE UP FROM THE WINTER.
AAAAAAAAA
...THE CLAS TRIA !!!
YA DIDN'T FORGET THE PART ABOUT "MUST NOT LET THE OTHER STUDENTS FIND
I STRONGLY ENDORSE THE HIBERNATION DIET. Y'ALL SHOULD GIVE IT A TRY THIS YEAR, ONCE THE SNOW STARTS FALLING.
HMM. COME TO THINK OF IT...DIDN'T THE ULTIMATE POP SENSATION AND THE ULTIMATE FASHIONISTA KICK THE BUCKET?
Y'KNOW, I BET BOTH OF *THEM* WERE INTO DIETS.

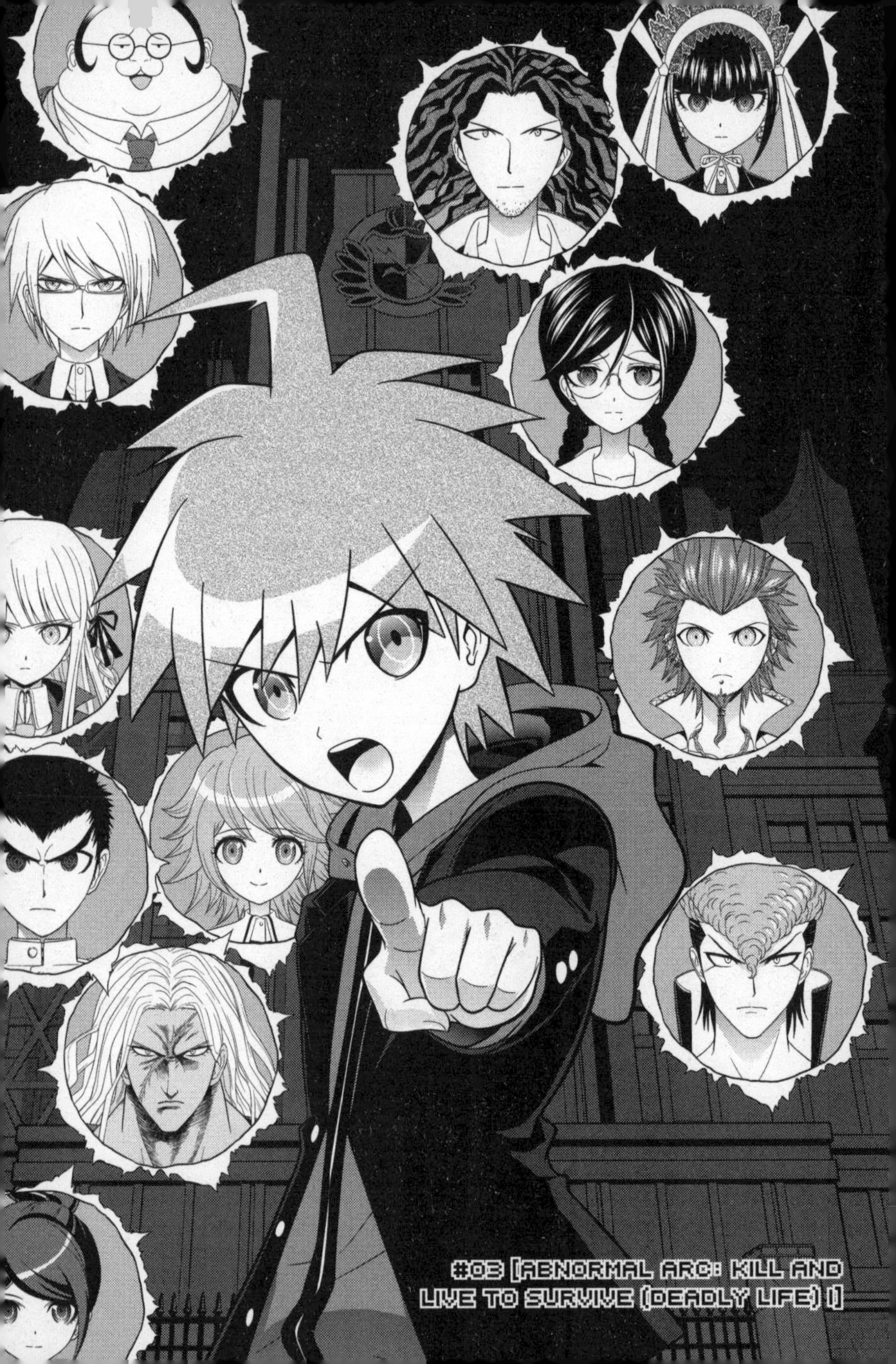
#03 [ABNORMAL ARC: KILL AND LIVE TO SURVIVE (DEADLY LIFE) I]

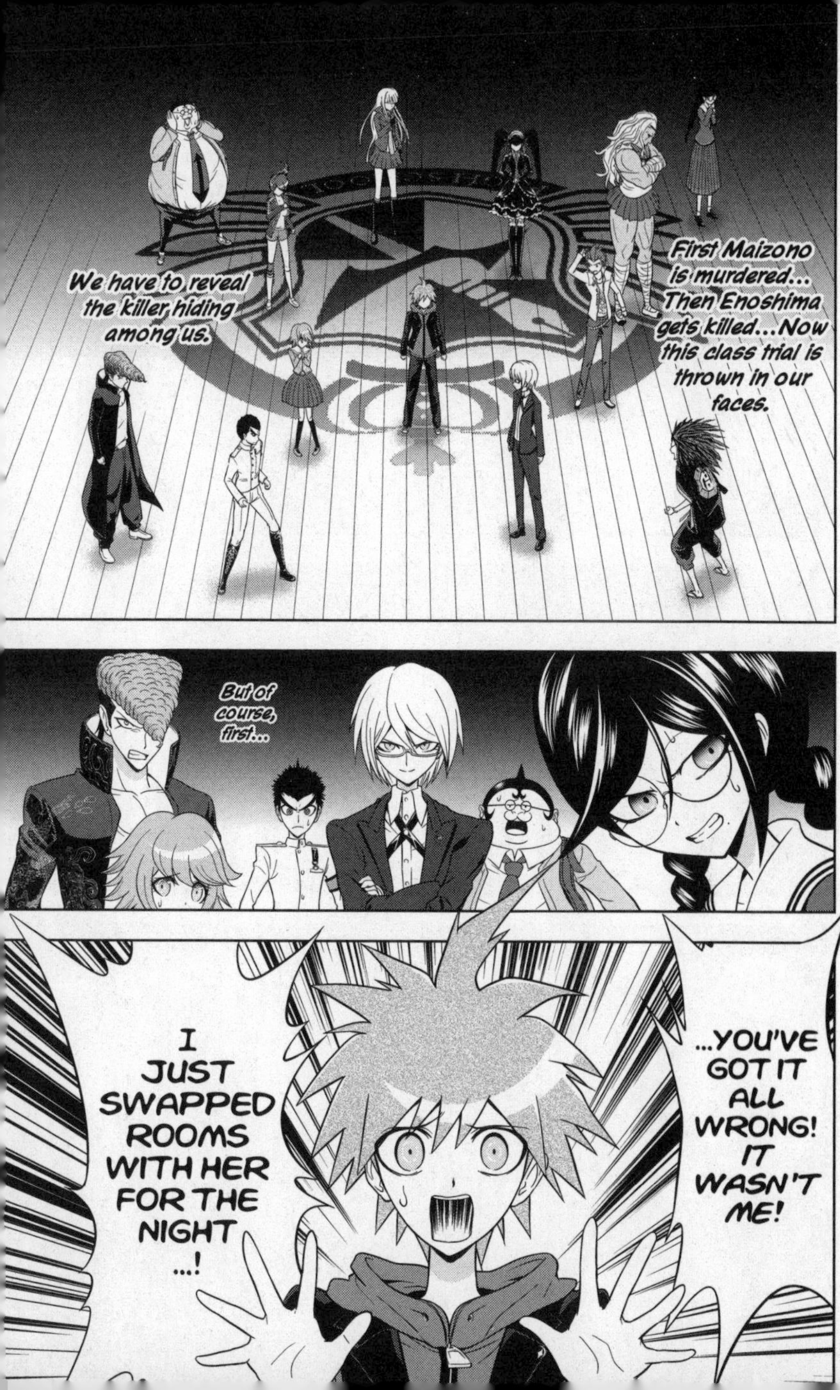
First Maizono is murdered... Then Enoshima gets killed...Now this class trial is thrown in our faces.
We have to reveal the killer hiding among us.
But of course, first...
...YOU'VE GOT IT ALL WRONG! IT WASN'T ME!
I JUST SWAPPED ROOMS WITH HER FOR THE NIGHT ...!

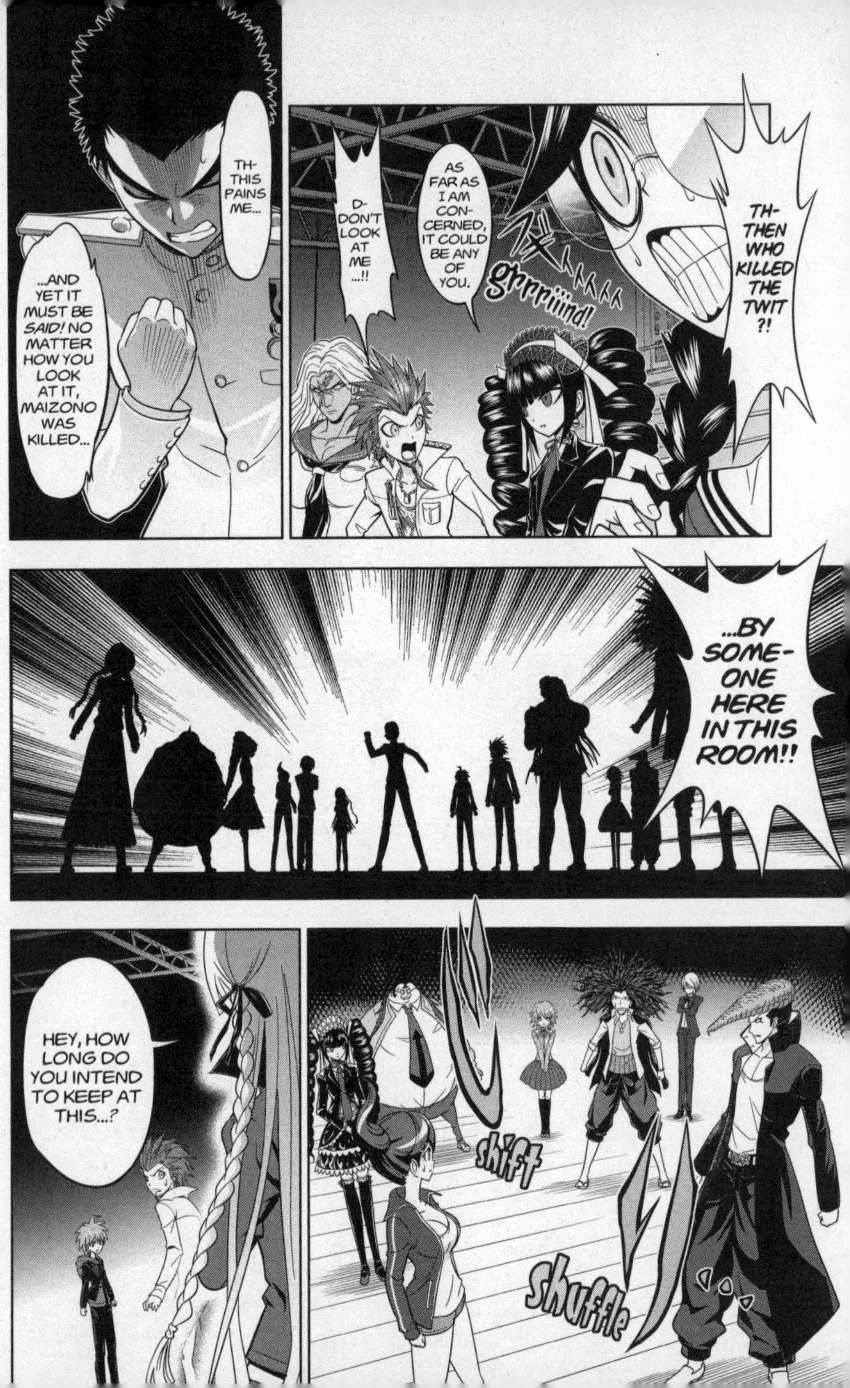
TH-THEN WHO KILLED THE TWIT?!
grrriiind!
AS FAR AS I AM CONCERNED, IT COULD BE ANY OF YOU.
D-DON'T LOOK AT ME ...!!
TH-THIS PAINS ME...
...AND YET IT MUST BE SAID! NO MATTER HOW YOU LOOK AT IT, MAIZONO WAS KILLED...
...BY SOMEONE HERE IN THIS ROOM!!
shift
shuffle
HEY, HOW LONG DO YOU INTEND TO KEEP AT THIS...?

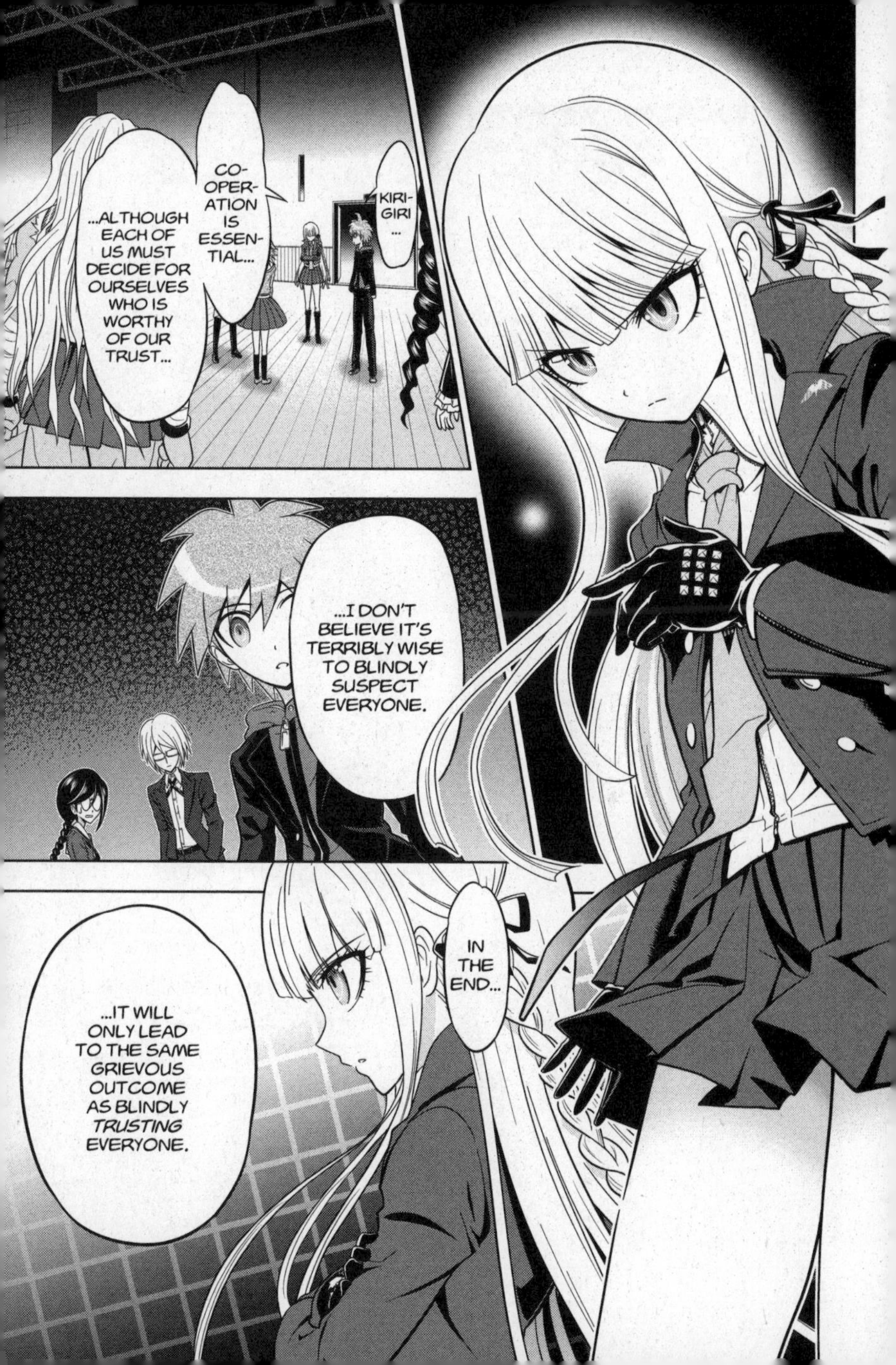
KIRI-GIRI...
CO-OPERATION IS ESSENTIAL...
...ALTHOUGH EACH OF US MUST DECIDE FOR OURSELVES WHO IS WORTHY OF OUR TRUST...
...I DON'T BELIEVE IT'S TERRIBLY WISE TO BLINDLY SUSPECT EVERYONE.
IN THE END...
...IT WILL ONLY LEAD TO THE SAME GRIEVOUS OUTCOME AS BLINDLY *TRUSTING* EVERYONE.

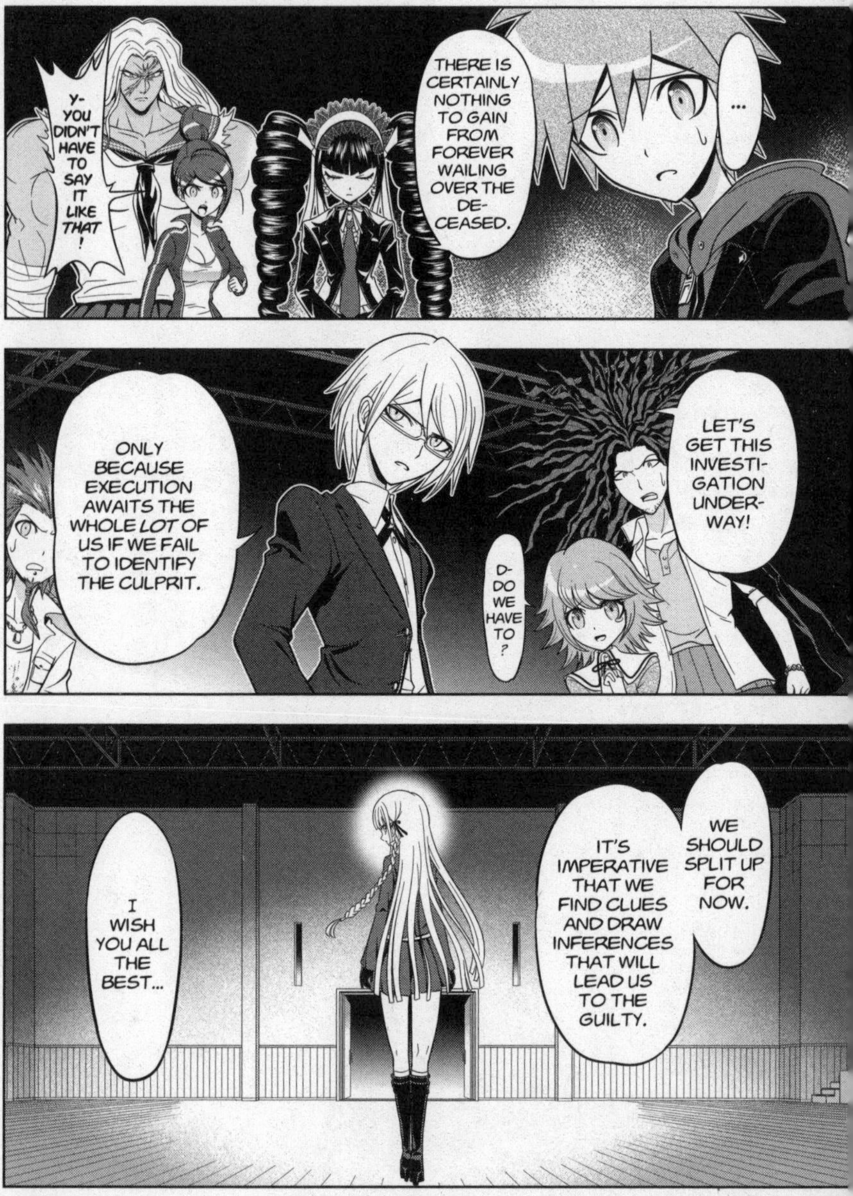
...
THERE IS CERTAINLY NOTHING TO GAIN FROM FOREVER WAILING OVER THE DECEASED.
Y-YOU DIDN'T HAVE TO SAY IT LIKE *THAT*!
LET'S GET THIS INVESTIGATION UNDERWAY!
D-DO WE HAVE TO?
ONLY BECAUSE EXECUTION AWAITS THE WHOLE *LOT* OF US IF WE FAIL TO IDENTIFY THE CULPRIT.
WE SHOULD SPLIT UP FOR NOW.
IT'S IMPERATIVE THAT WE FIND CLUES AND DRAW INFERENCES THAT WILL LEAD US TO THE GUILTY.
I WISH YOU ALL THE BEST...

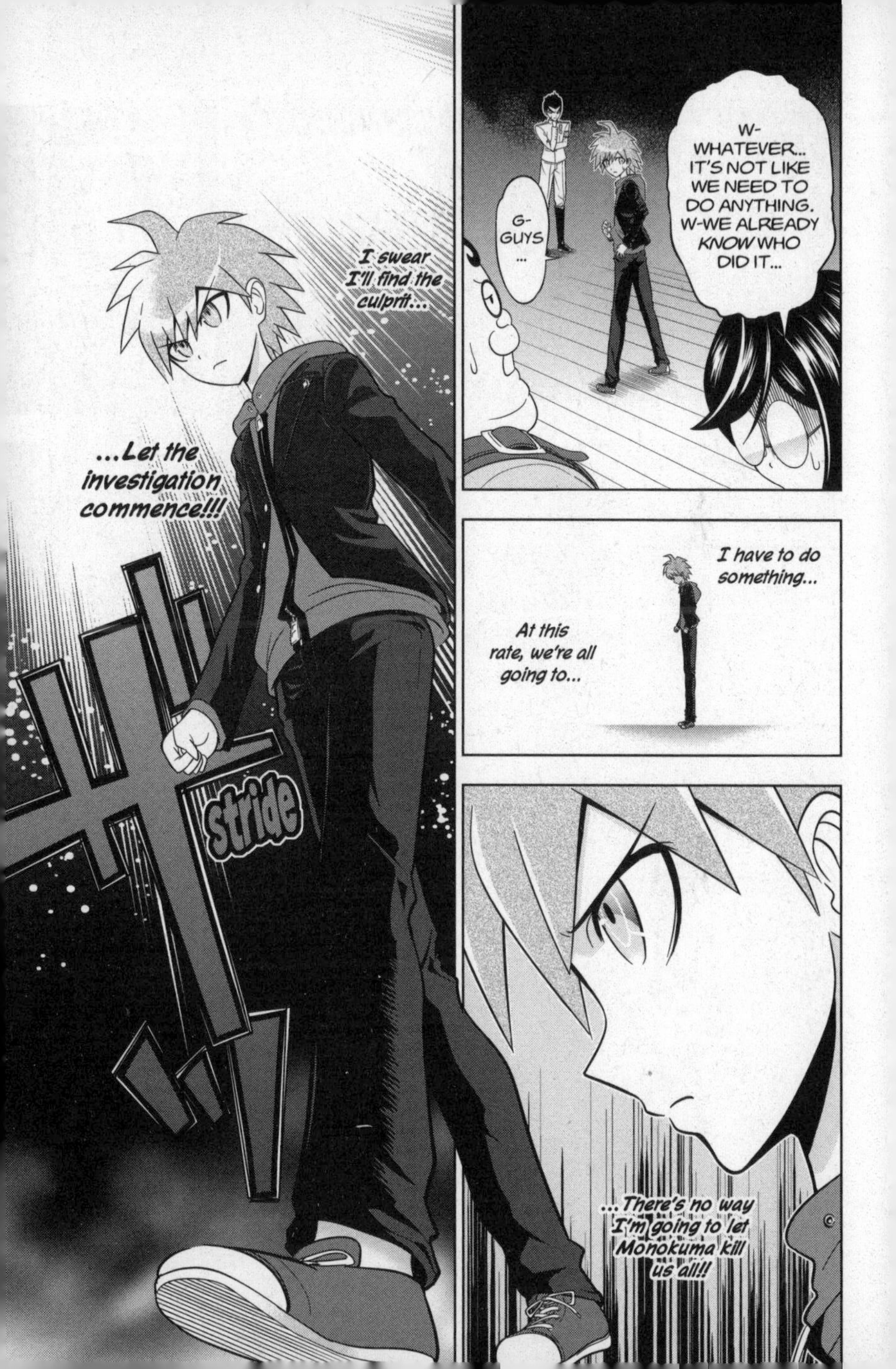
W- WHATEVER... IT'S NOT LIKE WE NEED TO DO ANYTHING. W-WE ALREADY KNOW WHO DID IT...
G- GUYS ...
I have to do something...
At this rate, we're all going to...
...There's no way I'm going to let Monokuma kill us all!!
I swear I'll find the culprit...
...Let the investigation commence!!!
stride

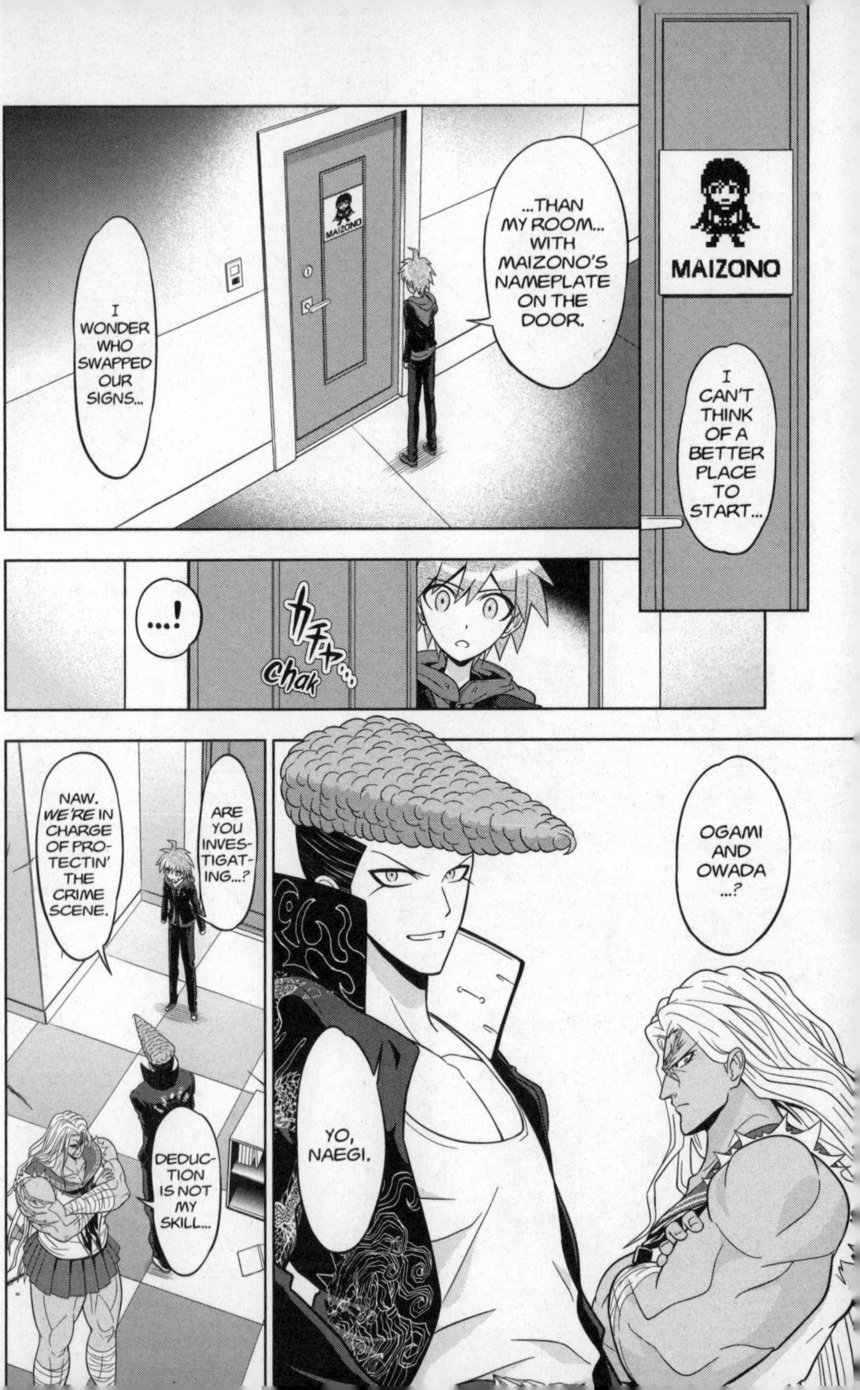
MAIZONO
I CAN'T THINK OF A BETTER PLACE TO START...
MAIZONO
...THAN MY ROOM... WITH MAIZONO'S NAMEPLATE ON THE DOOR.
I WONDER WHO SWAPPED OUR SIGNS...
カチャ...
Chak
...!
OGAMI AND OWADA ...?
YO, NAEGI.
ARE YOU INVESTIGATING...?
NAW. WE'RE IN CHARGE OF PROTECTIN' THE CRIME SCENE.
DEDUCTION IS NOT MY SKILL...

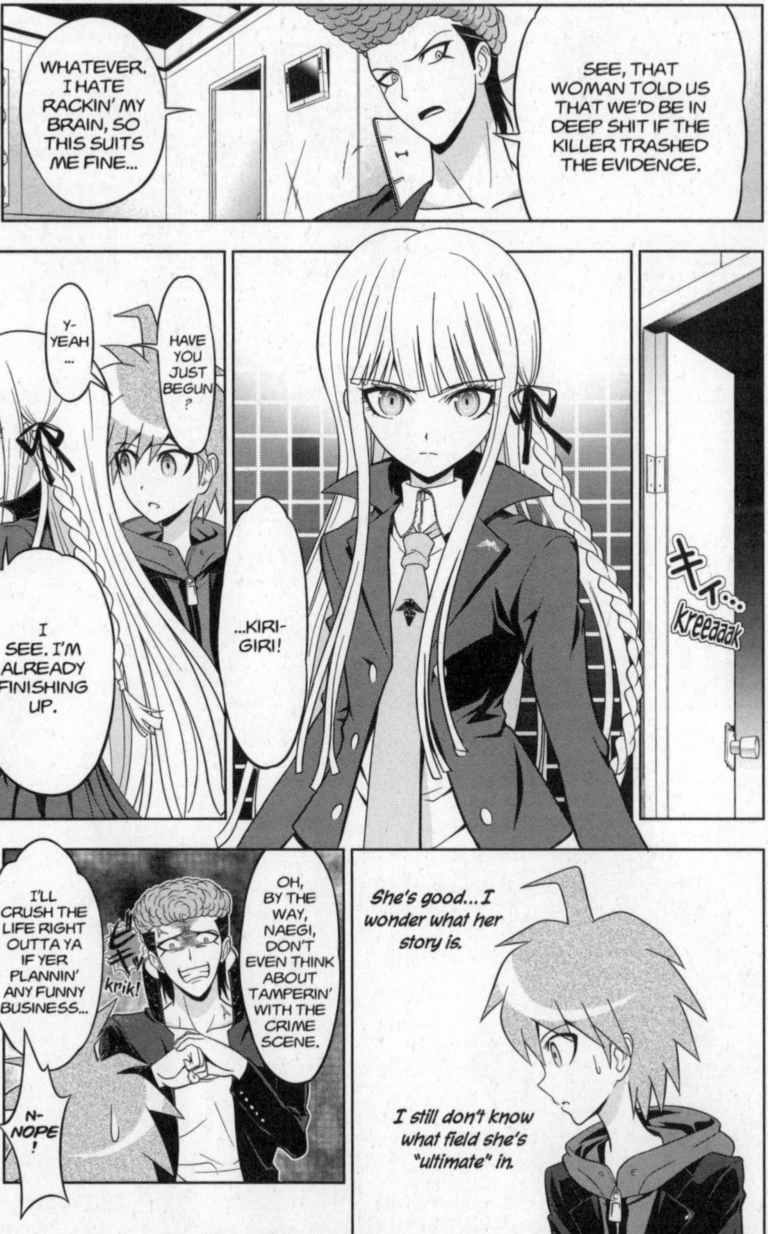
SEE, THAT WOMAN TOLD US THAT WE'D BE IN DEEP SHIT IF THE KILLER TRASHED THE EVIDENCE.
WHATEVER. I HATE RACKIN' MY BRAIN, SO THIS SUITS ME FINE...
キィ…
kreeaaak
...KIRI-GIRI!
HAVE YOU JUST BEGUN?
Y-YEAH...
I SEE. I'M ALREADY FINISHING UP.
She's good... I wonder what her story is.
I still don't know what field she's "ultimate" in.
OH, BY THE WAY, NAEGI, DON'T EVEN THINK ABOUT TAMPERIN' WITH THE CRIME SCENE.
I'LL CRUSH THE LIFE RIGHT OUTTA YA IF YER PLANNIN' ANY FUNNY BUSINESS...
krik!
N-NOPE!

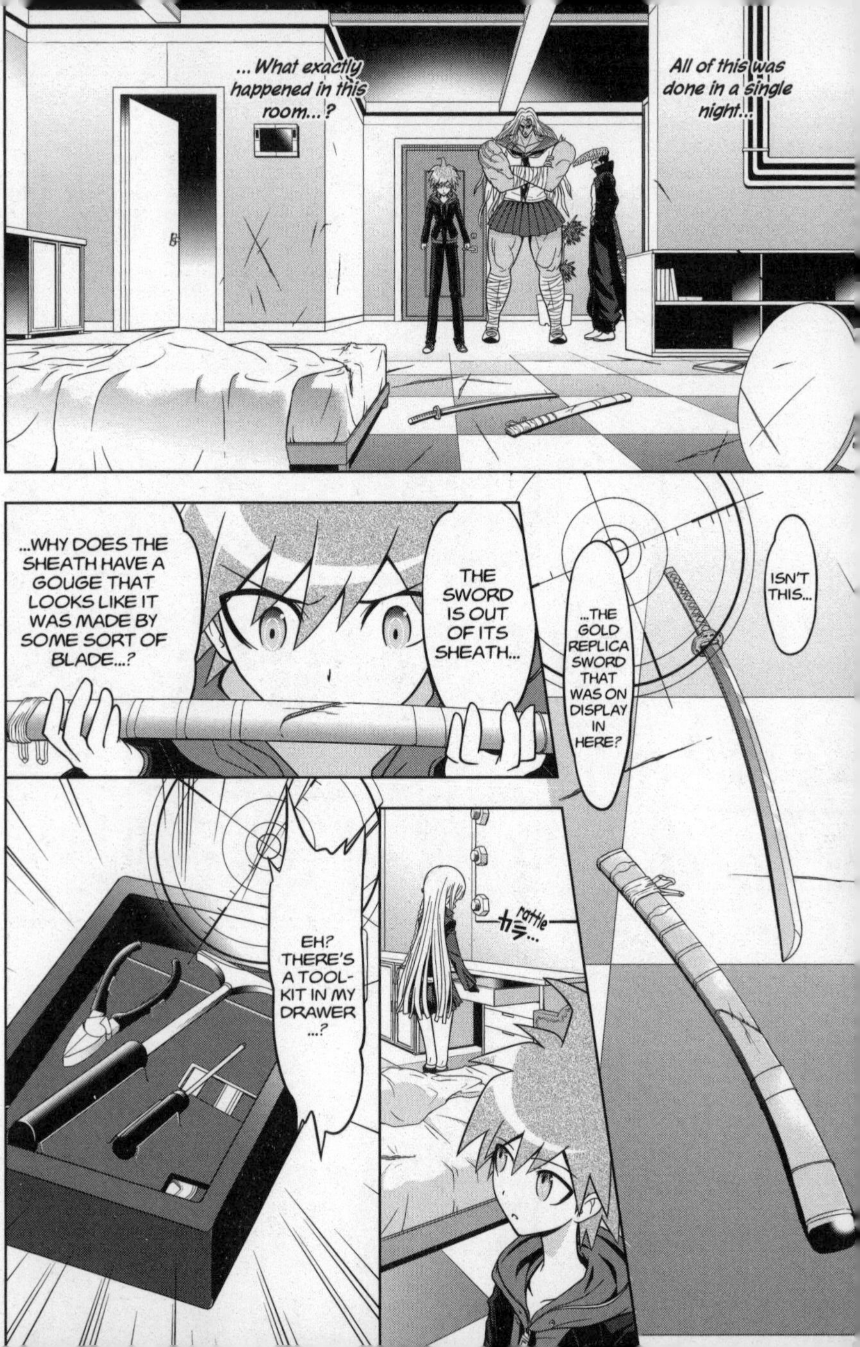
All of this was done in a single night...
... What exactly happened in this room...?
ISN'T THIS...
...THE GOLD REPLICA SWORD THAT WAS ON DISPLAY IN HERE?
THE SWORD IS OUT OF ITS SHEATH...
...WHY DOES THE SHEATH HAVE A GOUGE THAT LOOKS LIKE IT WAS MADE BY SOME SORT OF BLADE...?
カラ... rattle
EH? THERE'S A TOOL-KIT IN MY DRAWER ...?

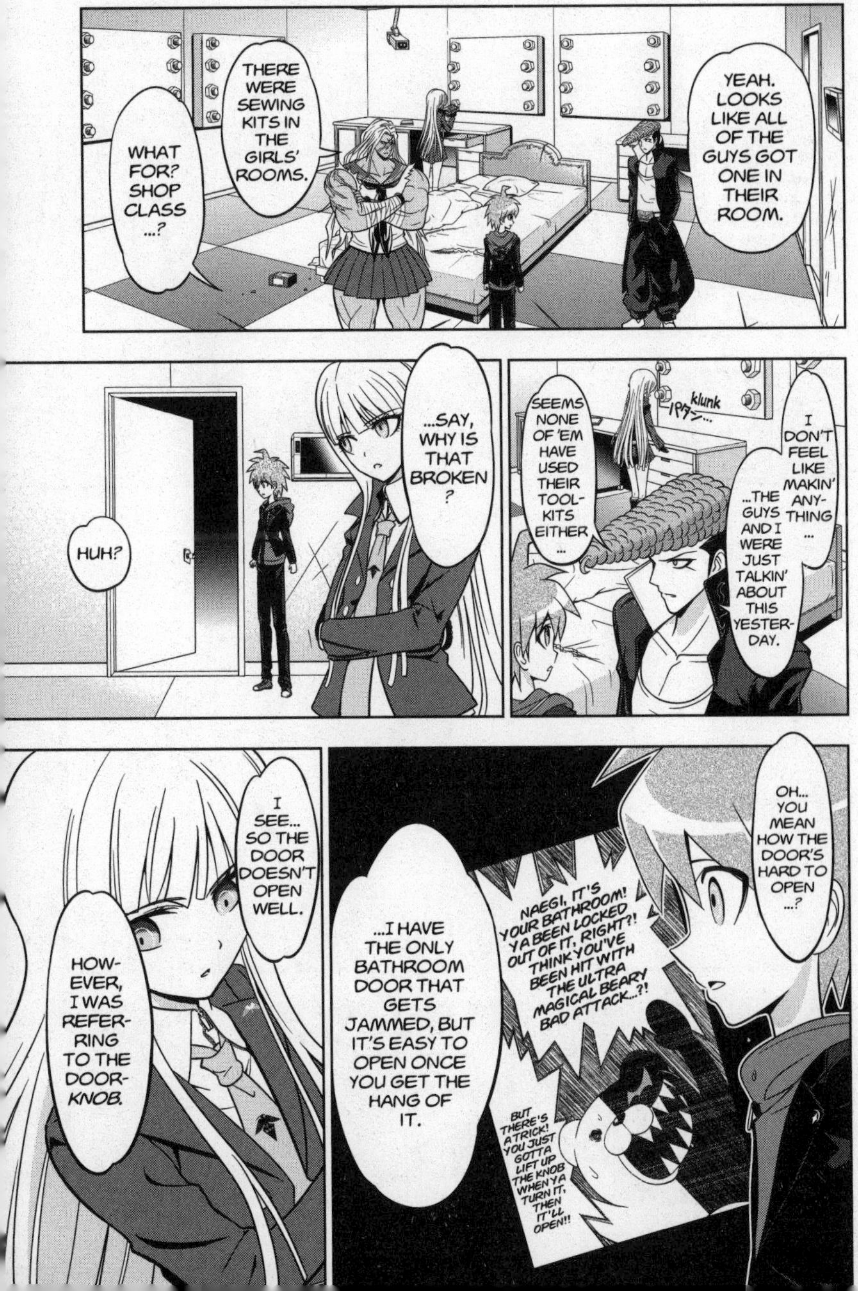
YEAH. LOOKS LIKE ALL OF THE GUYS GOT ONE IN THEIR ROOM.
THERE WERE SEWING KITS IN THE GIRLS' ROOMS.
WHAT FOR? SHOP CLASS ...?
I DON'T FEEL LIKE MAKIN' ANYTHING ...
...THE GUYS AND I WERE JUST TALKIN' ABOUT THIS YESTERDAY.
SEEMS NONE OF 'EM HAVE USED THEIR TOOLKITS EITHER ...
klunk
パタン...
...SAY, WHY IS THAT BROKEN?
HUH?
OH... YOU MEAN HOW THE DOOR'S HARD TO OPEN ...?
NAEGI, IT'S YOUR BATHROOM! YA BEEN LOCKED OUT OF IT, RIGHT?! THINK YOU'VE BEEN HIT WITH THE ULTRA MAGICAL BEARY BAD ATTACK...?!
BUT THERE'S A TRICK! YOU JUST GOTTA LIFT UP THE KNOB WHEN YA TURN IT, THEN IT'LL OPEN!!
...I HAVE THE ONLY BATHROOM DOOR THAT GETS JAMMED, BUT IT'S EASY TO OPEN ONCE YOU GET THE HANG OF IT.
I SEE... SO THE DOOR DOESN'T OPEN WELL.
HOWEVER, I WAS REFERRING TO THE DOORKNOB.

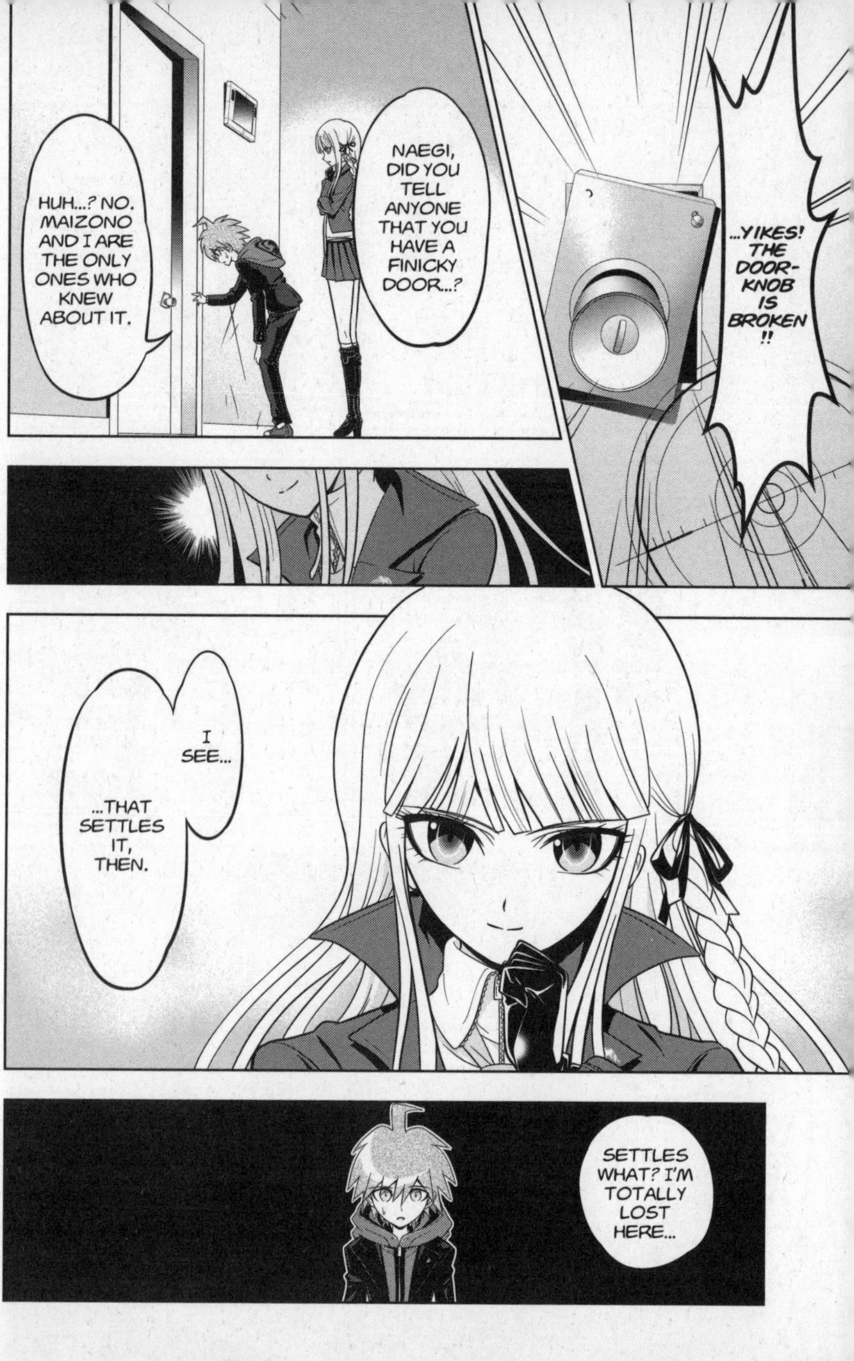
...YIKES! THE DOOR-KNOB IS BROKEN!!
NAEGI, DID YOU TELL ANYONE THAT YOU HAVE A FINICKY DOOR...?
HUH...? NO. MAIZONO AND I ARE THE ONLY ONES WHO KNEW ABOUT IT.
I SEE...
...THAT SETTLES IT, THEN.
SETTLES WHAT? I'M TOTALLY LOST HERE...

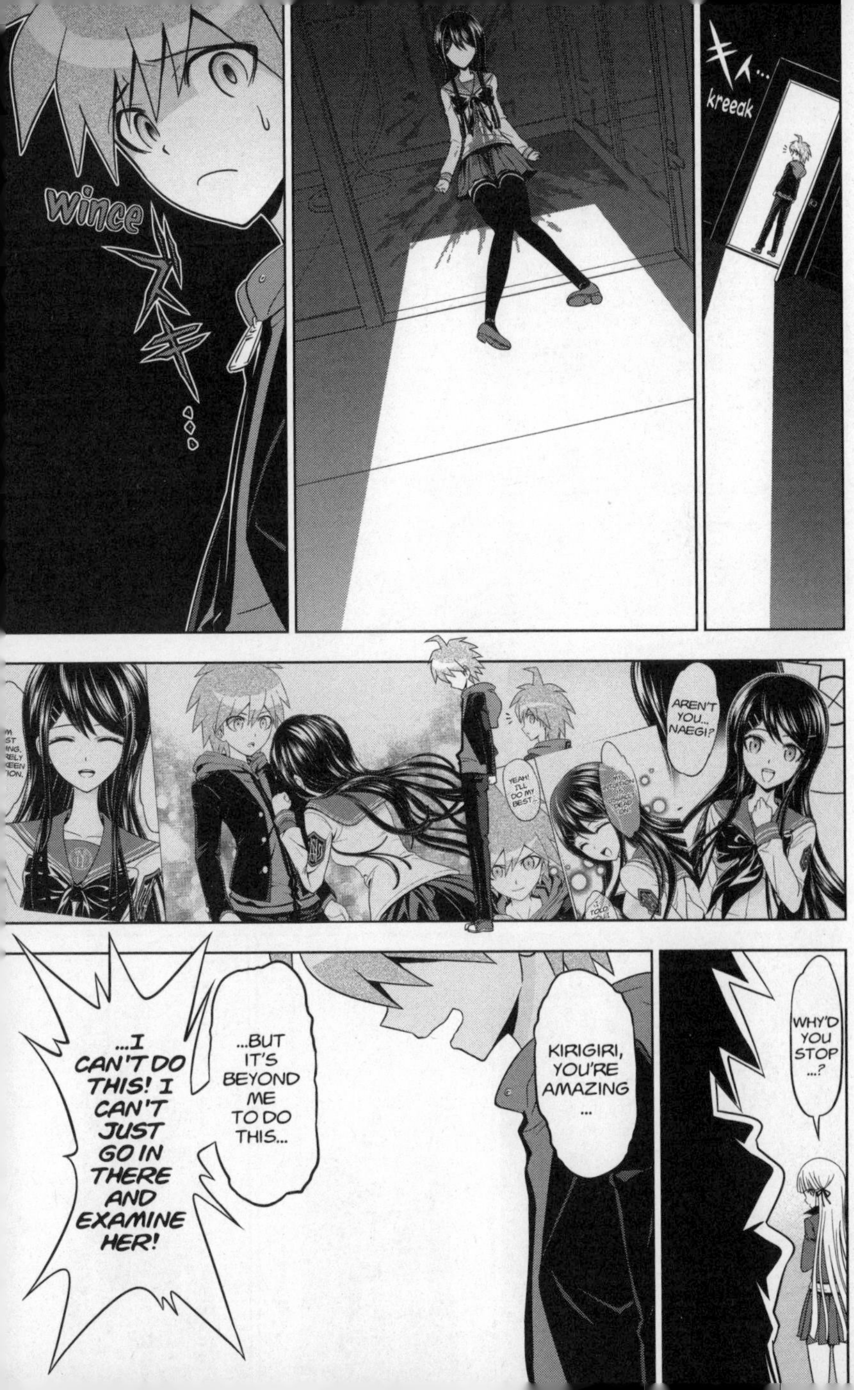
kreeak
wince
AREN'T YOU... NAEGI?
MY INTUITION IS USUALLY DEAD ON!
YEAH! I'LL DO MY BEST...
WHY'D YOU STOP ...?
KIRIGIRI, YOU'RE AMAZING ...
...BUT IT'S BEYOND ME TO DO THIS...
...I CAN'T DO THIS! I CAN'T JUST GO IN THERE AND EXAMINE HER!

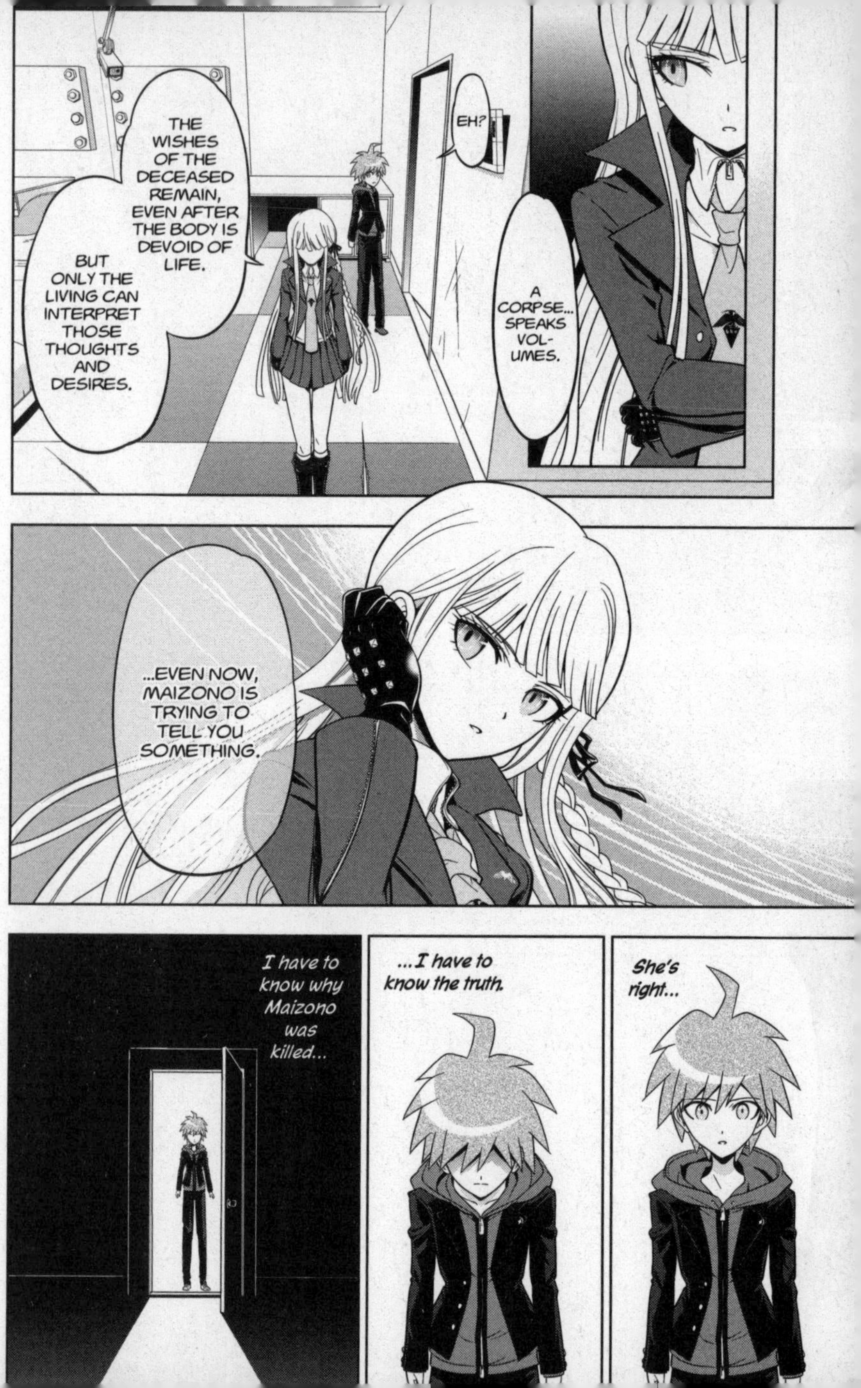
A CORPSE... SPEAKS VOLUMES.
EH?
THE WISHES OF THE DECEASED REMAIN, EVEN AFTER THE BODY IS DEVOID OF LIFE.
BUT ONLY THE LIVING CAN INTERPRET THOSE THOUGHTS AND DESIRES.
...EVEN NOW, MAIZONO IS TRYING TO TELL YOU SOMETHING.
She's right...
...I have to know the truth.
I have to know why Maizono was killed...

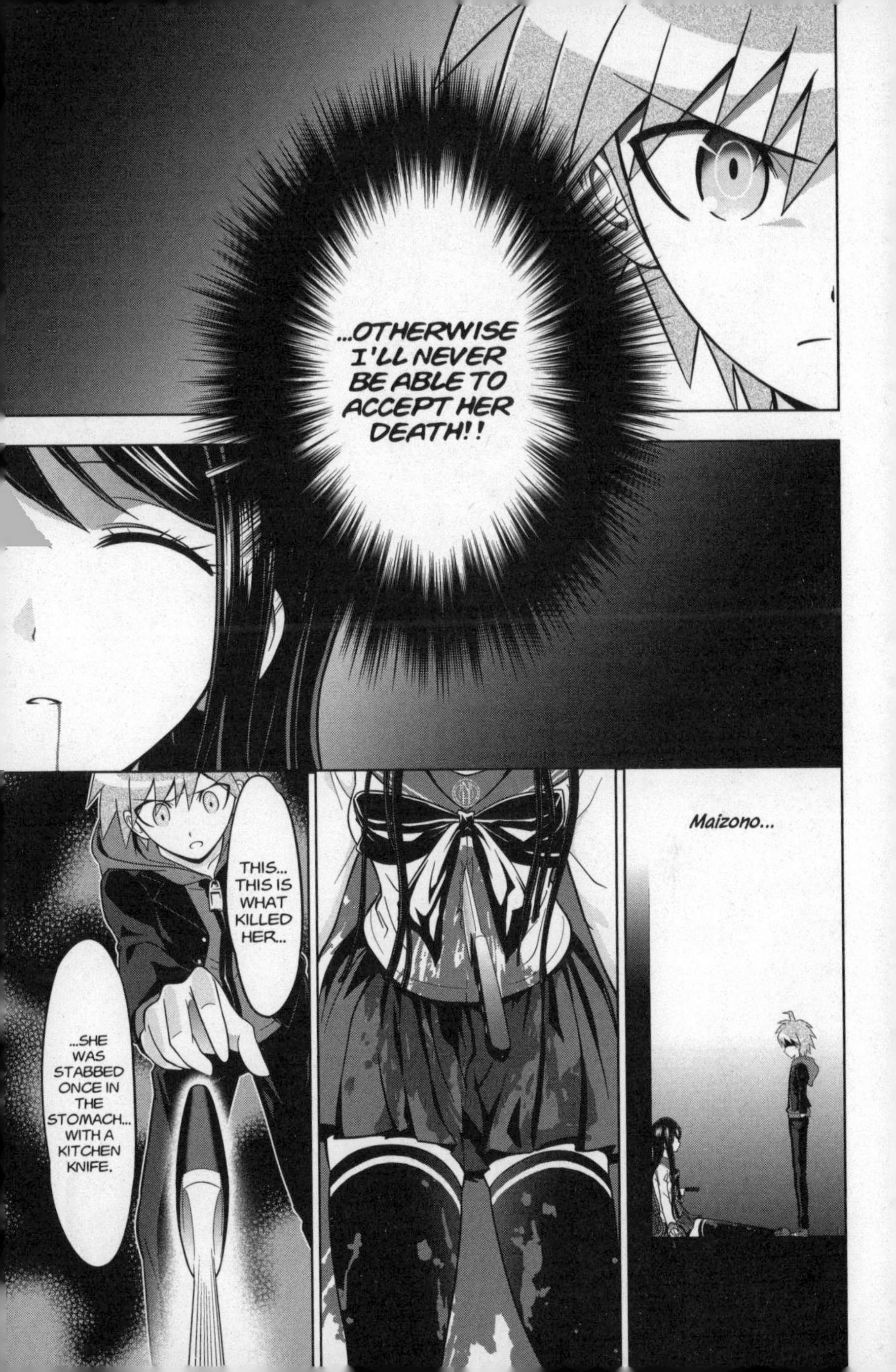

...OTHERWISE I'LL NEVER BE ABLE TO ACCEPT HER DEATH!!
Maizono...
THIS... THIS IS WHAT KILLED HER...
...SHE WAS STABBED ONCE IN THE STOMACH... WITH A KITCHEN KNIFE.

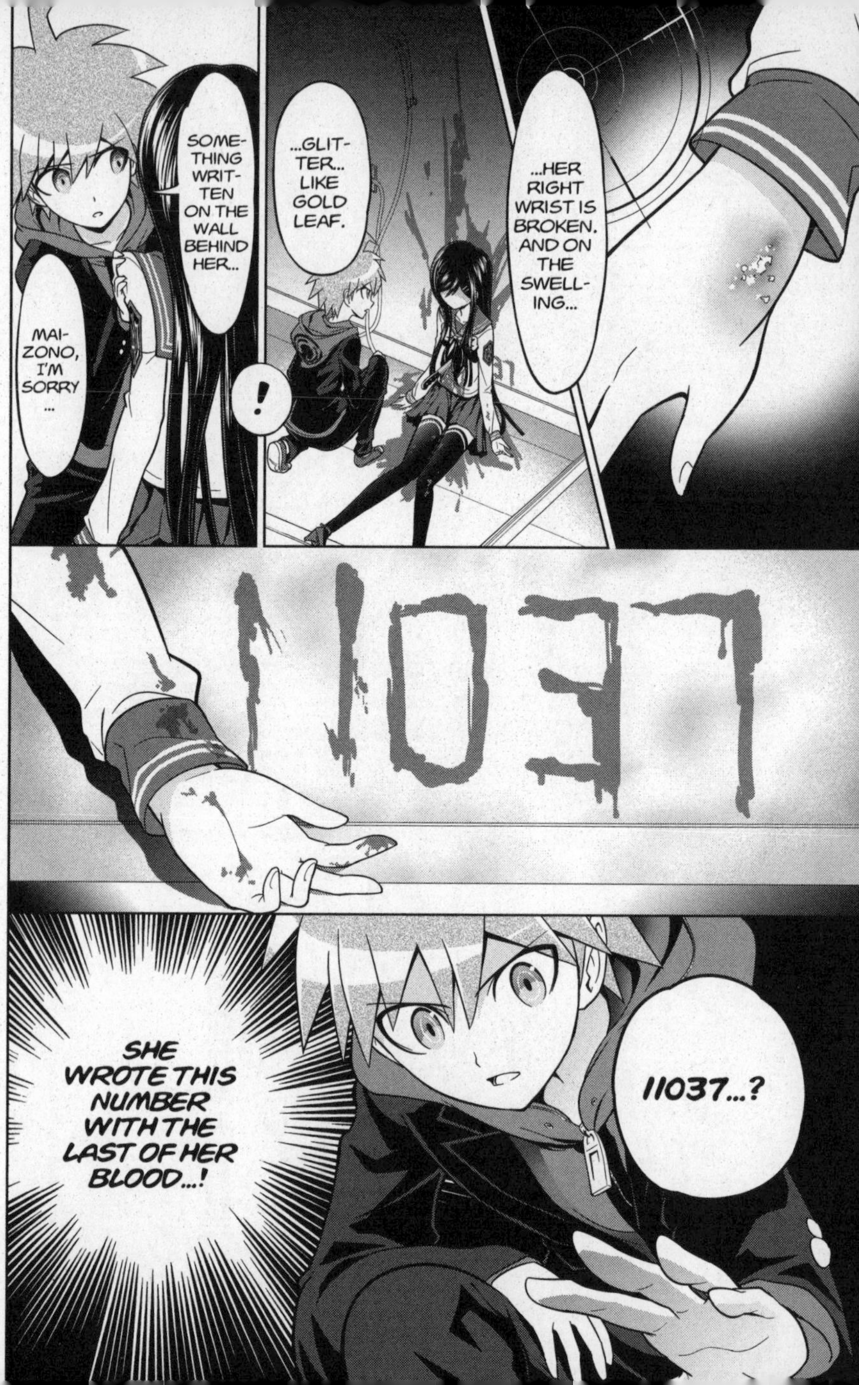

...HER RIGHT WRIST IS BROKEN. AND ON THE SWELLING...
...GLITTER... LIKE GOLD LEAF.
!
SOMETHING WRITTEN ON THE WALL BEHIND HER...
MAIZONO, I'M SORRY...
11037...?
SHE WROTE THIS NUMBER WITH THE LAST OF HER BLOOD...!

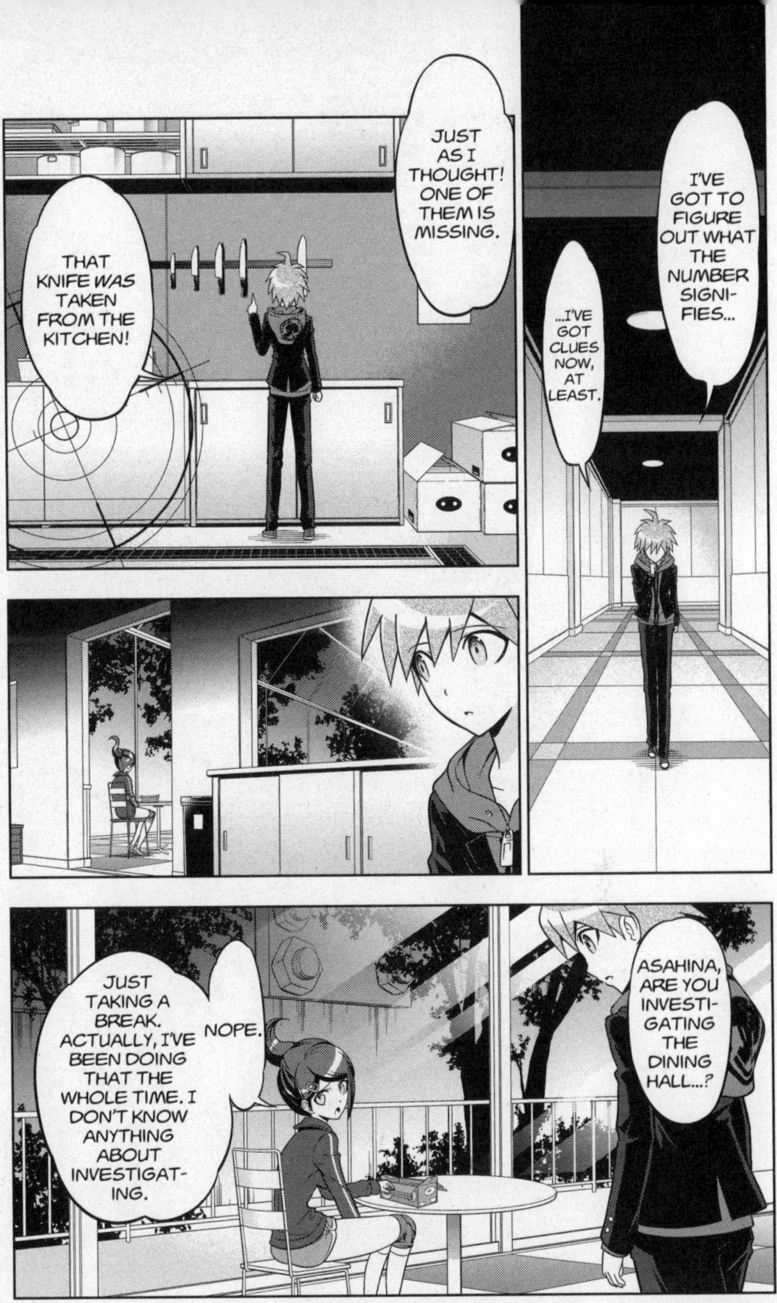
I'VE GOT TO FIGURE OUT WHAT THE NUMBER SIGNIFIES...
...I'VE GOT CLUES NOW, AT LEAST.
JUST AS I THOUGHT! ONE OF THEM IS MISSING.
THAT KNIFE *WAS* TAKEN FROM THE KITCHEN!
ASAHINA, ARE YOU INVESTIGATING THE DINING HALL...?
NOPE.
JUST TAKING A BREAK. ACTUALLY, I'VE BEEN DOING THAT THE WHOLE TIME. I DON'T KNOW ANYTHING ABOUT INVESTIGATING.

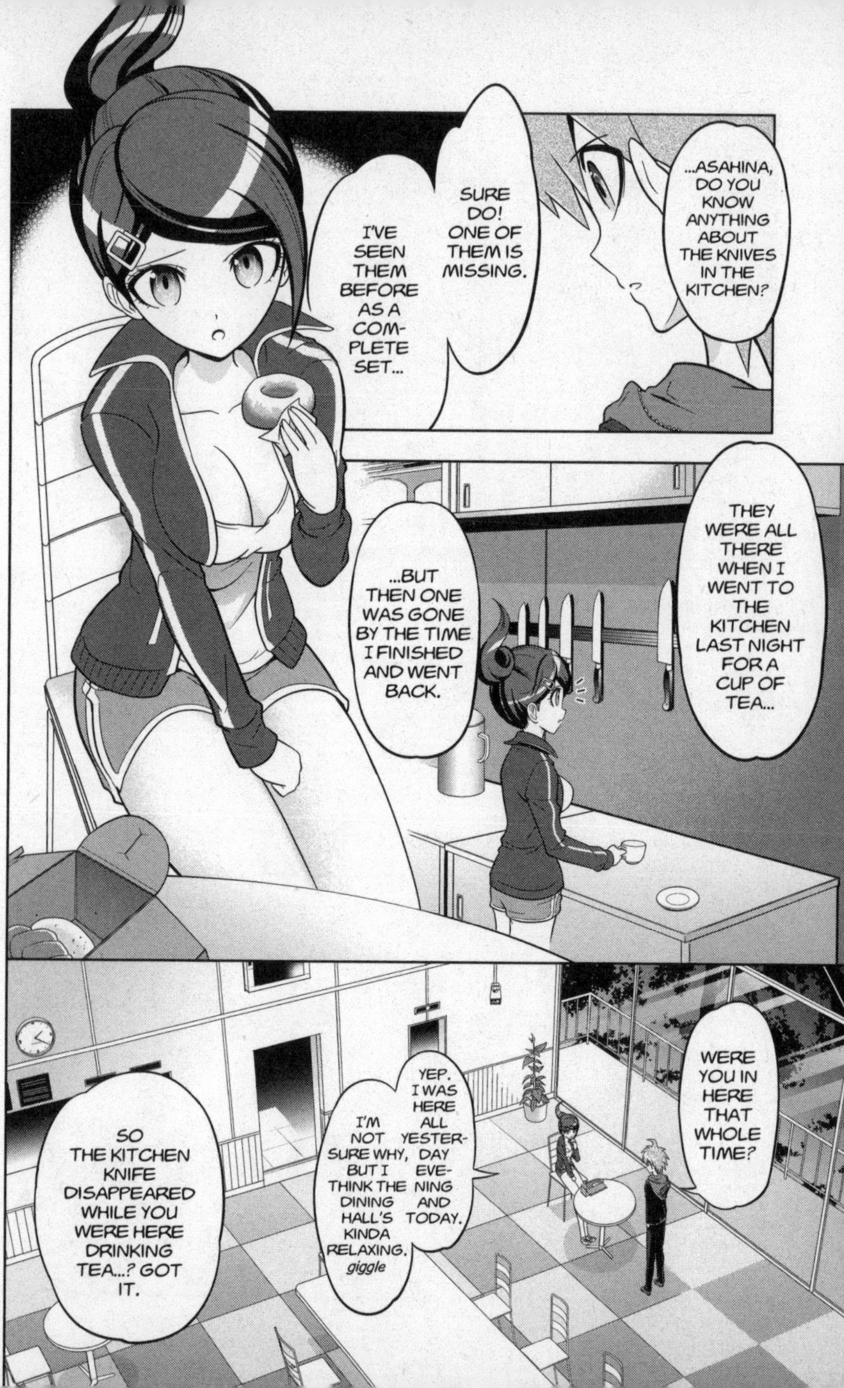
...ASAHINA, DO YOU KNOW ANYTHING ABOUT THE KNIVES IN THE KITCHEN?
SURE DO! ONE OF THEM IS MISSING.
I'VE SEEN THEM BEFORE AS A COMPLETE SET...
THEY WERE ALL THERE WHEN I WENT TO THE KITCHEN LAST NIGHT FOR A CUP OF TEA...
...BUT THEN ONE WAS GONE BY THE TIME I FINISHED AND WENT BACK.
WERE YOU IN HERE THAT WHOLE TIME?
YEP. I WAS HERE ALL YESTERDAY EVENING AND TODAY.
I'M NOT SURE WHY, BUT I THINK THE DINING HALL'S KINDA RELAXING.
giggle
SO THE KITCHEN KNIFE DISAPPEARED WHILE YOU WERE HERE DRINKING TEA...? GOT IT.

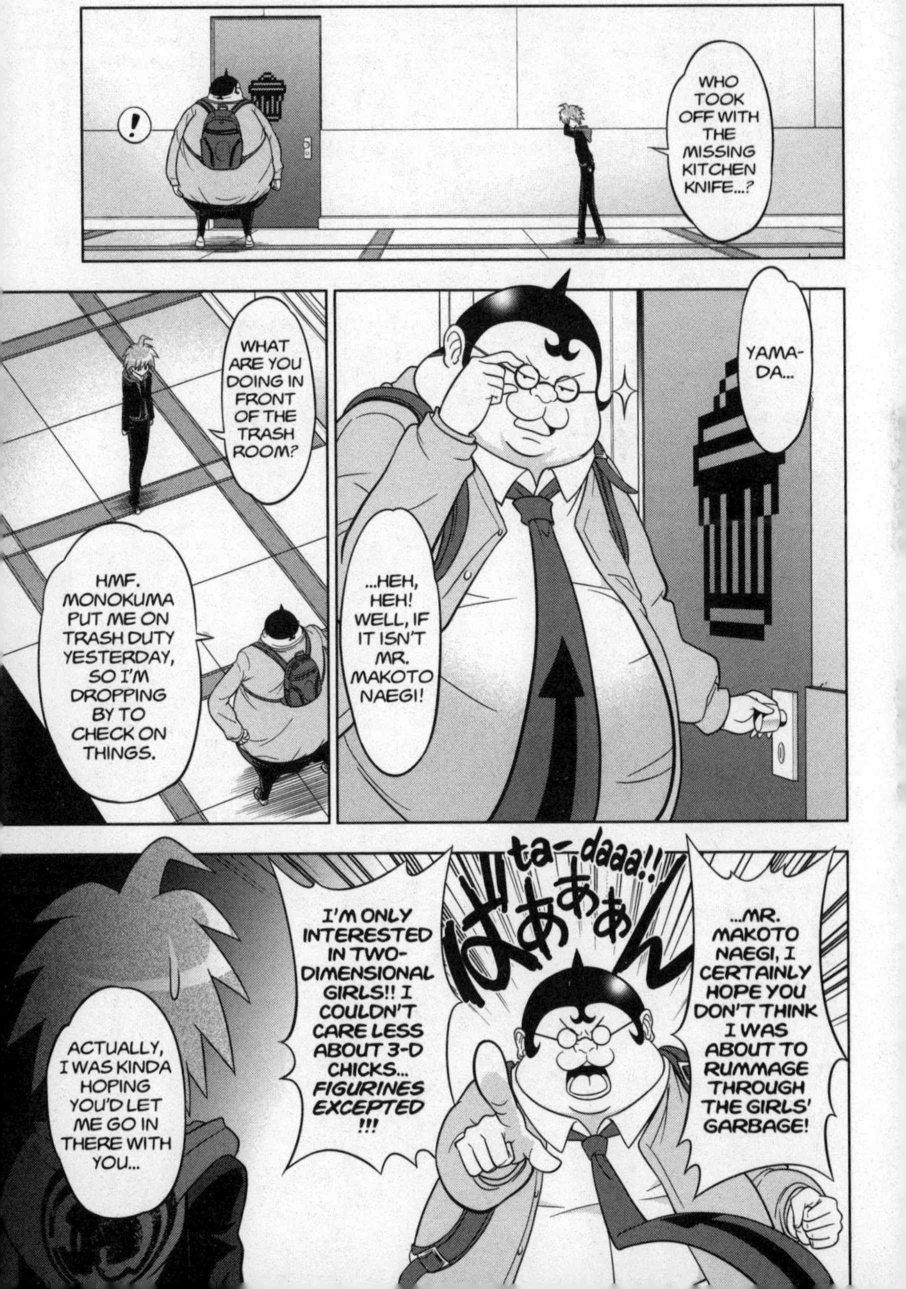
WHO TOOK OFF WITH THE MISSING KITCHEN KNIFE...?
!
YAMA-DA...
...HEH, HEH! WELL, IF IT ISN'T MR. MAKOTO NAEGI!
WHAT ARE YOU DOING IN FRONT OF THE TRASH ROOM?
HMF. MONOKUMA PUT ME ON TRASH DUTY YESTERDAY, SO I'M DROPPING BY TO CHECK ON THINGS.
...MR. MAKOTO NAEGI, I CERTAINLY HOPE YOU DON'T THINK I WAS ABOUT TO RUMMAGE THROUGH THE GIRLS' GARBAGE!
ta-daaa!!
ばあぁぁん
I'M ONLY INTERESTED IN TWO-DIMENSIONAL GIRLS!! I COULDN'T CARE LESS ABOUT 3-D CHICKS... *FIGURINES EXCEPTED*!!!
ACTUALLY, I WAS KINDA HOPING YOU'D LET ME GO IN THERE WITH YOU...

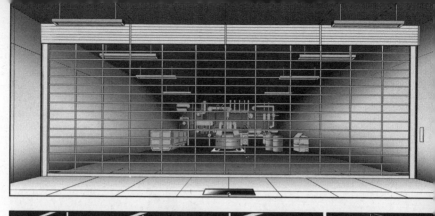

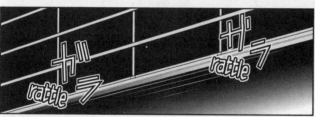

IT'S INSANE HOW HUGE THIS ROOM IS...
ガラ rattle
ガラ rattle
AND I'VE GOT THE ONE AND ONLY KEY TO THE SHUTTERS!
WHAT ?!?
THE INCINERATOR'S BEEN LEFT ON!!!
AND LOOK AT THAT JUNK LYING THERE...!

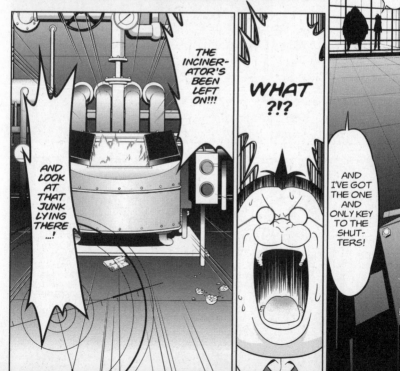

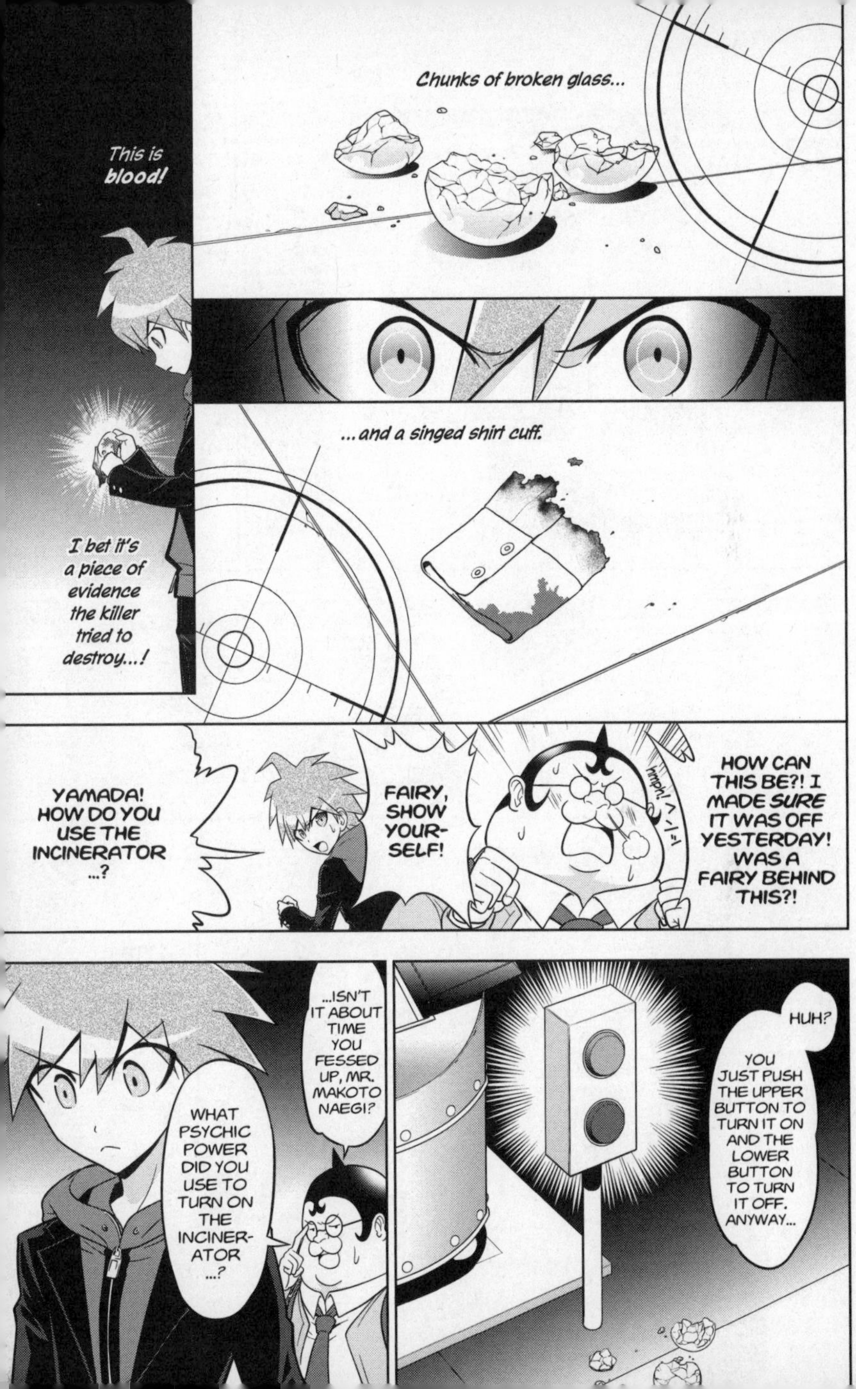
Chunks of broken glass...
...and a singed shirt cuff.
This is blood!
I bet it's a piece of evidence the killer tried to destroy...!
HOW CAN THIS BE?! I MADE SURE IT WAS OFF YESTERDAY! WAS A FAIRY BEHIND THIS?!
FAIRY, SHOW YOURSELF!
YAMADA! HOW DO YOU USE THE INCINERATOR ...?
HUH?
YOU JUST PUSH THE UPPER BUTTON TO TURN IT ON AND THE LOWER BUTTON TO TURN IT OFF. ANYWAY...
...ISN'T IT ABOUT TIME YOU FESSED UP, MR. MAKOTO NAEGI?
WHAT PSYCHIC POWER DID YOU USE TO TURN ON THE INCINERATOR ...?

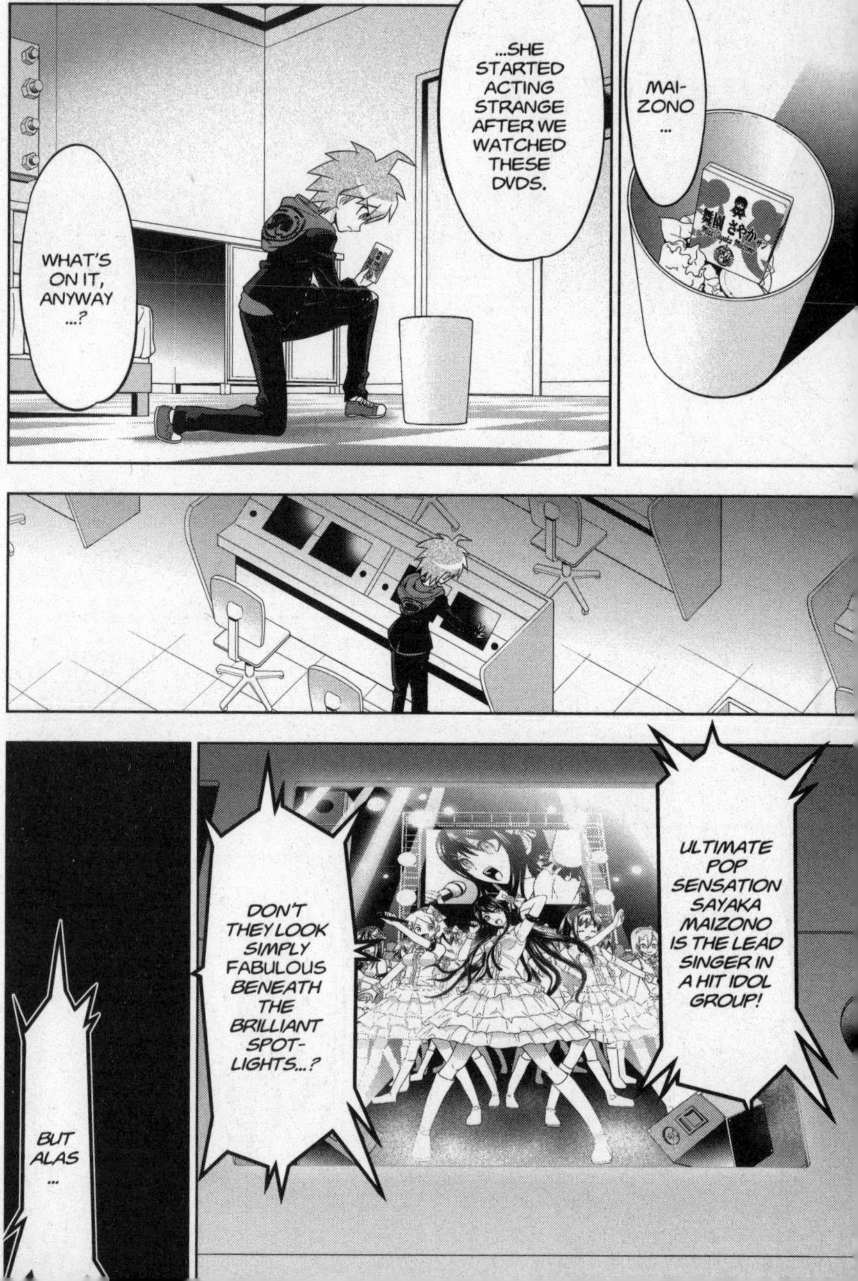
MAI-ZONO...
...SHE STARTED ACTING STRANGE AFTER WE WATCHED THESE DVDS.
WHAT'S ON IT, ANYWAY...?
ULTIMATE POP SENSATION SAYAKA MAIZONO IS THE LEAD SINGER IN A HIT IDOL GROUP!
DON'T THEY LOOK SIMPLY FABULOUS BENEATH THE BRILLIANT SPOT-LIGHTS...?
BUT ALAS...

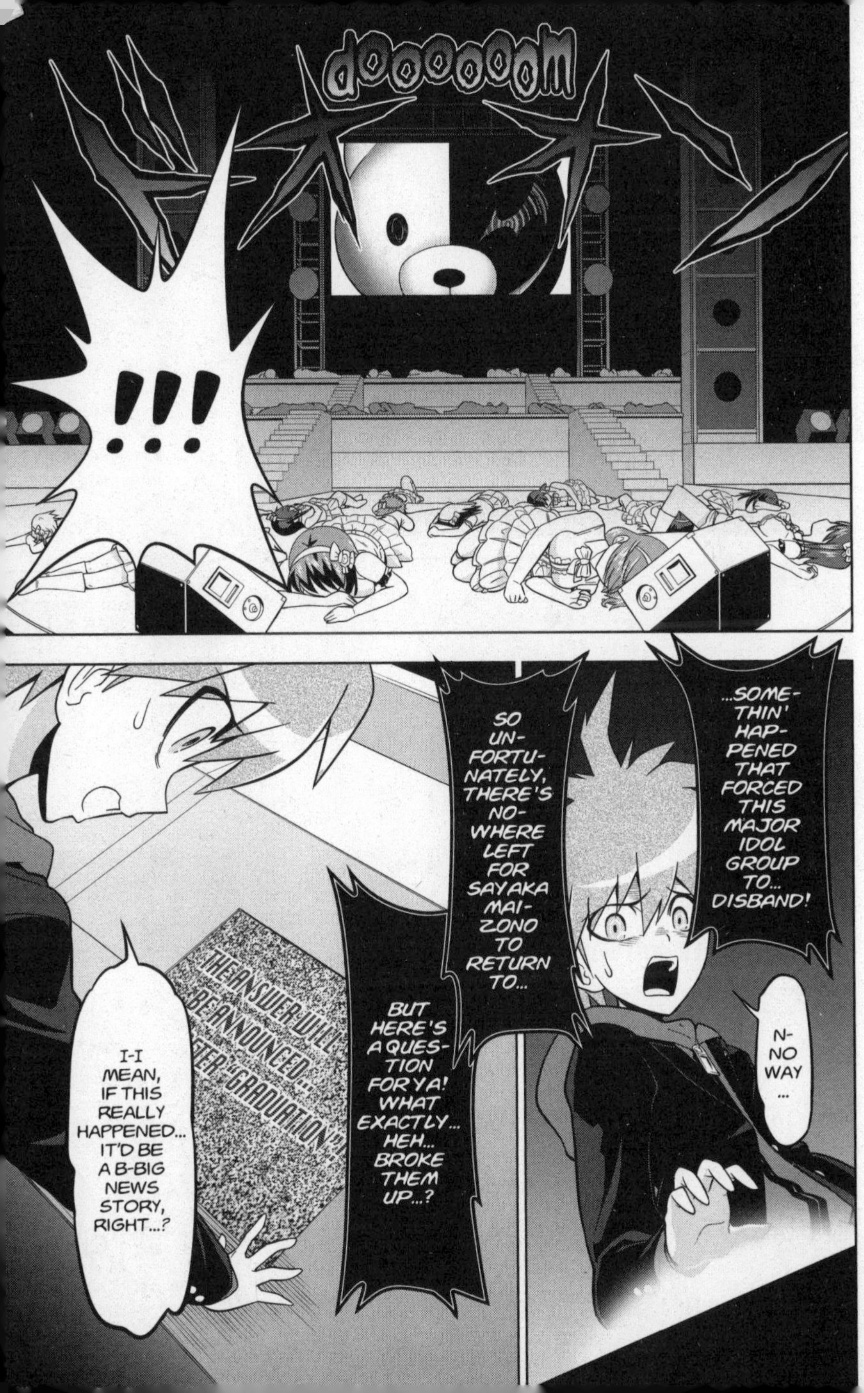
dOOOOOOM
!!!...
...SOMETHIN' HAPPENED THAT FORCED THIS MAJOR IDOL GROUP TO... DISBAND!
SO UNFORTUNATELY, THERE'S NOWHERE LEFT FOR SAYAKA MAIZONO TO RETURN TO...
N-NO WAY...
BUT HERE'S A QUESTION FOR YA! WHAT EXACTLY... HEH... BROKE THEM UP...?
THE ANSWER WILL BE ANNOUNCED... ...TER "GRADUATION"!
I-I MEAN, IF THIS REALLY HAPPENED... IT'D BE A B-BIG NEWS STORY, RIGHT...?

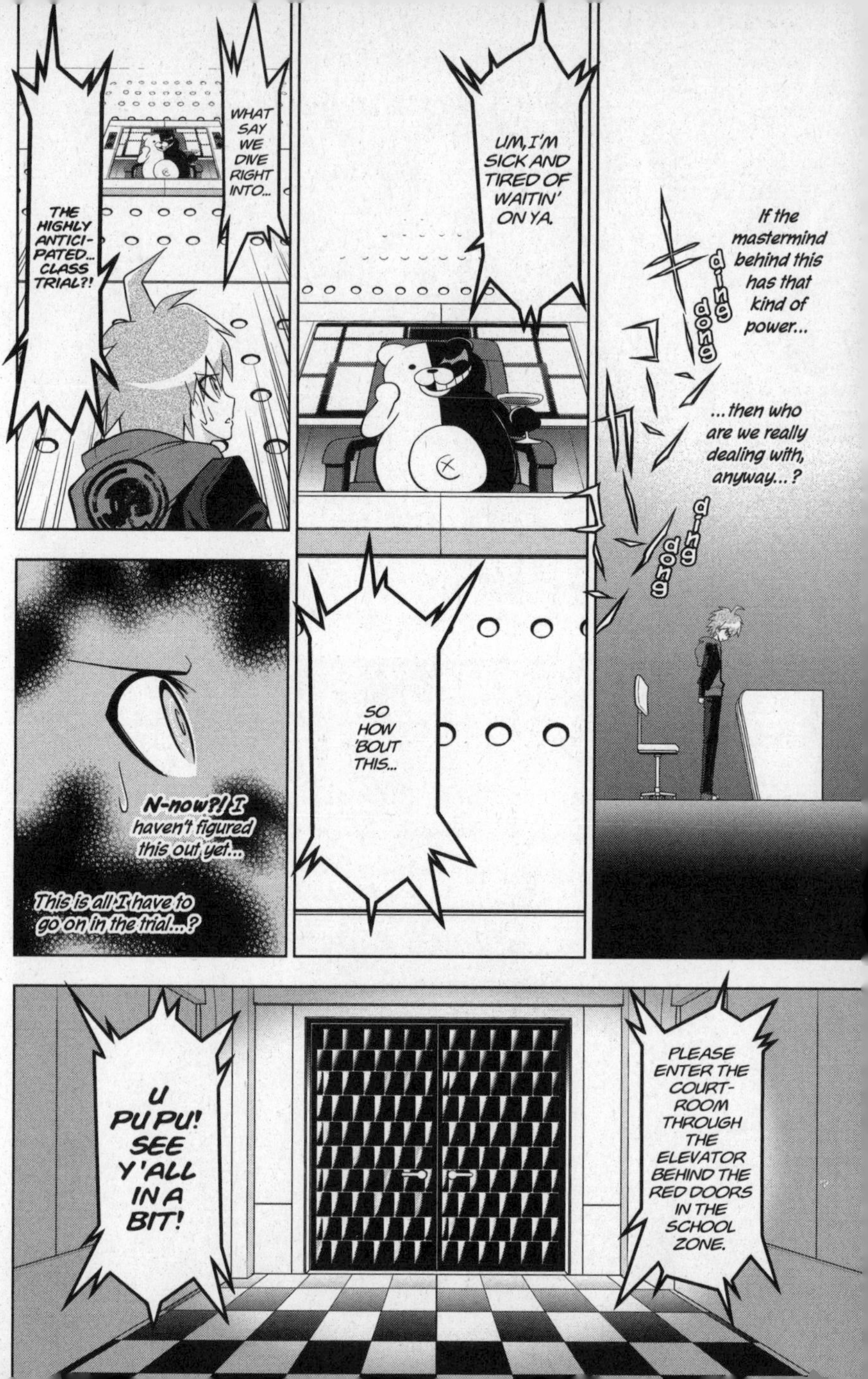
ding dong
ding dong
If the mastermind behind this has that kind of power...
...then who are we really dealing with, anyway...?
UM, I'M SICK AND TIRED OF WAITIN' ON YA.
WHAT SAY WE DIVE RIGHT INTO...
THE HIGHLY ANTICI-PATED... CLASS TRIAL?!
SO HOW 'BOUT THIS...
N-now?! I haven't figured this out yet...
This is all I have to go on in the trial...?
PLEASE ENTER THE COURT-ROOM THROUGH THE ELEVATOR BEHIND THE RED DOORS IN THE SCHOOL ZONE.
U PU PU! SEE Y'ALL IN A BIT!

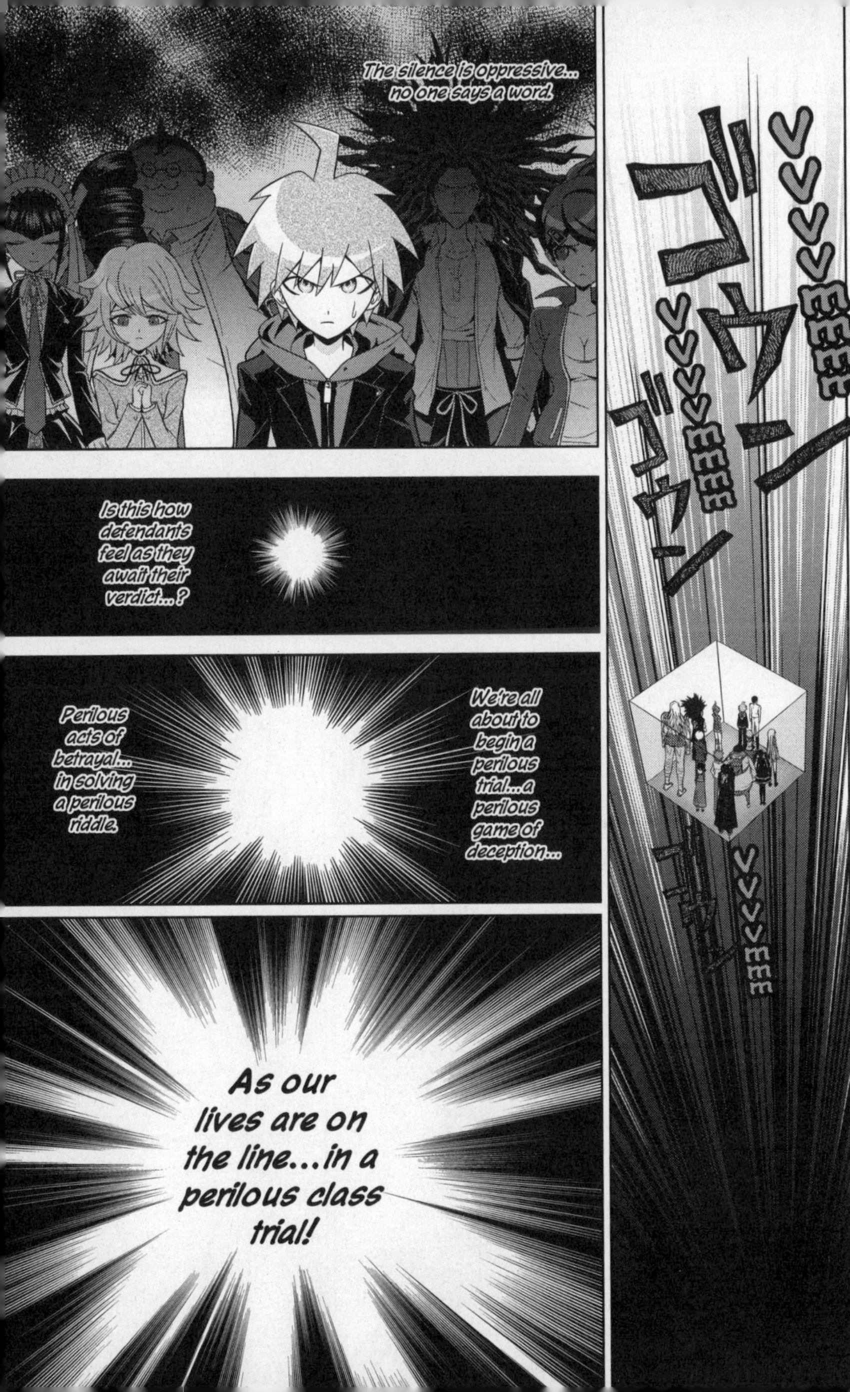
VVVVVMMMM
ゴウンー
VVVVVMMMM
ゴウンー
VVVVMMM
The silence is oppressive... no one says a word.
Is this how defendants feel as they await their verdict...?
We're all about to begin a perilous trial...a perilous game of deception...
Perilous acts of betrayal... in solving a perilous riddle.
As our lives are on the line...in a perilous class trial!

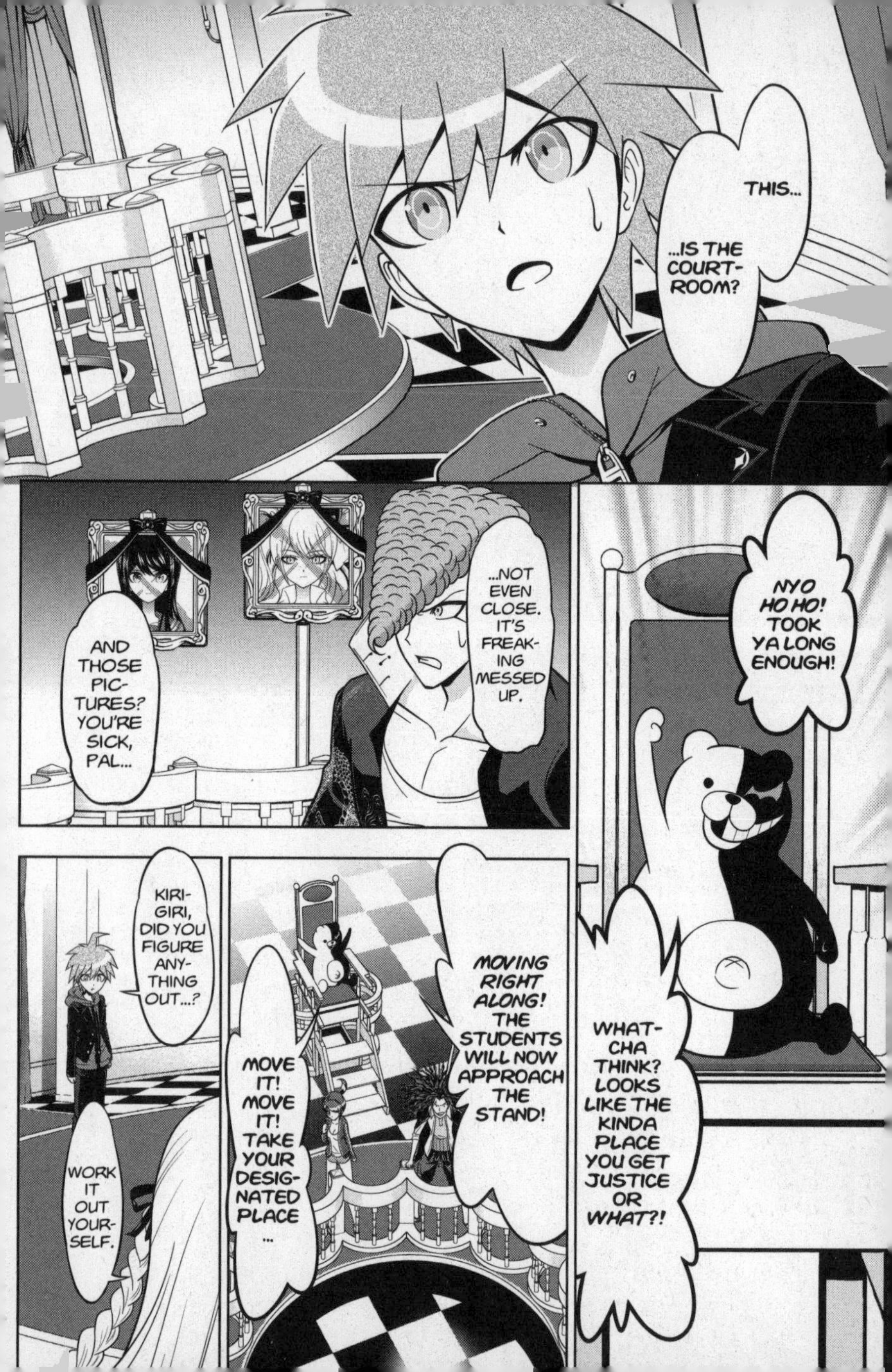
THIS...
...IS THE COURTROOM?
NYO HO HO! TOOK YA LONG ENOUGH!
WHATCHA THINK? LOOKS LIKE THE KINDA PLACE YOU GET JUSTICE OR WHAT?!
...NOT EVEN CLOSE. IT'S FREAKING MESSED UP.
AND THOSE PICTURES? YOU'RE SICK, PAL...
MOVING RIGHT ALONG! THE STUDENTS WILL NOW APPROACH THE STAND!
MOVE IT! MOVE IT! TAKE YOUR DESIGNATED PLACE ...
KIRIGIRI, DID YOU FIGURE ANYTHING OUT...?
WORK IT OUT YOURSELF.

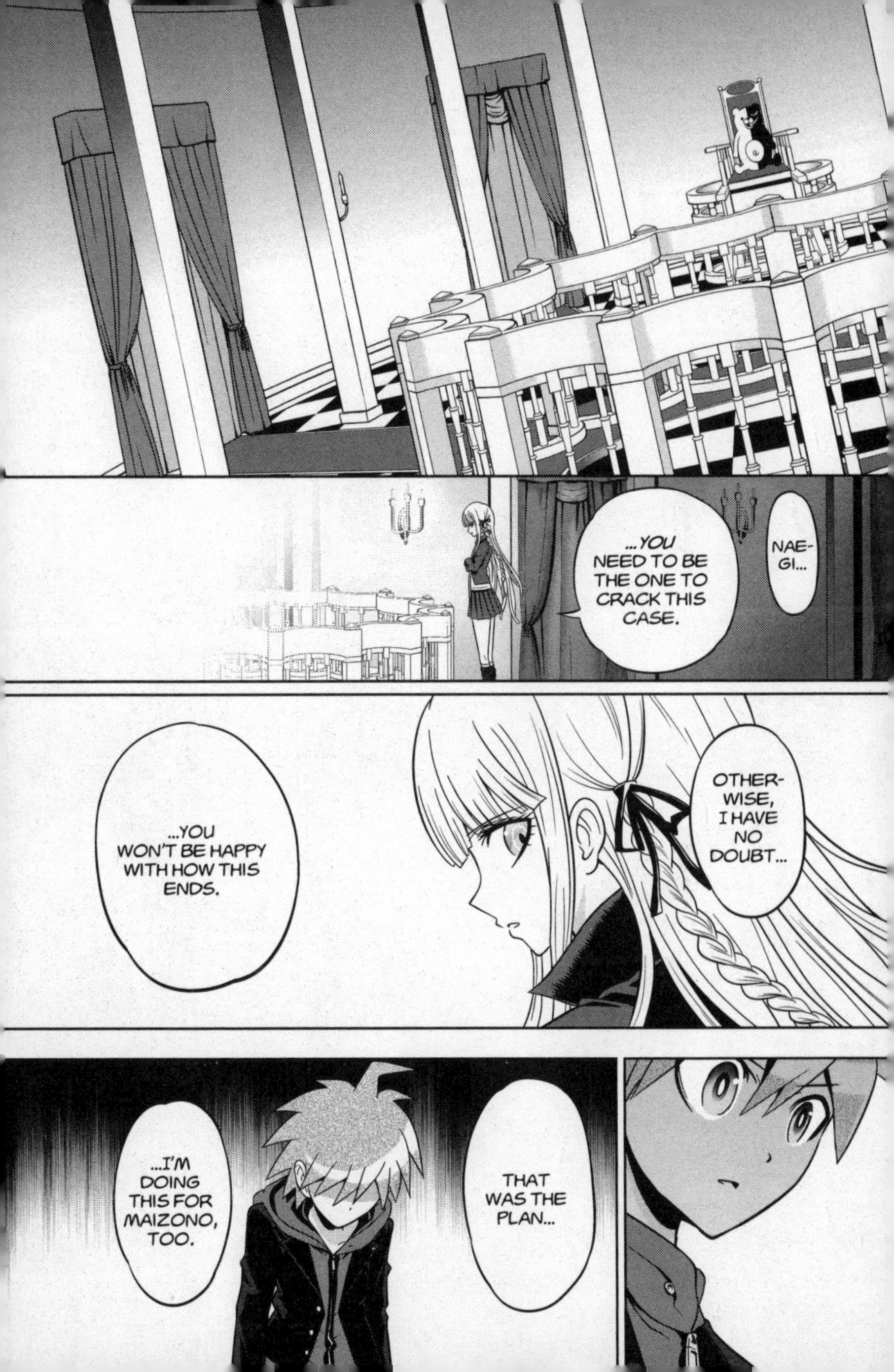
NAE-GI...
...YOU NEED TO BE THE ONE TO CRACK THIS CASE.
OTHER-WISE, I HAVE NO DOUBT...
...YOU WON'T BE HAPPY WITH HOW THIS ENDS.
THAT WAS THE PLAN...
...I'M DOING THIS FOR MAIZONO, TOO.

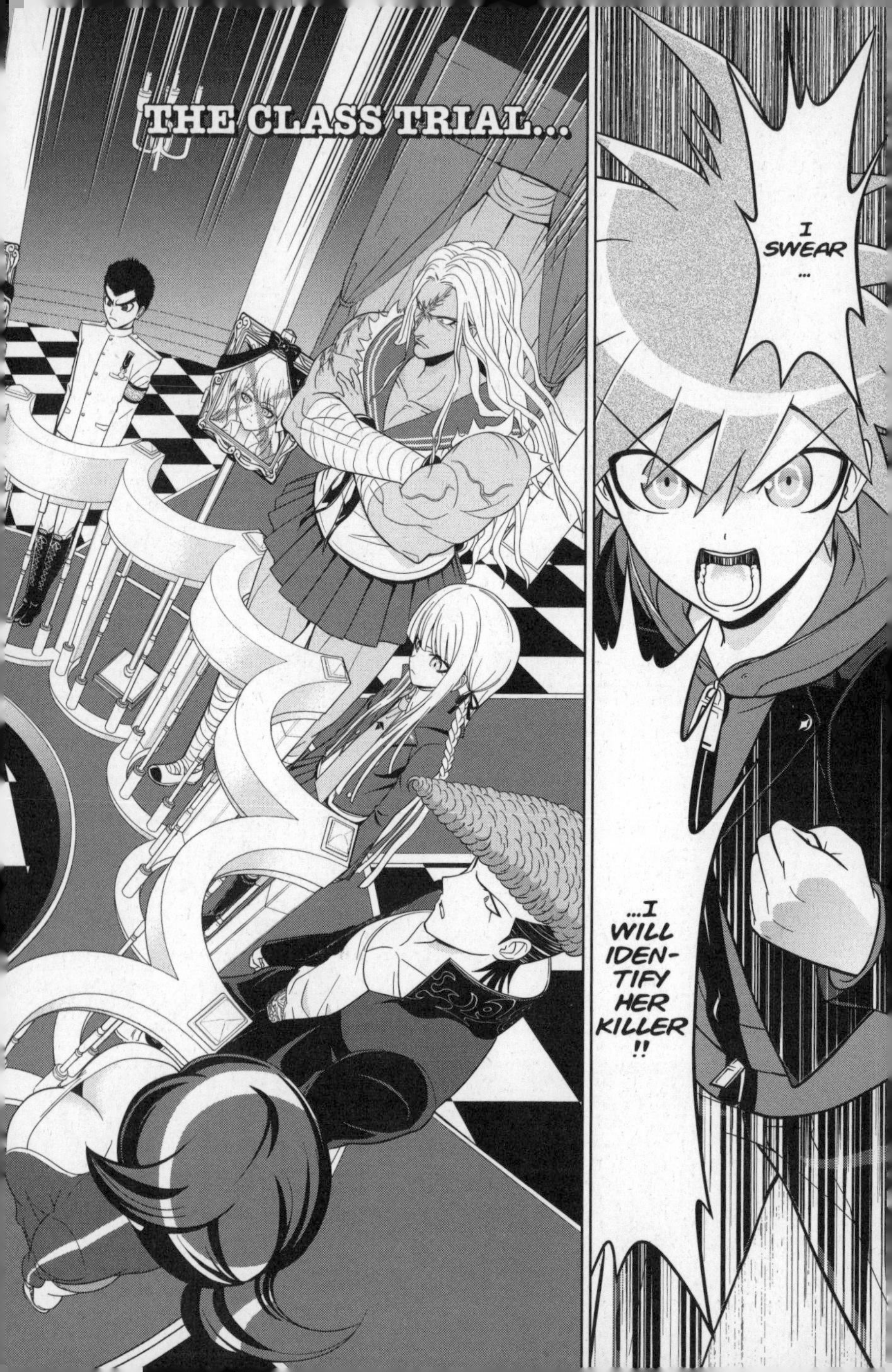
I SWEAR ...
...I WILL IDEN-TIFY HER KILLER !!
THE CLASS TRIAL...

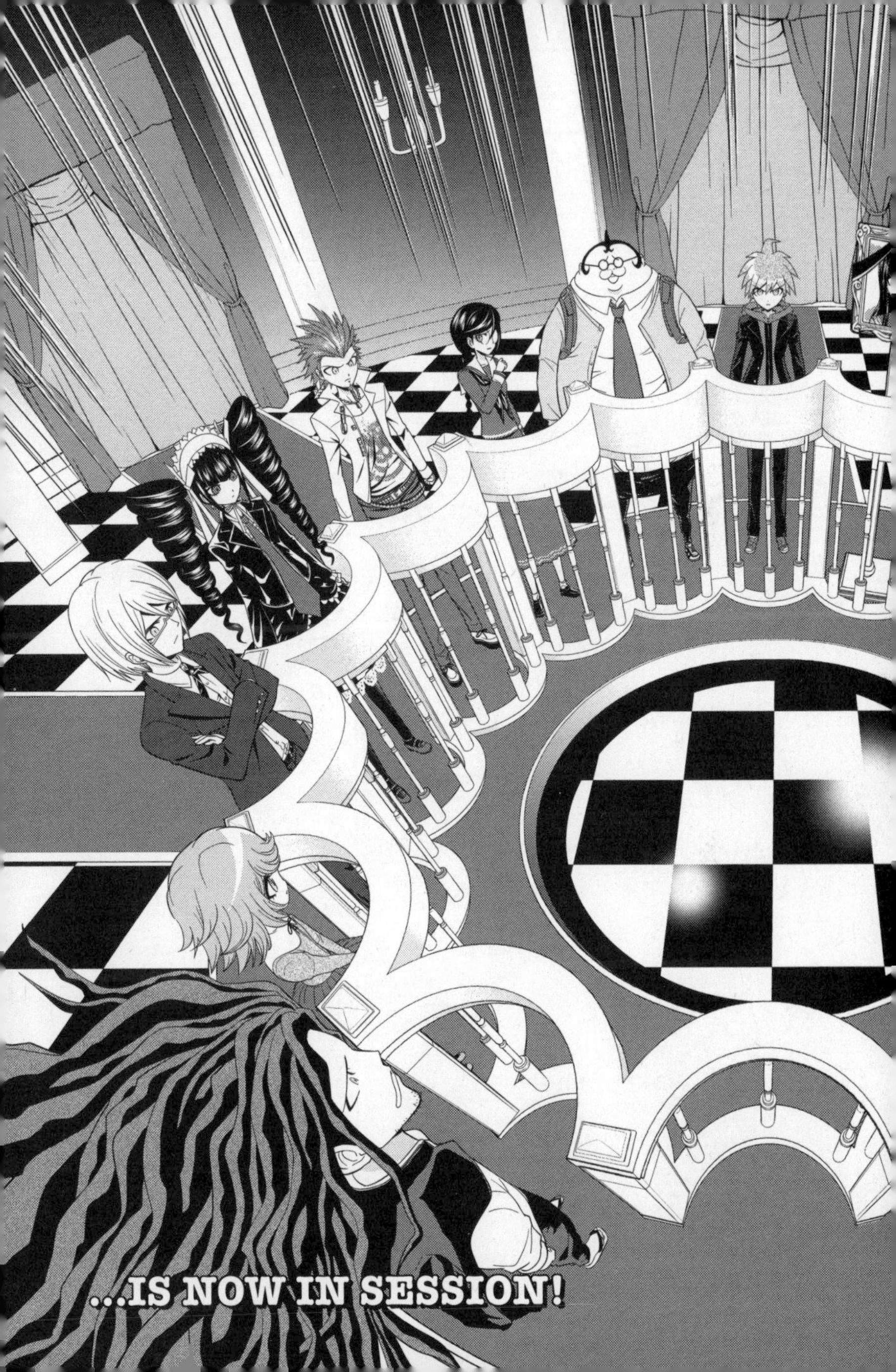
...IS NOW IN SESSION!

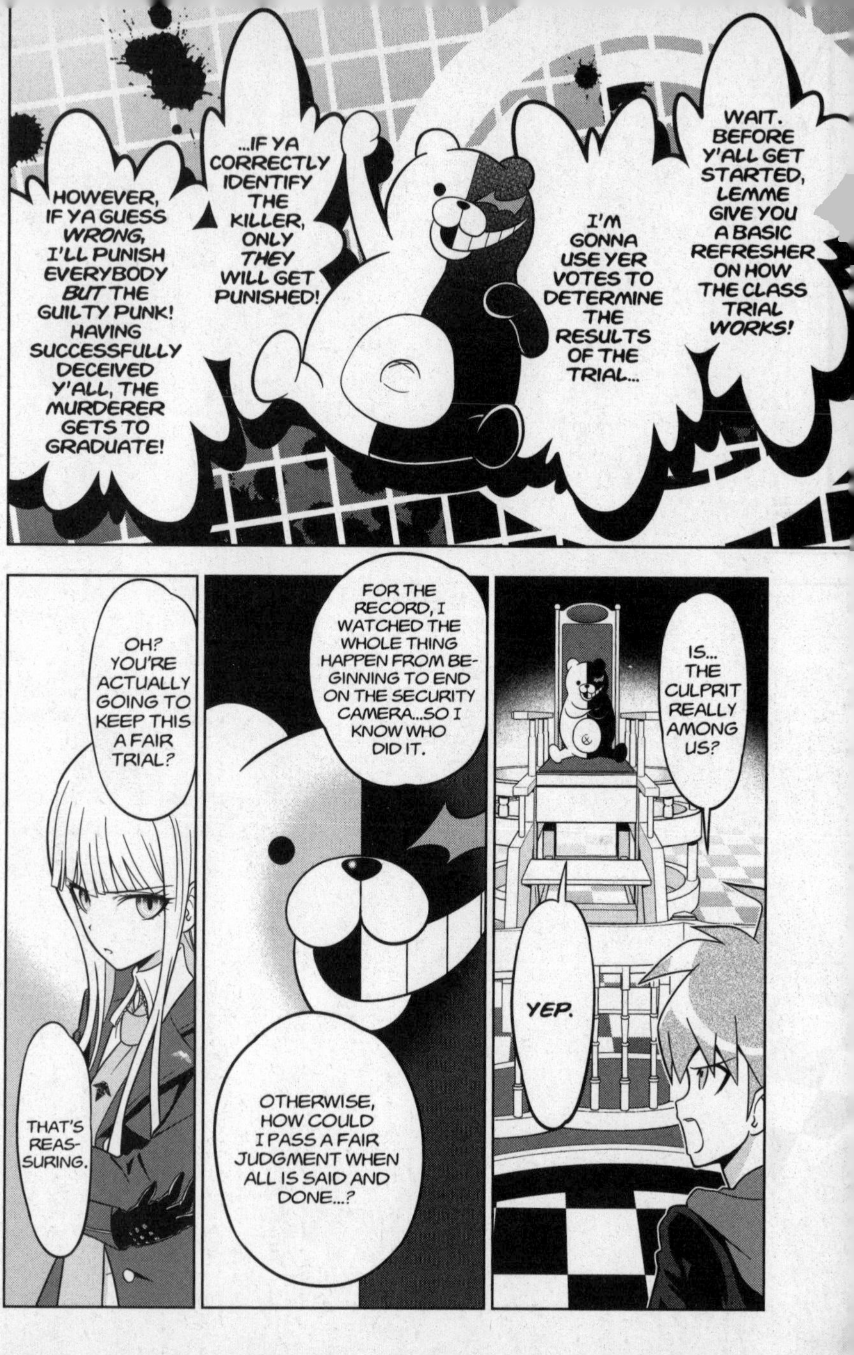
WAIT. BEFORE Y'ALL GET STARTED, LEMME GIVE YOU A BASIC REFRESHER ON HOW THE CLASS TRIAL WORKS!
I'M GONNA USE YER VOTES TO DETERMINE THE RESULTS OF THE TRIAL...
...IF YA CORRECTLY IDENTIFY THE KILLER, ONLY *THEY* WILL GET PUNISHED!
HOWEVER, IF YA GUESS *WRONG*, I'LL PUNISH EVERYBODY *BUT* THE GUILTY PUNK! HAVING SUCCESSFULLY DECEIVED Y'ALL, THE MURDERER GETS TO GRADUATE!
IS... THE CULPRIT REALLY AMONG US?
YEP.
FOR THE RECORD, I WATCHED THE WHOLE THING HAPPEN FROM BEGINNING TO END ON THE SECURITY CAMERA...SO I KNOW WHO DID IT.
OTHERWISE, HOW COULD I PASS A FAIR JUDGMENT WHEN ALL IS SAID AND DONE...?
OH? YOU'RE ACTUALLY GOING TO KEEP THIS A FAIR TRIAL?
THAT'S REASSURING.

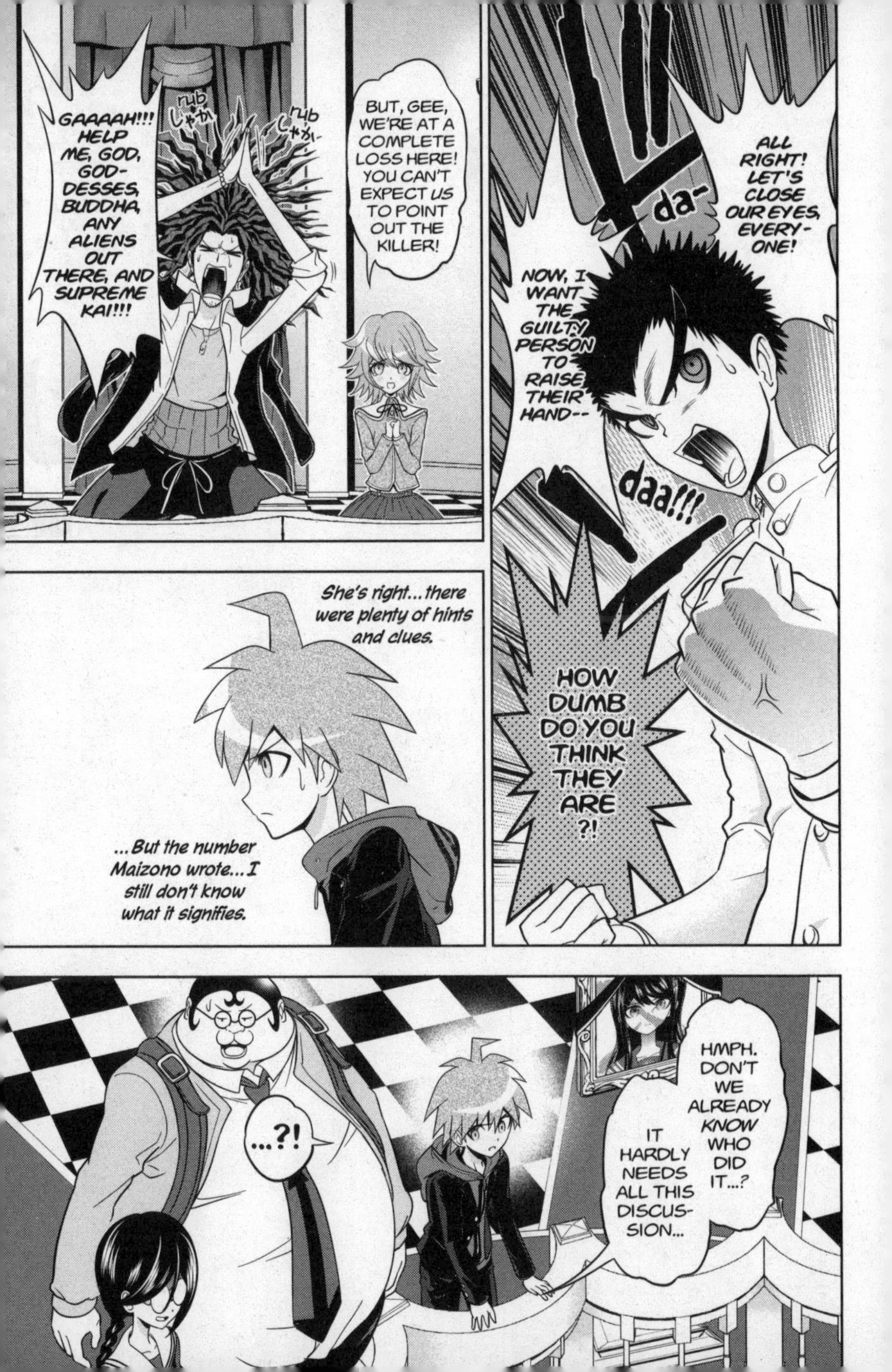
ALL RIGHT! LET'S CLOSE OUR EYES, EVERY-ONE!
da-
NOW, I WANT THE GUILTY PERSON TO RAISE THEIR HAND--
daa!!!
HOW DUMB DO YOU THINK THEY ARE?!
BUT, GEE, WE'RE AT A COMPLETE LOSS HERE! YOU CAN'T EXPECT US TO POINT OUT THE KILLER!
rub
rub
GAAAAH!!! HELP ME, GOD, GOD-DESSES, BUDDHA, ANY ALIENS OUT THERE, AND SUPREME KAI!!!
She's right... there were plenty of hints and clues.
...But the number Maizono wrote... I still don't know what it signifies.
HMPH. DON'T WE ALREADY KNOW WHO DID IT...?
IT HARDLY NEEDS ALL THIS DISCUS-SION...
...?!

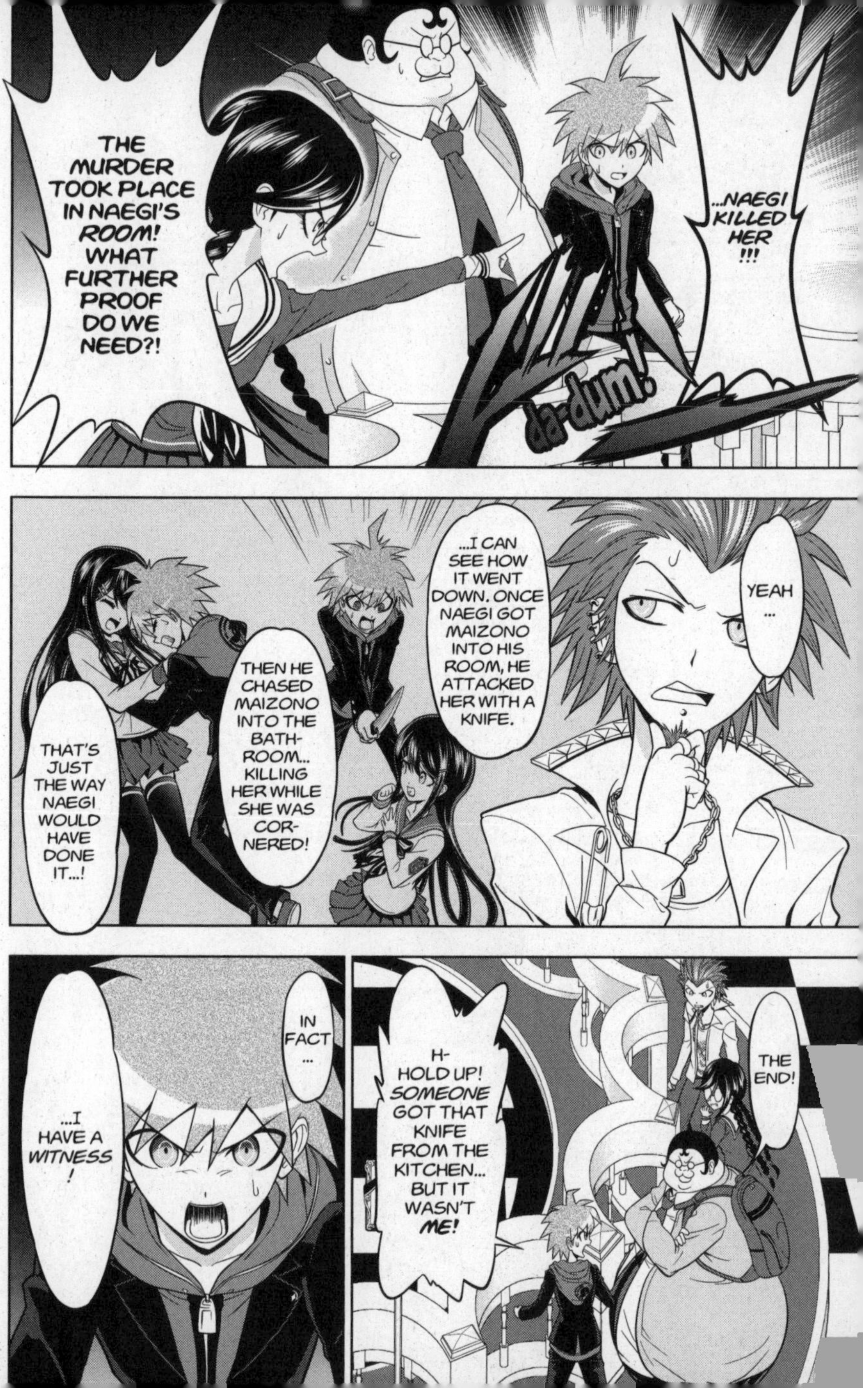
...NAEGI KILLED HER !!!
THE MURDER TOOK PLACE IN NAEGI'S ROOM! WHAT FURTHER PROOF DO WE NEED?!
da-dum!
YEAH ...
...I CAN SEE HOW IT WENT DOWN. ONCE NAEGI GOT MAIZONO INTO HIS ROOM, HE ATTACKED HER WITH A KNIFE.
THEN HE CHASED MAIZONO INTO THE BATH-ROOM... KILLING HER WHILE SHE WAS COR-NERED!
THAT'S JUST THE WAY NAEGI WOULD HAVE DONE IT...!
THE END!
H- HOLD UP! SOMEONE GOT THAT KNIFE FROM THE KITCHEN... BUT IT WASN'T ME!
IN FACT ...
...I HAVE A WITNESS !

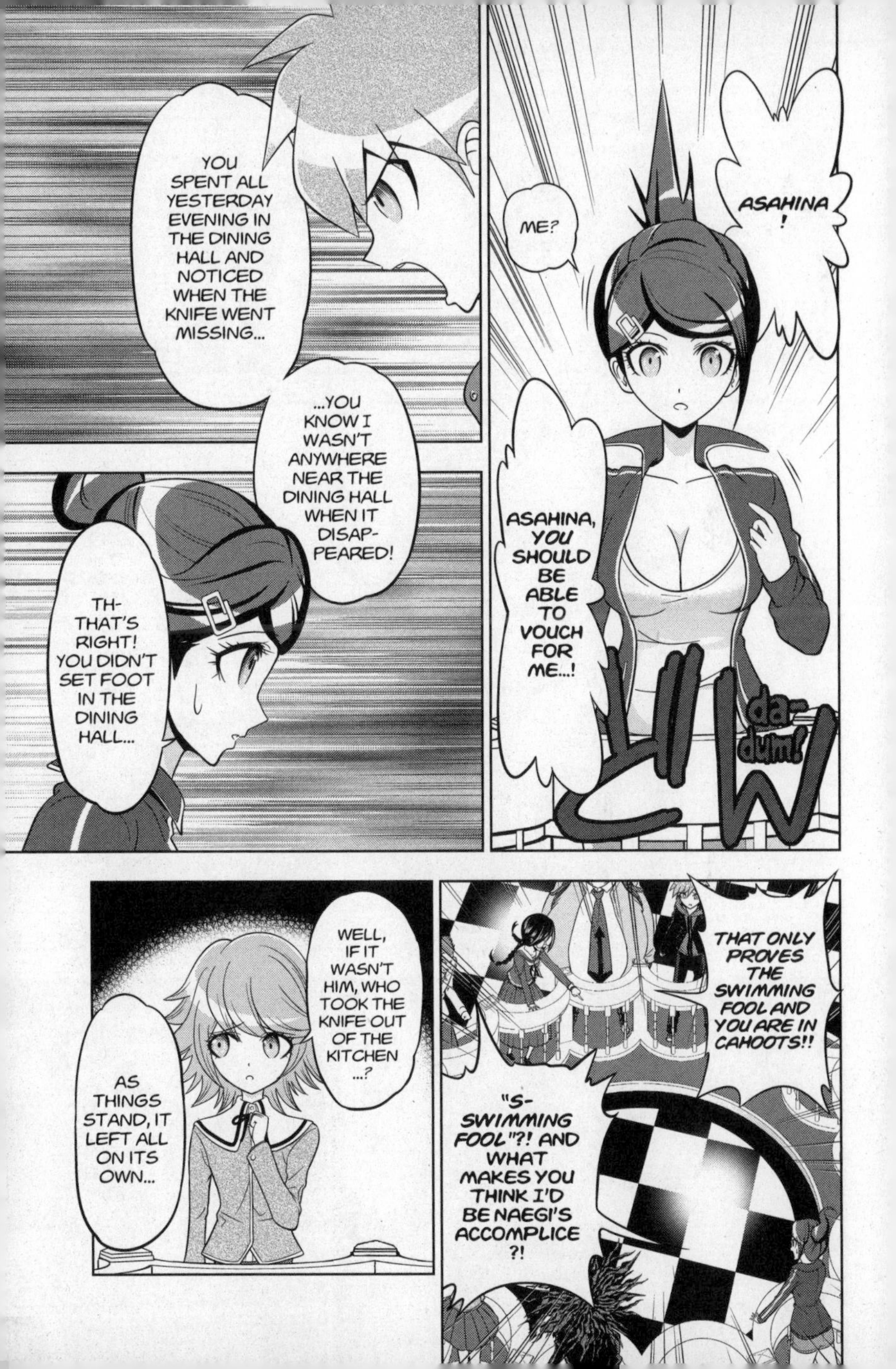
ASAHINA!
ME?
ASAHINA, YOU SHOULD BE ABLE TO VOUCH FOR ME...!
da-dum!
YOU SPENT ALL YESTERDAY EVENING IN THE DINING HALL AND NOTICED WHEN THE KNIFE WENT MISSING...
...YOU KNOW I WASN'T ANYWHERE NEAR THE DINING HALL WHEN IT DISAP-PEARED!
TH-THAT'S RIGHT! YOU DIDN'T SET FOOT IN THE DINING HALL...
THAT ONLY PROVES THE SWIMMING FOOL AND YOU ARE IN CAHOOTS!!
"S-SWIMMING FOOL"?! AND WHAT MAKES YOU THINK I'D BE NAEGI'S ACCOMPLICE?!
WELL, IF IT WASN'T HIM, WHO TOOK THE KNIFE OUT OF THE KITCHEN...?
AS THINGS STAND, IT LEFT ALL ON ITS OWN...

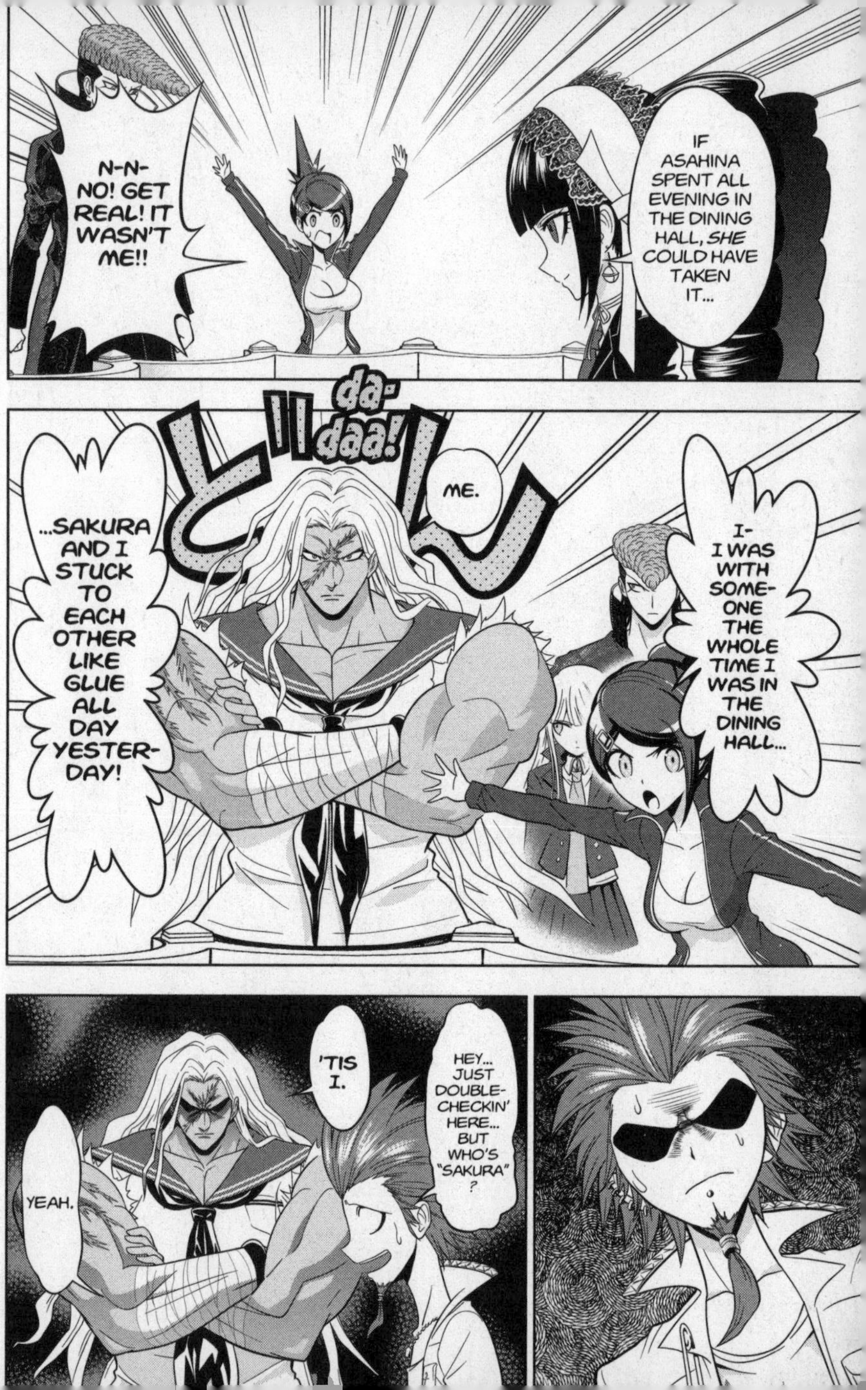
IF ASAHINA SPENT ALL EVENING IN THE DINING HALL, *SHE* COULD HAVE TAKEN IT...
N-N-NO! GET REAL! IT WASN'T ME!!
I- I WAS WITH SOMEONE THE WHOLE TIME I WAS IN THE DINING HALL...
da-daa!
ME.
...SAKURA AND I STUCK TO EACH OTHER LIKE GLUE ALL DAY YESTERDAY!
HEY... JUST DOUBLE-CHECKIN' HERE... BUT WHO'S "SAKURA"?
'TIS I.
YEAH.

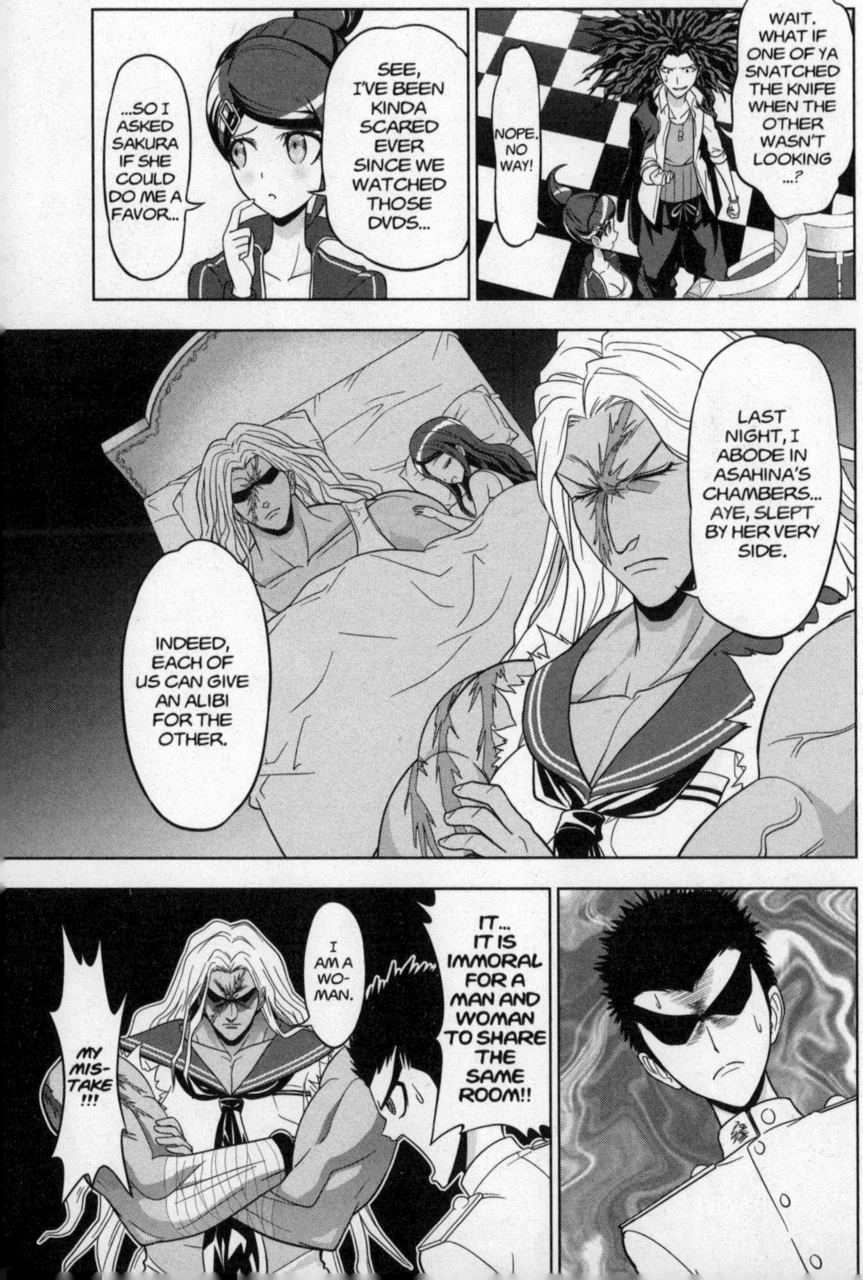
WAIT. WHAT IF ONE OF YA SNATCHED THE KNIFE WHEN THE OTHER WASN'T LOOKING ...?
NOPE. NO WAY!
SEE, I'VE BEEN KINDA SCARED EVER SINCE WE WATCHED THOSE DVDS...
...SO I ASKED SAKURA IF SHE COULD DO ME A FAVOR...
LAST NIGHT, I ABODE IN ASAHINA'S CHAMBERS... AYE, SLEPT BY HER VERY SIDE.
INDEED, EACH OF US CAN GIVE AN ALIBI FOR THE OTHER.
IT... IT IS IMMORAL FOR A MAN AND WOMAN TO SHARE THE SAME ROOM!!
I AM A WO-MAN.
MY MIS-TAKE!!!

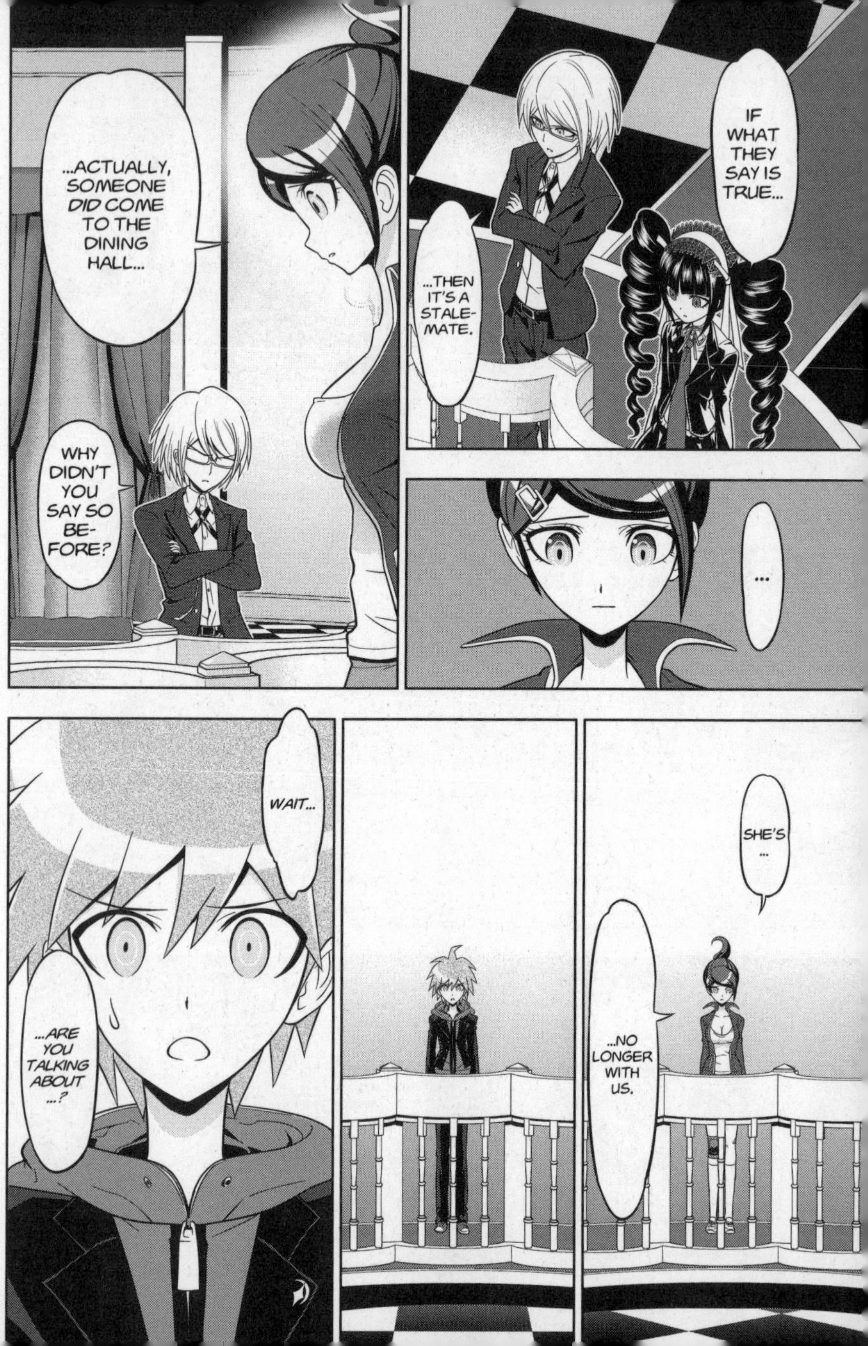
IF WHAT THEY SAY IS TRUE...
...THEN IT'S A STALEMATE.
...
...ACTUALLY, SOMEONE DID COME TO THE DINING HALL...
WHY DIDN'T YOU SAY SO BE-FORE?
SHE'S ...
...NO LONGER WITH US.
WAIT...
...ARE YOU TALKING ABOUT ...?

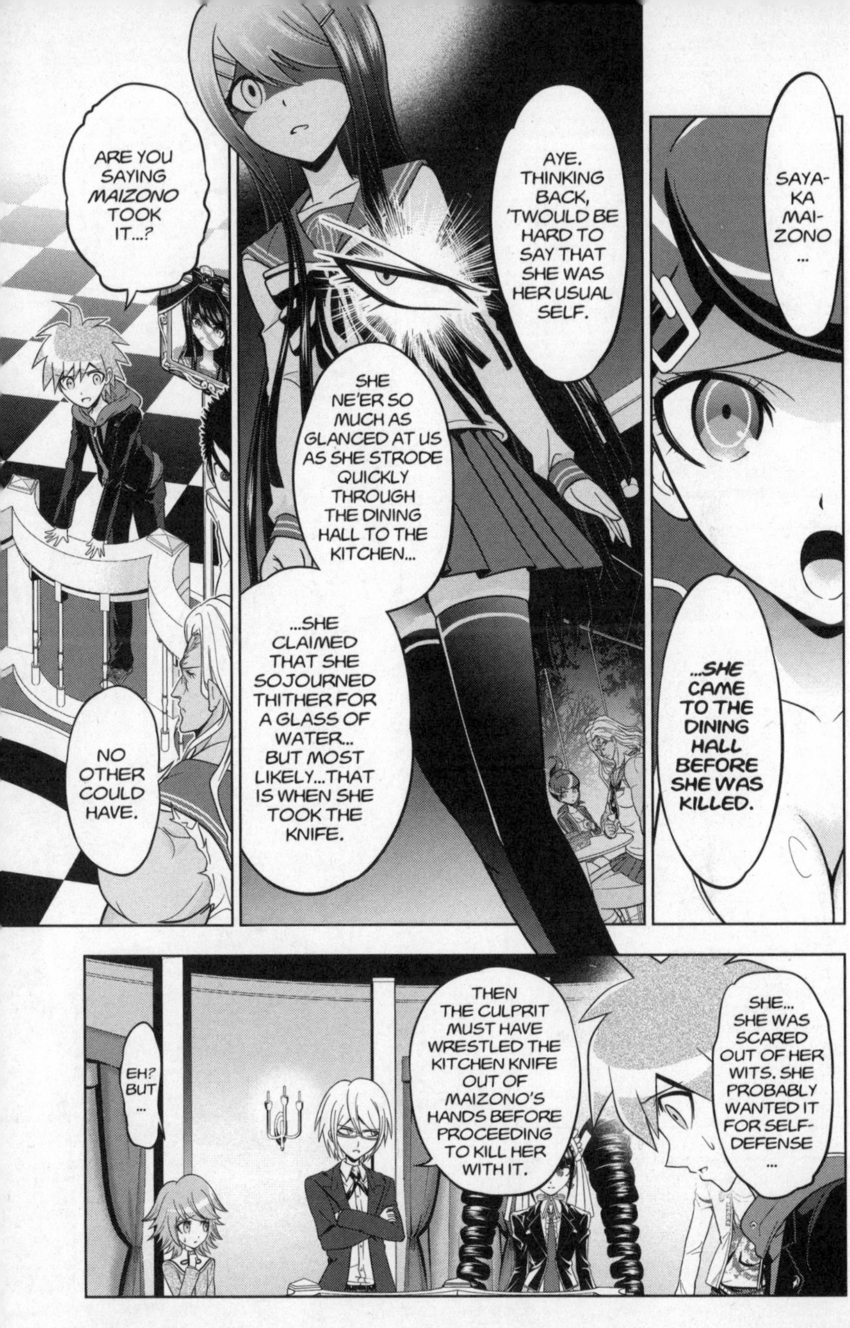
SAYAKA MAIZONO ...
...SHE CAME TO THE DINING HALL BEFORE SHE WAS KILLED.
AYE. THINKING BACK, 'TWOULD BE HARD TO SAY THAT SHE WAS HER USUAL SELF.
SHE NE'ER SO MUCH AS GLANCED AT US AS SHE STRODE QUICKLY THROUGH THE DINING HALL TO THE KITCHEN...
...SHE CLAIMED THAT SHE SOJOURNED THITHER FOR A GLASS OF WATER... BUT MOST LIKELY...THAT IS WHEN SHE TOOK THE KNIFE.
ARE YOU SAYING MAIZONO TOOK IT...?
NO OTHER COULD HAVE.
SHE... SHE WAS SCARED OUT OF HER WITS. SHE PROBABLY WANTED IT FOR SELF-DEFENSE ...
THEN THE CULPRIT MUST HAVE WRESTLED THE KITCHEN KNIFE OUT OF MAIZONO'S HANDS BEFORE PROCEEDING TO KILL HER WITH IT.
EH? BUT ...

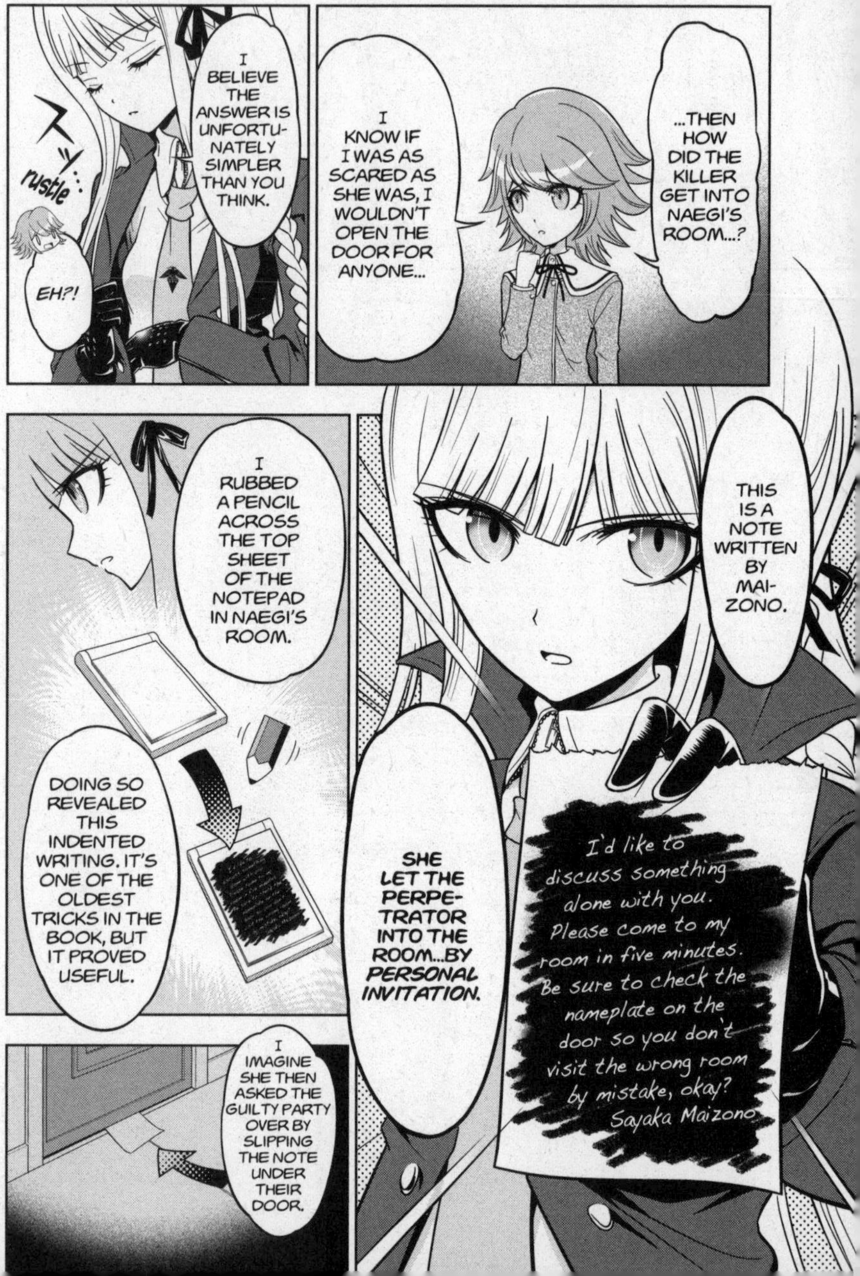
...THEN HOW DID THE KILLER GET INTO NAEGI'S ROOM...?
I KNOW IF I WAS AS SCARED AS SHE WAS, I WOULDN'T OPEN THE DOOR FOR ANYONE...
I BELIEVE THE ANSWER IS UNFORTUNATELY SIMPLER THAN YOU THINK.
スッ
rustle
EH?!
THIS IS A NOTE WRITTEN BY MAIZONO.
SHE LET THE PERPETRATOR INTO THE ROOM...BY PERSONAL INVITATION.
I'd like to discuss something alone with you. Please come to my room in five minutes. Be sure to check the nameplate on the door so you don't visit the wrong room by mistake, okay?
Sayaka Maizono
I RUBBED A PENCIL ACROSS THE TOP SHEET OF THE NOTEPAD IN NAEGI'S ROOM.
DOING SO REVEALED THIS INDENTED WRITING. IT'S ONE OF THE OLDEST TRICKS IN THE BOOK, BUT IT PROVED USEFUL.
I IMAGINE SHE THEN ASKED THE GUILTY PARTY OVER BY SLIPPING THE NOTE UNDER THEIR DOOR.

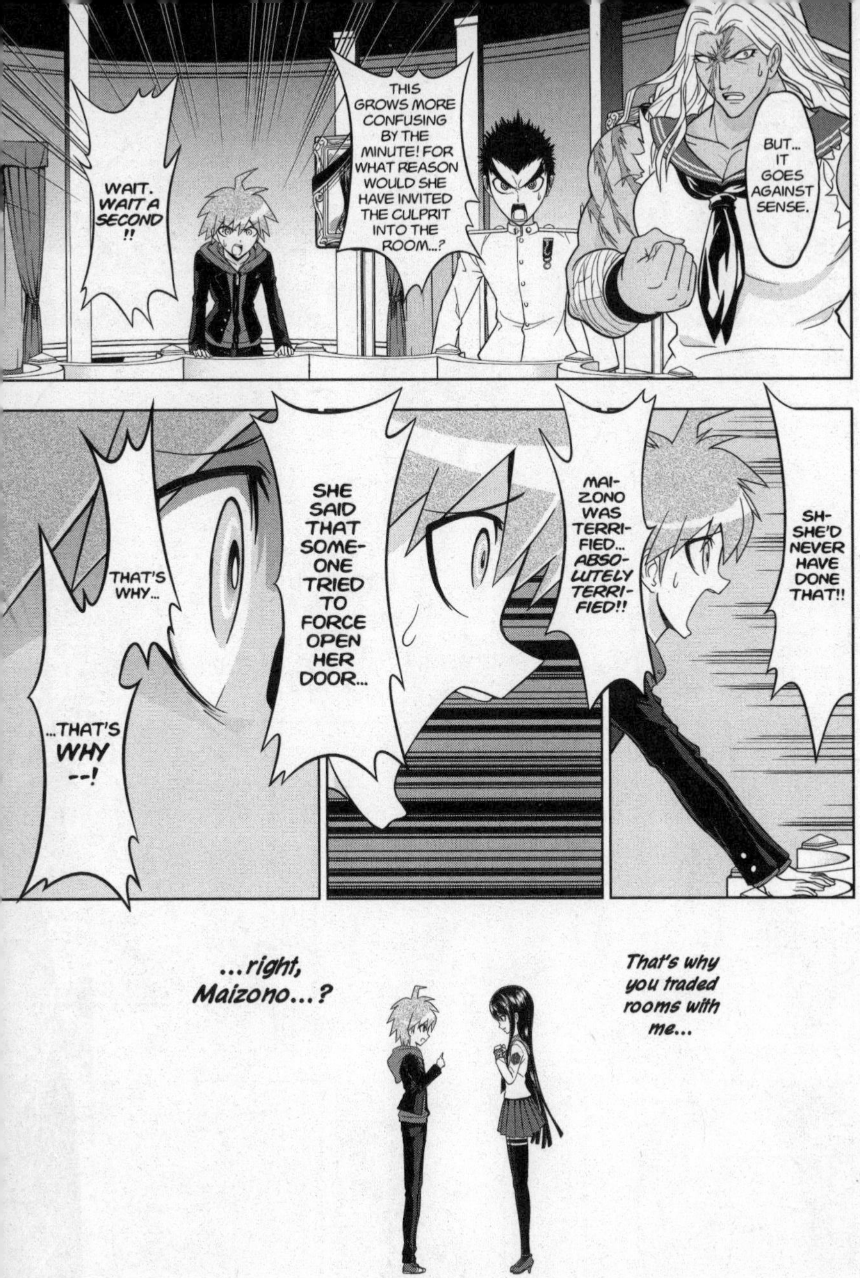
BUT... IT GOES AGAINST SENSE.
THIS GROWS MORE CONFUSING BY THE MINUTE! FOR WHAT REASON WOULD SHE HAVE INVITED THE CULPRIT INTO THE ROOM...?
WAIT. WAIT A SECOND!!
SH-SHE'D NEVER HAVE DONE THAT!!
MAI-ZONO WAS TERRI-FIED... ABSO-LUTELY TERRI-FIED!!
SHE SAID THAT SOME-ONE TRIED TO FORCE OPEN HER DOOR...
THAT'S WHY...
...THAT'S WHY --!
That's why you traded rooms with me...
...right, Maizono...?

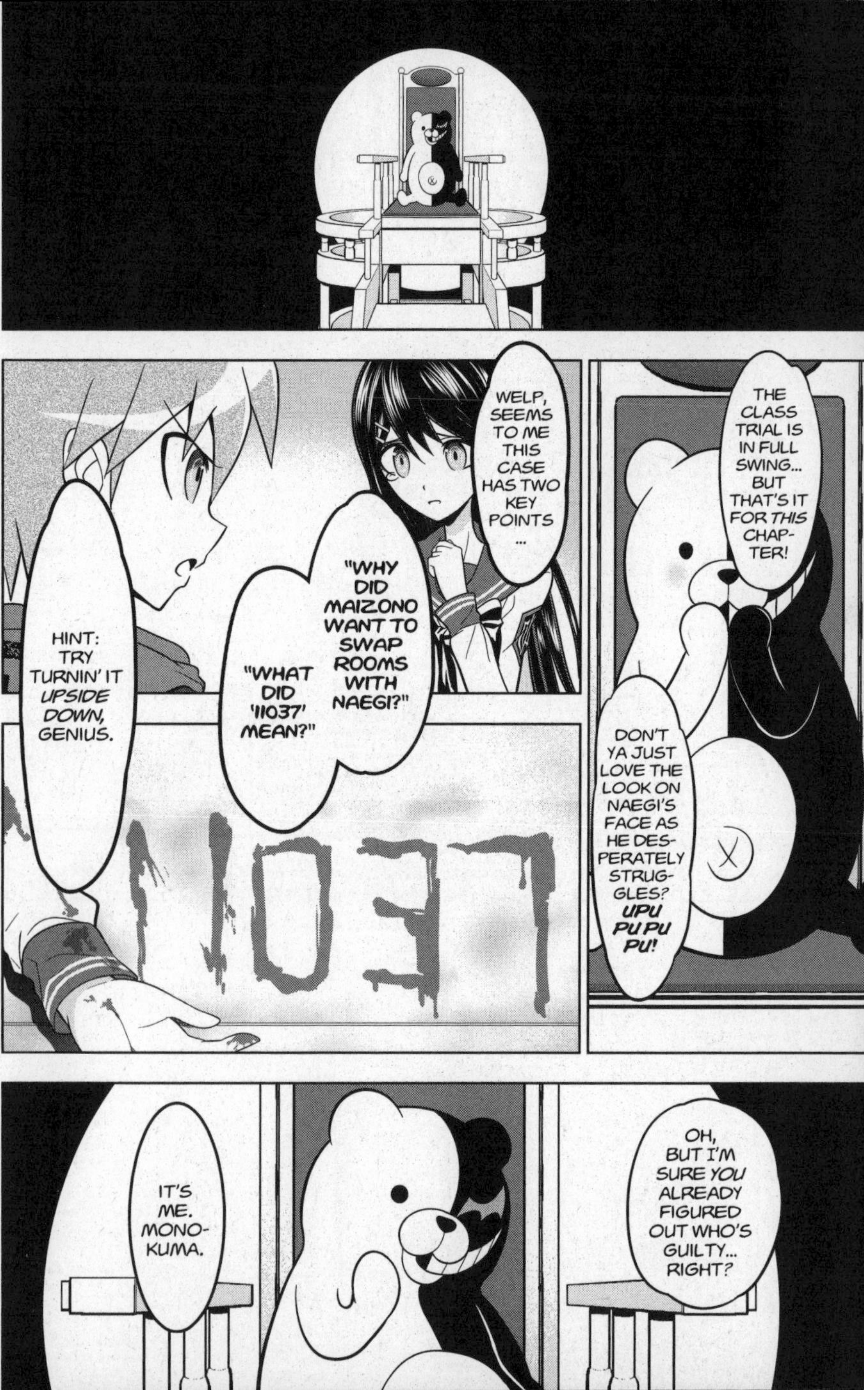

THE CLASS TRIAL IS IN FULL SWING... BUT THAT'S IT FOR *THIS* CHAPTER!
DON'T YA JUST LOVE THE LOOK ON NAEGI'S FACE AS HE DESPERATELY STRUGGLES? ***UPU PU PU PU!***
WELP, SEEMS TO ME THIS CASE HAS TWO KEY POINTS ...
"WHY DID MAIZONO WANT TO SWAP ROOMS WITH NAEGI?"
"WHAT DID '11037' MEAN?"
HINT: TRY TURNIN' IT *UPSIDE DOWN*, GENIUS.
OH, BUT I'M SURE *YOU* ALREADY FIGURED OUT WHO'S GUILTY... RIGHT?
IT'S ME. MONOKUMA.

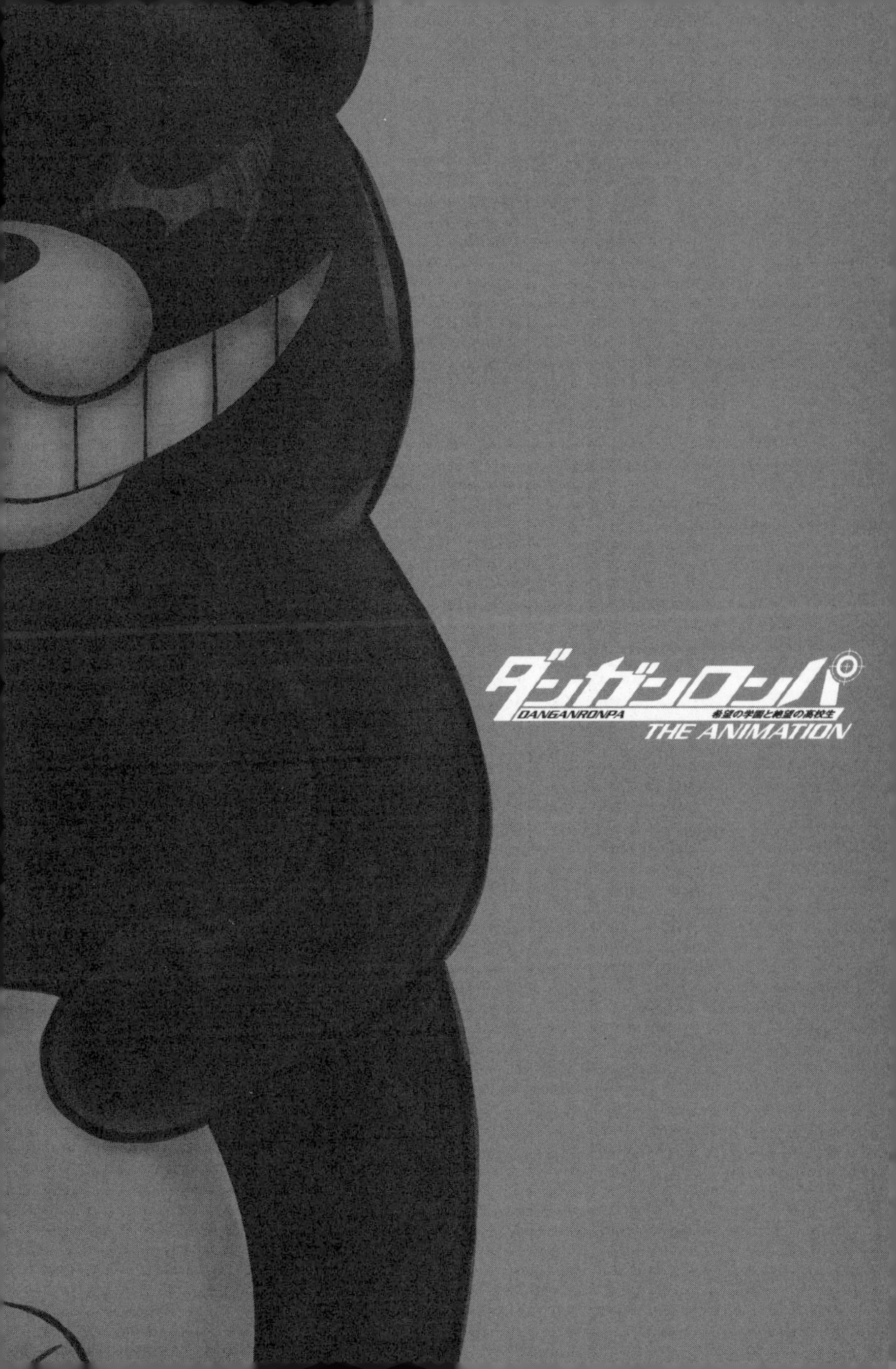
ダンガンロンパ
DANGANRONPA
希望の学園と絶望の高校生
THE ANIMATION

DANGANRONPA
A SCHOOL OF HOPE . . . WITH STUDENTS OF DESPAIR!
THE ANIMATION

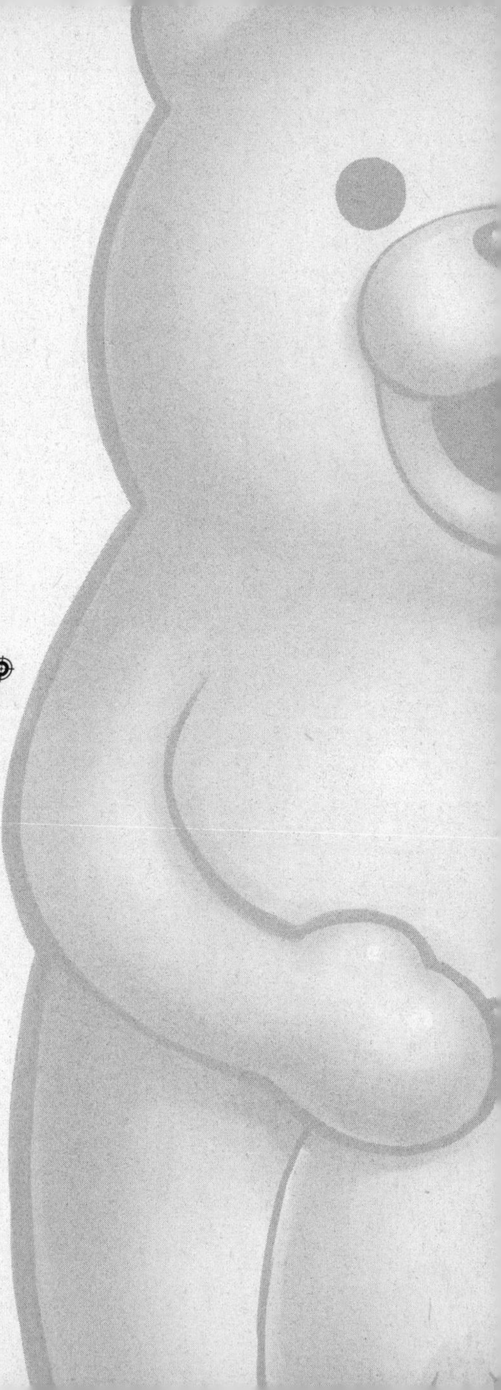

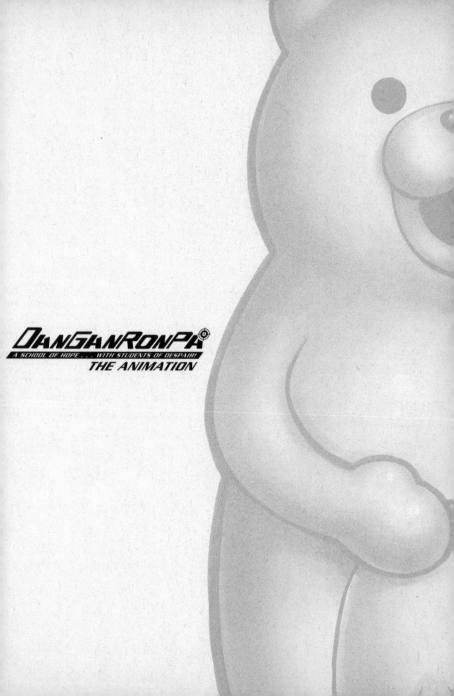

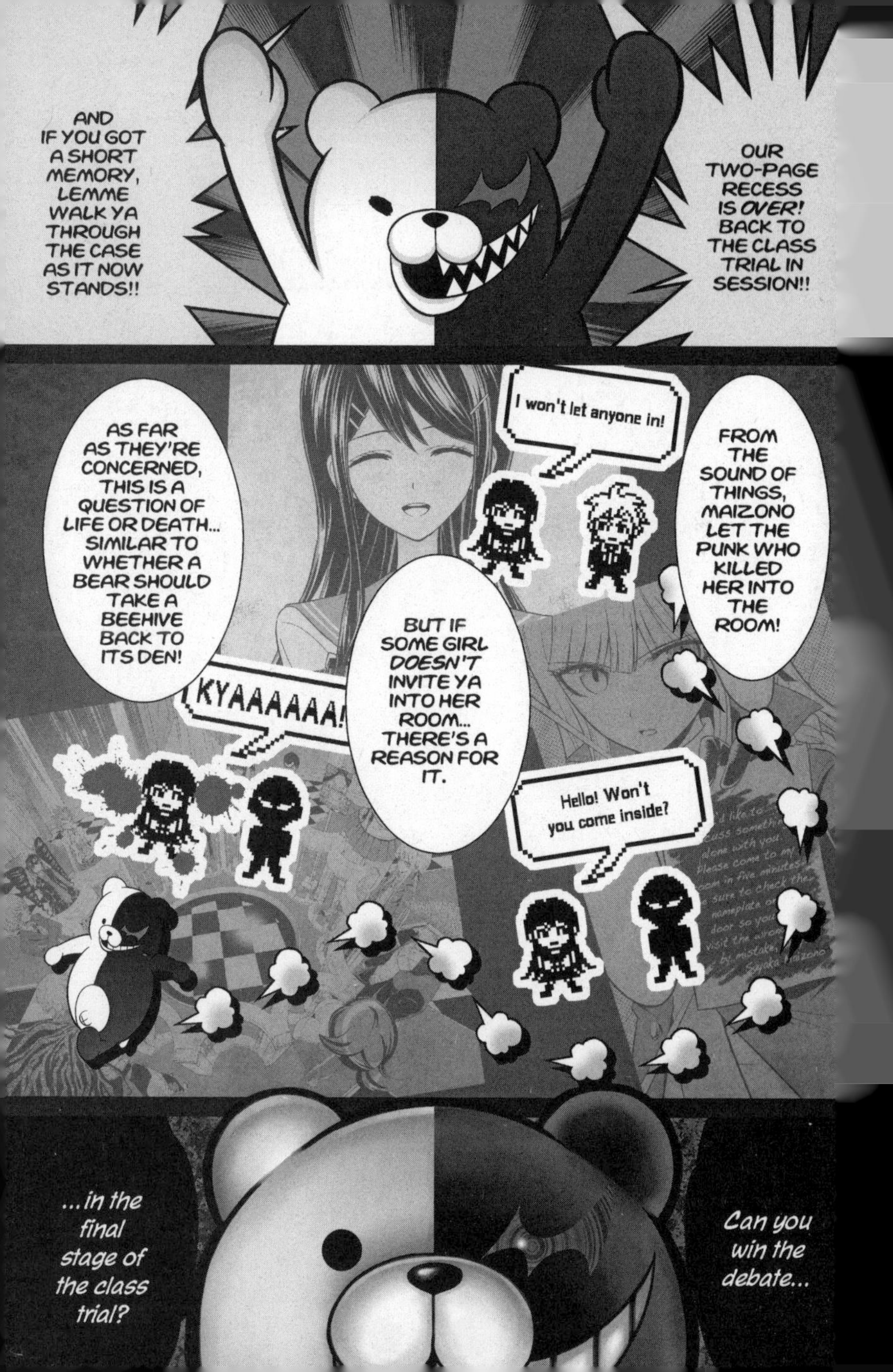
OUR TWO-PAGE RECESS IS OVER! BACK TO THE CLASS TRIAL IN SESSION!!
AND IF YOU GOT A SHORT MEMORY, LEMME WALK YA THROUGH THE CASE AS IT NOW STANDS!!
FROM THE SOUND OF THINGS, MAIZONO LET THE PUNK WHO KILLED HER INTO THE ROOM!
I won't let anyone in!
AS FAR AS THEY'RE CONCERNED, THIS IS A QUESTION OF LIFE OR DEATH... SIMILAR TO WHETHER A BEAR SHOULD TAKE A BEEHIVE BACK TO ITS DEN!
BUT IF SOME GIRL DOESN'T INVITE YA INTO HER ROOM... THERE'S A REASON FOR IT.
Hello! Won't you come inside?
KYAAAAAAA!
Can you win the debate...
...in the final stage of the class trial?

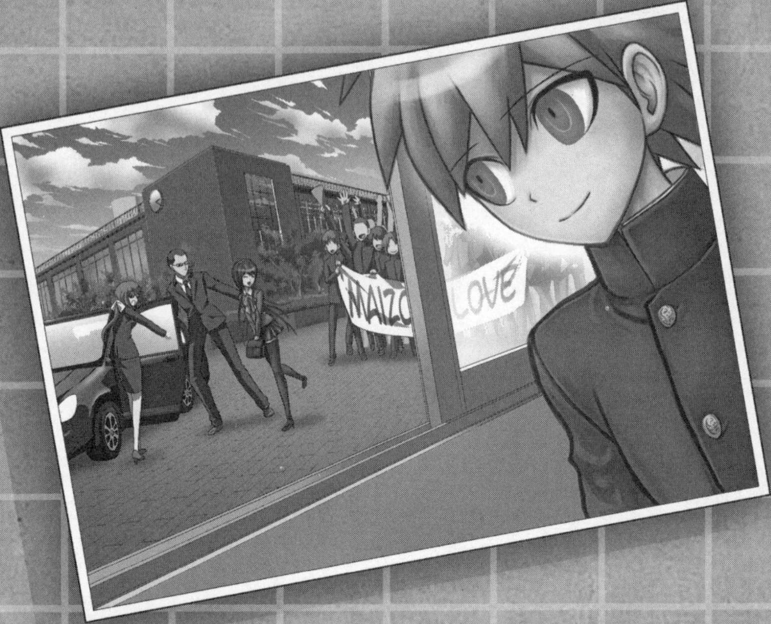
MAIZO
LOVE

#04 [ABNORMAL ARC: KILL AND LIVE TO SURVIVE (DEADLY LIFE) II]

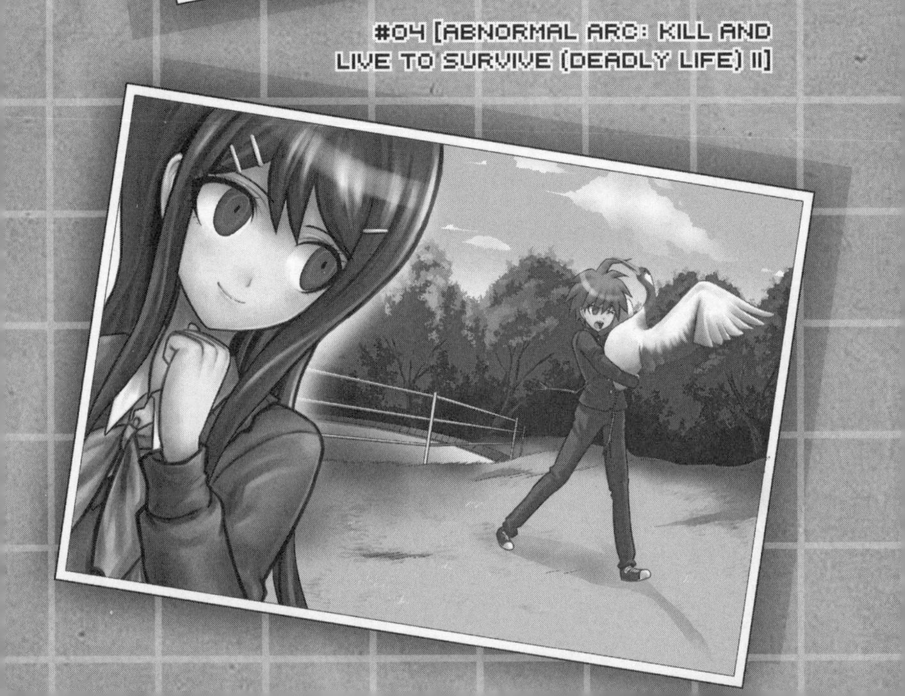

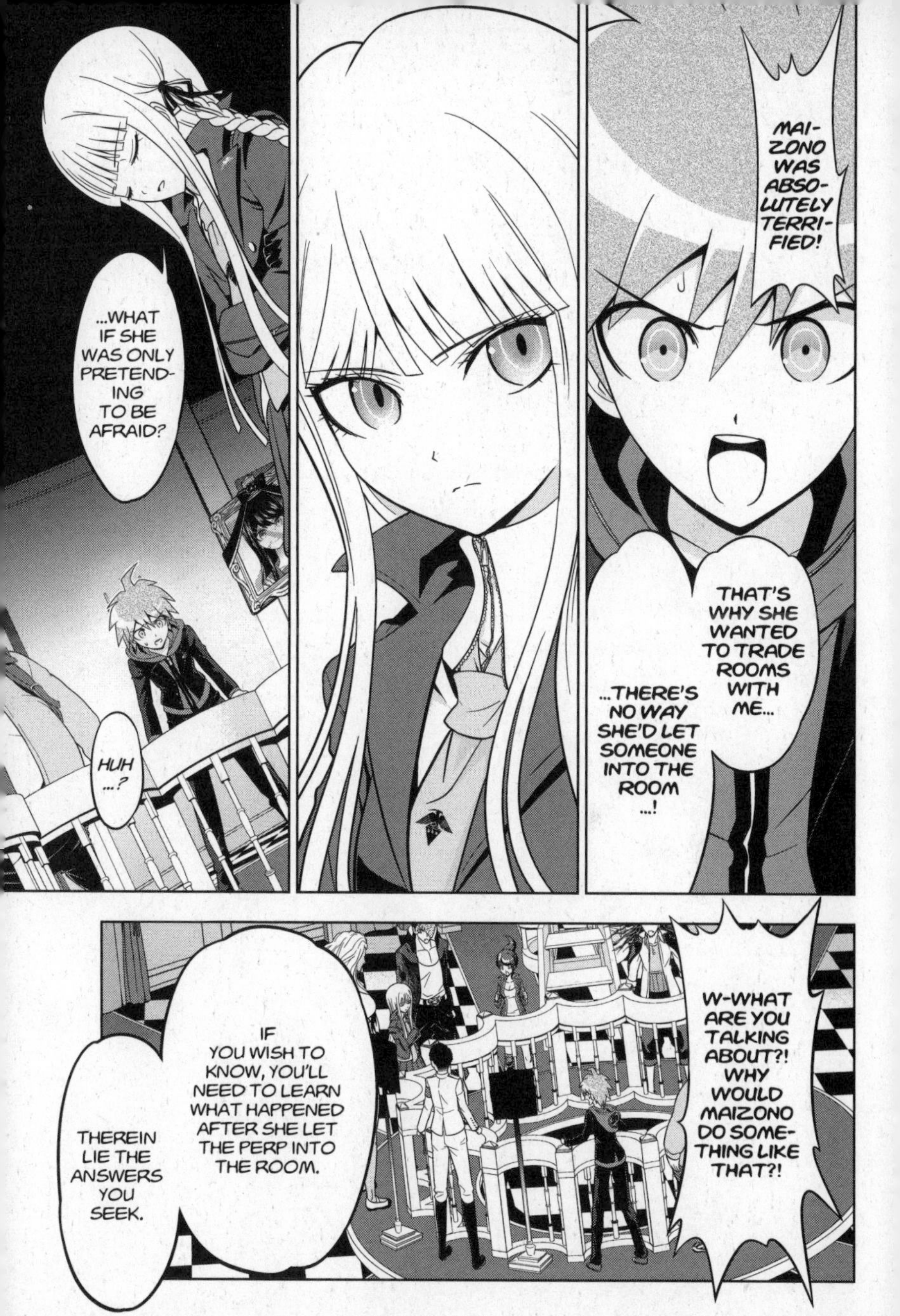
MAIZONO WAS ABSOLUTELY TERRIFIED!
THAT'S WHY SHE WANTED TO TRADE ROOMS WITH ME...
...THERE'S NO WAY SHE'D LET SOMEONE INTO THE ROOM ...!
...WHAT IF SHE WAS ONLY PRETENDING TO BE AFRAID?
HUH ...?
W-WHAT ARE YOU TALKING ABOUT?! WHY WOULD MAIZONO DO SOMETHING LIKE THAT?!
IF YOU WISH TO KNOW, YOU'LL NEED TO LEARN WHAT HAPPENED AFTER SHE LET THE PERP INTO THE ROOM.
THEREIN LIE THE ANSWERS YOU SEEK.

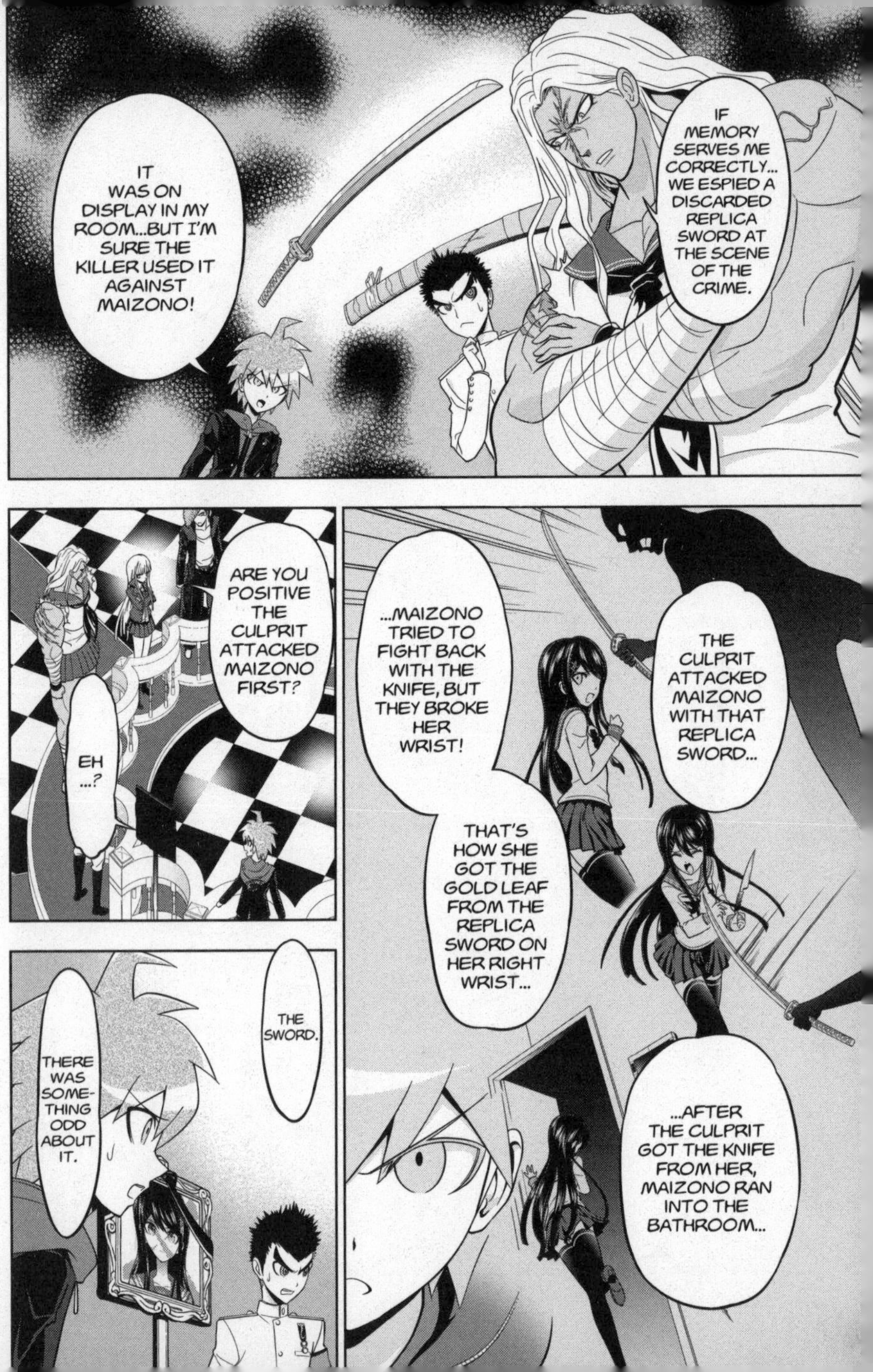
IF MEMORY SERVES ME CORRECTLY... WE ESPIED A DISCARDED REPLICA SWORD AT THE SCENE OF THE CRIME.
IT WAS ON DISPLAY IN MY ROOM...BUT I'M SURE THE KILLER USED IT AGAINST MAIZONO!
THE CULPRIT ATTACKED MAIZONO WITH THAT REPLICA SWORD...
...MAIZONO TRIED TO FIGHT BACK WITH THE KNIFE, BUT THEY BROKE HER WRIST!
THAT'S HOW SHE GOT THE GOLD LEAF FROM THE REPLICA SWORD ON HER RIGHT WRIST...
...AFTER THE CULPRIT GOT THE KNIFE FROM HER, MAIZONO RAN INTO THE BATHROOM...
ARE YOU POSITIVE THE CULPRIT ATTACKED MAIZONO FIRST?
EH ...?
THE SWORD.
THERE WAS SOME-THING ODD ABOUT IT.

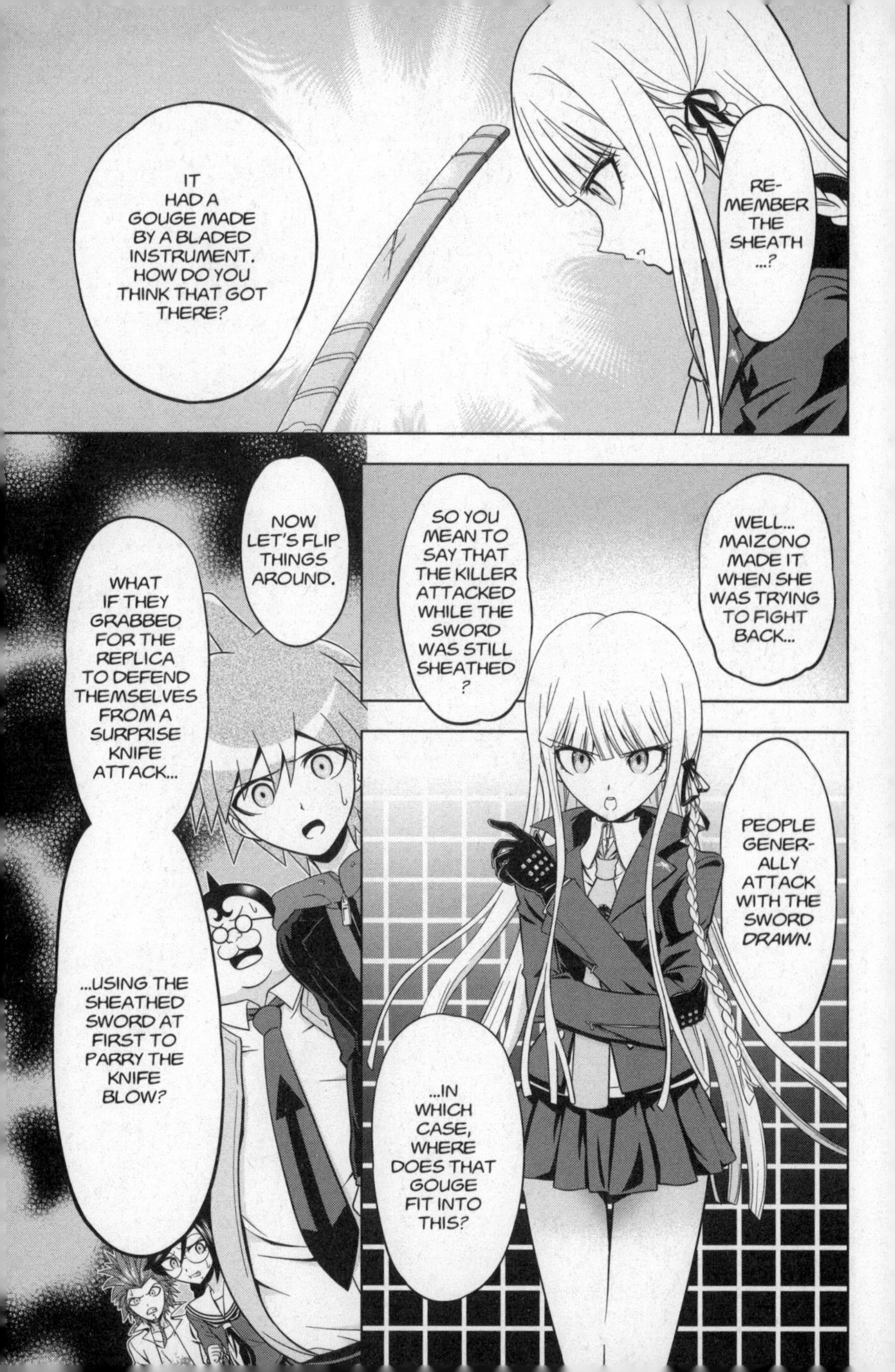
RE-MEMBER THE SHEATH ...?
IT HAD A GOUGE MADE BY A BLADED INSTRUMENT. HOW DO YOU THINK THAT GOT THERE?
WELL... MAIZONO MADE IT WHEN SHE WAS TRYING TO FIGHT BACK...
SO YOU MEAN TO SAY THAT THE KILLER ATTACKED WHILE THE SWORD WAS STILL SHEATHED ?
PEOPLE GENER-ALLY ATTACK WITH THE SWORD *DRAWN.*
...IN WHICH CASE, WHERE DOES THAT GOUGE FIT INTO THIS?
NOW LET'S FLIP THINGS AROUND.
WHAT IF THEY GRABBED FOR THE REPLICA TO DEFEND THEMSELVES FROM A SURPRISE KNIFE ATTACK...
...USING THE SHEATHED SWORD AT FIRST TO PARRY THE KNIFE BLOW?

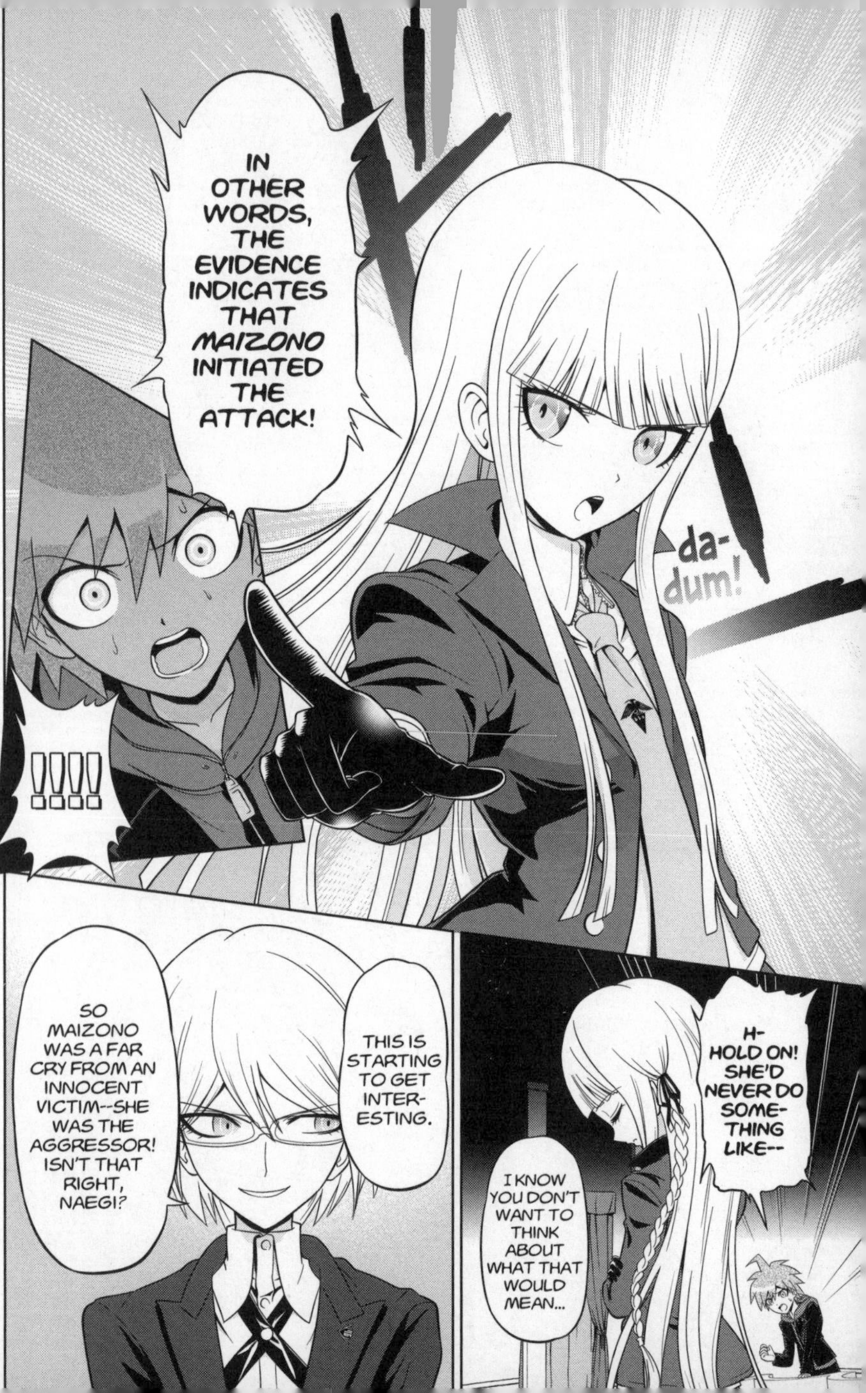
IN OTHER WORDS, THE EVIDENCE INDICATES THAT *MAIZONO* INITIATED THE ATTACK!
da-dum!
!!!!
H-HOLD ON! SHE'D NEVER DO SOME-THING LIKE--
I KNOW YOU DON'T WANT TO THINK ABOUT WHAT THAT WOULD MEAN...
THIS IS STARTING TO GET INTER-ESTING.
SO MAIZONO WAS A FAR CRY FROM AN INNOCENT VICTIM--SHE WAS THE AGGRESSOR! ISN'T THAT RIGHT, NAEGI?

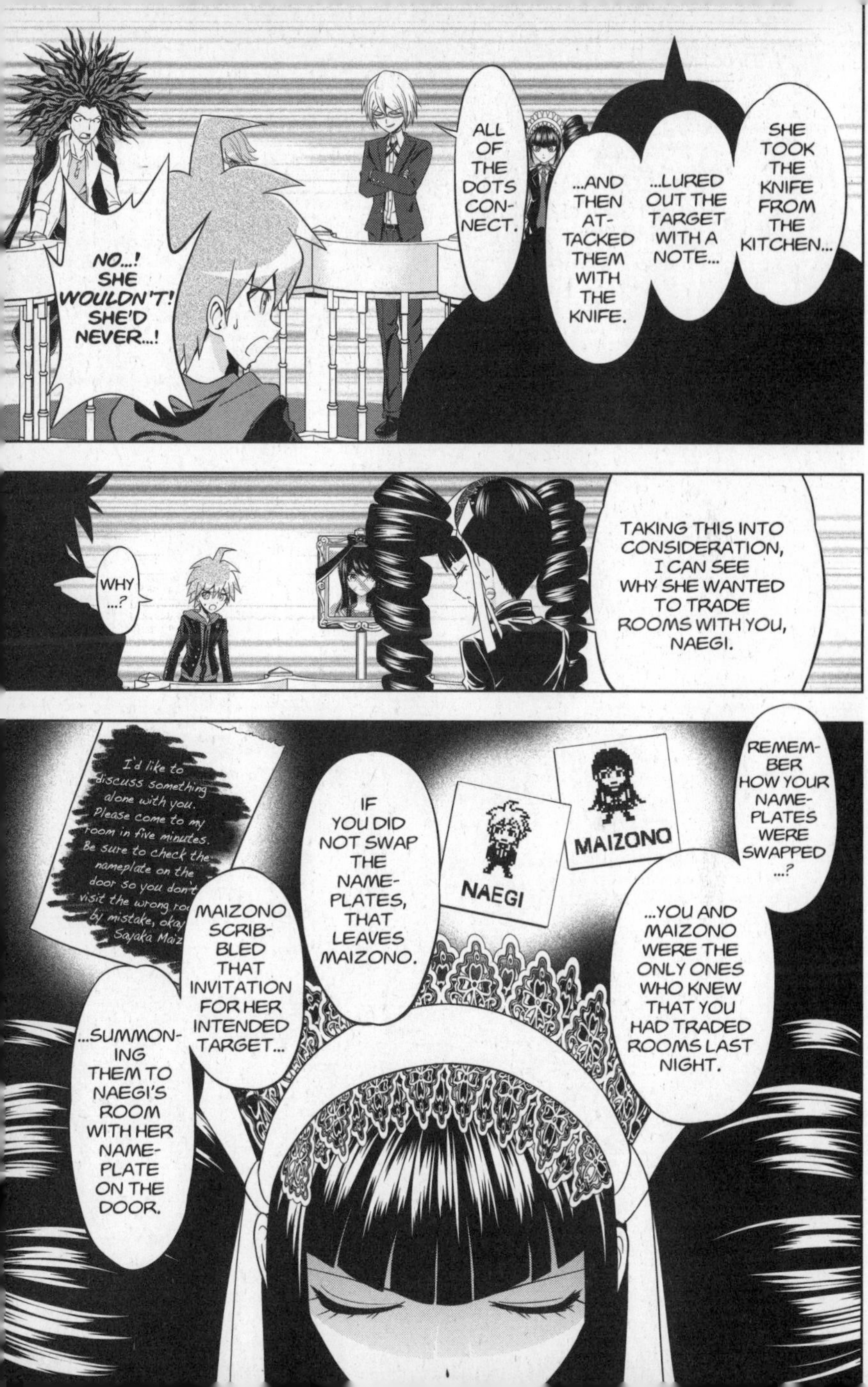
SHE TOOK THE KNIFE FROM THE KITCHEN...
...LURED OUT THE TARGET WITH A NOTE...
...AND THEN ATTACKED THEM WITH THE KNIFE.
ALL OF THE DOTS CONNECT.
NO...! SHE WOULDN'T! SHE'D NEVER...!
TAKING THIS INTO CONSIDERATION, I CAN SEE WHY SHE WANTED TO TRADE ROOMS WITH YOU, NAEGI.
WHY ...?
REMEMBER HOW YOUR NAMEPLATES WERE SWAPPED ...?
MAIZONO
NAEGI
...YOU AND MAIZONO WERE THE ONLY ONES WHO KNEW THAT YOU HAD TRADED ROOMS LAST NIGHT.
IF YOU DID NOT SWAP THE NAMEPLATES, THAT LEAVES MAIZONO.
I'd like to discuss something alone with you. Please come to my room in five minutes. Be sure to check the nameplate on the door so you don't visit the wrong ro by mistake, okay Sayaka Maiz
MAIZONO SCRIBBLED THAT INVITATION FOR HER INTENDED TARGET...
...SUMMONING THEM TO NAEGI'S ROOM WITH HER NAMEPLATE ON THE DOOR.

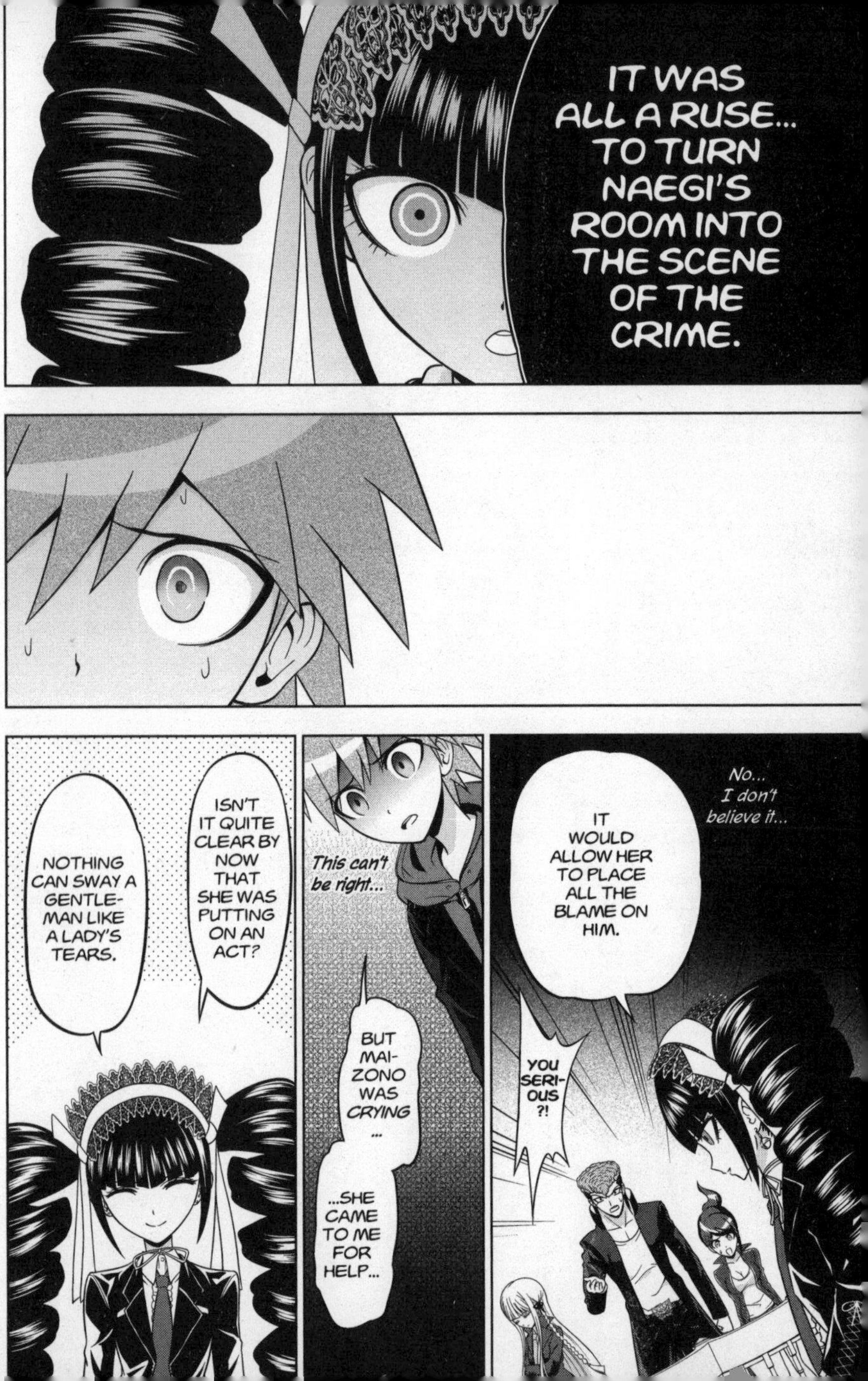
IT WAS ALL A RUSE... TO TURN NAEGI'S ROOM INTO THE SCENE OF THE CRIME.
No... I don't believe it...
IT WOULD ALLOW HER TO PLACE ALL THE BLAME ON HIM.
YOU SERIOUS?!
This can't be right...
BUT MAIZONO WAS CRYING...
...SHE CAME TO ME FOR HELP...
ISN'T IT QUITE CLEAR BY NOW THAT SHE WAS PUTTING ON AN ACT?
NOTHING CAN SWAY A GENTLEMAN LIKE A LADY'S TEARS.

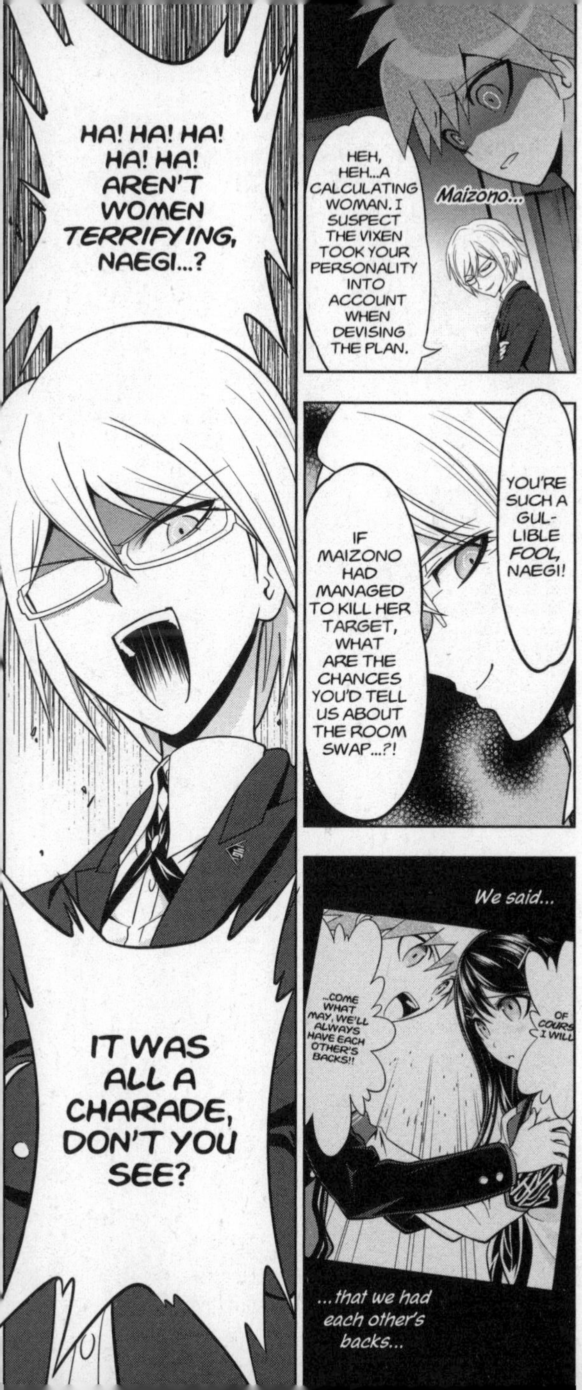
HEH, HEH...A CALCULATING WOMAN. I SUSPECT THE VIXEN TOOK YOUR PERSONALITY INTO ACCOUNT WHEN DEVISING THE PLAN.
Maizono...
YOU'RE SUCH A GUL-LIBLE FOOL, NAEGI!
IF MAIZONO HAD MANAGED TO KILL HER TARGET, WHAT ARE THE CHANCES YOU'D TELL US ABOUT THE ROOM SWAP...?!
We said...
...COME WHAT MAY, WE'LL ALWAYS HAVE EACH OTHER'S BACKS!!
OF COURS I WILL
...that we had each other's backs...
HA! HA! HA! HA! HA! AREN'T WOMEN TERRIFYING, NAEGI...?
IT WAS ALL A CHARADE, DON'T YOU SEE?

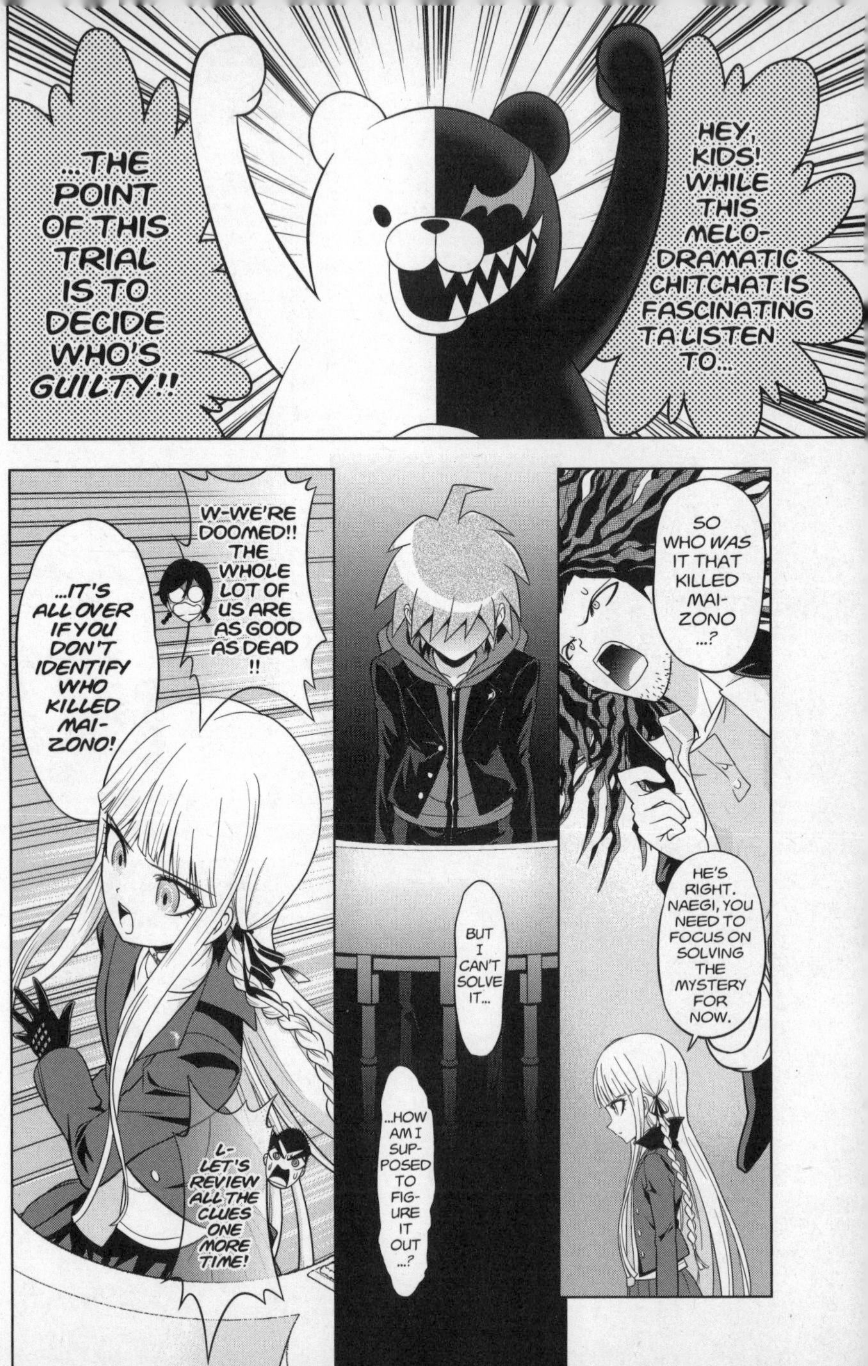
HEY, KIDS! WHILE THIS MELODRAMATIC CHITCHAT IS FASCINATING TA LISTEN TO...
...THE POINT OF THIS TRIAL IS TO DECIDE WHO'S GUILTY!!
SO WHO WAS IT THAT KILLED MAIZONO ...?
HE'S RIGHT. NAEGI, YOU NEED TO FOCUS ON SOLVING THE MYSTERY FOR NOW.
BUT I CAN'T SOLVE IT...
...HOW AM I SUPPOSED TO FIGURE IT OUT ...?
W-WE'RE DOOMED!! THE WHOLE LOT OF US ARE AS GOOD AS DEAD !!
...IT'S ALL OVER IF YOU DON'T IDENTIFY WHO KILLED MAIZONO!
L-LET'S REVIEW ALL THE CLUES ONE MORE TIME!

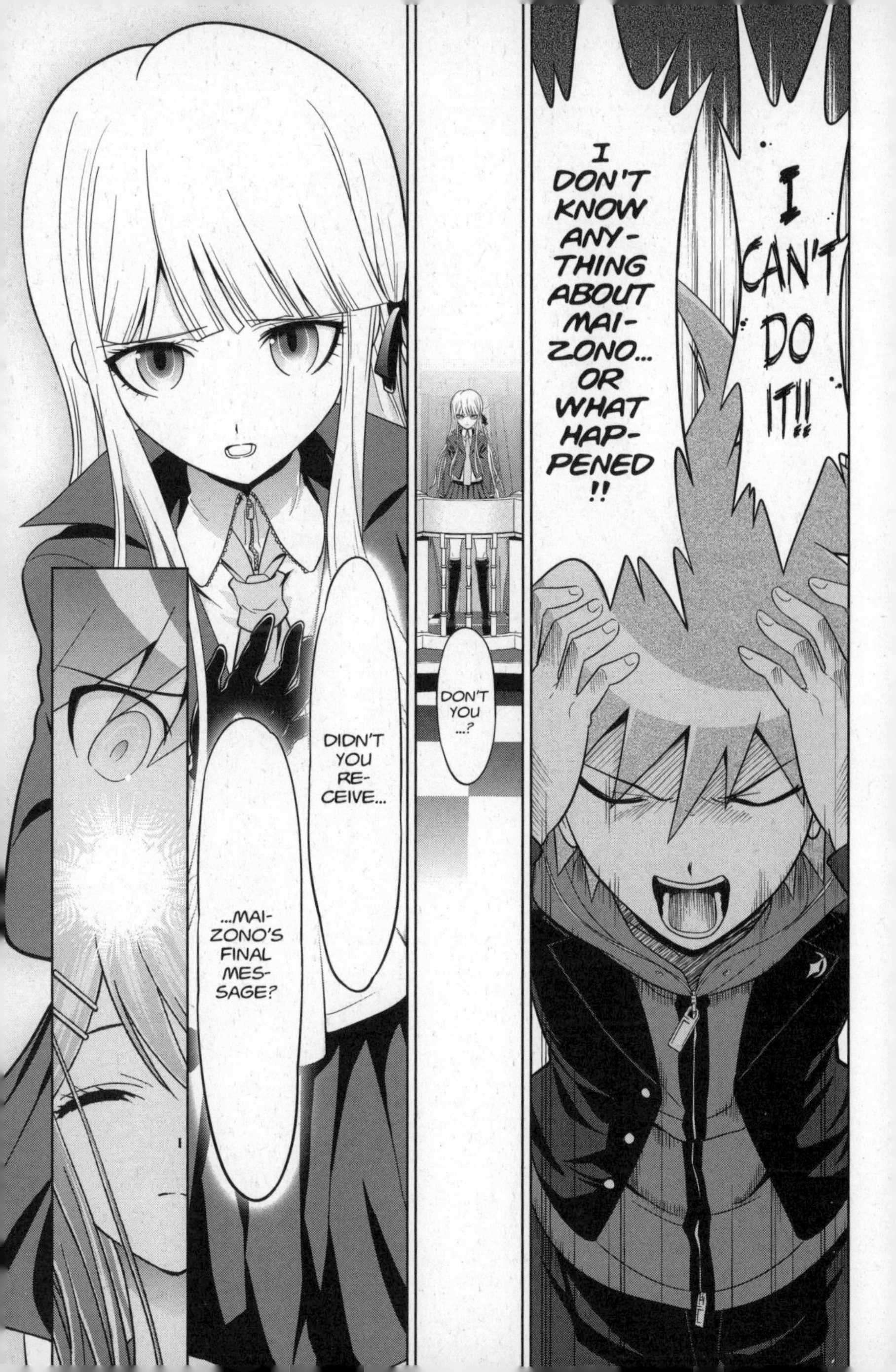
I CAN'T DO IT!!
I DON'T KNOW ANY-THING ABOUT MAI-ZONO... OR WHAT HAP-PENED!!
DON'T YOU ...?
DIDN'T YOU RE-CEIVE...
...MAI-ZONO'S FINAL MES-SAGE?

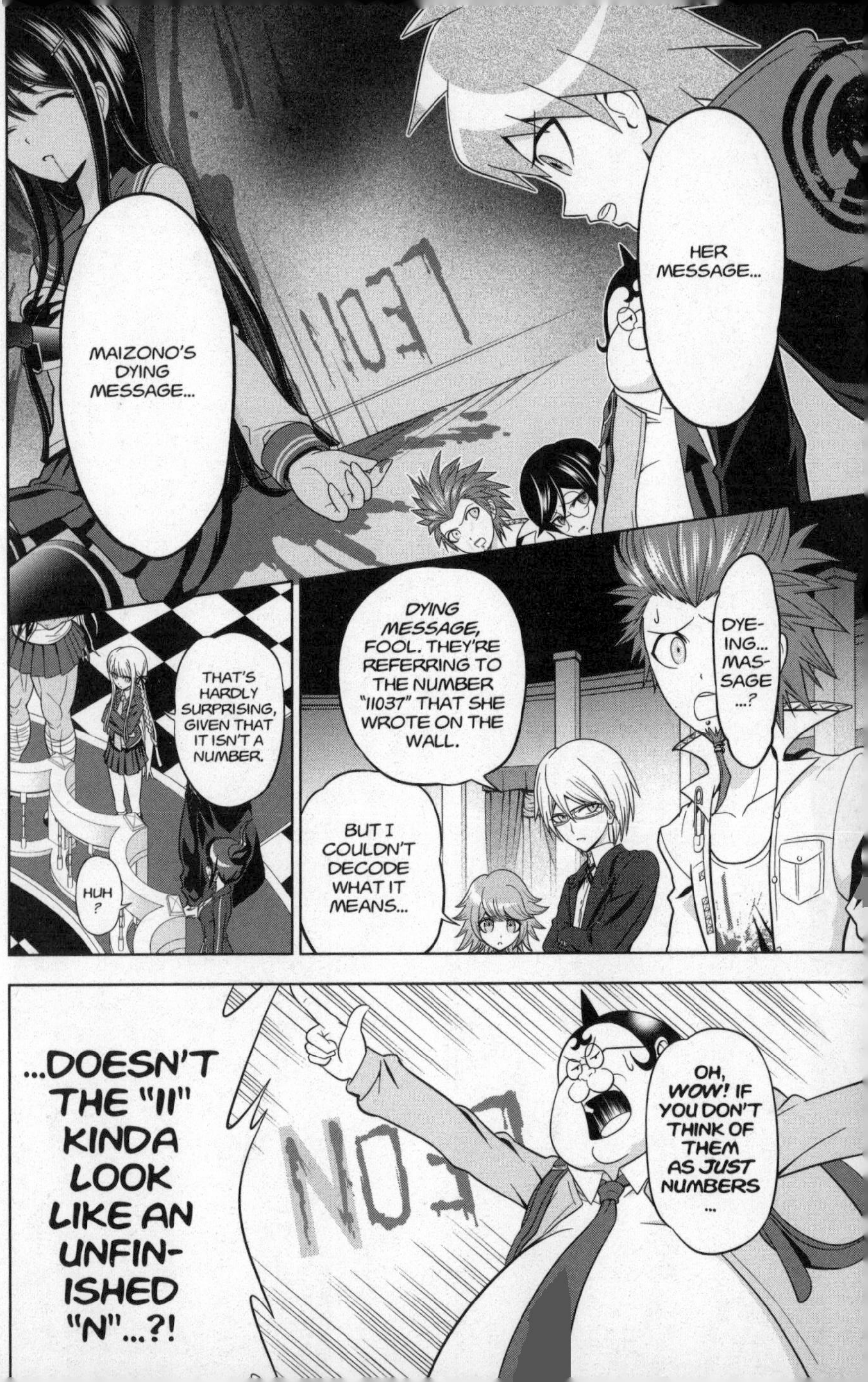
HER MESSAGE...
MAIZONO'S DYING MESSAGE...
DYE-ING... MAS-SAGE ...?
DYING MESSAGE, FOOL. THEY'RE REFERRING TO THE NUMBER "11037" THAT SHE WROTE ON THE WALL.
BUT I COULDN'T DECODE WHAT IT MEANS...
THAT'S HARDLY SURPRISING, GIVEN THAT IT ISN'T A NUMBER.
HUH?
OH, WOW! IF YOU DON'T THINK OF THEM AS JUST NUMBERS...
...DOESN'T THE "II" KINDA LOOK LIKE AN UNFIN-ISHED "N"...?!

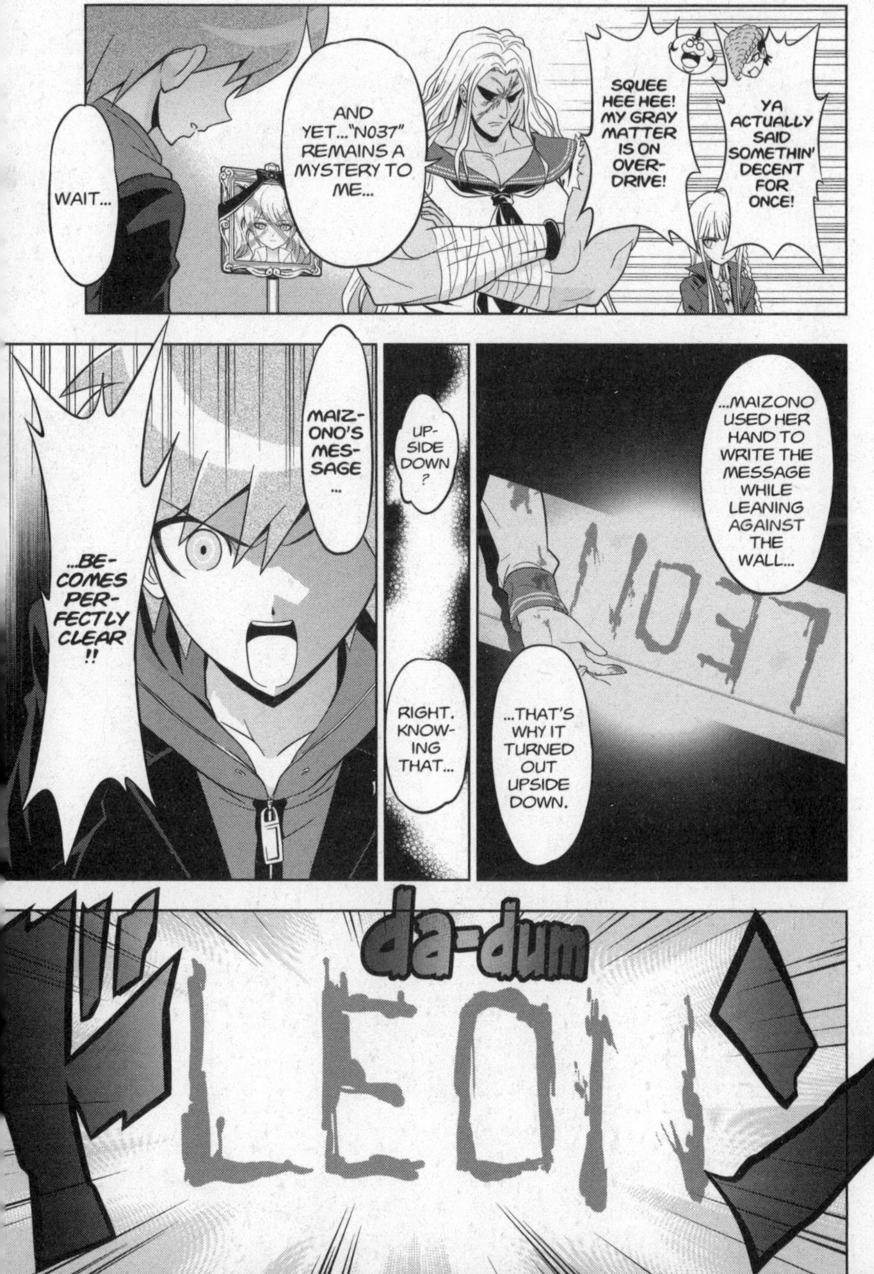
YA ACTUALLY SAID SOMETHIN' DECENT FOR ONCE!
SQUEE HEE HEE! MY GRAY MATTER IS ON OVER-DRIVE!
AND YET..."N037" REMAINS A MYSTERY TO ME...
WAIT...
...MAIZONO USED HER HAND TO WRITE THE MESSAGE WHILE LEANING AGAINST THE WALL...
...THAT'S WHY IT TURNED OUT UPSIDE DOWN.
UP-SIDE DOWN?
RIGHT. KNOWING THAT...
MAIZ-ONO'S MES-SAGE...
...BE-COMES PER-FECTLY CLEAR!!
da-dum

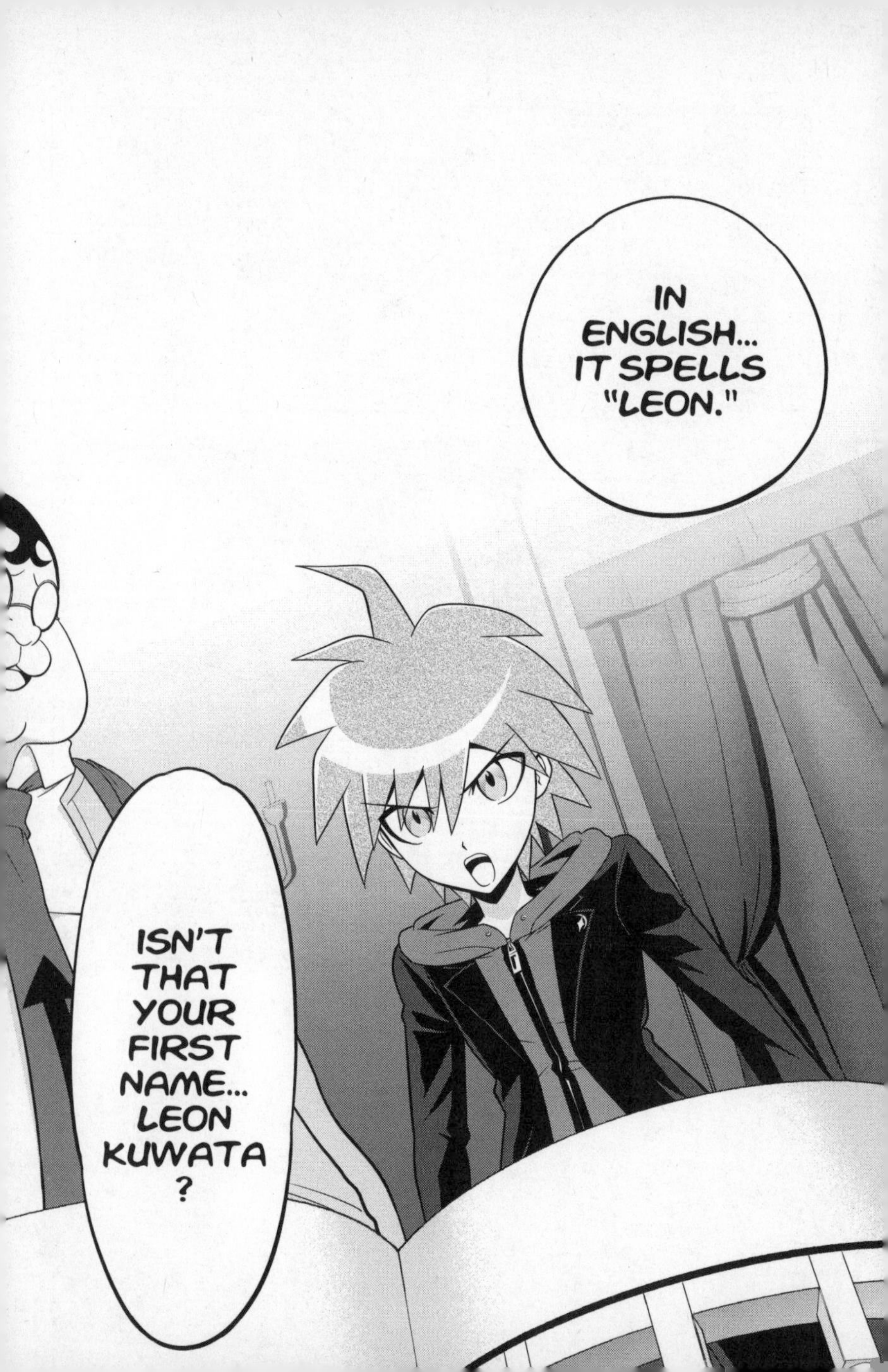
IN ENGLISH... IT SPELLS "LEON."
ISN'T THAT YOUR FIRST NAME... LEON KUWATA ?

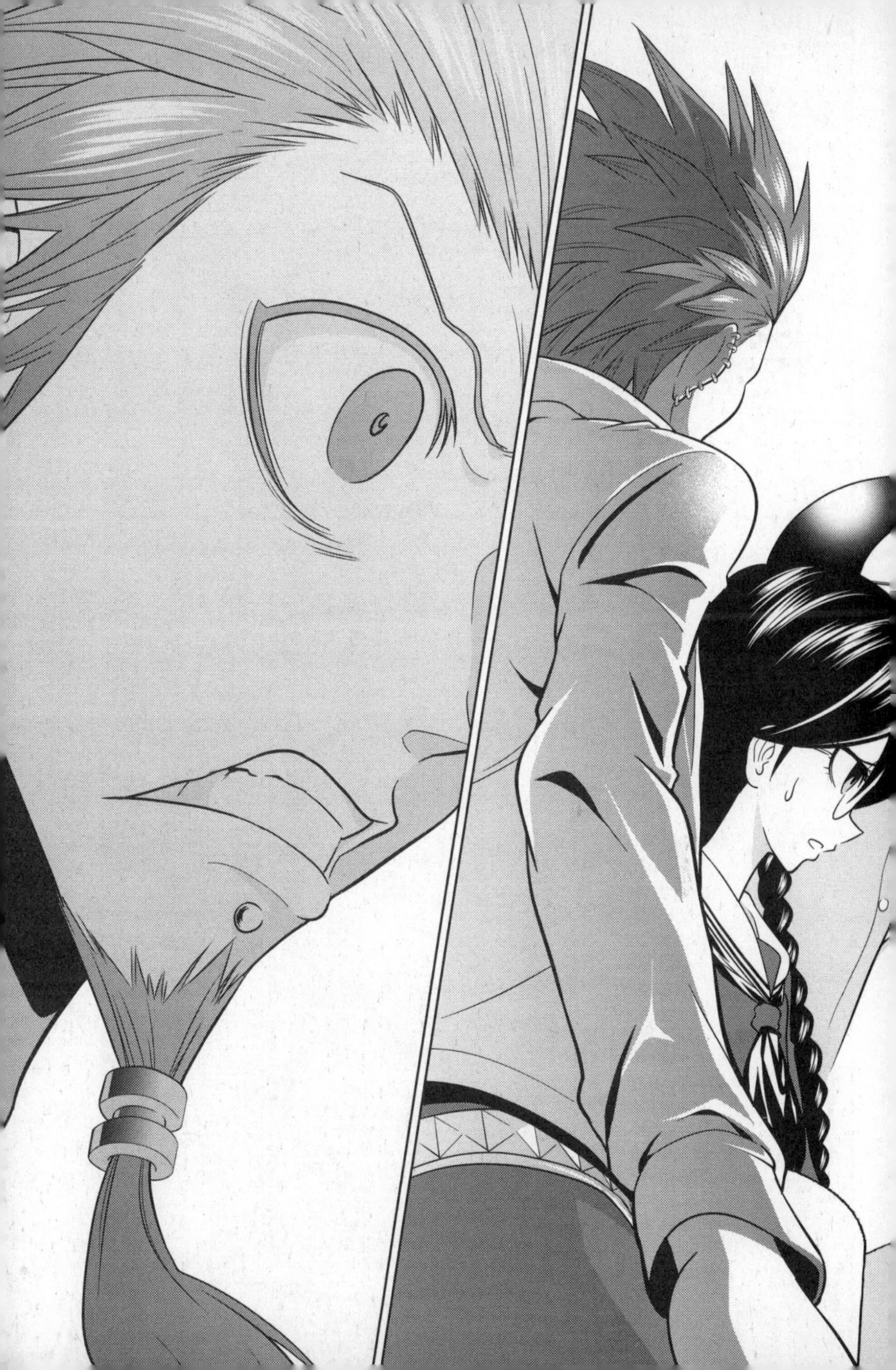

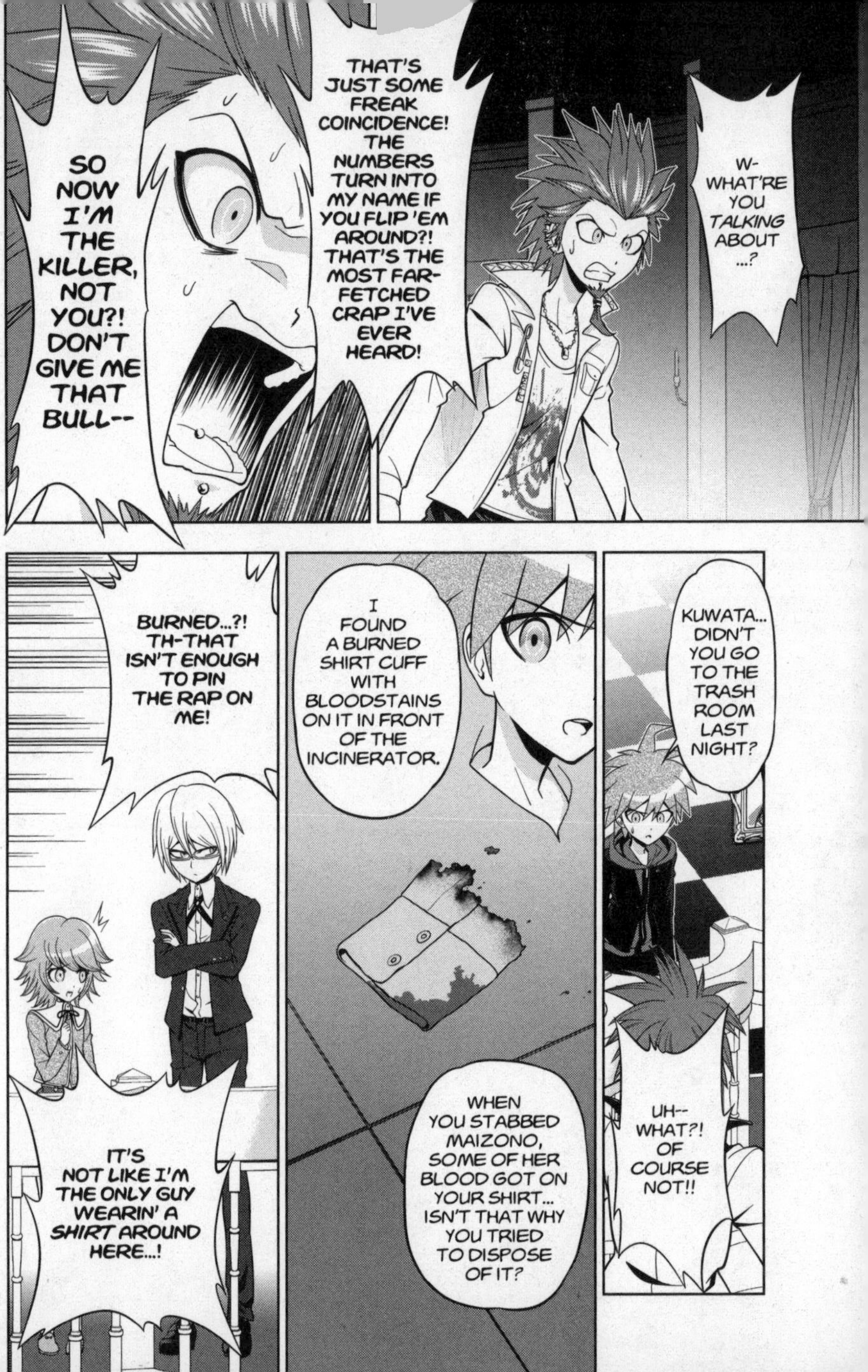
W-WHAT'RE YOU TALKING ABOUT ...?
THAT'S JUST SOME FREAK COINCIDENCE! THE NUMBERS TURN INTO MY NAME IF YOU FLIP 'EM AROUND?! THAT'S THE MOST FAR-FETCHED CRAP I'VE EVER HEARD!
SO NOW I'M THE KILLER, NOT YOU?! DON'T GIVE ME THAT BULL--
KUWATA... DIDN'T YOU GO TO THE TRASH ROOM LAST NIGHT?
UH-- WHAT?! OF COURSE NOT!!
I FOUND A BURNED SHIRT CUFF WITH BLOODSTAINS ON IT IN FRONT OF THE INCINERATOR.
WHEN YOU STABBED MAIZONO, SOME OF HER BLOOD GOT ON YOUR SHIRT... ISN'T THAT WHY YOU TRIED TO DISPOSE OF IT?
BURNED...?! TH-THAT ISN'T ENOUGH TO PIN THE RAP ON ME!
IT'S NOT LIKE I'M THE ONLY GUY WEARIN' A SHIRT AROUND HERE...!

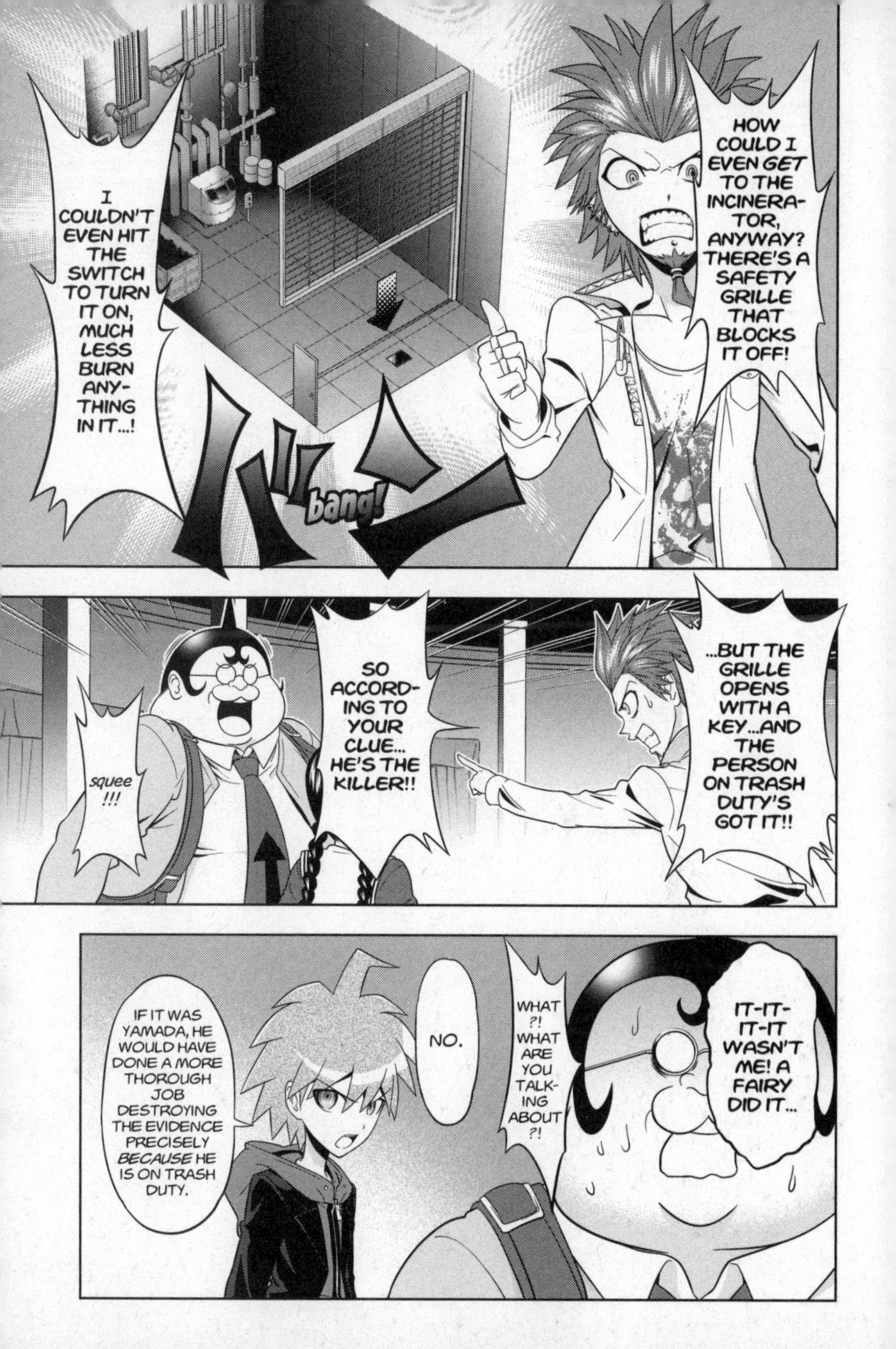
HOW COULD I EVEN *GET* TO THE INCINERATOR, ANYWAY? THERE'S A SAFETY GRILLE THAT BLOCKS IT OFF!
I COULDN'T EVEN HIT THE SWITCH TO TURN IT ON, MUCH LESS BURN ANYTHING IN IT...!
bang!
...BUT THE GRILLE OPENS WITH A KEY...AND THE PERSON ON TRASH DUTY'S GOT IT!!
SO ACCORDING TO YOUR CLUE... HE'S THE KILLER!!
squee !!!
IT-IT-IT-IT WASN'T ME! A FAIRY DID IT...
WHAT?! WHAT ARE YOU TALKING ABOUT?!
NO.
IF IT WAS YAMADA, HE WOULD HAVE DONE A MORE THOROUGH JOB DESTROYING THE EVIDENCE PRECISELY *BECAUSE* HE IS ON TRASH DUTY.

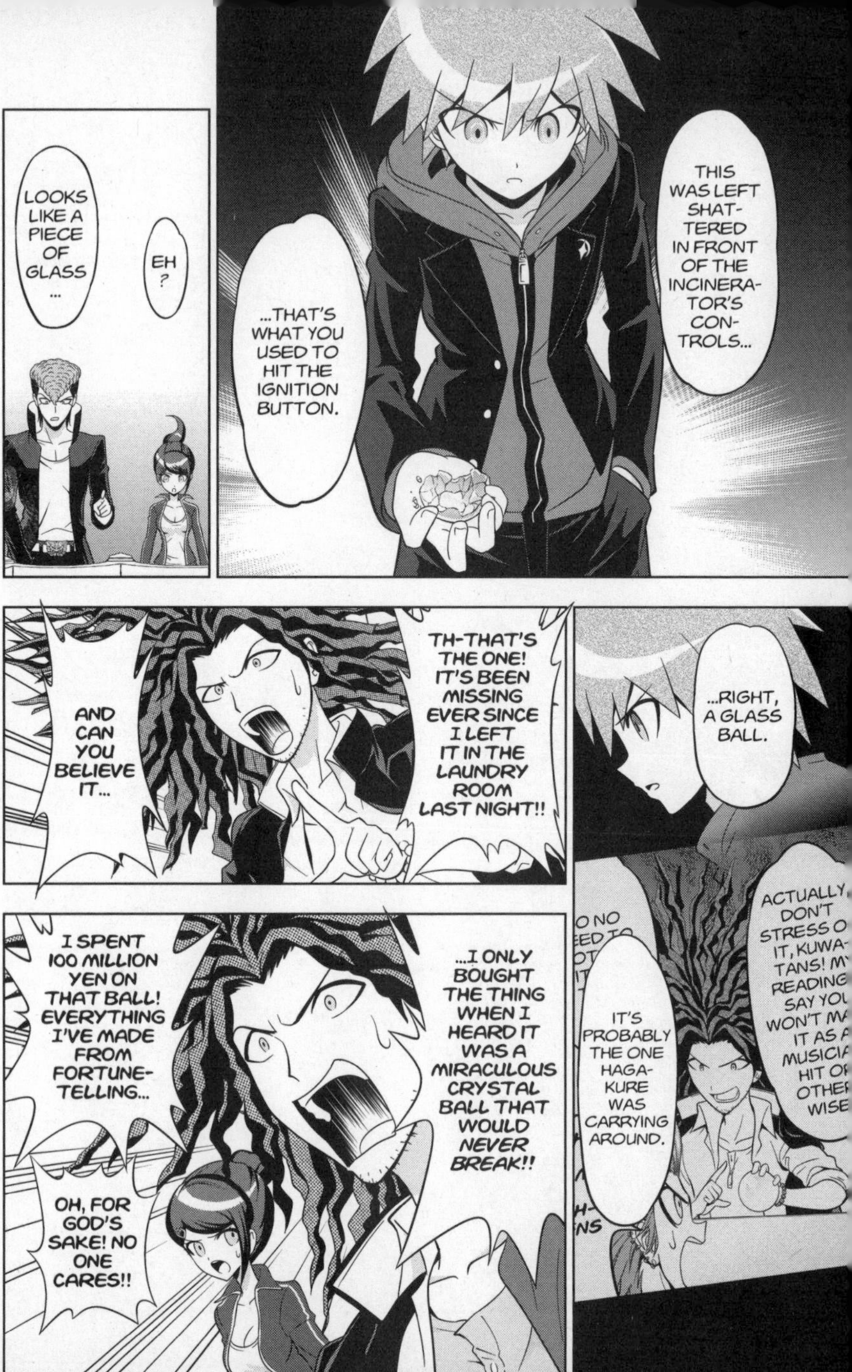
THIS WAS LEFT SHATTERED IN FRONT OF THE INCINERATOR'S CONTROLS...
...THAT'S WHAT YOU USED TO HIT THE IGNITION BUTTON.
LOOKS LIKE A PIECE OF GLASS...
EH?
...RIGHT, A GLASS BALL.
TH-THAT'S THE ONE! IT'S BEEN MISSING EVER SINCE I LEFT IT IN THE LAUNDRY ROOM LAST NIGHT!!
AND CAN YOU BELIEVE IT...
ACTUALLY, DON'T STRESS O IT, KUWA-TANS! M READING SAY YOU WON'T MA IT AS A MUSICIA HIT OR OTHER WISE
IT'S PROBABLY THE ONE HAGAKURE WAS CARRYING AROUND.
...I ONLY BOUGHT THE THING WHEN I HEARD IT WAS A MIRACULOUS CRYSTAL BALL THAT WOULD NEVER BREAK!!
I SPENT 100 MILLION YEN ON THAT BALL! EVERYTHING I'VE MADE FROM FORTUNE-TELLING...
OH, FOR GOD'S SAKE! NO ONE CARES!!

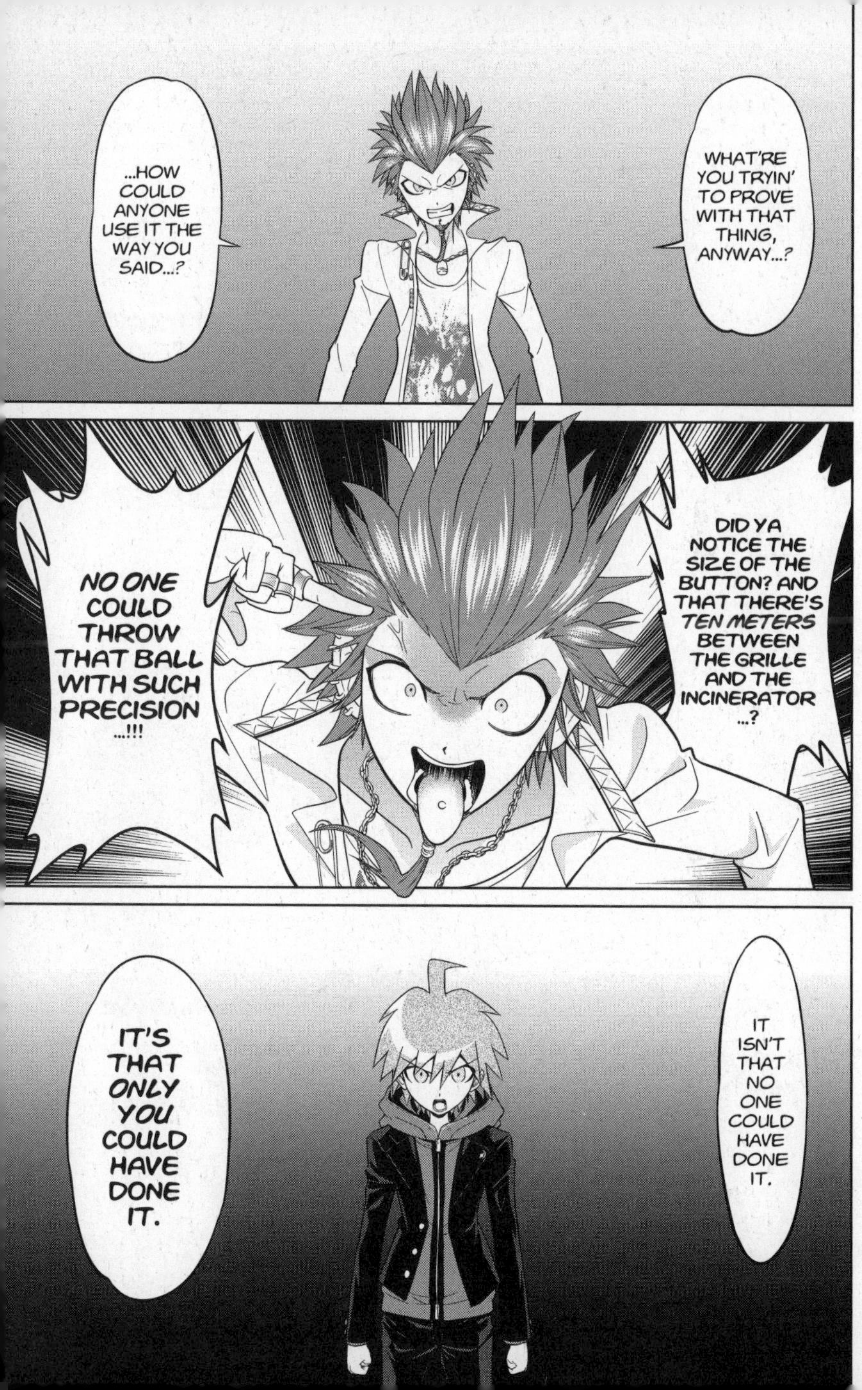
WHAT'RE YOU TRYIN' TO PROVE WITH THAT THING, ANYWAY...?
...HOW COULD ANYONE USE IT THE WAY YOU SAID...?
DID YA NOTICE THE SIZE OF THE BUTTON? AND THAT THERE'S *TEN METERS* BETWEEN THE GRILLE AND THE INCINERATOR ...?
NO ONE COULD THROW THAT BALL WITH SUCH PRECISION ...!!!
IT ISN'T THAT NO ONE COULD HAVE DONE IT.
IT'S THAT *ONLY YOU* COULD HAVE DONE IT.

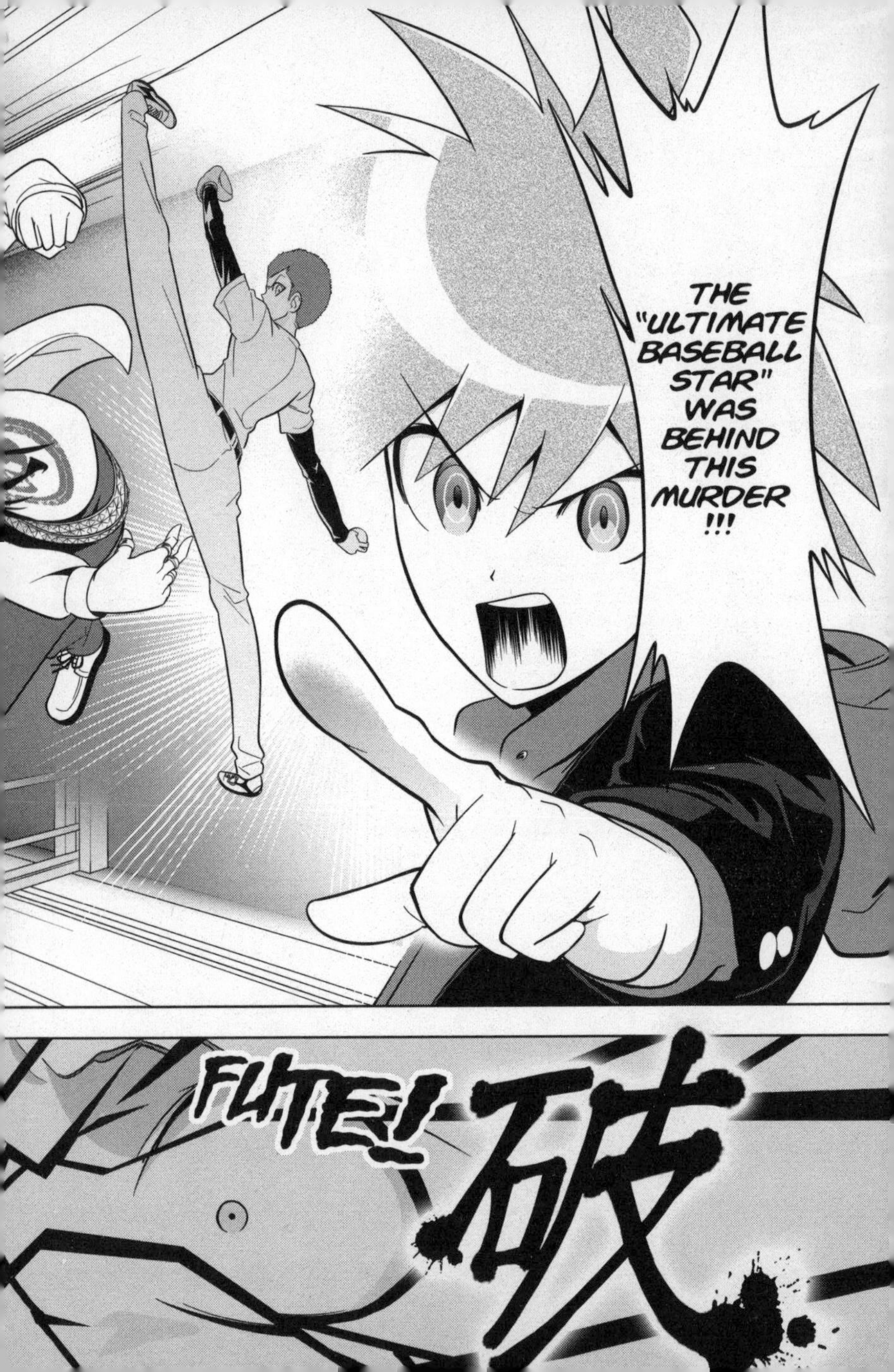
THE "ULTIMATE BASEBALL STAR" WAS BEHIND THIS MURDER !!!
FUTE! 破

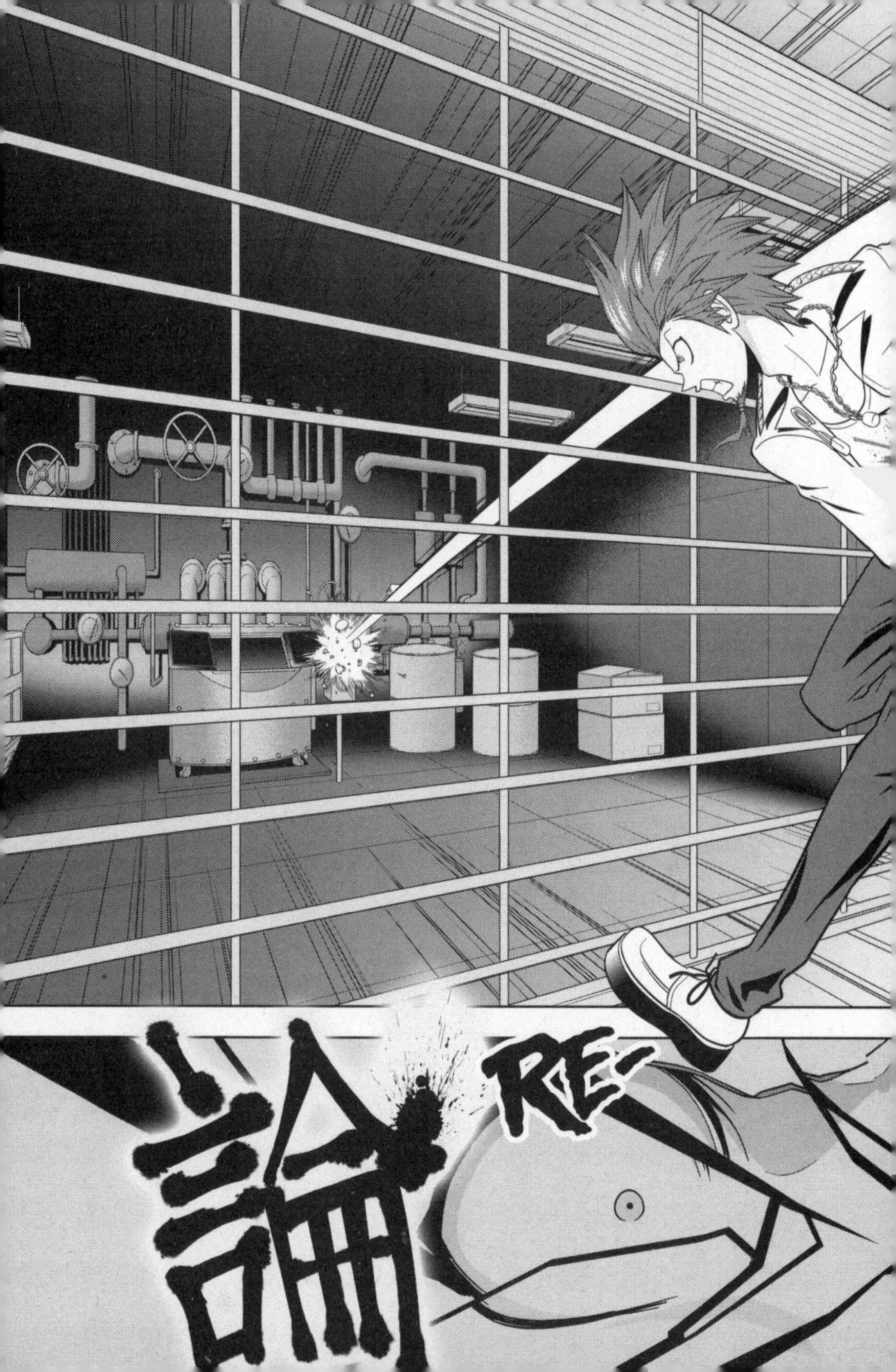
RE-
論

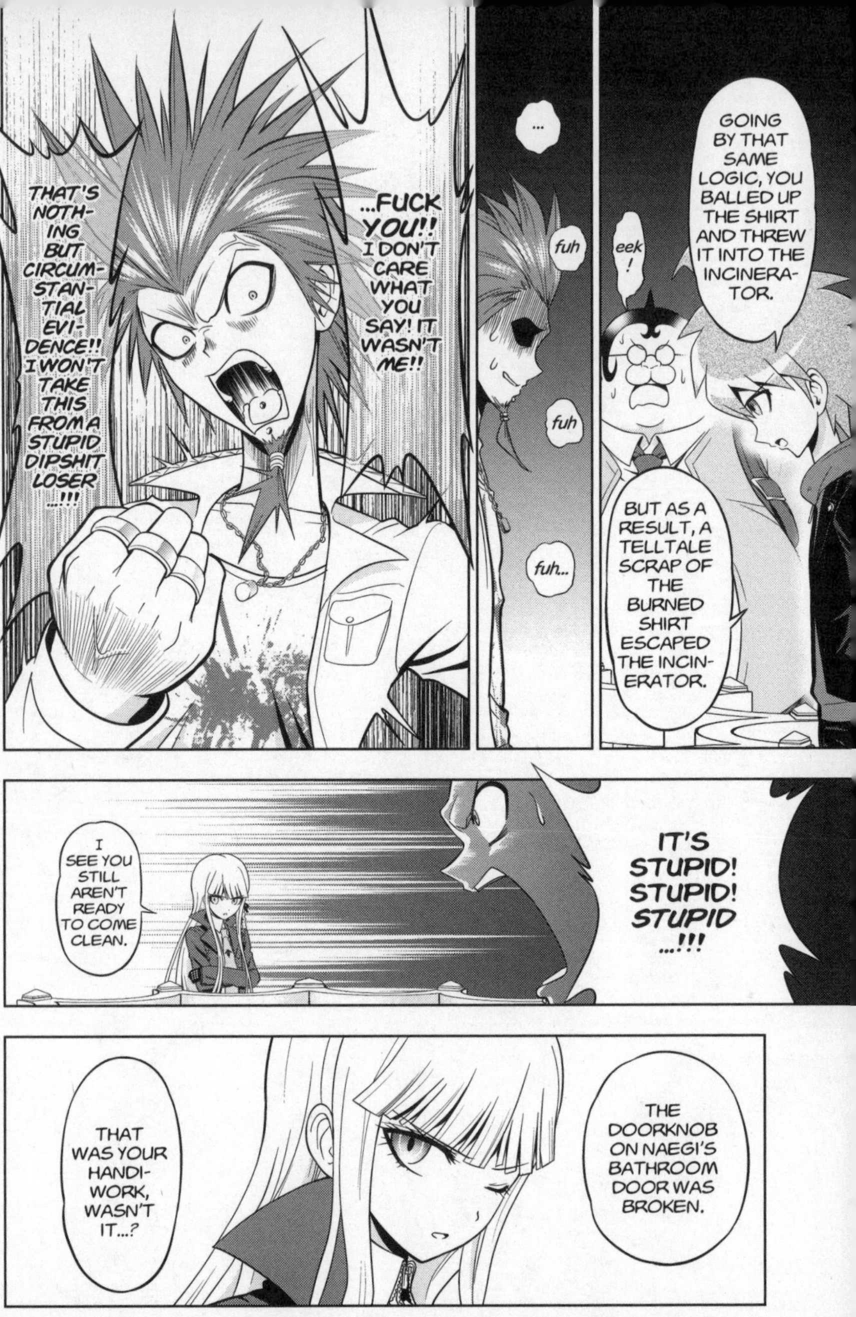
GOING BY THAT SAME LOGIC, YOU BALLED UP THE SHIRT AND THREW IT INTO THE INCINERATOR.
eek!
BUT AS A RESULT, A TELLTALE SCRAP OF THE BURNED SHIRT ESCAPED THE INCINERATOR.
...
fuh
fuh
fuh...
...FUCK YOU!! I DON'T CARE WHAT YOU SAY! IT WASN'T ME!!
THAT'S NOTHING BUT CIRCUMSTANTIAL EVIDENCE!! I WON'T TAKE THIS FROM A STUPID DIPSHIT LOSER...!!!
IT'S STUPID! STUPID! STUPID...!!!
I SEE YOU STILL AREN'T READY TO COME CLEAN.
THE DOORKNOB ON NAEGI'S BATHROOM DOOR WAS BROKEN.
THAT WAS YOUR HANDIWORK, WASN'T IT...?

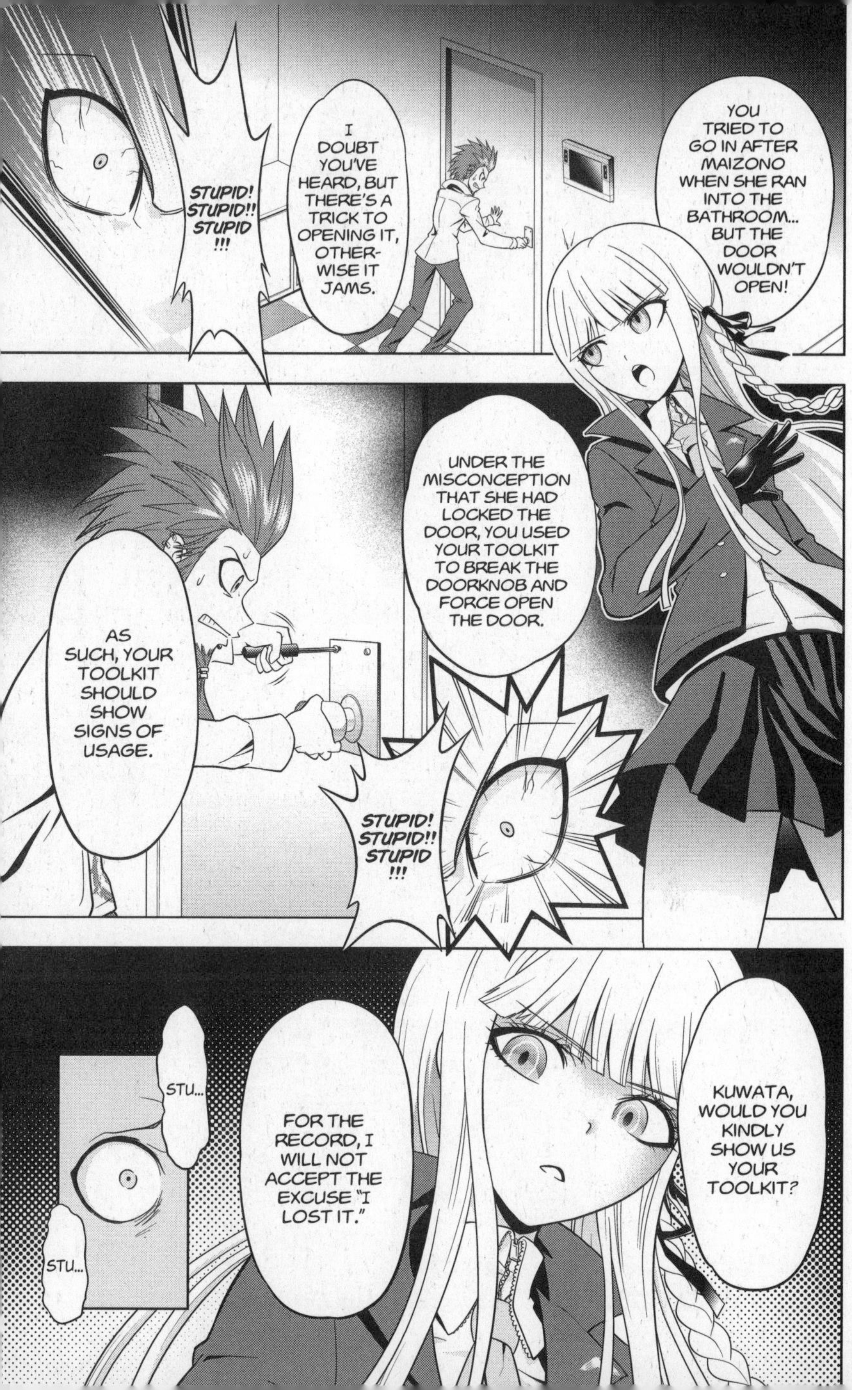
YOU TRIED TO GO IN AFTER MAIZONO WHEN SHE RAN INTO THE BATHROOM... BUT THE DOOR WOULDN'T OPEN!
I DOUBT YOU'VE HEARD, BUT THERE'S A TRICK TO OPENING IT, OTHER-WISE IT JAMS.
STUPID! STUPID!! STUPID !!!
UNDER THE MISCONCEPTION THAT SHE HAD LOCKED THE DOOR, YOU USED YOUR TOOLKIT TO BREAK THE DOORKNOB AND FORCE OPEN THE DOOR.
AS SUCH, YOUR TOOLKIT SHOULD SHOW SIGNS OF USAGE.
STUPID! STUPID!! STUPID !!!
KUWATA, WOULD YOU KINDLY SHOW US YOUR TOOLKIT?
FOR THE RECORD, I WILL NOT ACCEPT THE EXCUSE "I LOST IT."
STU...
STU...

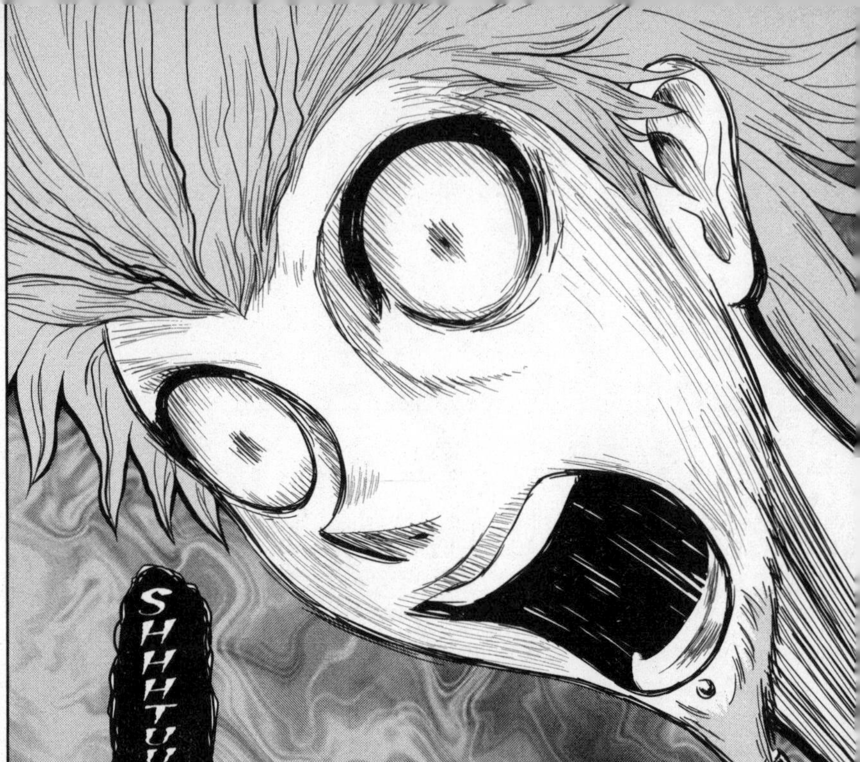
SHHTUUPID!
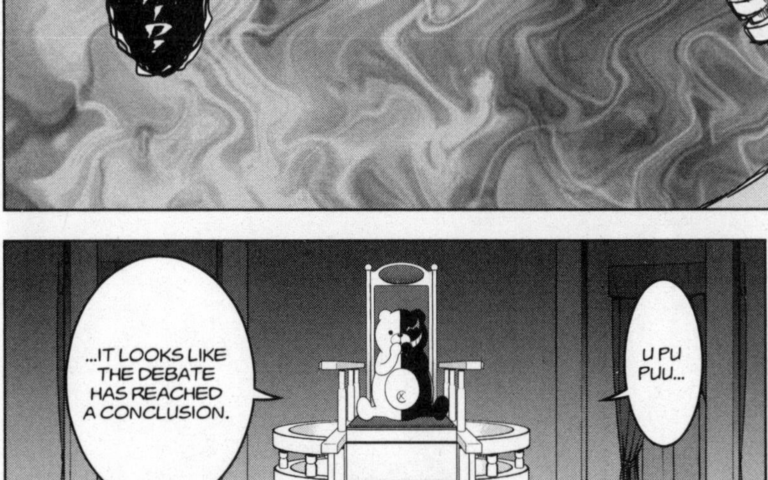
U PU PUU...
...IT LOOKS LIKE THE DEBATE HAS REACHED A CONCLUSION.

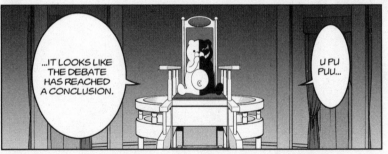

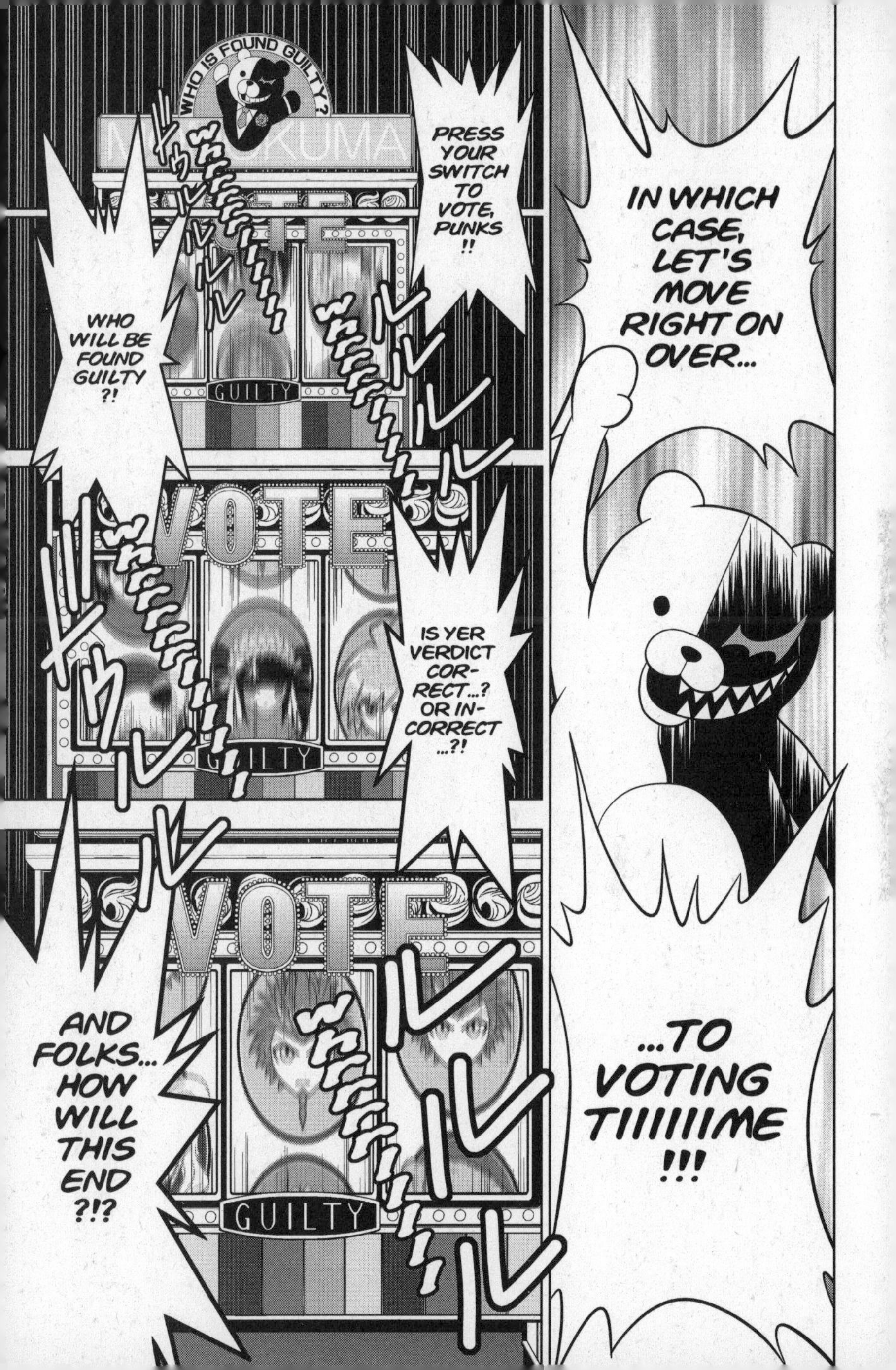
IN WHICH CASE, LET'S MOVE RIGHT ON OVER...
...TO VOTING TIIIIIIME !!!
WHO IS FOUND GUILTY?
PRESS YOUR SWITCH TO VOTE, PUNKS !!
WHO WILL BE FOUND GUILTY ?!
GUILTY
VOTE
IS YER VERDICT COR-RECT...? OR IN-CORRECT ...?!
GUILTY
VOTE
AND FOLKS... HOW WILL THIS END ?!?
GUILTY

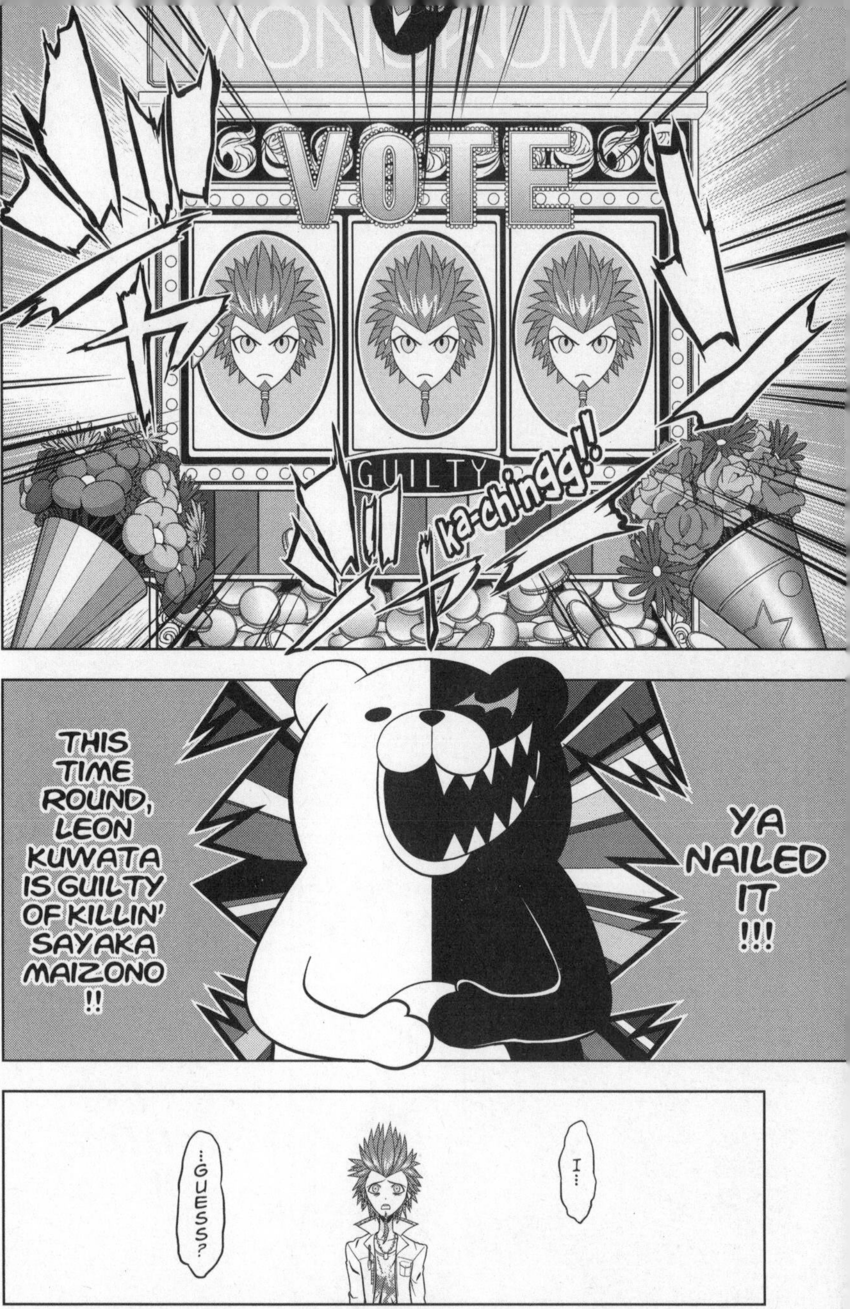
VOTE
GUILTY
ka-chingg!!
YA NAILED IT !!!
THIS TIME ROUND, LEON KUWATA IS GUILTY OF KILLIN' SAYAKA MAIZONO !!
I...
...GUESS?

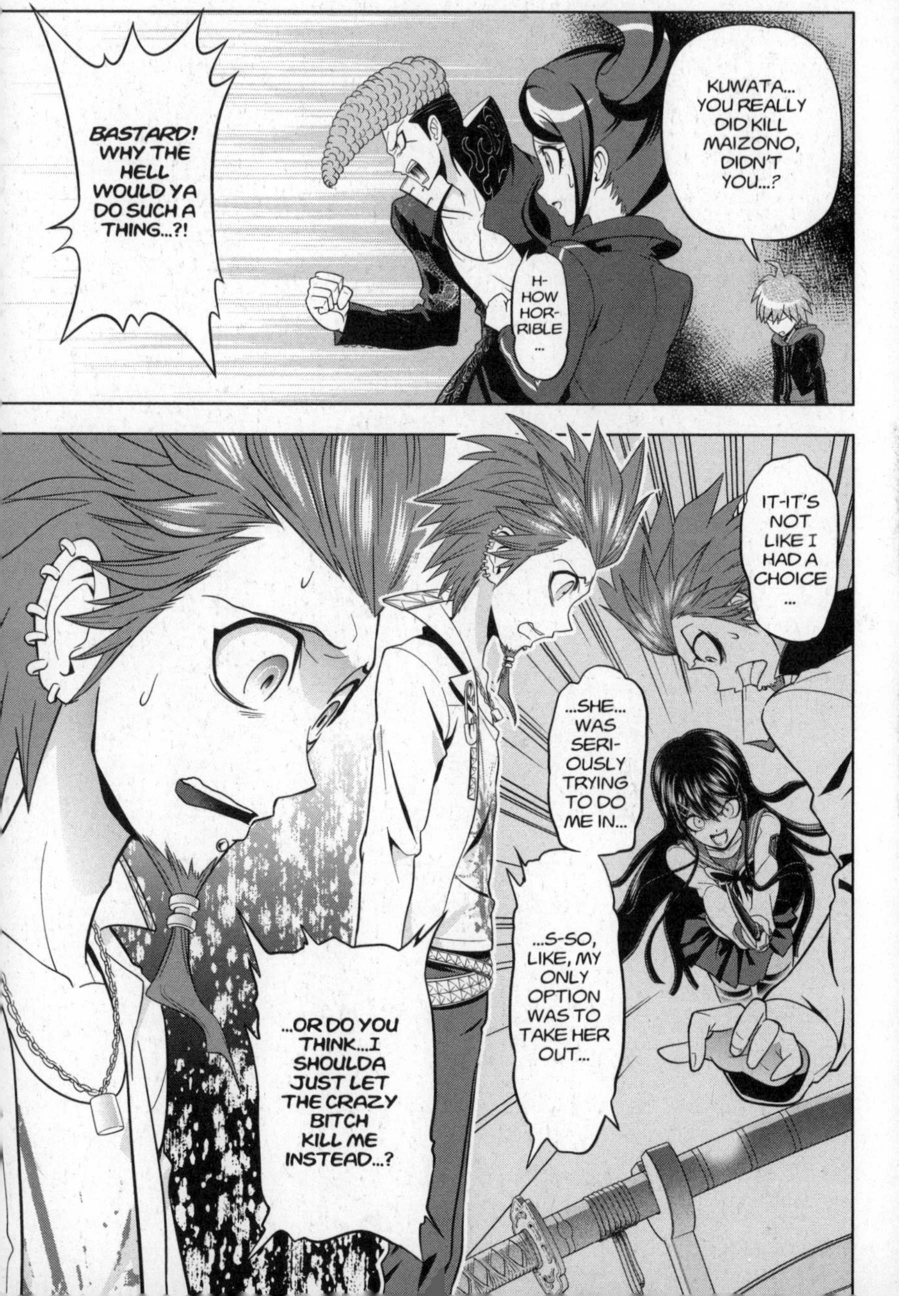
KUWATA... YOU REALLY DID KILL MAIZONO, DIDN'T YOU...?
H-HOW HOR-RIBLE...
BASTARD! WHY THE HELL WOULD YA DO SUCH A THING...?!
IT-IT'S NOT LIKE I HAD A CHOICE...
...SHE... WAS SERI-OUSLY TRYING TO DO ME IN...
...S-SO, LIKE, MY ONLY OPTION WAS TO TAKE HER OUT...
...OR DO YOU THINK...I SHOULDA JUST LET THE CRAZY BITCH KILL ME INSTEAD...?

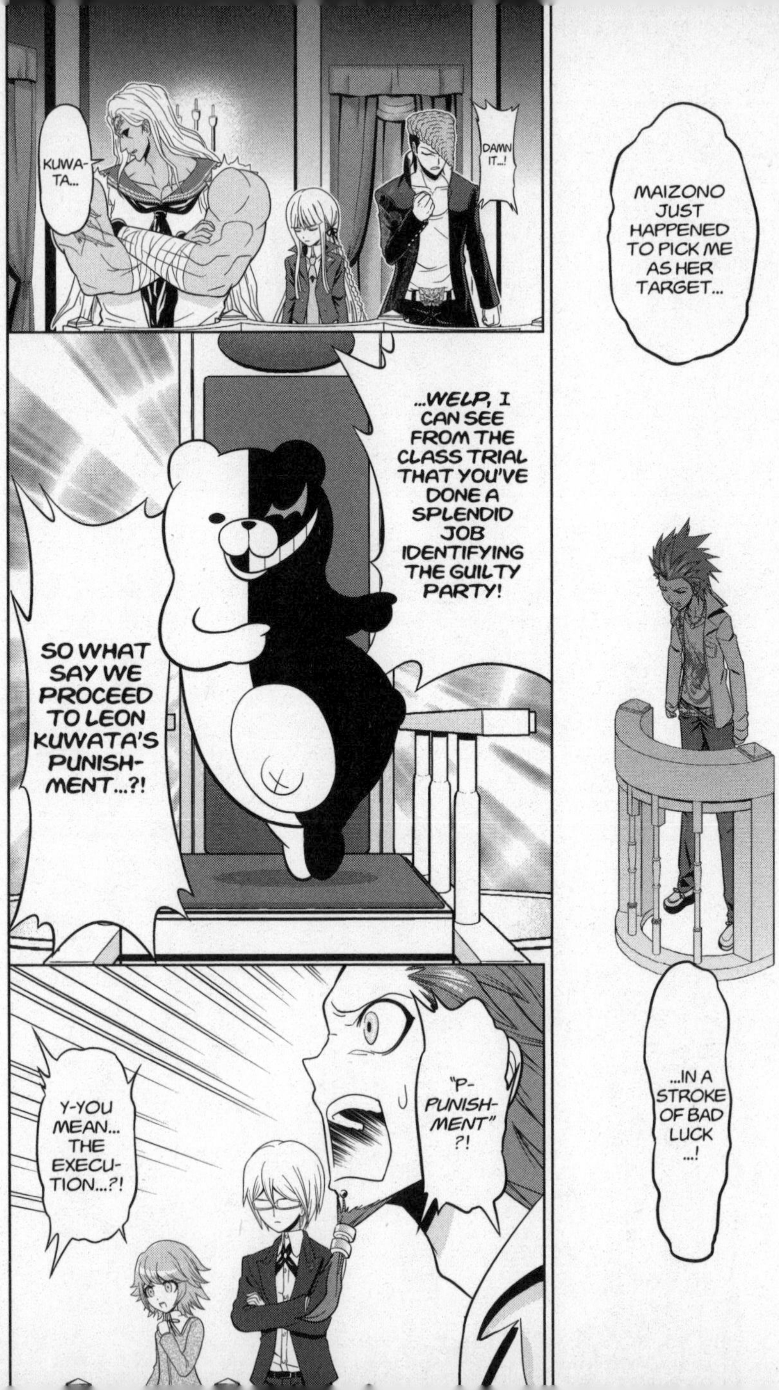
MAIZONO JUST HAPPENED TO PICK ME AS HER TARGET...
...IN A STROKE OF BAD LUCK ...!
DAMN IT...!
KUWATA...
...WELP, I CAN SEE FROM THE CLASS TRIAL THAT YOU'VE DONE A SPLENDID JOB IDENTIFYING THE GUILTY PARTY!
SO WHAT SAY WE PROCEED TO LEON KUWATA'S PUNISHMENT...?!
"P-PUNISHMENT"?!
Y-YOU MEAN... THE EXECUTION...?!

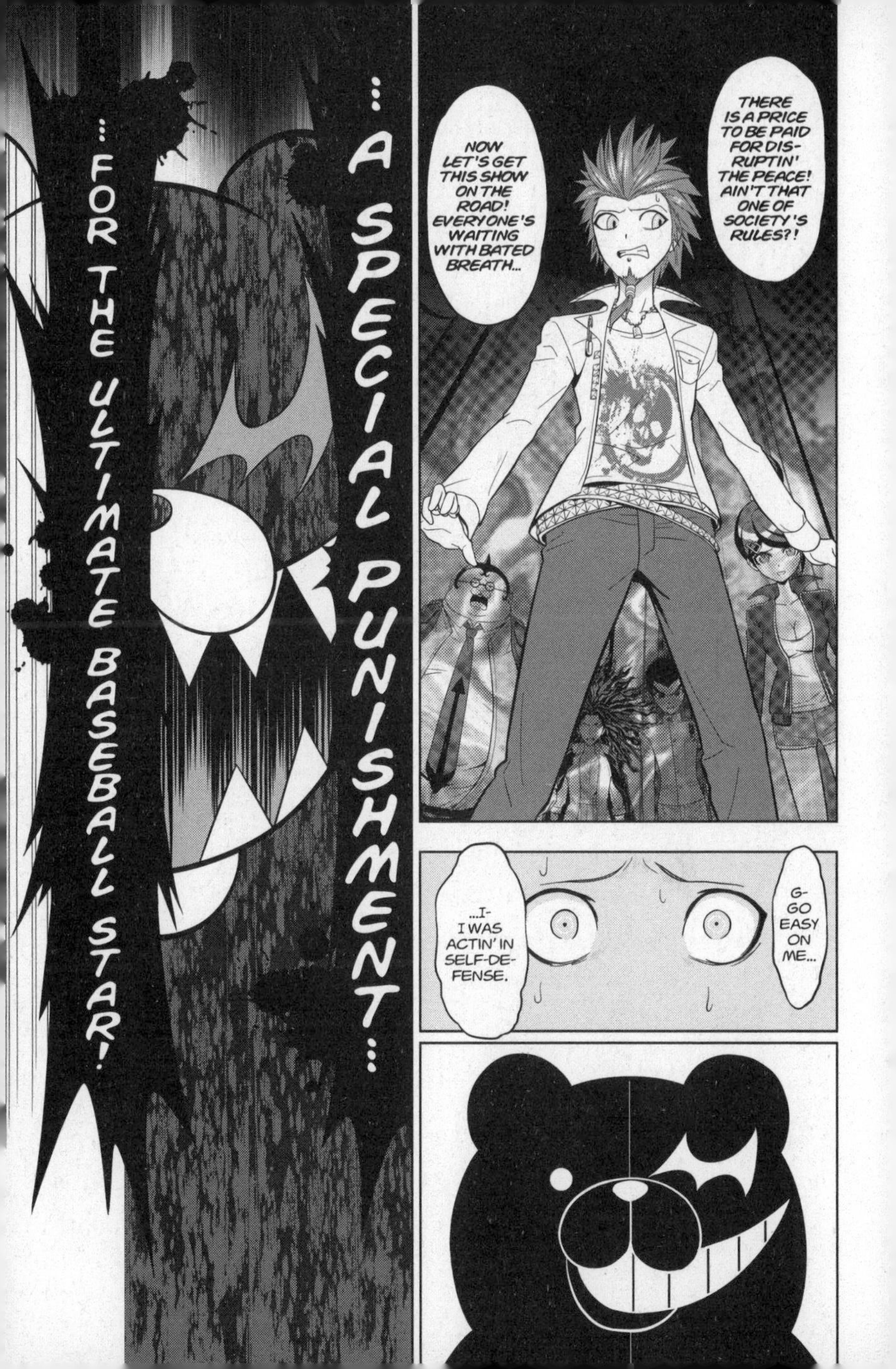
THERE IS A PRICE TO BE PAID FOR DIS-RUPTIN' THE PEACE! AIN'T THAT ONE OF SOCIETY'S RULES?!
NOW LET'S GET THIS SHOW ON THE ROAD! EVERYONE'S WAITING WITH BATED BREATH...
G-GO EASY ON ME...
...I-I WAS ACTIN' IN SELF-DE-FENSE.
...A SPECIAL PUNISHMENT...
...FOR THE ULTIMATE BASEBALL STAR!

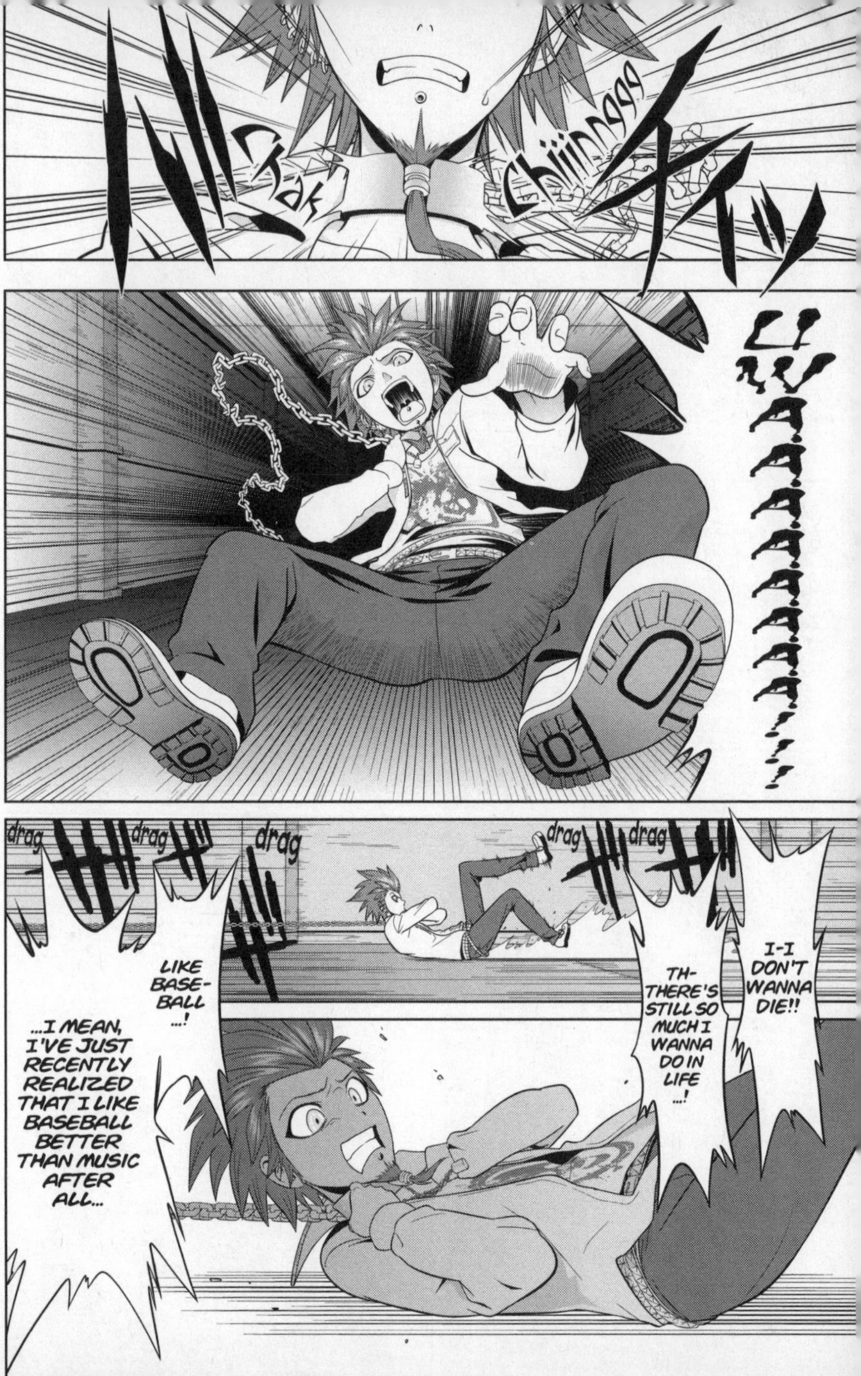
Chiiinggg
Chak
UWAAAAAAAA!!!
drag
drag
drag
drag
drag
I-I DON'T WANNA DIE!!
TH-THERE'S STILL SO MUCH I WANNA DO IN LIFE...!
LIKE BASE-BALL...!
...I MEAN, I'VE JUST RECENTLY REALIZED THAT I LIKE BASEBALL BETTER THAN MUSIC AFTER ALL...

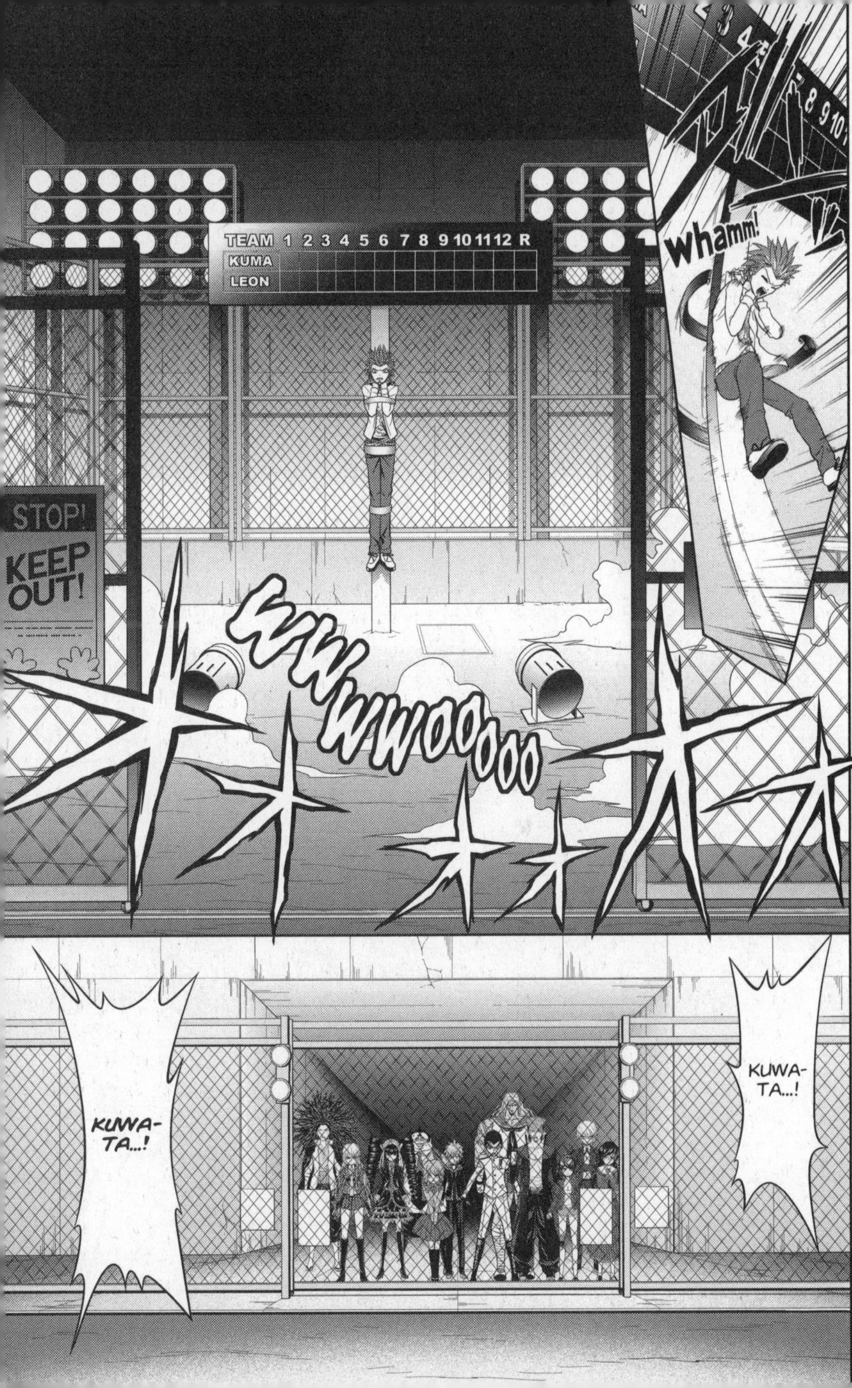
Whamm!
TEAM 1 2 3 4 5 6 7 8 9 10 11 12 R
KUMA
LEON
STOP!
KEEP OUT!
WWWWOOOooo
KUWA-TA...!
KUWA-TA...!

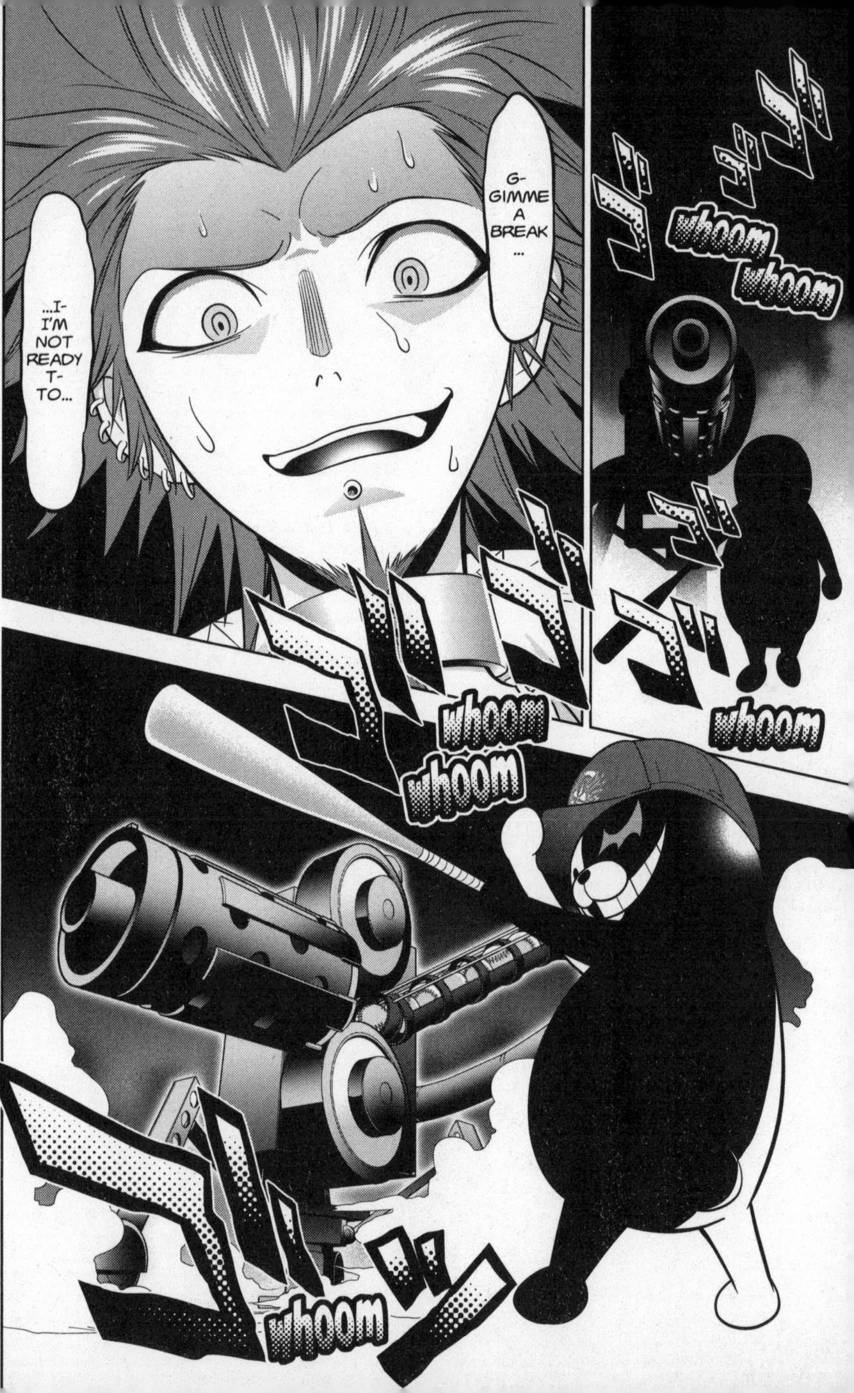
whoom whoom
whoom
G-GIMME A BREAK...
...I-I'M NOT READY T-TO...
whoom whoom
whoom

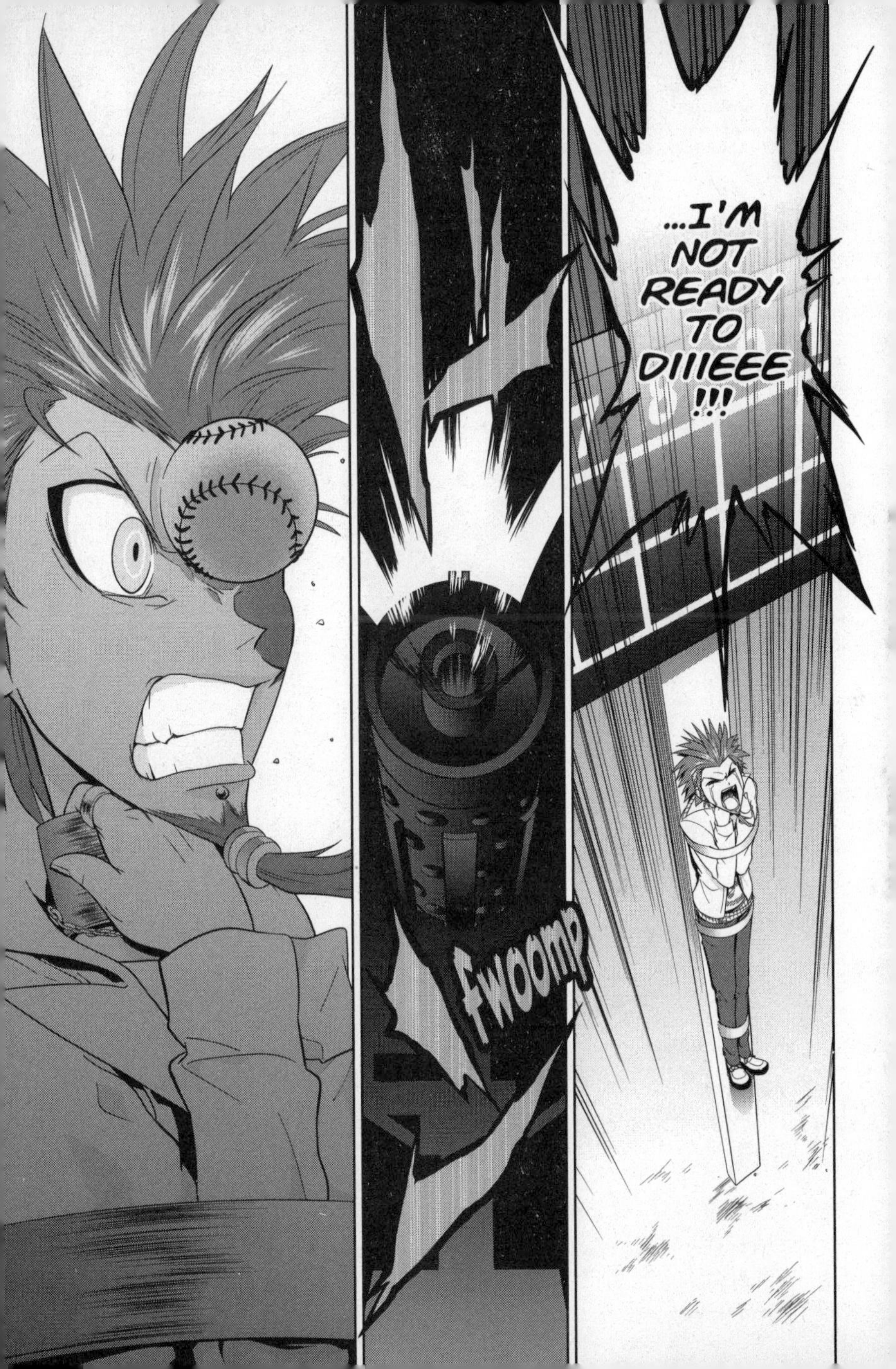
...I'M NOT READY TO DIIIEEE!!!
FWOOMP

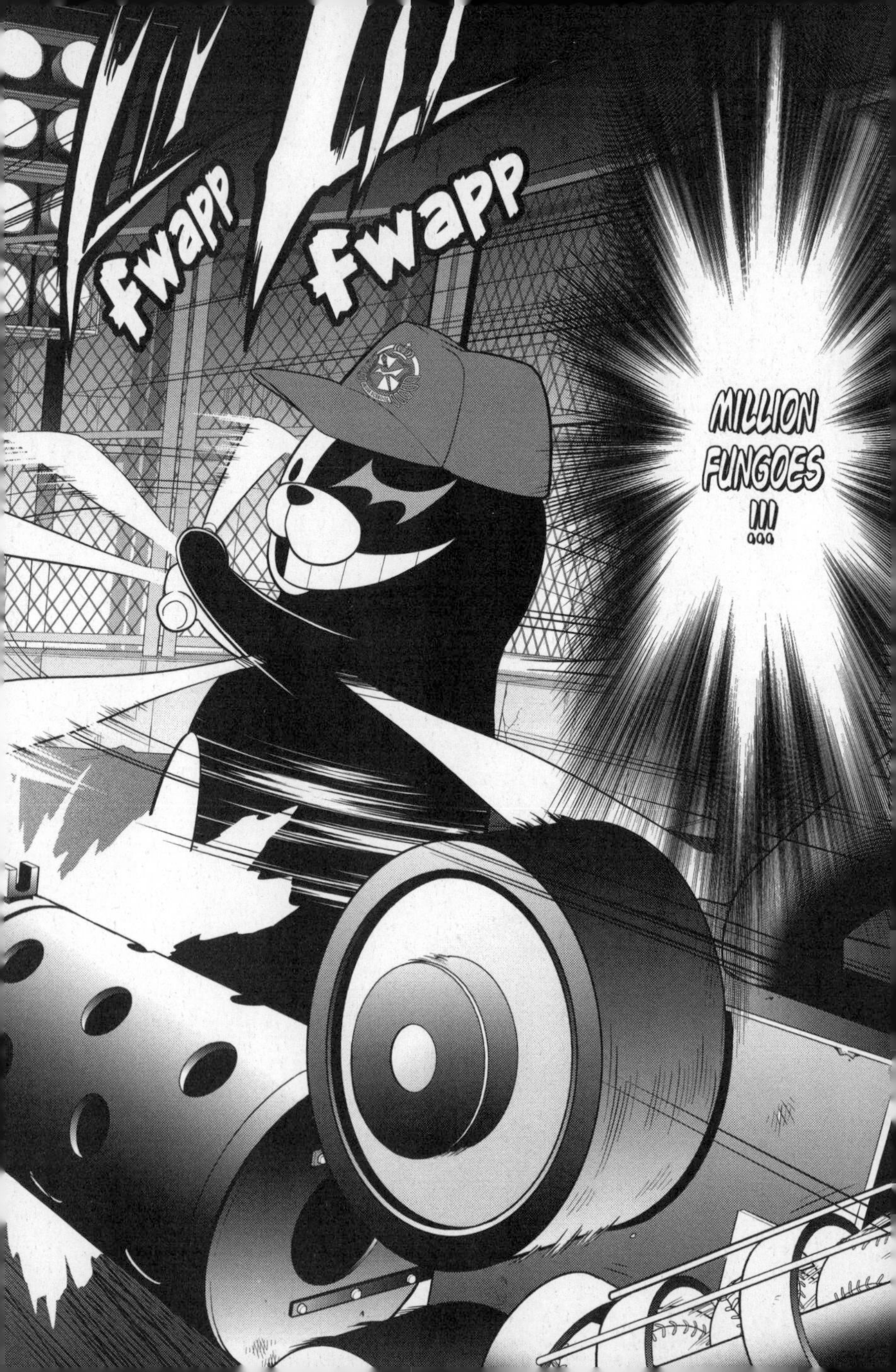
MILLION FUNGOES !!!
fwapp
fwapp

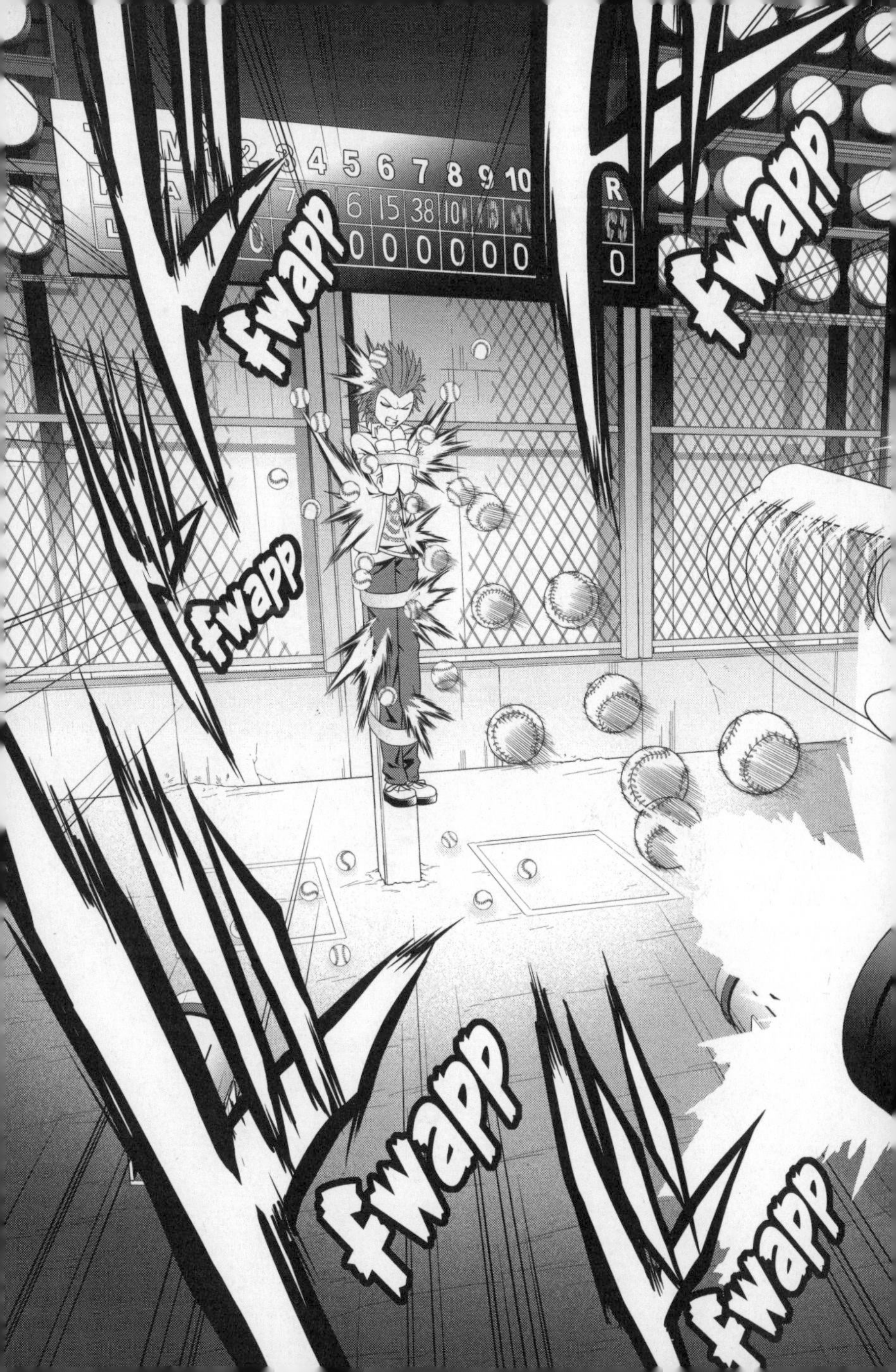
fwapp
fwapp
fwapp
fwapp
fwapp

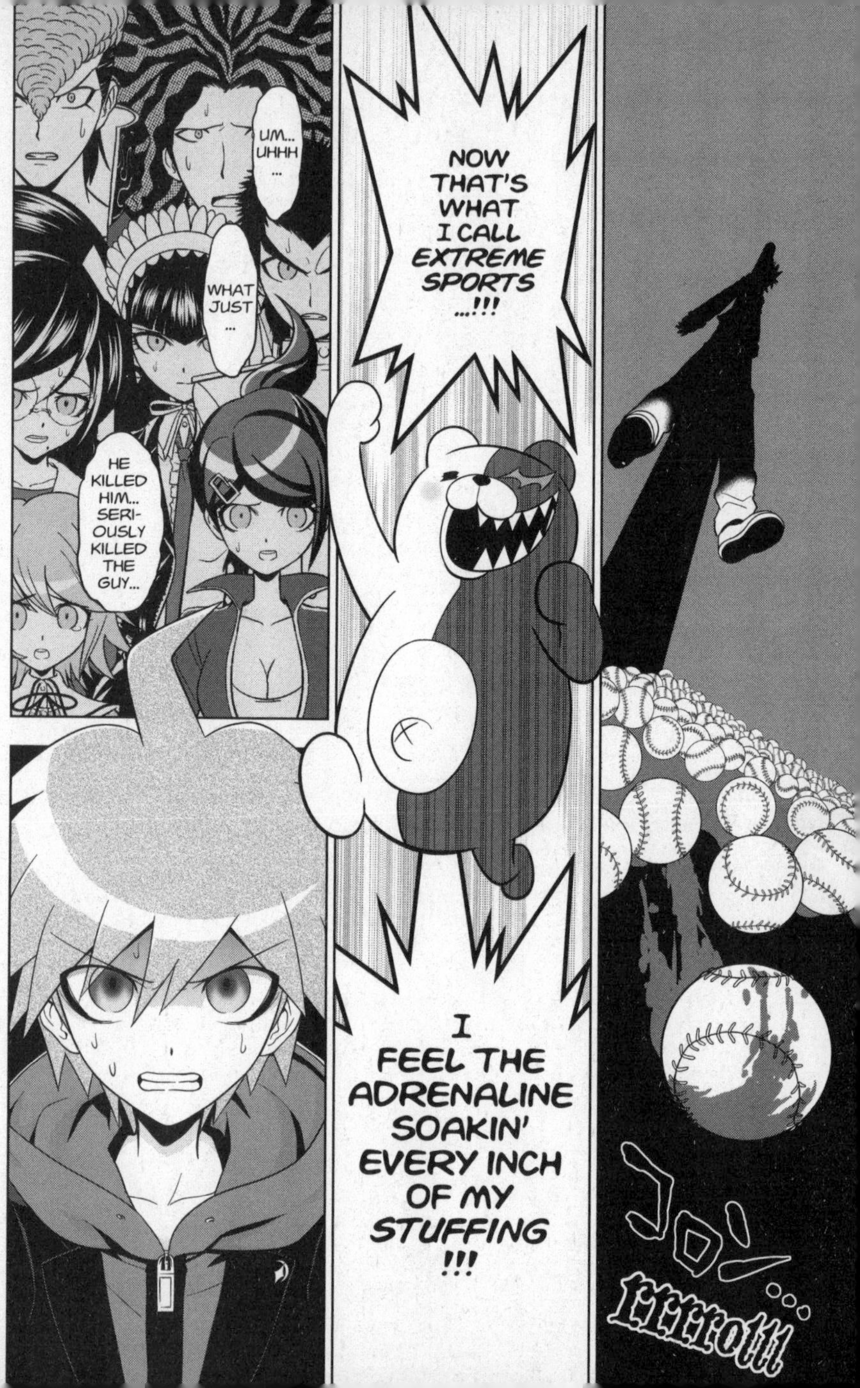
コロン…
rrrrolll
NOW THAT'S WHAT I CALL EXTREME SPORTS ...!!!
I FEEL THE ADRENALINE SOAKIN' EVERY INCH OF MY STUFFING !!!
UM... UHHH ...
WHAT JUST ...
HE KILLED HIM... SERIOUSLY KILLED THE GUY...

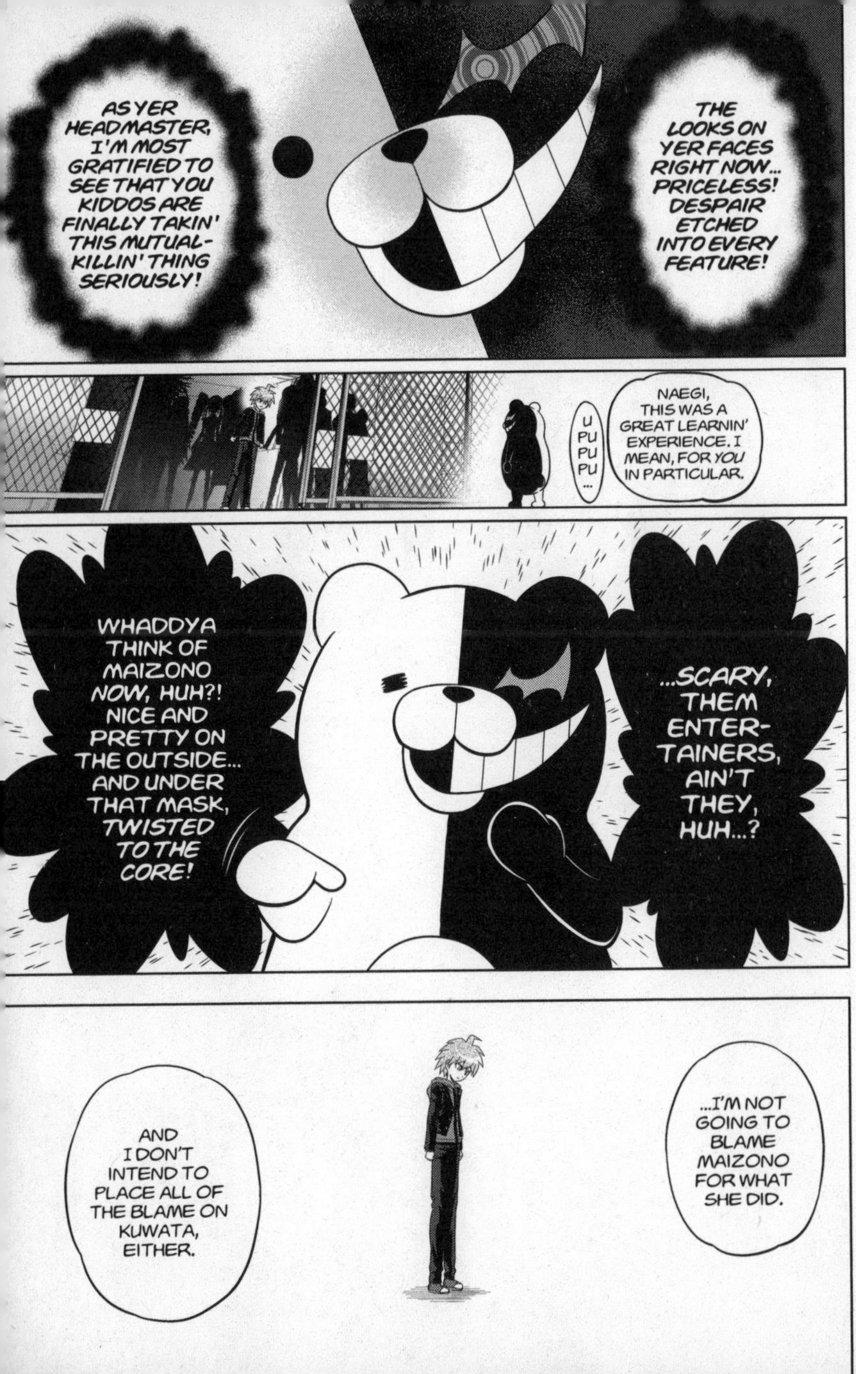
THE LOOKS ON YER FACES RIGHT NOW... PRICELESS! DESPAIR ETCHED INTO EVERY FEATURE!
AS YER HEADMASTER, I'M MOST GRATIFIED TO SEE THAT YOU KIDDOS ARE FINALLY TAKIN' THIS MUTUAL-KILLIN' THING SERIOUSLY!
NAEGI, THIS WAS A GREAT LEARNIN' EXPERIENCE. I MEAN, FOR *YOU* IN PARTICULAR.
UPUPUPU...
...SCARY, THEM ENTERTAINERS, AIN'T THEY, HUH...?
WHADDYA THINK OF MAIZONO NOW, HUH?! NICE AND PRETTY ON THE OUTSIDE... AND UNDER THAT MASK, TWISTED TO THE CORE!
...I'M NOT GOING TO BLAME MAIZONO FOR WHAT SHE DID.
AND I DON'T INTEND TO PLACE ALL OF THE BLAME ON KUWATA, EITHER.

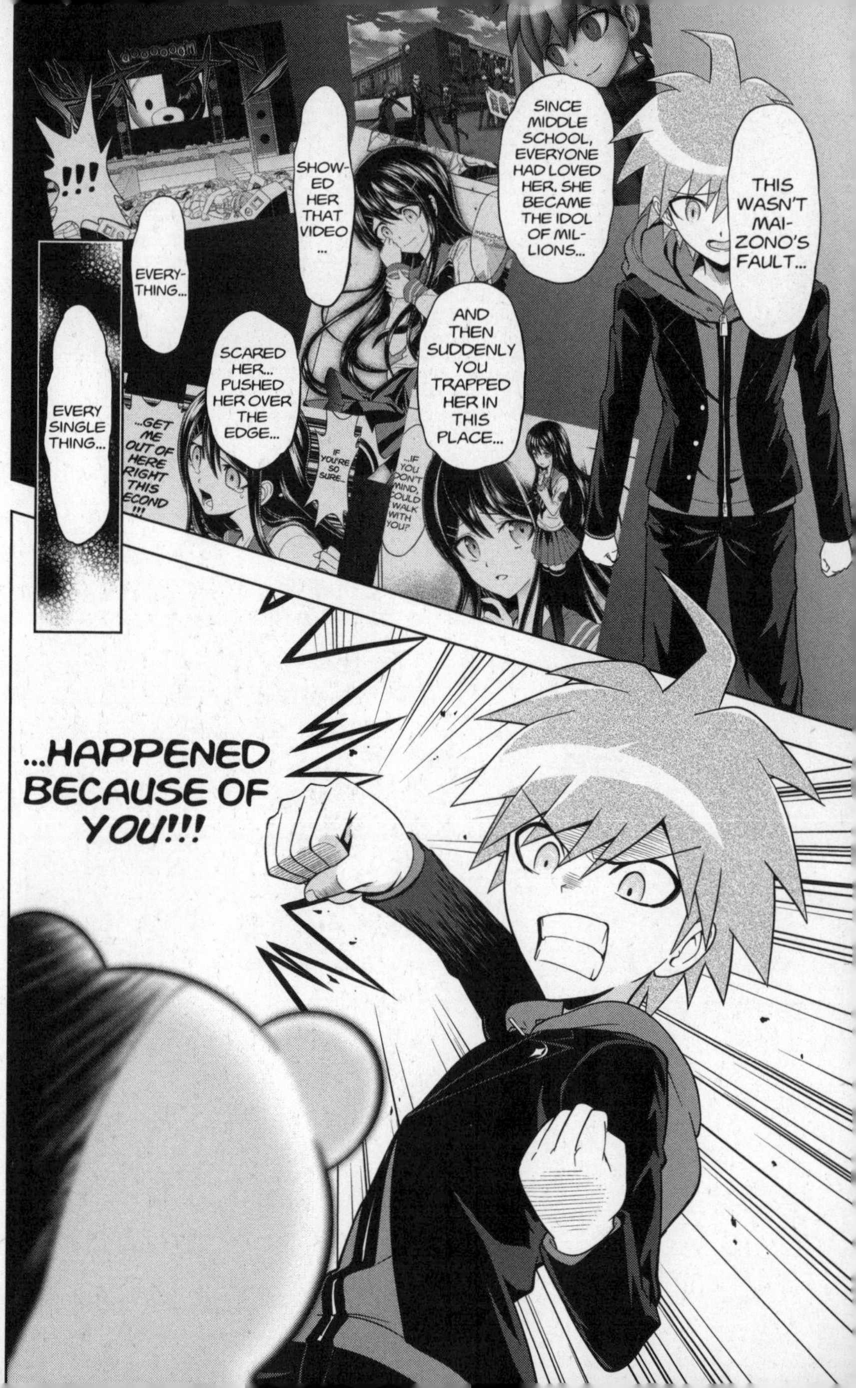
THIS WASN'T MAI-ZONO'S FAULT...
SINCE MIDDLE SCHOOL, EVERYONE HAD LOVED HER. SHE BECAME THE IDOL OF MIL-LIONS...
AND THEN SUDDENLY YOU TRAPPED HER IN THIS PLACE...
...IF YOU DON'T MIND, COULD WALK WITH YOU?
SHOW-ED HER THAT VIDEO...
SCARED HER... PUSHED HER OVER THE EDGE...
IF YOU'RE SO SURE...
...GET ME OUT OF HERE RIGHT THIS ECOND!!!
!!!
EVERY-THING...
EVERY SINGLE THING...
...HAPPENED BECAUSE OF YOU!!!

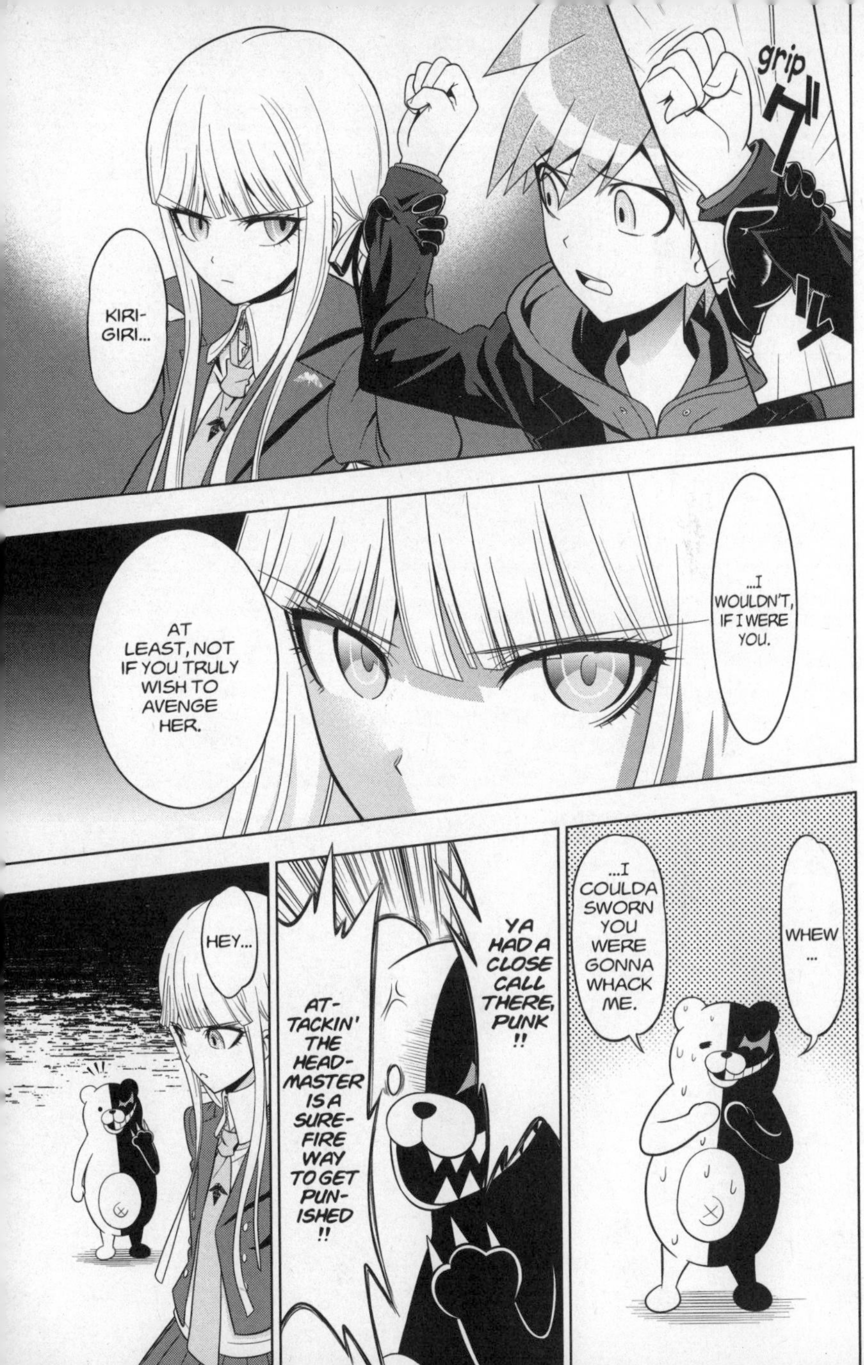
grip
KIRI-GIRI...
...I WOULDN'T, IF I WERE YOU.
AT LEAST, NOT IF YOU TRULY WISH TO AVENGE HER.
WHEW ...
...I COULDA SWORN YOU WERE GONNA WHACK ME.
YA HAD A CLOSE CALL THERE, PUNK!!
AT-TACKIN' THE HEAD-MASTER IS A SURE-FIRE WAY TO GET PUN-ISHED!!
HEY...

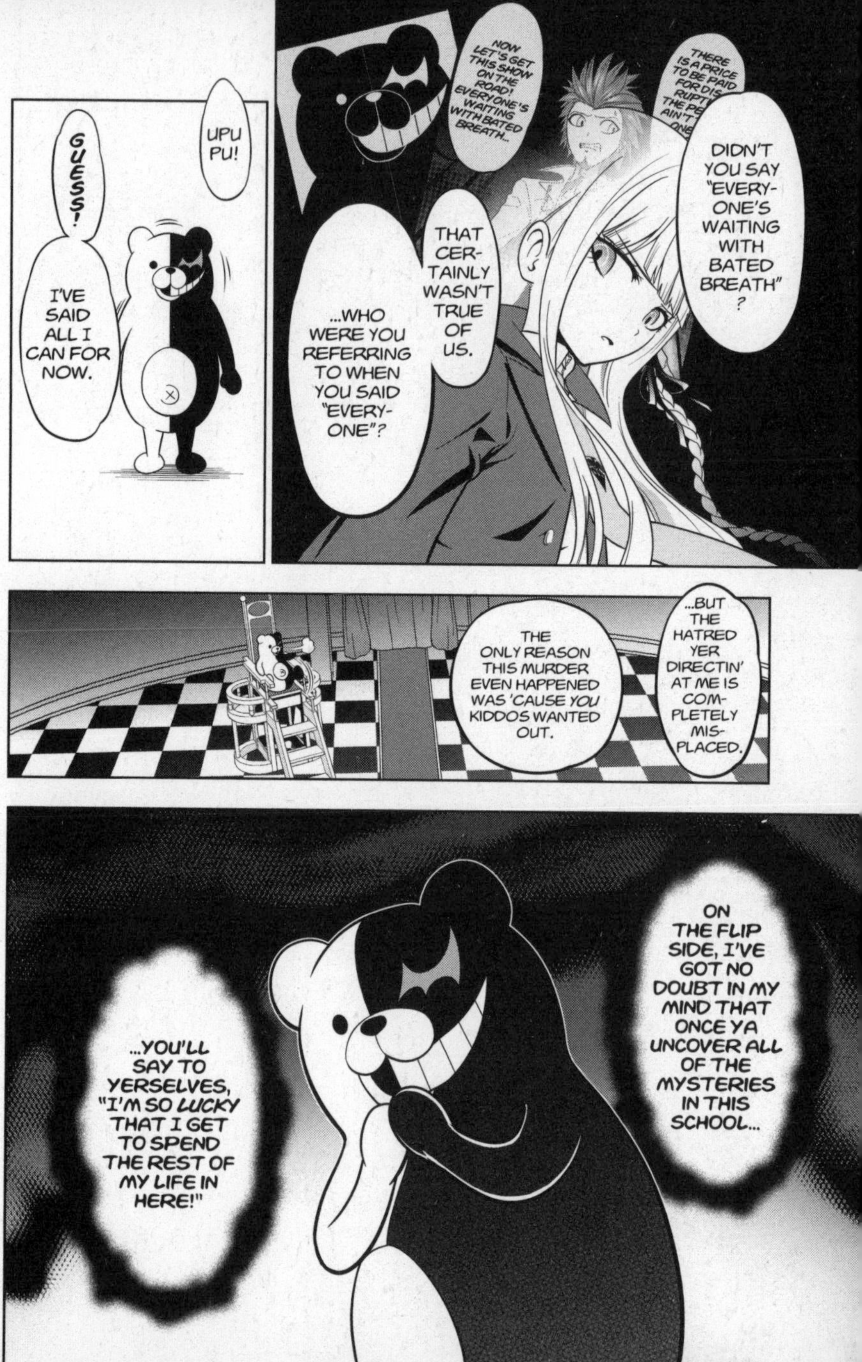
DIDN'T YOU SAY "EVERYONE'S WAITING WITH BATED BREATH"?
NOW LET'S GET THIS SHOW ON THE ROAD! EVERYONE'S WAITING WITH BATED BREATH...
THAT CERTAINLY WASN'T TRUE OF US.
...WHO WERE YOU REFERRING TO WHEN YOU SAID "EVERYONE"?
UPU PU!
GUESS!
I'VE SAID ALL I CAN FOR NOW.
...BUT THE HATRED YER DIRECTIN' AT ME IS COMPLETELY MISPLACED.
THE ONLY REASON THIS MURDER EVEN HAPPENED WAS 'CAUSE YOU KIDDOS WANTED OUT.
ON THE FLIP SIDE, I'VE GOT NO DOUBT IN MY MIND THAT ONCE YA UNCOVER ALL OF THE MYSTERIES IN THIS SCHOOL...
...YOU'LL SAY TO YERSELVES, "I'M SO LUCKY THAT I GET TO SPEND THE REST OF MY LIFE IN HERE!"

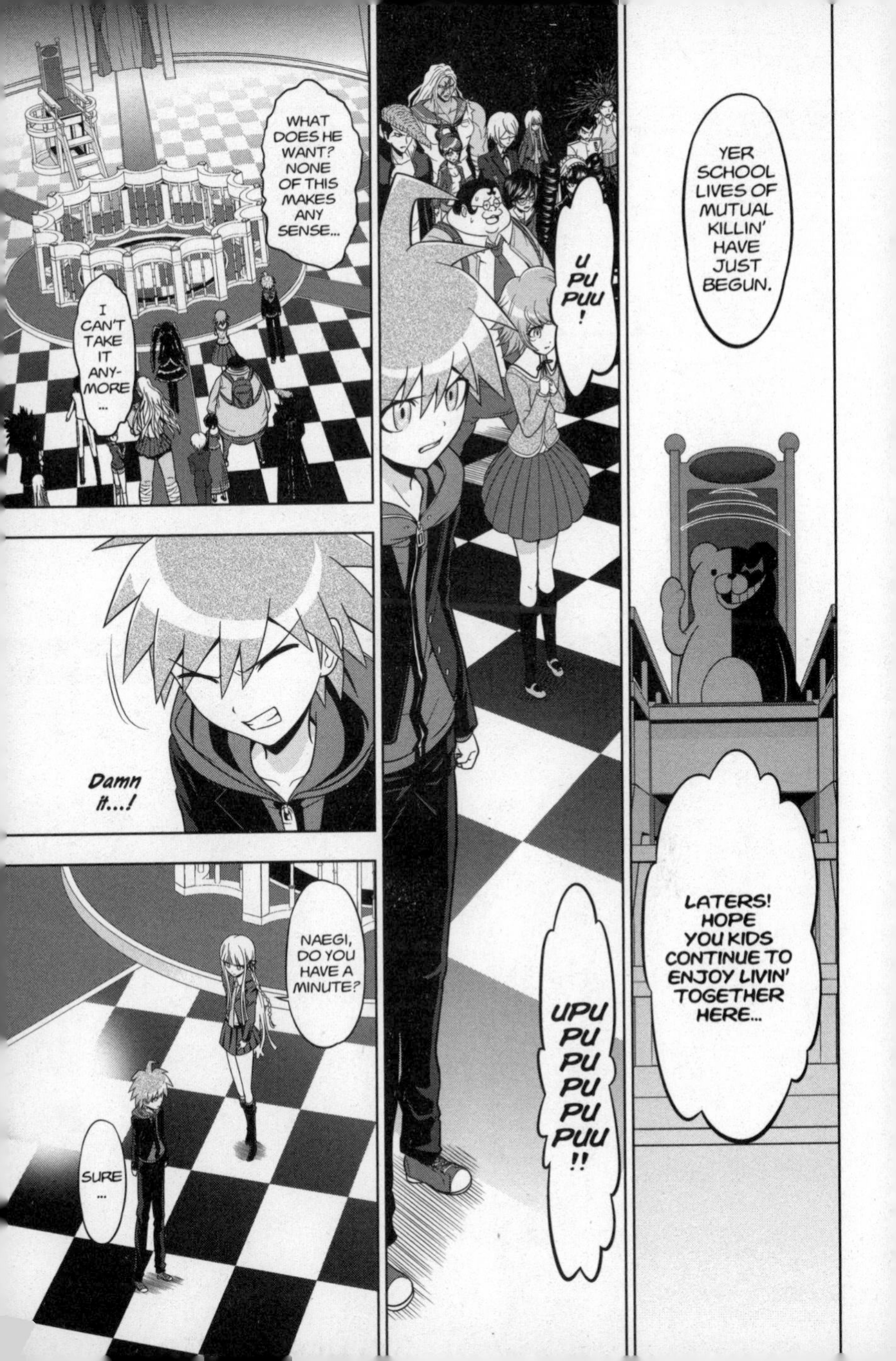
YER SCHOOL LIVES OF MUTUAL KILLIN' HAVE JUST BEGUN.
LATERS! HOPE YOU KIDS CONTINUE TO ENJOY LIVIN' TOGETHER HERE...
U PU PUU!
UPU PU PU PU PU PUU!!
WHAT DOES HE WANT? NONE OF THIS MAKES ANY SENSE...
I CAN'T TAKE IT ANY-MORE...
Damn it...!
NAEGI, DO YOU HAVE A MINUTE?
SURE...

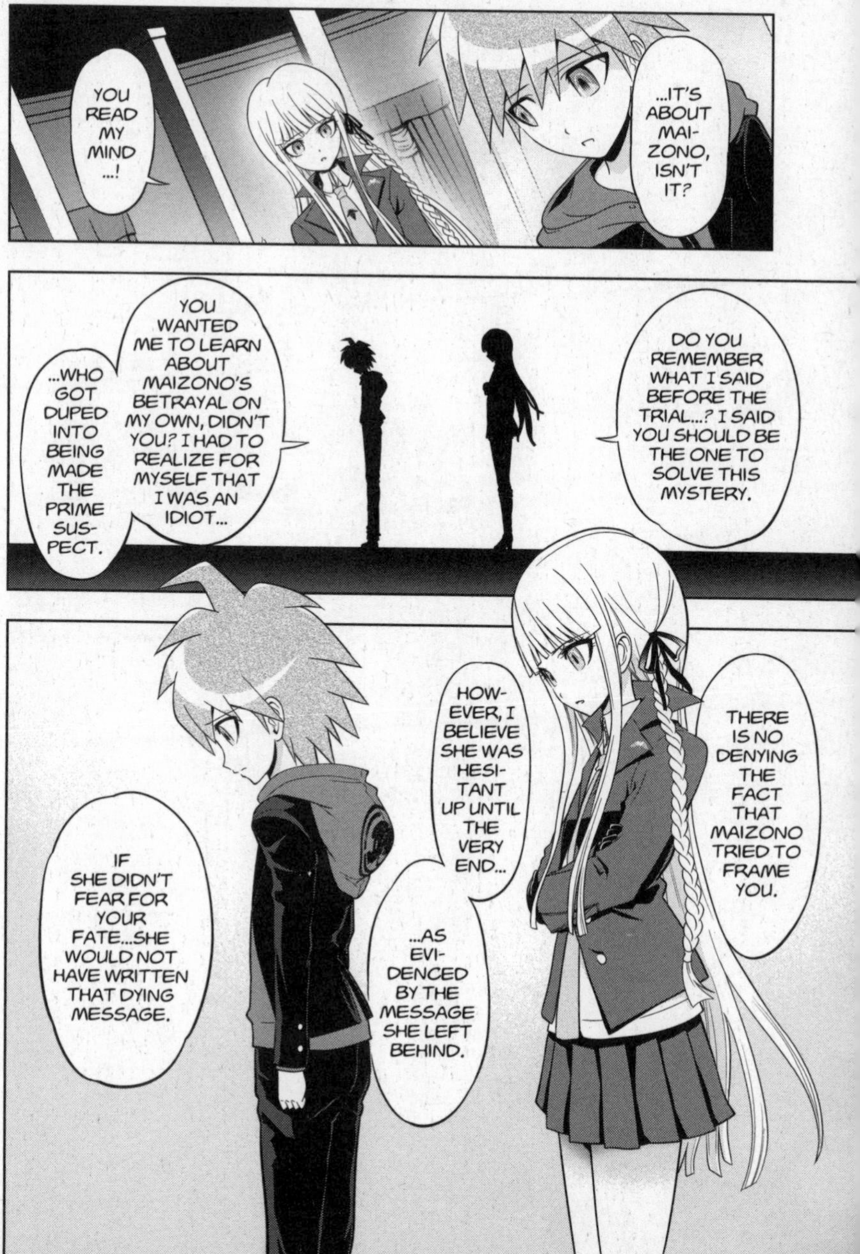
...IT'S ABOUT MAI-ZONO, ISN'T IT?
YOU READ MY MIND ...!
DO YOU REMEMBER WHAT I SAID BEFORE THE TRIAL...? I SAID YOU SHOULD BE THE ONE TO SOLVE THIS MYSTERY.
YOU WANTED ME TO LEARN ABOUT MAIZONO'S BETRAYAL ON MY OWN, DIDN'T YOU? I HAD TO REALIZE FOR MYSELF THAT I WAS AN IDIOT...
...WHO GOT DUPED INTO BEING MADE THE PRIME SUS-PECT.
THERE IS NO DENYING THE FACT THAT MAIZONO TRIED TO FRAME YOU.
HOW-EVER, I BELIEVE SHE WAS HESI-TANT UP UNTIL THE VERY END...
...AS EVI-DENCED BY THE MESSAGE SHE LEFT BEHIND.
IF SHE DIDN'T FEAR FOR YOUR FATE...SHE WOULD NOT HAVE WRITTEN THAT DYING MESSAGE.

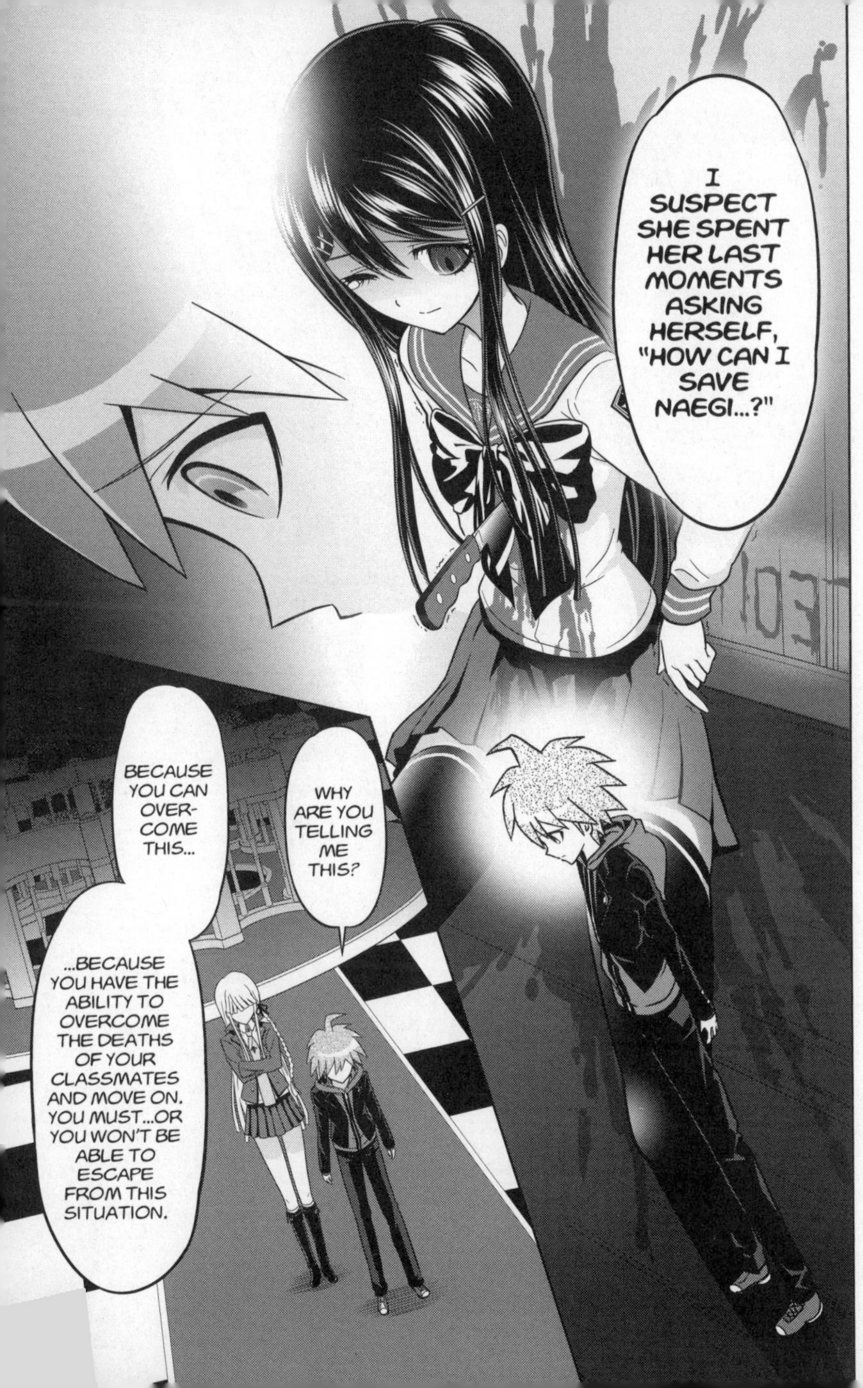
I SUSPECT SHE SPENT HER LAST MOMENTS ASKING HERSELF, "HOW CAN I SAVE NAEGI...?"
WHY ARE YOU TELLING ME THIS?
BECAUSE YOU CAN OVER-COME THIS...
...BECAUSE YOU HAVE THE ABILITY TO OVERCOME THE DEATHS OF YOUR CLASSMATES AND MOVE ON. YOU MUST...OR YOU WON'T BE ABLE TO ESCAPE FROM THIS SITUATION.

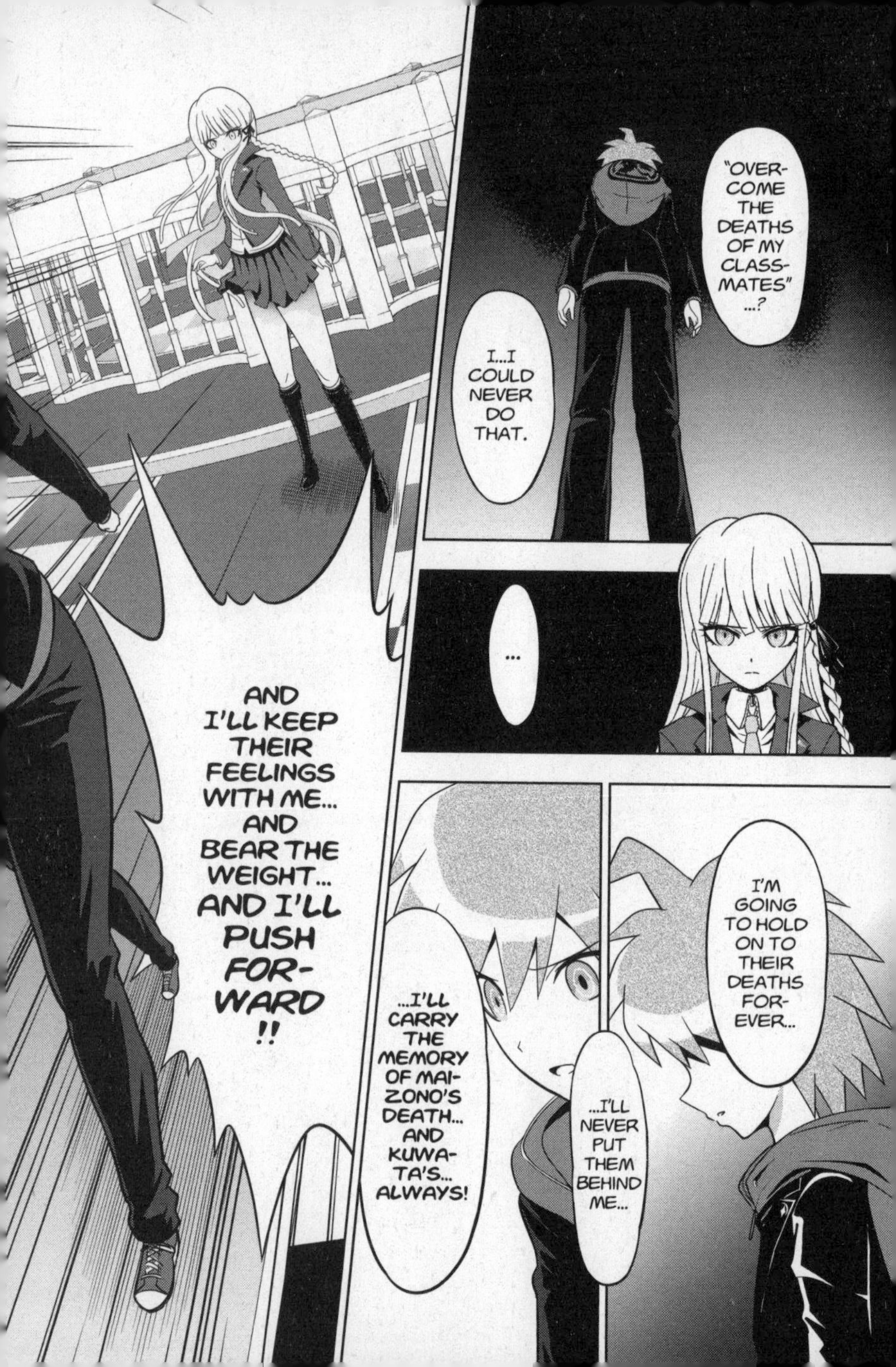
"OVER-COME THE DEATHS OF MY CLASS-MATES" ...?
I...I COULD NEVER DO THAT.
...
I'M GOING TO HOLD ON TO THEIR DEATHS FOR-EVER...
...I'LL NEVER PUT THEM BEHIND ME...
...I'LL CARRY THE MEMORY OF MAI-ZONO'S DEATH... AND KUWA-TA'S... ALWAYS!
AND I'LL KEEP THEIR FEELINGS WITH ME... AND BEAR THE WEIGHT... AND I'LL PUSH FOR-WARD!!

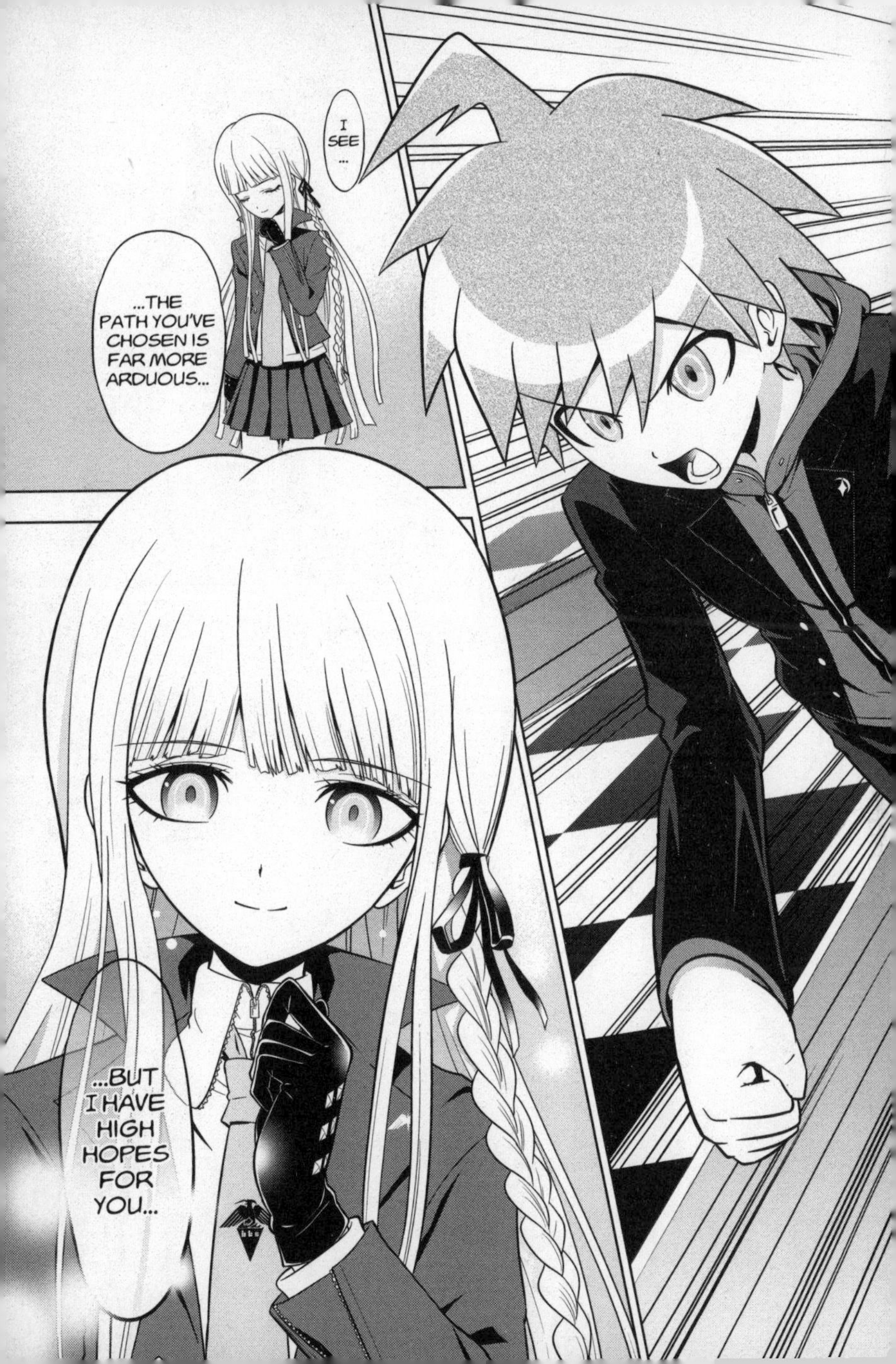
I SEE...
...THE PATH YOU'VE CHOSEN IS FAR MORE ARDUOUS...
...BUT I HAVE HIGH HOPES FOR YOU...

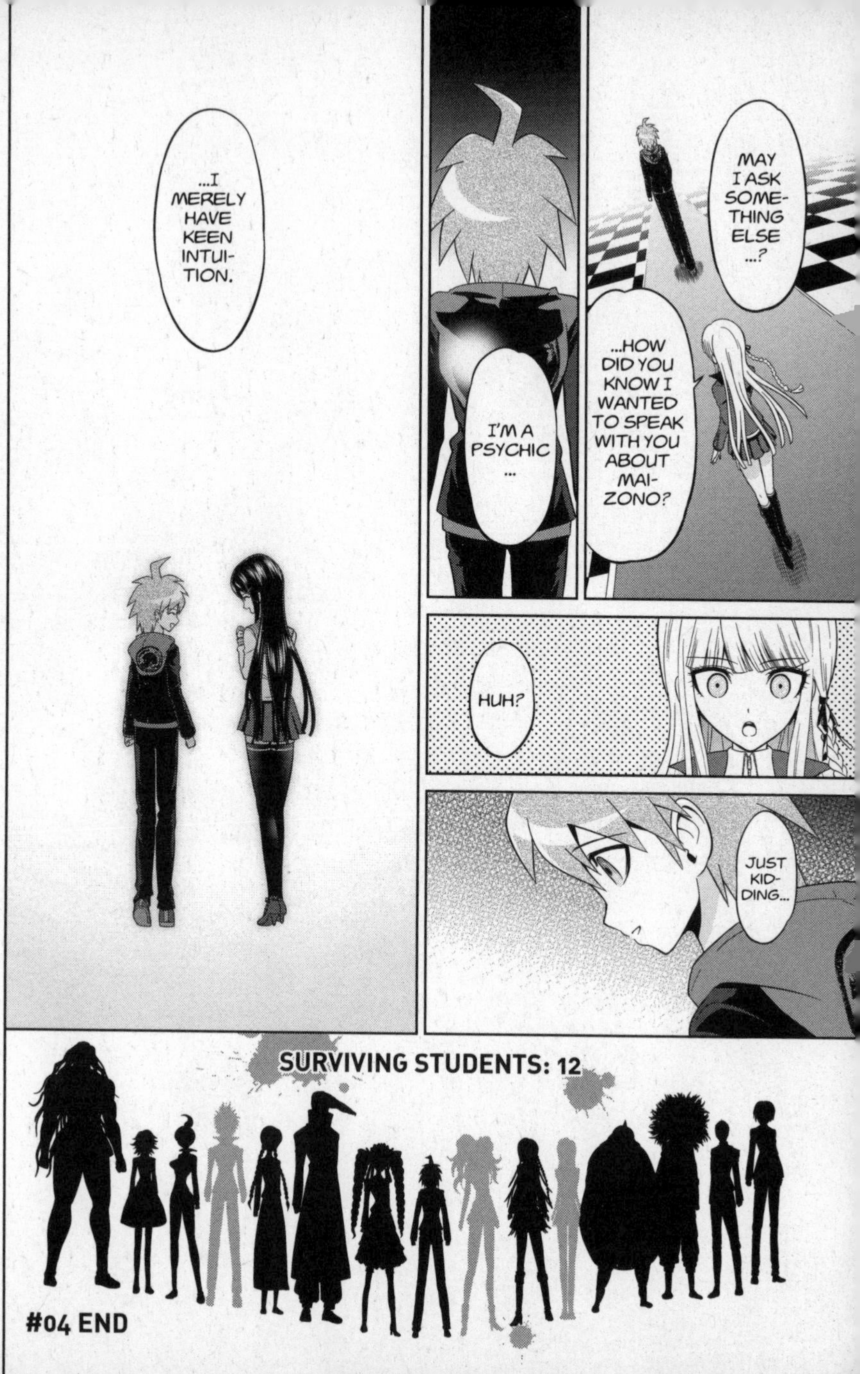
MAY I ASK SOME-THING ELSE ...?
...HOW DID YOU KNOW I WANTED TO SPEAK WITH YOU ABOUT MAI-ZONO?
I'M A PSYCHIC ...
HUH?
JUST KID-DING...
...I MERELY HAVE KEEN INTUI-TION.
SURVIVING STUDENTS: 12
#04 END

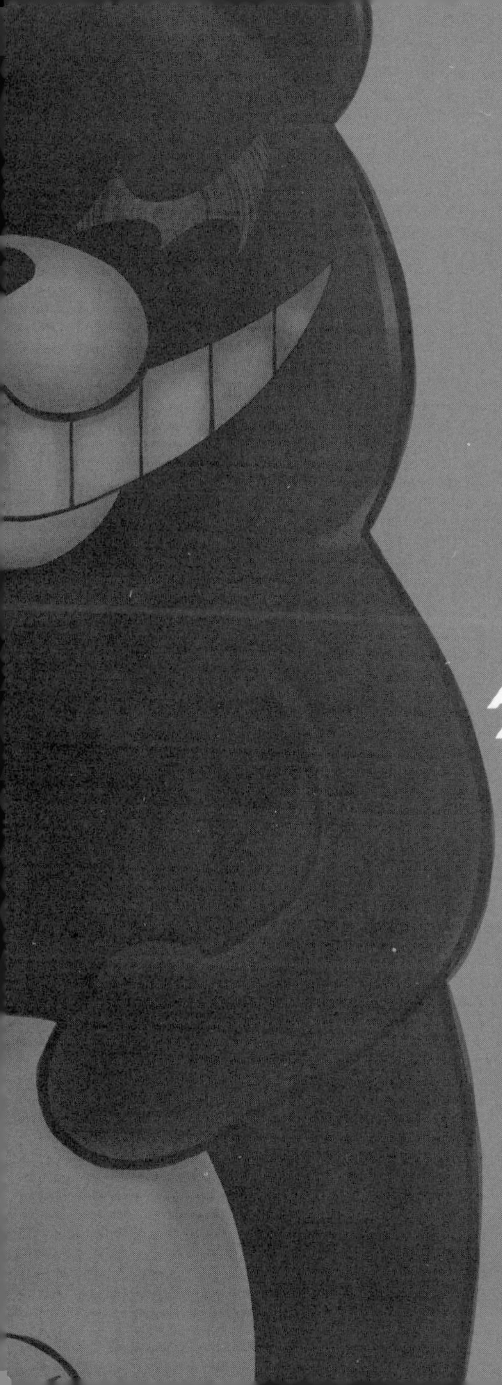

ダンガンロンパ
DANGANRONPA 希望の学園と絶望の高校生
THE ANIMATION

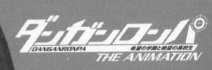

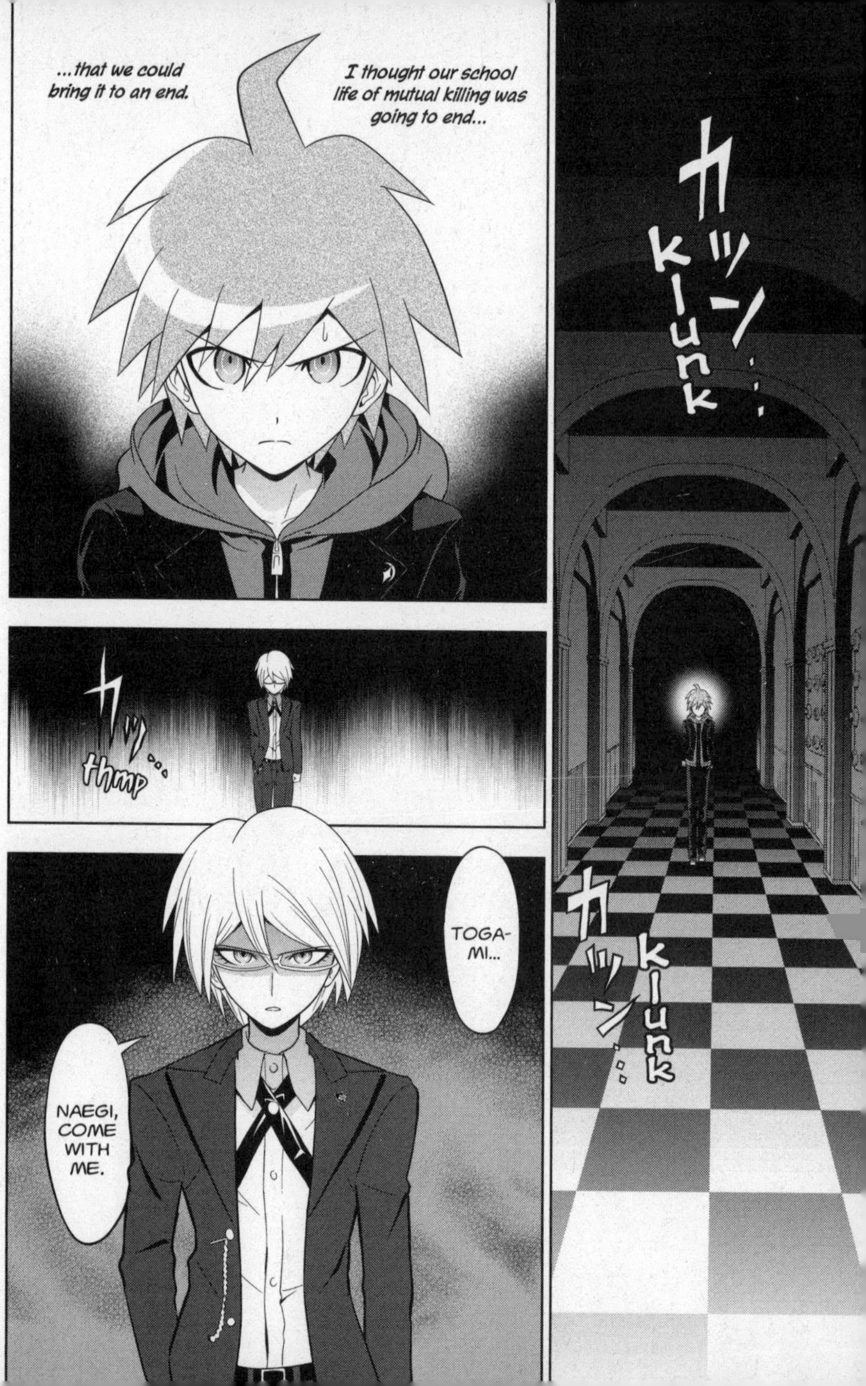
カッン…
klunk
カッン…
klunk
I thought our school life of mutual killing was going to end...
...that we could bring it to an end.
カッ…
thmp
TOGA-MI...
NAEGI, COME WITH ME.

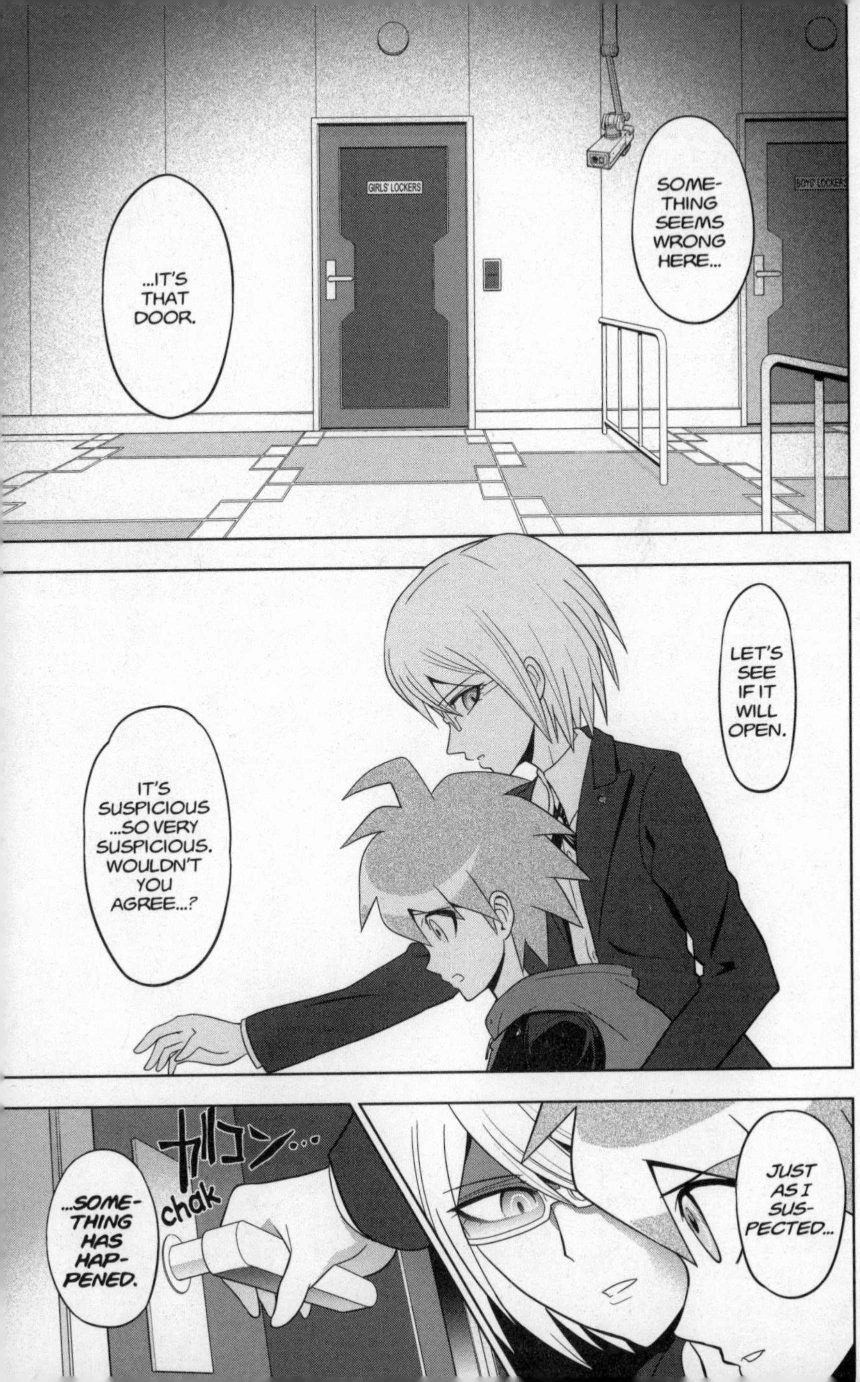
BOYS' LOCKERS
SOME-THING SEEMS WRONG HERE...
GIRLS' LOCKERS
...IT'S THAT DOOR.
LET'S SEE IF IT WILL OPEN.
IT'S SUSPICIOUS ...SO VERY SUSPICIOUS. WOULDN'T YOU AGREE...?
JUST AS I SUS-PECTED...
ガコン…
chak
...SOME-THING HAS HAP-PENED.

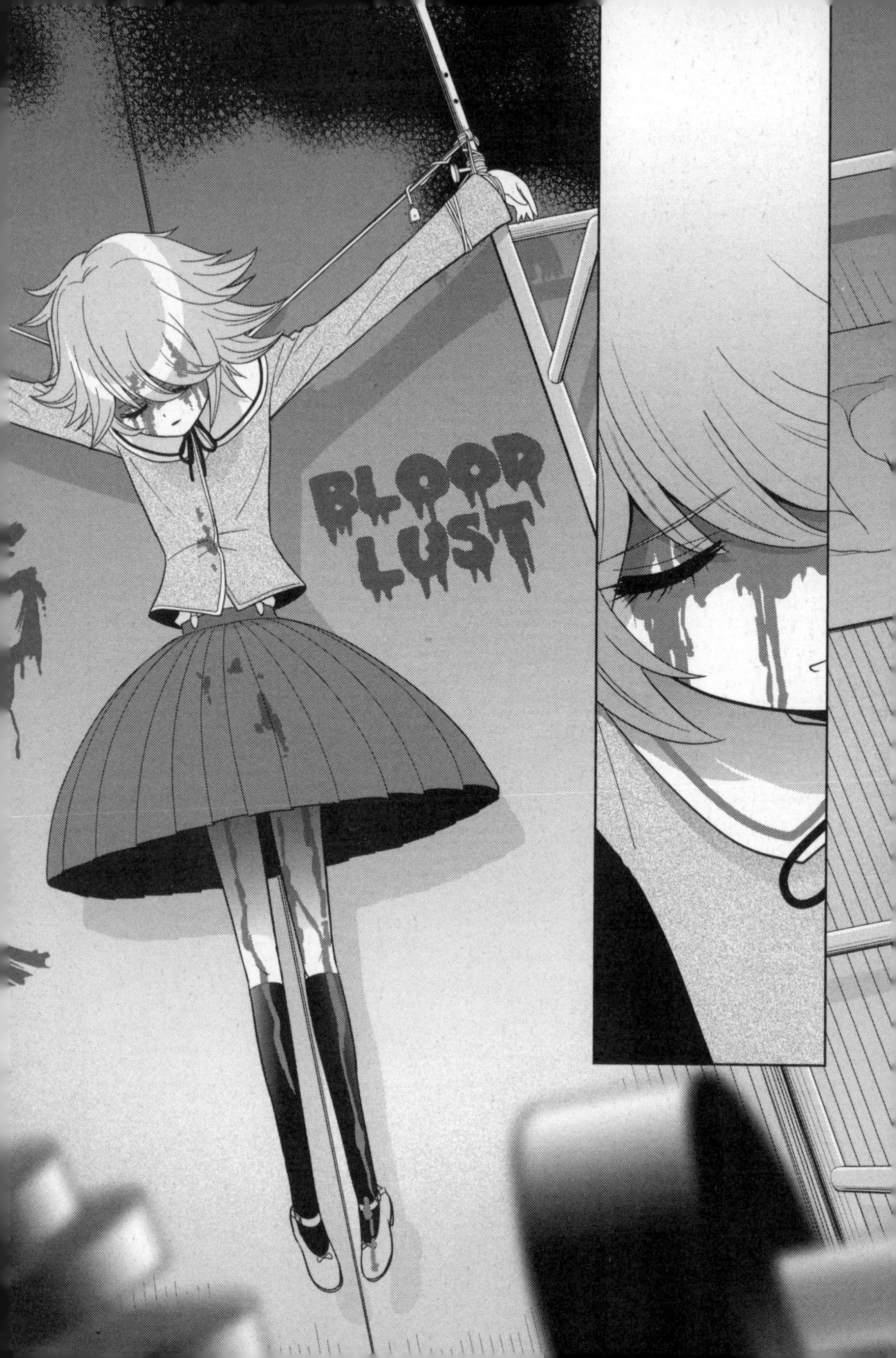
BLOOD LUST

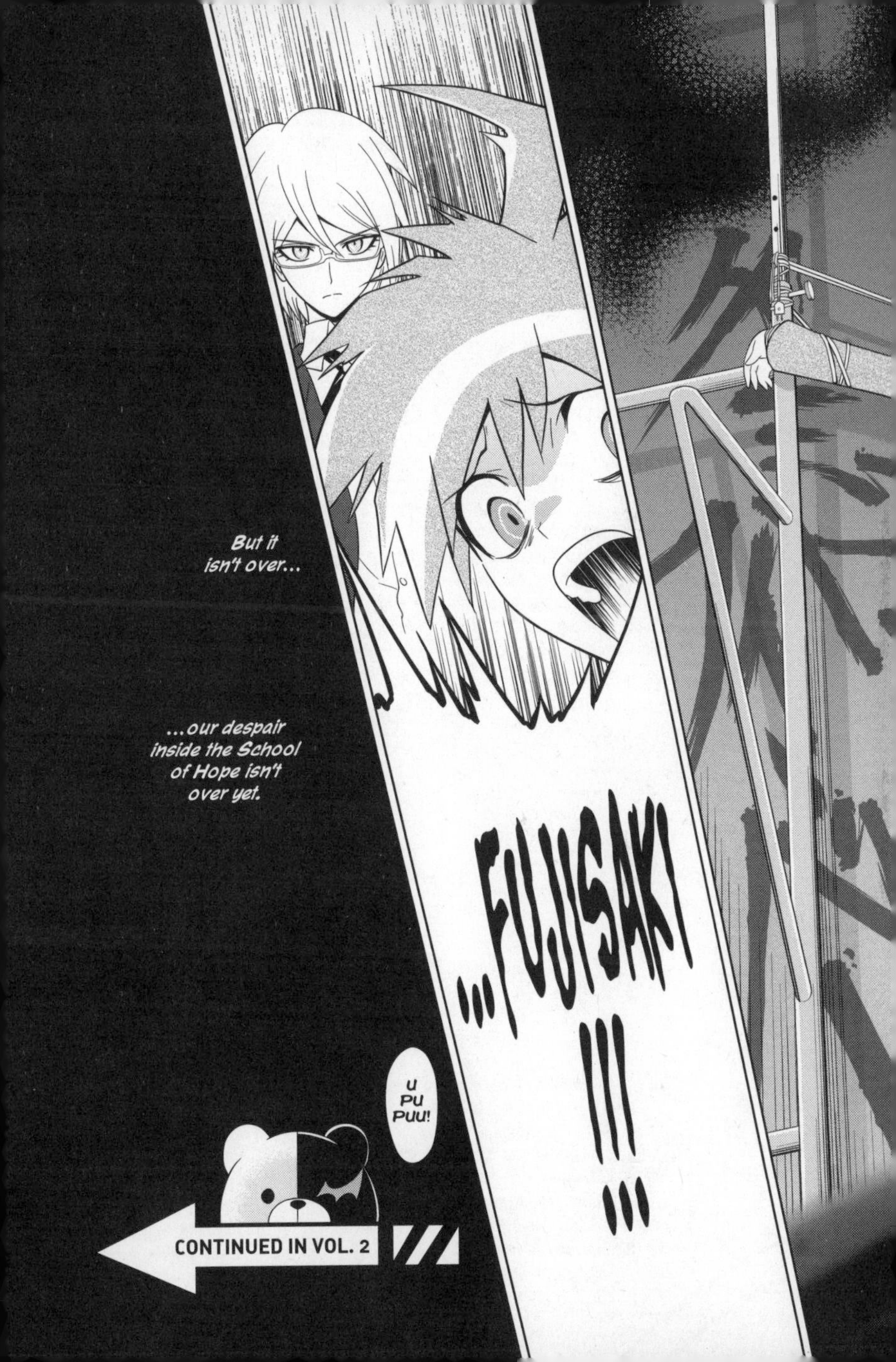
...FUJISAKI!!!
But it isn't over...
...our despair inside the School of Hope isn't over yet.
U PU PUU!
CONTINUED IN VOL. 2

president and publisher
MIKE RICHARDSON

designer
SARAH TERRY

ultimate digital art technician
CHRISTINA McKENZIE

English-language version produced by Dark Horse Comics

DANGANRONPA: THE ANIMATION VOLUME 1

Published by
Dark Horse Manga
A division of Dark Horse Comics LLC
10956 SE Main Street
Milwaukie, OR 97222

DarkHorse.com

To find a comics shop in your area, visit comicshoplocator.com

First edition: March 2016
ISBN 978-1-61655-928-1

11 12 13 14 15 16 17 18 19 20

Printed in the United States of America

DESPAIR MAIL

c/o Dark Horse Comics | 10956 SE Main St. | Milwaukie, OR 97222 | danganronpa@darkhorse.com

Welcome to Despair Mail, the place for Ultimate Danganronpa Fans! If you'd like to share your thoughts or comments on Danganronpa . . . pictures of your Danganronpa cosplay . . . or your Danganronpa fan art—this is the place for you! Send it to the address or e-mail at the top of the page, and remember to use high resolution (300 dpi or better) for your photos or images, so it'll look good in print!

We have three fans who were kind enough to write in early to kick off Danganronpa Vol. 1, so let's start! We begin with a letter from Mark Zilberts:

I've been a fan of *Danganronpa* for quite some time now, and when I first got into the series I already had the unfortunate knowledge of the murderer of the first trial, Leon Kuwata. The reason for this comes down to the game's advertising.

The Japanese trailer for the PS Vita release of *Danganronpa* contained several shots of Leon being dragged away with chains. This doesn't leave much up to the imagination and as a result, we are led to be suspicious toward the character. What makes this worse is the roll call of characters that has everyone looking straight toward the camera—taken from the game as they are reacting to Leon's execution—except for Leon, who is positioned in a different way with his eyes rolling back. Comparing this to the original Japanese PSP trailer, they used shots from a different build of the game and yet still ended it with Leon being dragged away. The English trailer does the same thing with the roll call, but coupled with a zooming target/crosshairs on his face, just to drill the suspicion in further.

I understand that it is hard to market a game that falls into the murder-mystery genre when the trial game play is the main focal point, but it's a shame because Leon is actually a pretty good character. Through the free-time events in the game, we learn that he actually wants to go into music and is tired of baseball, which ties into the irony that one of the reasons he was caught is because it could only have been him—the Ultimate Baseball Star—that could have thrown Yasuhiro's crystal ball through the small gaps in the grate with such accuracy.

The original Japanese trailer for *Danganronpa: The Animation* did not contain any spoilers, as they actually

drew scenes for both the trailer and the opening that featured the entire cast regardless of situation; the roll call for the trailer featured Leon in the same style as everyone else and the opening for every episode featured the trial room spinning, with every character present. Unfortunately the same cannot be said about the English trailer for *Danganronpa: The Animation* . . . I recommend anyone trying to get into the series ignore all forms of advertising from this English dub for the anime; the trailer genuinely spoils everything.

There was a demo for *Danganronpa* that was only available in Japanese that acted as a spoiler-free way to let people try out the game. In this demo it was in fact Yasuhiro that died in the bathroom, in much the same way, except that he did not write anything on the walls like Sayaka did that led to the downfall of Leon. This leads to us actually getting to play some parts of the first trial with Sayaka being involved. It also hinted that the culprit for the first trial is not Leon but instead Hifumi due to various mentions of potato grease on the floor in the bedroom along with Hifumi's constant talk about potato chips. Although this is mostly speculation as far as I can tell, aside from a one-volume manga that apparently confirms it, it is still interesting to see the different ways that the series has been advertised!

Thank you for bringing this manga into English! I hope that it can bring some more fans into the series who might expand into the rest of the *Danganronpa* universe as a result. ^^

It can be tricky sometimes to promote a work without showing some of its dramatic scenes, which then risk giving away too much of the plot. We can see this in a lot of Hollywood movie trailers, too. You're right about the conflict between trying to promote the "murder mystery" vs. the "trial" aspects of Danganronpa. Courtroom cross-examination can be dramatic, but murder is more dramatic still, and I guess you can argue that the murders come first in Danganronpa, because without the crime, you don't have the trial confronting the crime.

When Dark Horse advertised Danganronpa Vol. 1 in Previews magazine, I don't think we did anything to reveal the identity of Maizono's murderer (i.e., Leon), but we did reveal that Maizono would be murdered, by using the image of Naegi screaming at the discovery of her body. So you could say that we spoiled the murder to some extent (I say "to some extent," because you can't explain what Danganronpa is like if you don't reveal the fact that people are going to get murdered), but we did not spoil the trial aspect of the story, which, as you say, is the focal point of the game play. It's the trial, of course, where Naegi reveals his special strength as a character—and as a hero. We could also say, of course, that by revealing that Maizono dies in vol. 1, we were just keeping to the style of the manga itself, which reveals in the preview for next time that Fujisaki dies in vol. 2.

I was trying to explain Danganronpa to some people who weren't familiar with anime, manga, or Japanese games. I told them it reminds me somewhat of those dystopian young adult novels that are so popular these days—you know the kind, where teenagers are forced into a situation where they have to kill each other or fight for their lives. But there's a big difference in style. How should I put it? Danganronpa can be grim and dark, but it's not grimdark. There's a strong sense of the absurd. To kick it old school, it's almost as if you got Monty Python to do some YA dystopia.

Above everything else, Danganronpa is its characters. You can be drawn into this series by a single line from a single character, captured in a single screencap. I would be afraid that if Hollywood ever adapted Danganronpa, they'd never let the characters be as gloriously weird, bizarre, and individual as the ultimate students of Hope's Peak are. "Uncool," "cool," "ugly," "pretty," "nice," "mean," "gender conforming," "gender nonconforming"—every student still has their own personal style that shines through. Identity and labels are one thing—but personal style is another. You sometimes see people who greet you in their profile with a long list of identity labels they put on themselves . . . yet somehow they still manage to sound like completely boring individuals. I like the Danganronpa approach better. Never mind those labels—have personal style instead. Don't give up all your clues about who you are at the start—if someone wants to get to know you, make them figure you out!

And that brings us to the "ordinary" Makoto Naegi, whose style doesn't get to show itself until he gets into the courtroom and reveals himself to be a natural-born trial attorney. This is actually a more exotic skill in the eyes of Danganronpa's original Japanese audience than it is to English-speaking fans. As you may know, Japan doesn't have the centuries-long tradition of cross-examinations in front of a jury that you find in common-law systems like those of the US, Canada, and the UK—Japan didn't even begin using jury trials until 2009 (instead, accused people faced a panel of judges), and even now the system still requires three judges to be members of the jury. On the other hand, members of a jury can do things in Japan that they can't do in America, such as ask questions directly of a witness. If you would like to see how a real murder trial might work in Japan (complete with clues and cross-examinations), check out vol. 13 of The Kurosagi Corpse Delivery Service from Dark Horse.

In addition to our first letter, we've also received our first fan art! The illustration of Junko Enoshima is by Shelby Goldsmith. The illustrations of Byakuya Togami and Toko Fukawa (also known as . . .) are by Amie Palmer-Cutter. Thank you both very much! And everyone else, please feel free to send in your own letters, art, cosplay photos, or anything Danganronpa related to Despair Mail! See you in vol. 2 (rhymes with U PU PUU!).

—CGH

P.S. I'm sure many fans are aware of this, but part of the dark humor of Danganronpa is that in the original Japanese version, Monokuma is voiced by Nobuyo Oyama, most famous for the also-cuddly (but much nicer) rotund robot cat, Doraemon. The manga is making reference to Doraemon on page 20, panel 1 and on page 69, panel 2 (and also in panel 3 to Korosuke, another character from the creator of Doraemon).

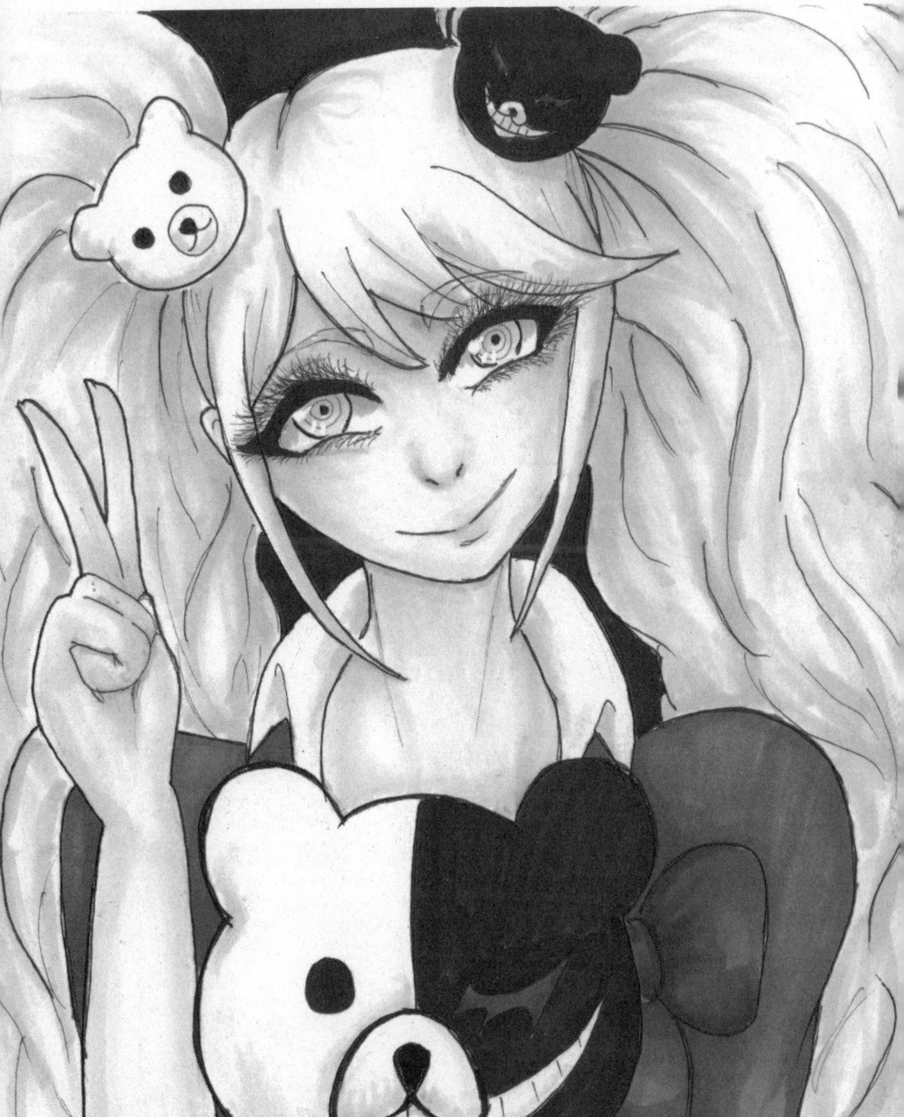

illustration by
Shelby Goldsmith

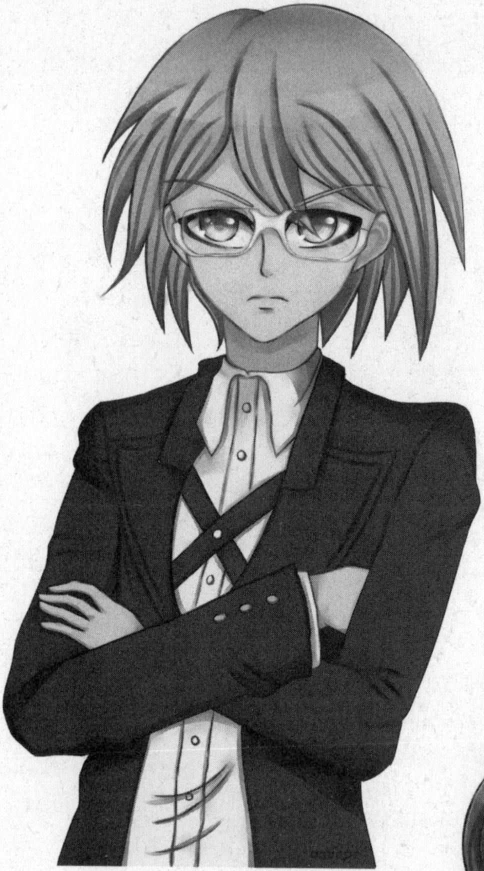

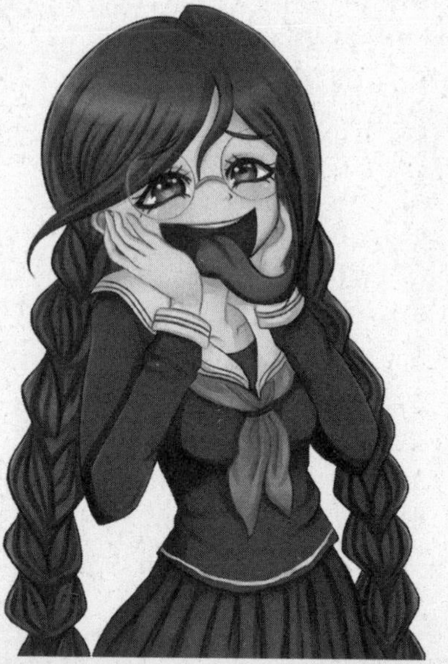

illustrations by

Amie Palmer-Cutter

Heroes Don't Save the World—Otakus Do.

Robotics;Notes ELITE & DasH

> The science itself may prove cynical. However, one mustn't forget that there is a scientific element in all things. The important truth is this: I am the master of my fate, I am the captain of my soul.

DOUBLE PACK

2 GAMES IN 1

Day One Edition includes 4 pin badges featuring main characters from both games!

ALL ART NOT FINAL

AVAILABLE 10.13.2020

COMING TO PS4   NINTENDO SWITCH   STEAM

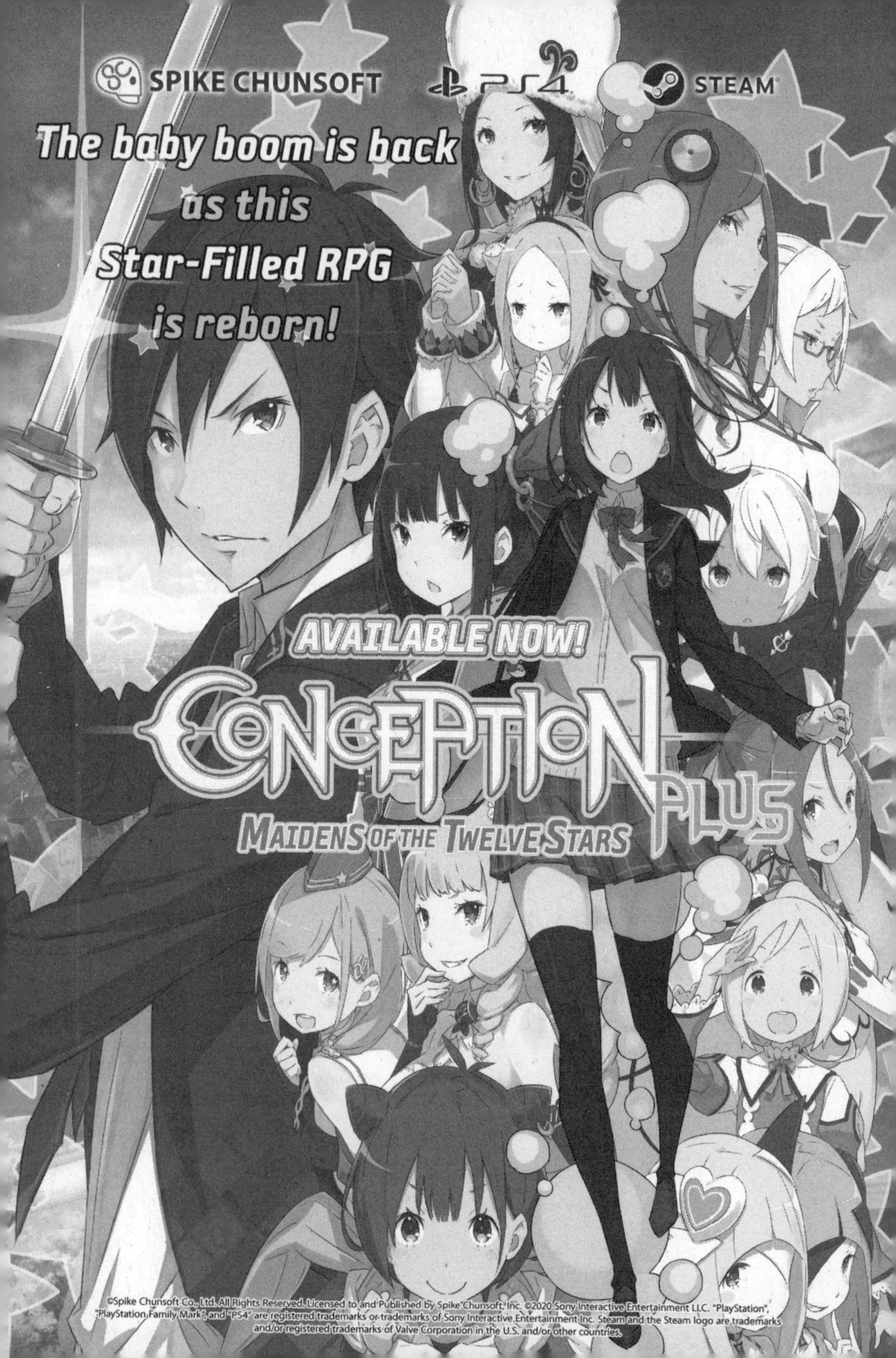
SPIKE CHUNSOFT
PS4
STEAM
The baby boom is back as this Star-Filled RPG is reborn!
AVAILABLE NOW!
CONCEPTION PLUS
MAIDENS OF THE TWELVE STARS
©Spike Chunsoft Co., Ltd. All Rights Reserved. Licensed to and Published by Spike Chunsoft, Inc. ©2020 Sony Interactive Entertainment LLC. "PlayStation", "PlayStation Family Mark", and "PS4" are registered trademarks or trademarks of Sony Interactive Entertainment Inc. Steam and the Steam logo are trademarks and/or registered trademarks of Valve Corporation in the U.S. and/or other countries.

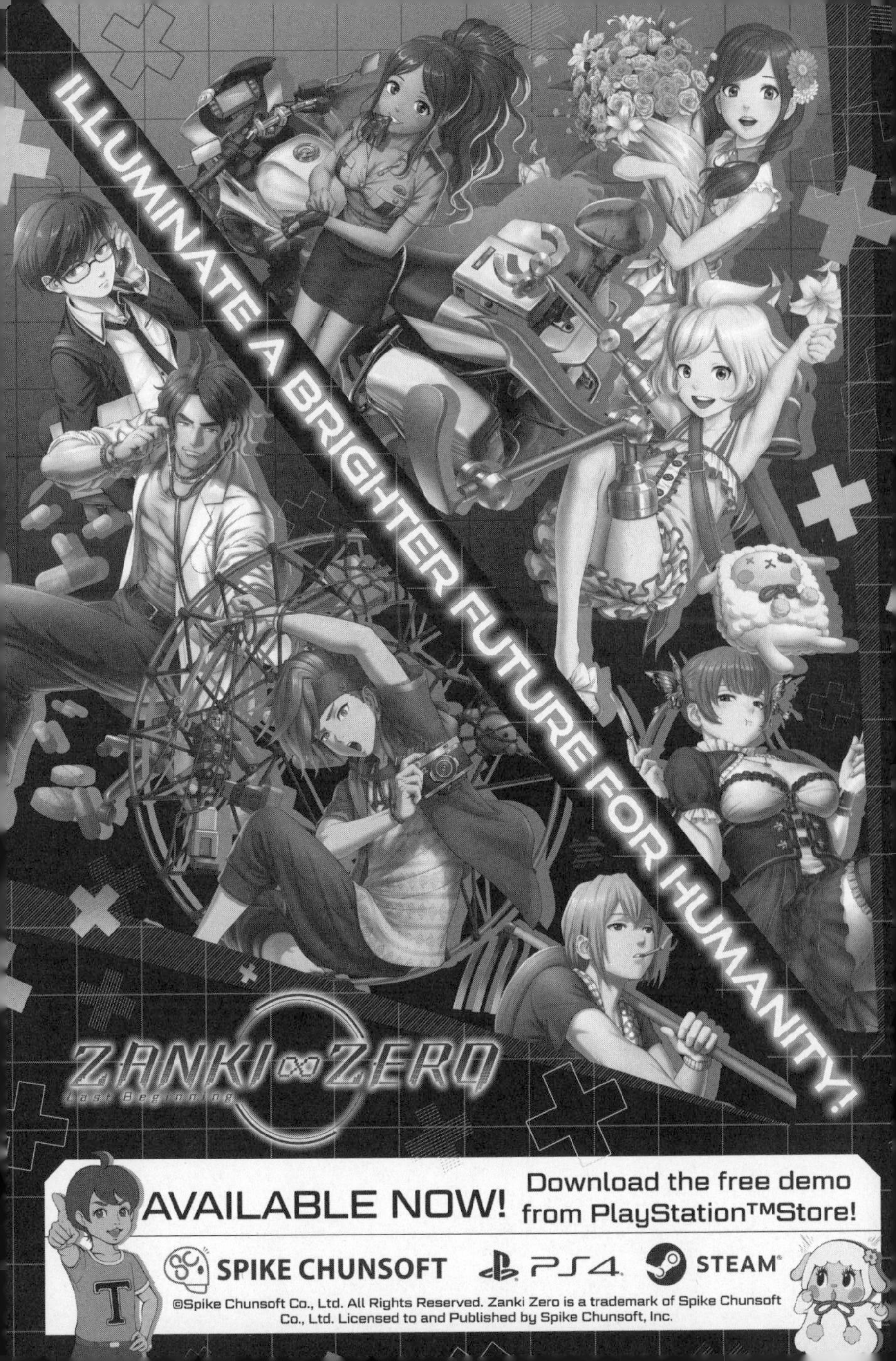
ILLUMINATE A BRIGHTER FUTURE FOR HUMANITY!
ZANKI ZERO
Last Beginning
AVAILABLE NOW!
Download the free demo from PlayStation™Store!
SPIKE CHUNSOFT
PS4
STEAM
©Spike Chunsoft Co., Ltd. All Rights Reserved. Zanki Zero is a trademark of Spike Chunsoft Co., Ltd. Licensed to and Published by Spike Chunsoft, Inc.

REPENT, SINNERS! THEY'RE BACK!

WHO'S THAT GIRL WITH THE LONG GREEN PONYTAILS YOU'VE BEEN SEEING EVERYWHERE? IT'S HATSUNE MIKU, THE VOCALOID—THE SYNTHESIZER SUPERSTAR WHO'S SINGING YOUR SONG!

AVAILABLE AT YOUR LOCAL COMICS SHOP OR BOOKSTORE

DarkHorse.com

HATSUNE MIKU: ACUTE
Art and story by Shiori Asahina
Miku, Kaito, and Luka! Once they were all friends making songs—but while Kaito might make a duet with Miku or a duet with Luka, a love song all three of them sing together can only end in sorrow!

ISBN 978-1-50670-341-1 | $10.99

HATSUNE MIKU: RIN-CHAN NOW!
Story by Sezu, Art by Hiro Tamura
Miku's sassy blond friend takes center stage in this series that took inspiration from the music video "Rin-chan Now!" The video is now a manga of the same name—written, drawn, and edited by the video creators!

VOLUME 1
978-1-50670-313-8 | $10.99

VOLUME 2
978-1-50670-314-5 | $10.99

VOLUME 3
978-1-50670-315-2 | $10.99

VOLUME 4
978-1-50670-316-9 | $10.99

HATSUNE MIKU: MIKUBON
Art and story by Ontama
Hatsune Miku and her friends Rin, Len, and Luka enroll at the St. Diva Academy for Vocaloids! At St. Diva, a wonderland of friendship, determination, and even love unfolds! But can they stay out of trouble, especially when the mad professor of the Hachune Miku Research Lab is nearby . . . ?

ISBN 978-1-50670-231-5 | $10.99

UNOFFICIAL HATSUNE MIX
Art and story by KEI
Miku's original illustrator, KEI, produced a best-selling omnibus manga of the musical adventures (and misadventures!) of Miku and her fellow Vocaloids Rin, Len, Luka, and more—in both beautiful black-and-white and charming color!

ISBN 978-1-61655-412-5 | $19.99

HATSUNE MIKU: FUTURE DELIVERY
Story by Satoshi Oshio, Art by Hugin Miyama
In the distant future, Asumi—a girl who has no clue to her memories but a drawing of a green-haired, ponytailed person—finds her only friend in Asimov, a battered old delivery robot. The strange companions travel the stars together in search of the mysterious "Miku," only to learn the legendary idol has taken different forms on many different worlds!

VOLUME 1
ISBN 978-1-50670-361-9 | $10.99

VOLUME 2
ISBN 978-1-50670-362-6 | $10.99

HATSUNE MIKU

TO FIND A COMICS SHOP IN YOUR AREA, VISIT COMICSHOPLOCATOR.COM. For more information or to order direct, visit DarkHorse.com